HISTO

OF THE

CHRISTIAN RELIGION

TO THE

YEAR TWO HUNDRED

By Charles B. Waite, A. M.

Fifth Edition — Revised and Updated

Containing much additional matter in Appendix.

THE BOOK TREE
San Diego, California

This edition first published 1900
C. V. Waite & Company
Chicago

New material and revisions
© 2014
The Book Tree
All rights reserved

ISBN 978-1-58509-357-1

Cover layout
Mike Sparrow

Cover art copyright 2013
by Vadim Petrakov

Cover Image: Dome at the Church of the Holy Sephulchre in Jerusalem, with obvious sun symbolism. Many researchers claim that a certain degree of sun worship and symbolism had been integrated into Christianity during its formative years to help pagans convert to the faith more comfortably. Directly below the dome is located what is believed to have been the tomb of Jesus, where, after his death, he "rose again."

Published by
The Book Tree
P.O. Box 16476
San Diego, CA 92176
www.thebooktree.com

We provide fascinating and educational products to help awaken the public to new ideas and information that would not be available otherwise.
Call 1 (800) 700-8733 for our *FREE BOOK TREE CATALOG*.

Introduction to the Sixth Printing

It has been my desire for a number of years to compile and publish a history of Christianity for the first two centuries. It has now been decided that it would be much better to reprint this work by Charles Waite. We believe this work to be the most complete, honest and best documented work available on the subject. We therefore present this work to the sincere seeker of truth, hoping that the facts presented will be more highly esteemed than common dogma and tradition.

Sincerely,
The Publisher – Dr. Carroll R. Biewbower
10090 Caves Highway
Cave Junction, OR 97523
1992

Introduction to the Seventh Printing

This book was out of print for almost a century until Dr. Carroll Biewbower privately printed 500 hard cover gold-embossed copies of this rare book in 1992. After about five years most had not sold so The Book Tree purchased the entire supply and carried on with the sales and marketing. Otherwise, there is a good chance this book may have been forgotten and lost to history. As with Dr. Biewbower, we recognized the immense importance of this work. Every serious researcher into the formation of Christianity should have a copy of this book, otherwise, your research will not be complete. Although those first 500 hard bound copies are gone, we will now be offering this important book in both paperback and e-book forms for many years to come.

Paul Tice, Publisher
The Book Tree
San Diego, CA
2014

PREFACE.

This volume is the result of an investigation, extending through several years, and instituted for the satisfaction of the author.

Two years of the time were spent in the Library of Congress, which is peculiarly rich in the department of Biblical Literature. It contains the writings of all the earlier fathers, in the original, and an immense collection of the works of later writers.

The intent to publish was formed upon ascertaining facts and arriving at conclusions which appeared of great importance, and which had never before been fully made known.

To the accomplished Librarian, who furnished the author with every facility for the prosecution of his work, and gave him much valuable information, he returns his sincere thanks; also to the assistant librarians, for the promptness with which the treasures of the Library were from time to time placed at his disposal.

It is believed that this will be found to be the most complete record of the events connected with the Christian religion during the first two centuries that has ever been presented to the public.

The time has been divided into six periods, and the different writers and events are carefully arranged in regular chronological order. In fixing the dates of the various writers, it was found that the subject was involved in much confusion. In each case, the different dates were carefully examined, and the one selected which appeared the most consistent, and supported by the most approved authorities.

A comprehensive view is given of the gospels of the first two centuries, with a brief sketch of those of a later date. The comparisons which have been instituted between the canonical and certain apocryphal gospels, constitute a peculiar feature of this work, and one which is believed to be of great importance in arriving at correct conclusions.

The Gospel of Marcion has been reproduced from the writings of the fathers, principally from the Greek of Epiphanius. This is something which, so far as the author is aware, has never before been attempted in this country.

The references to authorities will be found useful to those who may desire to pursue further the investigation of the questions discussed.

The reader will find considerable repetition in the following pages. The importance of the subject, and the necessity of examining many of the questions from different points of view, would seem to justify, if not absolutely to demand, a restatement, from time to time, of the same facts and propositions in different chapters.

In the preparation and publication of this work, the author has proceeded upon the assumption that the ascertainment of the truth is all important, and that its promulgation cannot fail to result in the permanent benefit of the human race.

The author is under special obligations to the Hon. William Birney, of Washington, formerly Professor in the University of France, who took a deep interest in the prosecution of the work, and devoted many hours to its examination and criticism.

The final result of the undertaking is submitted to the public, in the hope that it may add something to the pages of reliable history.

FROM PREFACE TO THIRD EDITION.

The History of the Christian Religion has met with a reception from the public, and especially from that great exponent of popular thought, the secular press, far more favorable than the author had expected. With but very few exceptions, the reviews have been fair and liberal in spirit, while many of them have been in the highest degree commendatory.

In this edition the author has availed himself of sundry criticisms, as well as of the kind suggestions of friends, in making some corrections, which, it is believed, will materially add to the value of the work.

The changes do not in any way affect the main propositions which peculiarly characterize the book, and which have given it such a hold upon the public mind. These remain unimpeached, and almost unassailed.

A writer of reputation in theological circles lately delivered a lecture upon the date of the canonical gospels, in which he asserted that there was no record of their introduction, and no evidence that they displaced older gospels. The fact is, there were various instances of the displacement of older gospels, and the substitution of the canonical in their

stead. Even as late as the fifth century Theodoret
found it necessary to suppress the Gospel of Tatian, and substitute in its place the four Gospels.

"I found myself," says Theodoret (A. D. 430), "upwards of two
hundred such books held in honor among your churches, and collecting them all together, I had them put aside, and instead introduced
the Gospels of the Four Evangelists."—[Hæret., Fab. 1. 20. See History, ch. 22.

Such points as appear worthy of attention in the
various criticisms which have thus far appeared
will be here briefly noticed :

CHRISHNA AND CHRIST.—It is claimed to have
been settled that the legends concerning Chrishna
have originated since the Christian era.

The author has yet to meet with a writer who has
produced any tangible evidence to sustain the position. The argument is based upon the facilities of
intercommunication between Palestine and India,
which would render interpolations possible, and
upon the fact that the legends of Chrishna are not
in some of the older sacred books of the Hindus.

The first branch of the argument neutralizes itself ; since the same facilities which would enable
the Hindus to interpolate from the Christian gospels, would furnish the Christian missionaries
equal opportunities to enrich their own gospels
from the Hindu writings. As to the omission of
the legends from the Vedas, that is no more strange
than the fact that the Christian Bible has an Old
and a New Testament. If the Chrishna stories are
later than the Vedas, that does not prove that they
are also later than Christ.

That they were anterior to the Christian era, is
maintained by Christian Lassen, an eminent Ger-

man scholar and Professor of Ancient Indian Language and Literature in the Royal University at Bonn. In the second volume of his Indian Antiquities, "Indische Alterthumskunde," pp. 1124 to 1128, he discusses the question fully, and comes to the following conclusion :

"I can discover no valid ground for the conjecture that Christian legends had then already [during the first three centuries of the Christian era] been transferred to Krishna."

"Kann ich keinen triftigen Grund fuer de Vermuthung entdecken, dass christliche Legenden damals schon auf Krishna uebertragen worden seien."—[Alterthumskunde, vol 2, p. 1128 2d ed.; p. 1109 of 1st edition.

Whether any such transfer was made at a later period, he does not discuss. But if the integrity of the Chrishna legends at any time after Christ be once established, the presumption of their continuance in the same form becomes exceedingly strong, and, in the absence of evidence of change, conclusive.

That Chrishna lived long before Christ is incontrovertible. Col. Wilford supposes him to have flourished about 1300 B. C.; while according to Col. Tod, he was born B. C. 1156. Sir Wm. Jones says the story of his birth is long anterior to the birth of Christ, and thinks it was probably at the time of Homer. Lassen places him in the period preceding the Pandava.—[Alterthumskunde, vol. 1, pp. 765–770.

That the history of Chrishna antedated Christianity was the opinion of Mr. H. T. Colebrook, Major Moor, and many others. That Chrishna himself was before Christ is conceded in the Religious Cyclopedia of McClintock and Strong.

Here, then, we have the older religion and the older god. This, in the absence of any evidence on either side, ought to settle the question. To assume without evidence that the older religion has been interpolated from the later, and that the legends of the older hero have been made to conform to the history of a later character, is worse than illogical —it is absurd. As well might one take a painting of one of the old masters, and claim that it has been retouched to make it resemble one known to have had a later origin.

THE DIVINITY OF CHRIST, AND HIS MIRACULOUS CONCEPTION.—Professor Elliott, of the Presbyterian Theological Seminary, quotes at some length from the History to show that according to the author certain doctrines were not taught in the first century; and assuming that the divinity of Christ was one of them, he makes quotations from Paul's writings apparently in favor of that doctrine. The author nowhere asserts that the divinity of Christ was not taught in the first century. On the contrary, he shows (chap. 33), that Pliny spoke of the Christians as singing hymns "to Christ as to God," and (on the preceding page) distinctly admits that such a doctrine was countenanced by Paul himself.

The author does maintain that there is no evidence of the doctrine of the miraculous conception in the first century, and the mistake of Professor Elliott arose from thinking this doctrine was necessarily involved in the other.

Marcion held that Christ in his conception and birth was entirely human, but that when he was baptized, preparatory to entering upon his ministry, the Holy Ghost descended upon him, and from that time he became divine. This doctrine he claimed to have received from Paul.

If the Epistles of Paul are studied in the light of this theory, it will be seen that all of the expressions implying the divinity of Christ find a full explanation; while, so far from believing in the miraculous conception, he says that Christ was of the seed of David, according to the flesh.

WHEN THE FOUR GOSPELS WERE WRITTEN.—The editor of the San Francisco Chronicle, in a learned and very favorable review of the History, says that to many, the views of the author in differing from eminent German scholars as to the date of the four gospels, will seem, at the outset, to savor of presumption.

Of this he is fully aware. He can only say that he has given his own convictions, after a careful and thorough examination. In so doing, he feels that he is more at liberty to differ from the German scholars alluded to, from the fact that they nearly all differ from each other. It is believed that in this work the solution of the question is made easier by the application of a principle to which sufficient attention has not heretofore been given; a principle designated as the law of accretion. This, properly applied, indicates for the four gospels a date late in the second century. The historical evidence points the same way.

Having arrived at his conclusions by evidence, both internal and external, the author feels justified in maintaining them, even against some eminent names. He is not, however, unsupported by high

German authority. Eichhorn and several others came to the conclusion that the four gospels did not come into use until near the close of the second century.

CREDIBILITY OF THE GOSPELS — ARGUMENT OF GREENLEAF.—The argument of Prof. Greenleaf has been reproduced by several of our critics. He undertook to apply to Matthew, Mark, Luke and John, as witnesses, certain presumptions and rules of evidence.

The first questions put to a witness are as to his name and place of residence, and his means of knowledge of the facts concerning which he is expected to testify. But what are the names and where were the residences of the men who wrote or compiled the four gospels? When did Matthew, Mark, Luke or John ever claim to have written a gospel? So far from claiming any such thing, if any one of them could be placed upon the witness stand to-day, and questioned, he would undoubtedly testify at once that he knew nothing about any gospel bearing his name, and never heard of it. There is, then, nobody in the witness box to whom these legal presumptions and rules of evidence can be applied.

As to the presumption of validity arising from the gospels being ancient, and being in the possession of the church, the law wisely provides for a record of title papers where the custodian is an interested party. Here there is no record, and the slight presumption arising from possession has been overthrown.

There have been many other criticisms, but these

are the most important. We must not pass, however, an allusion by one critic to the discrepancy between Josephus and the gospel historians, in reference to the person whose wife had been taken by Herod. He says a glance at Smith's Bible Dictionary will explain the apparent diversity. Certainly; and how is it explained? Simply by adding to Philip another name, to make the name of this prince accord with the gospel narrative. This mode of making history conform to theology, is at least to be admired for its simplicity, and is not infrequent in our religious and semi-religious cyclopedias.

In conclusion, we again call attention to the fact that none of the main propositions of this work have been in the slightest degree impeached; much less, overthrown.

Nearly every one of these propositions is of a negative character. A single positive fact upon the other side would be sufficient for disproof. For instance, it is stated that no reference is made to the miracles of Christ by any writer, Christian, heathen or Jewish, until nearly a hundred years after they are said to have been performed. A single well attested passage from any writer would disprove the assertion. Why is no such passage produced? Simply because it cannot be found.

Until these propositions are overthrown, this work will remain, as it has thus far proved to be, an obstacle in the path of superstition, and an aid to the free searcher after truth.   C. B. W.

PREFACE TO FIFTH EDITION.

It is now nearly twelve years since the fourth edition of this work was exhausted. So many inquiries have been made for it during that time, that a fifth edition has become an imperative necessity. This would have been issued long since but for the unfortunate loss of the plates, which necessitated an entire republication.

The author has availed himself of this opportunity to make a careful and thorough revision of the entire work.

Though the History of the Christian Religion has been before the public for a number of years, and has been extensively and sometimes adversely criticised, it can be safely asserted that no single statement of fact contained in it has been successfully controverted. This is the more remarkable, since the book is a magazine of facts from beginning to end. In such a multitude of statements, it would not have been strange if some error had been found. That there has not been, is the strongest possible evidence of the correctness and reliability of the entire work. Having passed through such an ordeal, the fifth edition will undergo no changes of consequence in the text. As a history, it will stand as it was written.

The value of the work will, however, be enhanced by the addition of an Appendix, in which will be discussed the following topics:

Was Jesus an Essene?

The Zealots;

The Inquisition;

all of them subjects of absorbing interest.

Other notes, also, have been added to those in the original appendix.

A new Index has been prepared, completely alphabetical, and some other changes and additions have been made, all adding to the value of the work, which has now about a hundred pages more than the earlier editions.

During the last twenty years great changes have been going on in the theological world, especially in the view taken of the origin and history of the gospels. The theory of the apostolic origin of these books—that they were written by eye-witnesses of the events therein related—is no longer insisted upon. On the contrary, it is now conceded that the gospels had their origin in tradition, partly oral, partly written. Evidence of this change of front is given in an article in the Appendix, entitled "Date of the Gospels," wherein quotations are made from late authors upon the subject.

The articles on the Essenes and the Zealots will be found to contain important matter not hitherto sufficiently understood.

The subject of the Inquisition has been treated in a new light, and its philosophical connection with the Christian religion has been shown. Instead of being, as has been maintained, an excrescence which originated some six or seven hundred years ago, it has been traced back to Jerome and Augustine, and its roots have been found in the teachings of Paul the apostle, with some sanction in the reported sayings of Jesus himself.

It is believed that in the present form, with the improvements and additions mentioned, this work will more than justify the many encomiums that have been passed upon it throughout this country and in Europe.

Chicago, October, 1900.

TABLE OF CONTENTS.

CONTENTS.

FIFTH PERIOD.

THE FOUR CANONICAL GOSPELS.—A. D. 170 TO 185.

CONTENTS.

CHAPTER XXXIV.

SIXTH PERIOD.

CLOSE OF THE SECOND CENTURY —A. D. 185 to A. D. 200.

CHAPTER XXXVI.

LIST OF CHRISTIAN WRITERS

AND WRITINGS, OF THE FIRST TWO CENTURIES.

——

CHRONOLOGICALLY ARRANGED.

——

	A. D
Oracles of Christ, by Matthew,	50
Gospel of Paul,	"
Gospel or Recollections of Peter,	"
PAUL'S EPISTLES. (See Note.)	
1. 2d Epistle to the Thessalonians,	52
2. 1st " " "	53
3. 1st " · " Corinthians,	57
4. 2d " " "	"
5. Epistle to the Galatians,	58
6. " " Romans,	"
7. " to Philemon,	62
8. " to the Colossians,	"
9. " " Philippians,	63
10. " " Ephesians,	"
The General Epistle of Peter, (1st Peter),	80
" James,	"
" Jude,	"
First Epistle of Clement of Rome, to the Corinthians,	97
Epistle of Ignatius to the Romans,	115
" " " Ephesians,	"
" " to Polycarp,	"
Gospel according to the Egyptians,	"
Epistle of Polycarp to the Philippians,	116
Proverbs of Xystus,	119
Menander, Prodicus,	120

A. D.

[Note. THE EPISTLES OF PAUL.—We have taken as genuine the ten epistles which constituted the Apostolicon of Marcion. The same course has been adopted by Dr. Davidson, except that he rejects, upon what appear insufficient grounds, the Epistle to the Ephesians.]

ROMAN EMPERORS

OF THE FIRST TWO CENTURIES.

		B. C.		A. D.
AUGUSTUS,		31	to	14
TIBERIUS,		A. D. 14	to	37
CALIGULA,		37	to	41
CLAUDIUS,		41	to	54
NERO,		54	to	68
GALBA,		68	to	69
OTHO,	January to April,			69
VITELLIUS,	April to December,			69
VESPASIAN,		69	to	79
TITUS,		79	to	81
DOMITIAN,		81	to	96
NERVA,		96	to	98
TRAJAN,		98	to	117
HADRIAN,		117	to	138
ANTONINUS PIUS,		138	to	161
MARCUS AURELIUS,		161	to	180
COMMODUS,		180	to	192
PERTINAX,	January to March,			193
JULIAN,	March to June,			193
SEPTIMIUS SEVERUS,		193	to	211

THE APOSTOLIC AGE.

CHAPTER I.

LOST GOSPELS OF THE FIRST CENTURY.

The Gospel of Paul—Gospel or Recollections of Peter —References and Citations by the Fathers of the Church—Views of Modern Writers—Oracles or Sayings of Christ, attributed to Matthew—These the Germs of the Synoptic Gospels, Luke, Mark and Matthew.

This is an attempt to write a history of the Christian religion during the first two centuries. Not a history of Christianity, which would require us to follow the principles of that religion, in their dissemination through various countries, and in their influence upon other institutions. Nor yet a history of the church ; which would make it necessary to examine questions of ecclesiastical polity, to trace the rise and progress of different forms of church government, and to notice the manners and customs of the early Cristians, and their treatment by the civil magistrates.

These are touched upon only in their bearing upon the main object of the inquiry ; which is, an examination into the principal doctrines distinctive of the Christian religion, so far as they were known and taught in the first two centuries; also the principal traditions and books by which those doctrines were disseminated.

The difficulty of the undertaking is great. The gospels of the first century are unfortunately lost. There are left, of that century, only the epistles of Paul, the one epistle of Clement of Rome, some slight notices by Jewish and heathen writers, and the few legends and traditions preserved in the writings of the fathers, and in the extant second century gospels. And when we enter upon the next century, though there is more remaining than of the first, still, the great body of the Christian literature of that age also, has been lost or destroyed.

Availing himself of what remains, the author will, though conscious of the magnitude of the task, enter upon it at least with fidelity to the truth, as he understands it.

The time will be divided into six periods, to be designated as follows:

FIRST PERIOD ...Apostolic Age.........A.D. 30 to A.D. 80.
SECOND PERIOD...Apostolic Fathers...... " 80 " " 120.
THIRD PERIOD....The Three Apocryphal
             Gospels........... " 120 " " 130.
FOURTH PERIOD..Forty Years of Christian
             Writers........... " 130 " " 170.
FIFTH PERIOD....The four Canonical Gos-
             pels.............. " 170 " " 185.
SIXTH PERIOD....Close of the Second Cen-
             tury .... " 185 " " 200.

FIRST PERIOD.

Lost Gospels of the First Century.

When Christianity had become partially established by the teaching of Christ and the preaching of his apostles and disciples, there arose among the Christians of the various churches a necessity, and hence a demand, for some written testimonies or records of the life and doctrines of their great master. But this need was not so apparent or pressing in the first century, and especially during the lifetime of those who had been with Jesus, and had been his followers and companions.

Of the numerous gospels which were in circulation in the second century, not more than three can with any certainty, or with any high degree of probability, be traced back to the times of the apostles. These are the Gospel of Paul, the Gospel or Recollections of Peter, and the Oracles or Sayings of Christ, attributed to Matthew.

THE GOSPEL OF PAUL.

Ewald, one of the best of the German critics, concludes that there was a Gospel of Paul; thinks it was in the Greek language, and that it may have been written by the evangelist Philip.[1]

It may be inferred that it afterward became incorporated into the Gospel of Marcion (A. D. 145), since Marcion was a follower of Paul, and for his own gospel claimed the sanction of that apostle.[2]

Marcion was a native of Sinope, a town of Asia

(1.) Jahrbuecher, 1848, 1849.
(2.) See Fabricius, Codex Apocryphus, Hamb. 1703, vol. 1, p. 372. Also History of the Canon, by Westcott, 3d ed. Lond. 1870, p. 282.

Minor, on the south shore of the Black Sea. It is supposed that the church at Sinope was furnished by Paul, at the time of its formation, with a collection such as he supplied to the other Asiatic churches; containing records of the life and teachings of Christ.

It was the opinion of Jerome, and of several other writers, that when Paul spoke of his gospel, (Rom. 2. 16; 16. 25; 2d Thess. 2. 14,) he referred to a written gospel then in circulation.

Paul may have had such a gospel in mind; but his language is not sufficiently explicit to justify us in concluding, with any certainty, that he meant any thing more than that gospel of which he was the great expounder.

There is, however, a more distinct trace of the Gospel of Paul in his First Epistle to the Corinthians, ch. 11, vv. 23 to 25. By comparing this passage with Luke 22. 19, 20, it will be seen that the language is almost identical; while the parallel passages, Matt. 26. 26 to 28, and Mark 14. 22 to 24, have no such complete similarity, though the idea is the same. The Gospel of Luke, whether directly, or through Marcion's, was founded partly upon the Gospel of Paul. That Paul had something to do with a written gospel, which now appears, in whole or in part, in the compilation of Luke, is generally acknowledged; and this passage in First Corinthians, taken in connection with the corresponding passage in Luke, is strong evidence that in Corinthians Paul refers to a written gospel, which he had "delivered" to the church at Corinth, and a portion of which written gospel appears in Luke 22. 19, 20.

Paul may have referred, also, to the same gospel in Galatians 2. 2.

This supposition receives countenance from a passage in Tertullian. In his work against Marcion (A. D. 200–210), after saying that Marcion did not ascribe his gospel to any author, and arguing thence that it was not authentic, he proceeds as follows :

"Had Marcion even published his gospel in the name of Paul himself, the single authority of the document, destitute of all support from preceding authorities, would not be a sufficient basis for our faith. There would still be wanting that gospel which Paul found in existence, to which he yielded his belief, and with which he so earnestly wished his own to agree, that he actually on that account went up to Jerusalem, to know and consult the apostles 'lest he should run or had been running in vain;' in other words, that the faith which he had learned and the gospel which he was preaching, might be in accordance with theirs. Then, at last, having conferred with the authors, and having agreed with them touching the rule of faith, they joined their hands in fellowship, and divided their labors thenceforth in the office of preaching the gospel, so that they were to go to the Jews, and Paul to the Jews and Gentiles. Inasmuch, therefore, as the enlightener of Luke himself desired the authority of his predecessors, for both his own faith and preaching, how much more may I not require from Luke's Gospel, that which was necessary for the gospel of his master."—[Tertullian adv. Marcion, bk. 4, ch. 2, Ante-Nicene Christian Library, vol. 7, p. 180.

From this passage of Tertullian it is manifest, first, that there was a Gospel of Paul, and the inference is very strong that it was in writing ; since Paul is represented as going to Jerusalem to compare his gospel with another, and while there, conferring with the "authors" of the other gospel ; secondly, that it was necessary, for the purpose of verification, that these two gospels should be compared ; and thirdly, that all this was anterior to the Gospel according to Luke. It might be inferred, from the closing portion of the paragraph, that Tertullian thought the Gospel of Luke itself stood in need of some verification.

It does not follow, however, that the gospel with which Paul was so anxious to compare his own, was written before his. The word "primitive" inserted by the Ante-Nicene translator, in brackets, before the word "authors," we have therefore discarded as unnecessary to the sense, and unauthorized.

The language of Tertullian is, "Denique, ut cum auctoribus contulit, et convenit de regula fidei, dexteras miscuere," etc.—[Tertull. Op, tom. 1, p. 251.

The opinion of Ewald is, that the Greek Gospel of Paul was the first ever written. There was probably no great length of time intervening between the origin of that and of the other two gospels of the first century.

The testimony of Irenæus (A. D. 190) concerning this gospel is, that it was written by Luke.

"Luke, also, the companion of Paul, recorded in a book the gospel preached by him."[1]

Notwithstanding the positive language here used, the statement is to be taken with some allowance. Irenæus was fully committed to the four gospels, and was engaged in endeavoring to give them authority. He may be said, in fact, to have introduced them to the notice of the literary world ; since he is the first author who mentions more than one of them. He speaks frequently of these gospels, and argues that they should be four in number, neither more nor less, because there are four universal winds, and four quarters of the world.

(1.) Irenæus v, Hær. bk. 3, ch. 1, Ante-Nic. vol. 5, p. 259.

Davidson calls him "credulous and blundering."[1]

Those who are so quick to receive the statement of Irenæus that the Gospel of Paul was written by Luke, a statement manifestly made to give apostolic sanction to the Gospel of Luke, are not prepared to accept so readily his assertion that the ministry of Jesus lasted twenty years, and that he was fifty years old at his crucifixion.[2]

THE GOSPEL OR RECOLLECTIONS OF PETER.

This was a book more generally known than the Gospel of Paul, and of the existence of which there can be no doubt.   In the year 190, a large number of these Gospels of Peter were found in use by the church of Rhossus, in Cilicia; and so much were the Christians of that church attached to them that it became necessary for Serapion, one of the bishops, to suppress them, and to substitute the canonical gospels in their stead.[3]

Another case of the suppression of older gospels in use in the churches, to make way for those which had been selected, will be noticed hereafter. (See Tatian.)

Eusebius (A. D. 325) speaking of the Gospel according to Peter, with other books, says :

"Neither among the ancient nor the ecclesiastical writers of our day, has there been one that has appealed to the testimony taken from them." Again, in book 3, chapter 25, he speaks of the Gospel of

(1.) Canon, p. 121.

(2.) Iren. v. Hær. 2. 22, Ante-Nic. vol. 5, p. 196.

(3.) Dr. Lardner's Works, vol. 4, p. 636; Theodoret, Fab. Hær. 2. 2; Euseb. Ecc. Hist. 6. 12; Lost and Hostile Gospels by S. Baring-Gould, p 245. Theodoret there says, the Nazarenes held that Christ was a just man, and they used the Gospel of Peter. He speaks as of his own day, A. D. 430.

Peter as among those that were "adduced by the heretics, under the name of the apostles," and "of which no one of those writers in the ecclesiastical succession, has condescended to make any mention in his works;" and says, "they are to be ranked not only among the spurious writings, but are to be rejected as altogether absurd and impious."—[Eccles. Hist. bk 3, ch. 3.

Eusebius had a peculiar faculty for diverging from the truth. Let us see how far from it he has gone in these assertions:

1. Justin Martyr, in the Dialogue, written about A. D. 160, says:

"The mention of the fact, that Christ changed the name of Peter, one of the apostles, and that the event had been recorded in his [Peter's] Memoirs, together with his having changed the name of two other brethren, who were sons of Zebedee, to Boanerges, tended to signify that he was the same through whom the surname Israel was given to Jacob, and Joshua to Hosea."—[Dialogue with Trypho, ch. 106.

The translation, as given in the Ante-Nicene Christian Library, vol. 2, p. 233, is as follows:

"And when it is said that he changed the name of one of the apostles to Peter, and when it is written in the memoirs of Him that this so happened, as well as that he changed the name of other two brothers," etc.

The word "Him," commencing with a capital letter, of course refers to Christ; thus making it read, the memoirs of Christ, and ignoring Peter as the author. The Greek is,

"*Kai to eipein metonomakenai auton Petron hena tone Apostolone, kai gegraphthai en tois apomneemoneumasin autou*," etc.

Such a construction, besides referring the pronoun autou (of him), at the close of the sentence, to the more distant antecedent, contrary to the rule in such cases, attributes to Justin language which he is not in the habit of using. Elsewhere, when speaking of the gospels which he cites so frequently, he calls them, not Memoirs of Christ, but "Memoirs of the Apostles." He has ten times "Memoirs of the Apostles," and five times "Memoirs;" not once "Memoirs of Christ."

For the rendering we have adopted we have the authority of Dr. Westcott[1] and other eminent scholars. Moreover, it is powerfully supported by the fact, that the only one of the canonical gospels which has this account of the change of the name of James and John to Boanerges, is Mark, which has such an intimate connection with the Gospel of Peter. (See Mark 3. 17.)

We conclude, therefore, that Justin Martyr here refers to the Memoirs or Recollections of Peter, which can be nothing else than the Gospel of Peter. It was probably a consideration of this passage which induced Credner to say that Justin made use of this gospel.[2]

2. The next writer who refers to the Gospel of Peter, is Turtullian (A. D. 200-210). He was one of the three fathers who were engaged in establishing the canonical gospels. And as Irenæus had undertaken to confound the Gospel of Paul with the Gospel of Luke, so Tertullian endeavors to identify the Gospel of Peter with the Gospel of Mark. He says:

"The Gospel which Mark published is affirmed to be Peter's, whose interpreter Mark was."[3]

Jones, who is unwilling to recognize the Gospel of Peter as authoritative, attempts to break the force of this testimony by interpolating, in the translation, the words "by some"; thus: "is af-

(1) Hist. of the Canon, p. 103.
(2) Geschicht. N. T. Kan. p. 22.
(3) Tert. ad. Marcion, 4. 5.

firmed by some to be Peter's." But this is entirely unauthorized.

The original is, "Evangelium quod edidit Marcus, Petri affirmatur, cujus interpres Marcus;"
translated in the Ante-Nicene collection, "That
[gospel] which Mark published, may be affirmed to
be Peter's, whose interpreter Mark was."

Tertullian manifestly intended to assert that in
his day the Gospel of Mark was understood to be
Peter's, or to have the Gospel of Peter for its original.

3. The third father who referred to this Gospel,
was Origen, A. D. 230.

"There are some," says he, "who say the brethren of Christ [here
mentioned] were the children of Joseph by a former wife, who lived
with him before Mary; and they are induced to this opinion by some
passages in that which is entitled the Gospel of Peter, or The Book
of James."—[Com. on Matt. 13. 55.

It must not be inferred that Origen here speaks
of the books as the same; but that the opinion was
held, in accordance with passages in the one book
or the other. In the Protevangelion, or Book of
James, as it was called, it is related, that when the
high priest told Joseph that he was the person selected to take the virgin, he demurred, saying, "I
am an old man and have children; but she is young,
and I fear lest I should appear ridiculous in Israel."

Though Origen was not fully prepared to accept
this statement, not seeing it in the canonical gospels, which had then, to use his own language, been
"chosen,"[1] and were thenceforth to be authoritative, yet the fact had become so well understood,

(1) "And that not four gospels but very many were written, out of which those we

from the previous use of the other gospels, that it was by most of the fathers, implicitly received as true, for a long time afterward. Epiphanius, Chrysostom, Cyril, Theophylact, Œcumenius, and all the Latin fathers till Ambrose, and the Greek fathers afterward, held to the opinion that Joseph was a widower, and had children by a former wife; showing that the Gospel of Peter and the Protevangelion were regarded as authority.

Thus we find the Gospel of Peter expressly referred to by three of the fathers before Eusebius, though that historian asserts that no one of them had condescended to make any mention of it.

Eusebius exhibited a still more reckless disregard for the truth, in regard to the Preaching of Peter. He made a similar sweeping assertion respecting that; while the fact was, it had been mentioned by Heraclion and Lactantius, and six times by Clement of Alexandria, and every time with indications of approval. It may be well to mention an error of some writers, in supposing the Preaching of Peter and the Preaching of Paul to be one book, or parts of the same book, merely from their being mentioned in the same connection by Lactantius. Such an inference is not authorized.

Other writers have mentioned this gospel. Theodoret (A. D. 430) says, "The Nazarenes are Jews who venerate Christ as a just man merely, and it is said they use the Gospel according to Peter."[1]

have were chosen, and delivered to the churches, we may perceive," etc.—[Origen, in Prœm. Lucæ, Hom. 1, t. 2, p. 210.

Again: "Four gospels only have been approved, out of which the doctrines of our Lord and Savior are to be learned."

These gospels were selected, or "separated" from others.—[Westcott, p. 317.

(1) Hær. Fab. 2. 2.

Credner thinks the gospel was one of the oldest writings of the church, and the source from which Justin Martyr drew many of his quotations; also that it was essentially identical with the Harmony of Tatian, and the Gospel according to the Hebrews.[1]

Dr. Mill[2] says it was publicly read by the Christians; and Mr. Whiston[3] asserts that it was probably, in some sense, a sacred book.

Jones, who wishes to discredit it, says it was interdicted by the decree of Pope Gelasius (A. D. 494), according to some copies; though he does not explain how the interdict crept into those copies, nor why it is not in the decree as generally published, and as it appears in his own work, vol. 1, p. 154.

The Gospel of Peter favored the opinions of the Docetæ, who held that Christ and Jesus were different; that Jesus really suffered, but Christ only in appearance.

Norton,[4] whose opinion is entitled to great weight, thinks this gospel was not a history of Christ's ministry.[4]

Rev. S. Baring-Gould asks the question, "Was this gospel a corrupted edition of St. Mark?" and answers it thus: "Probably not. We have not much ground on which to base an opinion, but there is just sufficient to make it likely that such was not the case."[5]

He considers the statement concerning the broth-

(1) Gesch. d. N. T. Kanon, p. 22.
(2) Prolegom. in Nov. Test., sec. 336.
(3) Essay on the Constitutions of the Apostles, p. 24.
(4) Evidences of the Genuineness of the Gospels, by Andrews Norton, Boston, 1837 vol. 1, p 234. Notes.
(5) Lost and Hostile Gospels, p. 221.

ers and sisters of Christ, as most valuable, as the gospel is "wholly unprejudiced, and of great antiquity."[1]

THE ORACLES OR SAYINGS OF CHRIST.

Our information concerning this collection, is exceedingly meager; being based entirely upon a passage in Eusebius, in which Papias is represented as saying, "Matthew set forth the Oracles in the Hebrew dialect, which every one interpreted as he was able."[2]

Eusebius says further, that Papias wrote five books of "Expositions of the Oracles of the Lord." These are a part of the multitude of lost writings of those times.

Baring-Gould thinks the Oracles consisted of five parts, ending at the following passages:

First, at Matthew ch. 7, v. 28; second, at Matt. 11. 1; third, at Matt. 13. 53; fourth, at Matt. 19. 1, and fifth, at Matt. 26. 1. Upon this theory, the Oracles were a compilation of different manuscripts. It is the generally received opinion that a number of older manuscripts have entered into the construction of the Gospel according to Matthew, and that this gospel was to some extent based upon the Oracles.

RECAPITULATION.

THE GOSPEL OF PAUL, though it does not stand out so clearly and indisputably as the Gospel of Peter, has yet sufficient evidence of having been one of the gospels of the first century. It is testified to by Marcion, and is apparently alluded to by Irenæ-

(1) P. 222.
(2) Euseb. Ecc. Hist., bk. 3, ch. 39.

us and Tertullian, and by Paul himself.   It was in the Greek language.

THE GOSPEL OR RECOLLECTIONS OF PETER, was a book well known, and of high authority among the ancient Christians.   Even after the introduction of the four gospels afterward made canonical, the Gospel of Peter maintained so firm a footing that it became necessary to suppress it in some of the churches.   It was retained and used by the Nazarenes, long afterward.

It is cited by Justin Martyr, and referred to by Tertullian and Origen.   The statement of Eusebius, that no one of the ecclesiastical writers had appealed to testimony taken from it, and that no one of them had condescended to make any mention of it, is untrue.   The passage in Justin Martyr is mistranslated in the Ante-Nicene collection, and the passage in Turtullian is mistranslated by Jones.

The statement contained in this gospel, that Joseph had children by a former wife, was generally received by the fathers, for several centuries.   The Gospel of Peter is highly spoken of by Dr. Mill, Mr. Whiston, and other eminent writers.   Credner, a German writer of high authority, thinks it was used by Justin Martyr, A. D. 150–160.

THE ORACLES, OR SAYINGS OF CHRIST, in the Aramaic language, we know but little about.   It has been generally conceded, on the authority of Eusebius, that Papias (A. D. 125) had such a book, and that he wrote commentaries upon it.

DOCTRINES.—There is no evidence that any of these gospels taught the miraculous conception, or the material resurrection of Christ, or contained any account of his miracles, or any reference to any book containing such accounts or teaching either of those doctrines.

It will be seen as we proceed, that the three gospels which have been considered, were the germs of the three synoptic gospels, respectively. That is, the Gospel of Paul was the germ of the Gospel according to Luke ; the Gospel of Peter, of the Gospel according to Mark ; and the Oracles, of the Gospel according to Matthew.

They cannot, however, in any sense, be considered the same. The synoptic gospels were undoubtedly written long afterward, and contained, in many respects, very different material. Moreover, the Gospel of Paul appears to have passed through the Gospel of Marcion before reaching the author of Luke, and the Oracles through the Gospel of the Hebrews before reaching the author of Matthew.

CHAPTER II.

JOHN THE BAPTIST—JESUS CHRIST—PAUL—PETER—JOHN—
THE JAMESES—THE JUDASES—THE OTHER APOSTLES—
EPISTLES OF THE NEW TESTAMENT—THE APOCALYPSE.

The first character in Christian history is John the Baptist.

What was his connection with Jesus, and what were his relations to the origin of the Christian religion?

Josephus, while he gives an account of John the Baptist baptizing and making converts, says nothing of his announcing the approach of a coming Messiah.[1]

The author of Luke commences his account of John the Baptist by saying that he appeared in the fifteenth year of the reign of Tiberius Cæsar, Pontius Pilate being Governor of Judea and Herod being Tetrarch of Galilee, his brother Philip Tetrarch of Iturea and of the region of Trachonitis, Lysanias Tetrarch of Abilene, Annas and Caiaphas being the high priests. (Luke 3. 1, 2.)

In the 23d verse of the same chapter, after relating the baptism of Jesus, he states that he began to be about thirty years of age.

(1) Antiquities, bk. 18, ch. 5, 2.

If by this language the author of Luke meant to say that Jesus was not then past thirty, did he not make a mistake of at least three years? Tiberius commenced reigning A. D. 14, and the fifteenth year of his reign would be A. D. 29, or when Jesus was thirty-three years of age, as he was four years old at the commencement of the Christian era.

We do not, however, look upon this as a very serious discrepancy, and think Dr. Lardner over-estimated the question when he spoke of it as one of "very great difficulty." The word "hosei," "about," used by the gospel historian, relieves him from any very exact criticism.

So of another objection; the statement that Annas and Caiaphas were high priests; it being notorious that the Jews never had but one high priest at a time. This has been partially explained by showing that Josephus, in one place, spoke of one as a high priest, who had held, but did not at the time referred to, hold that office. The language here is somewhat more definite, and appears more plainly to intimate that two did actually hold the position the same year.

This would indicate that this portion of the book was written long afterward, by one not acquainted with Jewish customs. Dr. Lardner says, "It would be extremely unreasonable to impute to St. Luke so great a mistake as the supposing there were properly two high priests among the Jews at the same time." The most effectual way of relieving him from the imputation is, not to charge upon him the authorship of a work which bears so many marks of having been written long after his day.

If the passage in Josephus concerning Christ were genuine, then the failure to connect him with John the Baptist, would be utterly incomprehensible. But since it is the general verdict of scholars that the paragraph in the 3d chapter of the 18th book of the Antiquities, wherein it is stated that Jesus was the Christ, etc., is an interpolated forgery, the matter appears very differently. It is easy to see that Josephus, retaining all his Jewish prejudices and antipathies, might have intentionally passed over the proclamation of the coming Messiah.

Pursuing the biography of John, as given in the gospel history, the next incident presents a difficulty of a more serious character.

It is stated that Herod the Tetrarch shut up John in prison, being reproved by him for Herodias, his brother Philip's wife. (Luke, 3. 19, 20; Mark, 6. 17–20; Matthew, 14. 3–5.) This Philip could be no other than Philip the Tetrarch of Trachonitis, men-mentioned in Luke 3. 1. He was the brother, or rather half-brother of Herod the Tetrarch, and Herod had no other brother Philip. They were both sons of Herod the Great.

But according to Josephus, Philip could not have been the former husband of Herodias. It was another Herod, half-brother of Herod the Tetrarch, having the same father, but not the same mother. The father of this Herod was Herod the Great, while his mother was Mariamne, daughter of Simon the high priest.[1]

Josephus could not well be mistaken in this mat-

_____
(1) Antiq., bk 18, ch. 5, sec. 1, and same, sec. 4.

ter, being himself a Jew, and all the parties occupying a high position among his people. Not only were all these sons of Herod the Great, but Herodias was sister of Agrippa the Great. The attention of the historian was particularly called to the transaction, and he relates in full the visit of Herod the Tetrarch to Herod, his half-brother, his falling in love with Herodias, his brother's wife, and their subsequent arrangement to be married. Also the difference that arose on this very account, between Herod the Tetrarch and Aretas, King of Petræa, father of the wife whom Herod put aside, in favor of Herodias; a difficulty which resulted in a war.

The gospel account of the death of John, is also very different from that of the historian. It does not appear in Luke, but in Mark and Matthew it is related that the daughter of Herodias danced before Herod, at a supper given by him on his birthday; (Mark, 6. 21, 22;) that Herod was pleased, and promised to give her whatever she should ask; and she, being instructed by her mother, asked the head of John the Baptist; that the king ordered it to be given her, and it was brought in a charger. (Mark, 6. 21–29; Matt., 14. 6–11).

The account by Josephus is, in substance:

That John was a good man; that he commanded the Jews to exercise virtue, and exhorted them to come to his baptism; that crowds came about him, much pleased at his discourses; that Herod feared that his great influence over the people might put it into his power and inclination to raise a rebellion, the people being ready to do anything he should advise; that to prevent any mischief he might do, and to put it out of his power to raise a rebellion, Herod had him thrown into prison at Macherus, and there put to death.

Though it might be possible, by the exercise of skill and ingenuity, to show that the accounts of John the Baptist, as given by Josephus on the one hand and the gospel historians on the other, are not absolutely contradictory, except as to the former husband of Herodias; yet the general tenor of the two biographies is so different, and the narratives so divergent, as to render it problematical whether John sustained any such relation to Jesus as is commonly supposed.

The Gospel of Marcion (A. D. 145), which, in other respects, was very similar to Luke, contained no such history of John. Marcion's Gospel was probably first written. The first two chapters of Luke were not in Marcion. In place of the 3d and 4th chapters, there was the first chapter in Marcion's Gospel, which commenced as follows:

"Now in the fifteenth year of Tiberius Cæsar, Pontius Pilate ruling in Judea, Jesus came down to Capernaum, a city of Galilee, and straightway on the sabbath days, going into the synagogue, he taught.

"2. And they were astonished at his doctrine, for his word was with power."

There was no statement in Marcion as to the age of Christ, nor concerning the two high priests, nor were there any contradictions of Josephus.

Before leaving the history of John the Baptist, we cannot refrain from referring to the grotesque incident of the daughter of Herodias dancing at a supper given by Herod to his lords, high captains and chief estates. This portion of the narrative caused a sore trial to the faith of the great Dr. Lardner.

" It may perhaps be expected," he says, " I should here produce an instance, about that time, of some lady of like station with Herodias' daughter, who danced at a public entertainment. But I must own, I am not furnished with any instance exactly parallel."

Although the Doctor did not hesitate to believe in miracles, yet, when any thing purported to be inside the bounds of nature, he desired to see it within the range of probability.

JESUS CHRIST.

The next character is Christ himself.

He is said to have been begotten of a virgin, by the overshadowing of the Holy Ghost.

This event does not appear to have been mentioned in heathen, Jewish or Christian history, until more than a hundred years after it is said to have taken place. The doctrine of the immaculate or miraculous conception, when it was promulgated to the Christians of the second century, was found to be so congenial to the prevailing disposition to deify Christ, that it was at once taken up by the bishops, and incorporated among the foundations of the grand religious structure then being erected.

Paul, who had already laid the foundations of the structure, seems to have known nothing of the doctrine.

It was somewhat incongruous to deify a person born in the ordinary course of generation. The miraculous conception was needed, to give form and consistency to the doctrine of the divinity of Jesus.

Many attempts have been made to write the life of Christ. But it is difficult to see where, outside the gospels, the material for such a work is to come from; while, if the gospels are to be taken as a basis, it is equally difficult to understand what is to be gained by rewriting what is contained in them. Any such attempt only brings out, in plainer light, the discrepancies in those accounts, and finally results in a mere display of ingenuity on the part of the biographer, in his efforts to reconcile them; or, as in the case of some writers, in a sublime unconsciousness of any discrepancies whatever.

We know of Christ historically, that he was a prominent moral and religious teacher; that he had the most devoted followers and disciples; that he was put to death in the reign of Tiberius Cæsar;[1] and that upon his doctrines and precepts, and upon a belief in his spiritual resurrection, Paul, the chief of his disciples, founded a new religion.

PAUL.

That Paul was the one who did the work, is manifest, from recorded tradition, and from those wonderful epistles, written in the first century, which are still extant, and the most of which are considered by scholars to be genuine.

Countless volumes have been written concerning Paul; works abounding in unmixed eulogy. It is the duty of the impartial historian, while appreciating and admiring those grand qualities which mark him as one of the greatest men of any age—

(1) See Appendix.

while conceding his intellectual and moral grandeur, his thorough conviction of the truth of the doctrines he was teaching, and the zeal and devotion which he manifested in their propagation, to point out, at the same time, some of the defects in his character.

The chief of these, which was the result of his excessive zeal, was an impatience, and even a vindictiveness, toward those who differed with him in opinion.

By an occasional outburst of that spirit of persecution under the influence of which he had so unrelentingly pursued the Christians, he demonstrates, that however thorough was his conversion, it had not eradicated or essentially changed those traits of character, and peculiarities of disposition, which distinguished him from other men. Commentators would have us believe, that when, in his Epistle to the Galatians, he said, "I would they were even cut off who trouble you," he meant nothing more than that they should be cut off from the church. But this he had power to have done; and did direct it, in addressing other churches. An examination of the context, and of the whole epistle, in the commencement of which he had anathematized any one who should preach any other doctrine, ("Let him be accursed,") together with the application of a careful and thorough philological analysis of the words used by the apostle, all combine to give to his language a deeper meaning; showing that in a moment of exasperation, he gave utterance to a sentiment, which, taken in connection with the teaching and practice of Peter, and the construction which was put upon some of the sayings of Christ, resulted in the most fearful and wide-spread persecutions, through subsequent ages.

It is not strange that the apostle should have such feelings toward those whom he saw endeavoring to remove some of the beautiful pillars from the splendid edifice he was constructing; but it is to be regretted that he did not foresee the use which could be made of his language in after times.

Again: notwithstanding the spirit of kindness, of brotherly love, and even of tenderness, pervading the letters of the apostle, there may be discovered occasionally, beneath it all, glimpses of an overbearing and tyrannical disposition. This is particularly noticeable in his injunctions to the female Christians, and in his determination to discountenance any ambition on their part to take an equal place with their brothers in the management of church affairs.

They were permitted to hold the position of deaconess, an office the functions of which consisted principally in ministering to the necessities of the saints. An office of labor and subserviency they could fill, but not one of honor; "I suffer not a woman to teach," said Paul; thus disclosing his domineering spirit, and his inability to rise above the prejudices of the age.

This prohibition of the apostle was scrupulously carried out; and in the Council of Laodicea, A. D. 365, the 11th canon forbade the ordination of women for the ministry, while the 44th canon prohibited them from entering into the altar. '

But the point upon which the fathers were most sensitive, in reference to the position of women in

(1) Landon's Manual of Councils, pp. 284 to 287.

the church, related to administering the rite of baptism. One of the earliest Chistian writings was the Acts of Paul and Thecla. It was a romance. Thecla, who was engaged to be married, had heard, from an upper window, Paul, preaching. She had fallen in love with him ; had deserted her lover and relatives, and had followed Paul ; had become a devoted Christian ; had baptized ; first baptizing herself. Then she worked miracles, became a saint, and finally a martyr. She was held in the highest veneration by the fathers. But the book gave implied sanction to the right of women to baptize. On that account it was declared heretical, and search was made for its author ; an unusual proceeding in those days. It was traced to a presbyter of one of the eastern churches, who acknowledged he had written it "for the honor of Paul." He was tried for the offense, and being convicted, was deposed from the ministry. [1]

The women claimed the right to baptize their own sex. But the bishops and presbyters did not care to be relieved from the pleasant duty of baptizing the female converts. [2]

Of the life of Paul we know but little. The accounts in the Acts of the Apostles, cannot, for reasons which will hereafter be given, be considered historical.

In the first epistle of .Clement of Rome, it is stated that Paul was seven times imprisoned. Dr.

(1) Tertullian, de Baptismo, ch. 17; Jerome, de Vir., 1. 7. Jerome states, erroneously, that Turtullian had said he was convicted before John.

(2) See Bunsen's Christianity and Mankind, vol. 7, pp. 386 to 393, published in the 3d volume of the Analecta. The converts were first exorcised of the evil spirits that were supposed to inhabit them; then, after undressing, and being baptized, they were anointed with oil. The custom may not have prevailed in the colder climates.

Doellinger says Paul was seven times imprisoned.[1]

WAS PAUL MARRIED?—Eusebius said,

" Paul does not demur, in a certain epistle, to mention his own wife, whom he did not take about with him, in order to expedite his ministry the better."

In saying this, Eusebius was quoting from the Stromata, of Clement of Alexandria (A. D. 200).

The full passage in Clement is as follows:

" Paul does not, indeed, in a certain epistle, fear to speak of his own wife, whom he did not take about with him, because it was not necessary for him, in the great work of the ministry. Therefore he says in a certain epistle, ' Have we not power to take about a sister wife, as also the other apostles?' For they, as was proper, while engaged in the ministry, because they could not keep them apart, were accustomed, doubtless as a matter of commendation, to take about with them female attendants, not as wives, but as sisters, who, together with the female servants, might be among the women who had charge of the house, by whom without any reprehension or suspicion of evil the doctrine of the Lord might be carried even to the secret apartments of the women."—[Strom., bk. 3, ch. 6, Latin Translation in Ante-Nicene Collection, vol. 12, p. 109.

Paul, according to the fathers, was martyred at Rome, A. D. 67 or 68.

An interesting story is preserved, of Paul and Perpetua. It is related that Perpetua, seeing Paul dragged along the streets of Rome, in irons, had compassion upon him, and wept bitterly. She had but one eye.

Paul asked her for her handkerchief. She gave it.

It was tied around Paul's head, and afterward returned to her, bloody. When she received it back, her other eye was restored. Perpetua was afterward thrown into prison, and tortured, and at last, with a great stone tied to her neck, was thrown over a precipice.

(1) First Age of the Church, p. 87.

There was between Paul and his followers on one side and Peter and his followers on the other, a strong antagonism, not generally understood in our day, and which, if properly taken into account, will explain several knotty points of scripture, and throw light upon many controverted questions in the early history of the church.   Paul was rejected by large bodies of Jewish Christians; and in the entire volume of the Recognitions, a Petrine work of the early ages, abounding in scripture quotations, there is not a single citation from Paul's epistles.

The controversy related principally, in the first instance, to the observance by the Christians of Jewish rites and ceremonies; but afterward it became hereditary and traditional.

The Ebionites claimed that Paul was an imposter; that he only became a convert for the purpose of obtaining a Jewish lady with whom he had fallen in love, and when he failed, he turned against the Jews, and opposed their observances and customs.

HIS EPISTLES.—Ten of the Epistles of Paul are probably genuine; though some of the German critics hold that we cannot be certain of more than four: Romans, 1st and 2d Corinthians, and Galatians.[1] The 15th and 16th Chapters of Romans, also, are disputed, or at least not considered part of the Epistle to the Romans; not only by German critics, but by many others.   Davidson and some others confine the objections to the 16th chapter.[2]

(1) See an interesting and well written work, entitled "What is the Bible?" by J. T. Sunderland, Chicago, 1878; where authorities are referred to.

(2) Davidson, Int. to N. T., 1, p. 137. Weiss, das Marc., 1872, p. 495.

Though all the fourteen epistles ascribed to Paul have maintained a place in the canon, many, even among evangelical writers, look with distrust upon the Epistle to the Hebrews, as having been admitted upon insufficient evidence.

Westcott states that at the close of the second century, it had not yet become established as authoritative in the churches.[1] It was not in the Latin version made by Tertullian, A. D. 210; Jerome speaks of it dubiously, and Toland says it was doubted by "the soundest part" of the ancients.[2] Dr. Doellinger says Paul did not write it.[3]

The New Testament as compiled by Marcion (A. D. 145) contained ten epistles of Paul. He knew of no epistles to Timothy, to Titus, or to the Hebrews; or if he did, he did not consider them genuine. Probably they were later productions.

The style of the Apostle Paul, though strong and concise, is sometimes elliptical and ambiguous. He indulges in mystical and allegorical expressions, and his applications are at times far-fetched and fanciful. "He often," says Doellinger, "gets more out of a passage than the words or historical sense convey." This author shows that in one place he applies to his argument a meaning precisely opposite to that of the passage quoted. The passage is Psalms 68. 18; where, instead of "Thou receivedst gifts among men," or, "Thou hast received gifts for men," Paul reads, "He gave gifts unto men." (Ephes., 4. 8.)

(1) History of the Canon, p. 306.
(2) Amyntor, p. 57.
(3) First Age of the Church, p. 83.

DOCTRINES.—The epistles of Paul being the oldest Christian writings extant, [1] their importance in the history of the Christian religion, cannot be over-estimated.

Paul believed in the resurrection of Christ, with a spiritual body. His idea of the resurrection, like that of Clement of Rome, was that the spiritual body arose from the decay of the natural body, as a plant from the decay of the seed sown to produce it. It is manifest that when Paul saw Jesus, he saw what appeared to be a spirit; since it was after the time when, as is alleged, Christ had ascended in the body. There is no evidence that Paul knew any thing of the canonical gospels; nor is there any reason to believe he had ever seen a gospel in which Jesus denied being a spirit, after the resurrection. With Paul, the resurrection and ascension were one and the same thing; and obviously meant, a manifestation from the spiritual world.

Paul believed that Christ, after his resurrection, or ascension, communicated to his disciples, by the agency of the Holy Spirit, through intercession with the Father, supernatural gifts; "charismata"; and that these gifts were imparted by the laying on of hands. The precise nature of these "charismata" has been the subject of much discussion. There is no doubt that in the view of Paul, they not only included some miraculous powers, but extended as well to the natural operations and processes of the mind; those involved in preaching and exhorting, as well as in interpreting, prophesying, etc. The assistance of this extraordinary gift ex-

---

[1] Origin of the Four Gospels, by Tischendorf, 1867, p. 24; Credibility of the Gospel History, by Dr. Lardner, vol. 3, p. 148.

tended to all the qualities necessary for the guidance as well as the edification of the church.

Whether Paul claimed to have himself performed miracles, is also a mooted question. He apparently makes such a claim, in Rom. 15. 18, 19, and in 2d Corinthians, 12. 12; but it has been contended that the original does not necessarily require that construction. [1]

Whatever Paul may claim for himself and his fellow-disciples, by virtue of the descent of the Holy Ghost, there is no reference in his epistles to any miracles performed by Jesus, during his earthly ministry, nor any evidence that Paul believed in any such miracles, or had ever heard of them.

It has often been asked, why did not any heathen or Jewish writer of the first century speak of the miracles of Christ? But a question arises which is equally suggestive, why does neither Paul nor Clement of Rome, the only Christian writers of the first century, make the slightest allusion to them?

The same is true of the miraculous conception. Justin Martyr is constantly referring to Christ as "born of a virgin." So with other writers of the second century. But in the epistles of Paul and Clement, though they abound continually in references to Christ, we look for that phrase in vain.

PETER.

If the fanatics of subsequent times could point to the sayings of Paul, as apparent authority for their excesses, they could, with still more confidence, turn to the teaching and example of Peter. " When," says Dr. Doellinger, "Ananias and Sapphira, through

(1) Supernatural Religion, vol. 3, pt. 2, ch. 2.

their hypocrisy and avaricious attempt at deception, had made the first assault on the authority of the apostles and the Holy Ghost ruling in the church, *St. Peter inflicted a terrible punishment upon them.*"[1]

When we meet with such language in a Christian writer of the nineteenth century, what might not be expected of the priests of the middle ages?

In the Epistle of Clement to James, in the Ante-Nicene collection, Clement describes his ordination.

He says, when Peter was about to die, the brethren being assembled (at Rome), he laid his hands on Clement as the bishop, and communicated to him the power of binding and loosing, etc.; and as to him who should grieve the president of the truth, after declaring that such a one sins against Christ, and offends the Father of all, Peter proceeded as follows:

" Wherefore, *he shall not live;* and therefore it becomes him who presides, to hold the place of a physician; and not to cherish the rage of an irrational beast."—[Ante-Nicene Christian Library, vol. 17, p. 7.

It does not require a forced construction to enable one to find the inquisition in this sentence. The genuineness of the epistle is not generally admitted by Protestants; but it appears among the ancient writings of the church. If its authenticity cannot be proved, the same may be said of other writings which are implicitly received as genuine.

But little is known of the personal history of Peter. His name was Simon. There has not been the same difficulty in distinguishing him from the Apostle Simon Zelotes, as in the case of the two apostles James, and the two apostles Judas. There

(1) First Age of the Church, by John Ignatius Doellinger, D. D., 2d London Edition, 1867, p. 44.

results, however, considerable confusion, when an attempt is made to identify Peter with the Cephas so often alluded to by Paul, and we are tempted to seek refuge from the dilemma, by assuming, with Eusebius, that Paul alludes to a person supposed to be one of the seventy ; not to Peter the Apostle.[1]

It is noticeable that in every place in the gospels but one (and the total number is nearly a hundred) where Peter is mentioned, the Greek name "Petros" is given, which is supposed to be used by Jews as well as others. This would indicate that all the canonical gospels, Matthew included, are original Greek productions.

So little is there authentic in the history of Peter, that to this day the learned cannot agree whether he ever went to Rome. Protestants generally do not admit that such a journey was made.[2]

Theodore of Mopsuestia, about A. D. 394, says, Peter went to Rome, the others elsewhere. But he probably took it from Eusebius. That writer does not hesitate to make the statement explicitly, and to give the most circumstantial evidence. But in this instance, as in so many others, his testimony is at second hand, from lost writings. He quotes from Caius, a writer whose works, if they ever existed, are now lost or destroyed, what he said disputing with Proclus, and Caius quotes from another writer whose works are lost, Dionysius of Corinth.[3]

(1) Eccles. Hist., i. 12, citing Clement of Alexandria.

(2) Rev. Dr. Sunderland, late Chaplain of the United States Senate, is said to have thanked the Lord, in a prayer, at a public meeting, that Paul had visited Rome, though Peter had not.

(3) Euseb. Eccles. Hist., 2. 25.

Going back 135 years, we find the same thing in Irenæus. He says:

"Matthew wrote a gospel for the Jews, and in the language of the Jews, at the same time when Peter and Paul founded the church at Rome."—[Iren. adv. Hær., 3. 1.

This complicates the question somewhat. Perhaps the easiest way to dispose of this testimony, would be to adopt the construction of Dupin, who, maintaining that Matthew wrote his gospel earlier, says the words of Irenæus are not to be understood in the literal sense.[1]

The journey of Peter to Rome, and his residence there, cannot be denied by Protestant writers, without rejecting the testimony of witnesses who, in other matters, are, by the same writers, relied upon with implicit confidence.

The received accounts of the miracles of Peter, are sufficient to excite our astonishment; but the most wonderful of all his miracles is related in the Acts of Peter and Andrew, where he is represented as making a camel go through the eye of a needle.

"After the needle had been brought, and all the multitude of the city were standing by to see, Peter looked up and saw a camel coming. And he ordered her to be brought. Then he fixed the needle in the ground, and cried out with a loud voice, saying: 'In the name of Jesus Christ, who was crucified under Pontius Pilate, I order thee, O camel, to go through the eye of the needle.' Then the eye of the needle was opened like a gate, and the camel went through it, and all the multitude saw it."—[Ante-Nicene, vol. 16, p. 371.

The miracle was repeated. Onisephorus, who would not believe, sent for another needle and another camel, with a woman sitting on the camel. "And they went through twice."

(1) Dupin, Eccles, Hist., vol. 1, p, 46.

HIS EPISTLES.—The First Epistle of Peter is not free from doubt, and the Second has long been a subject of controversy.

It was omitted in the Latin Version of Tertullian of Africa, (A. D. 210,)[1] in the Muratorian Fragment,[2] in the Peshito Version, used in the east in ancient times;[3] and as Mr. Toland says, was doubted by the soundest part of the ancient writers.

Westcott cannot trace it back earlier than A. D. 170,[4] and says it was not authoritative until near the close of the second century.[5]

Davidson says it was the last of the New Testament documents,[6] and Norton declares that there is no historical evidence to justify us in believing it to be the work of the Apostle Peter.[7]

DOCTRINES.—There is too little extant which can be relied upon as the genuine writing of Peter, to throw much light upon the history of Christian doctrine. The two epistles ascribed to him are as silent as those of Paul concerning the miracles of Christ, or the material resurrection, or the miraculous conception.

If we could only rely upon the Clementine writings as authority for the views of Peter, we might infer that he did not look upon Jesus as equal to the Father.

"Our Lord," he is represented as saying, "neither asserted that there were gods, except the Creator of all, nor did he proclaim himself to be God, but he pronounced him blessed who called him the Son of that God who ordered the universe."—[Clementine Homilies, 16. 15.

(1) Westcott, History of Canon, p. 234.
(2) McClintock and Strong.
(3) Westcott, p. 221.   (4) p. 234.   (5) p. 306.
(6) Canon, p. 85.
(7) Genuineness of the Gospels, vol. 2, p. 162.

JOHN.

John is the only one of the twelve apostles whose life appears to extend into the region of authentic history. And of him, this can only be said of the latter portion of his life. He is supposed to have been driven to Patmos, by some persecution, but the learned cannot agree what emperor it was under; the range being from Claudius to Domitian. In the persecution under Domitian he was taken to Rome. There, it is said, the boiling oil into which he was thrown had no power to hurt him. [1]

The account of his living to an old age, at Ephesus, has been universally received, and may be considered historic. Irenæus says that at Ephesus John leaped out of a public bath, with horror, when he saw Cerinthus, the heretic, entering it. Cerinthus flourished about the middle of the second century. Some ecclesiastical historians, in aid of Irenæus, have tried to bring Cerinthus within the first century.

THE WRITINGS OF JOHN.—Probably none of the writings attributed to the Apostle John are entitled to be considered genuine.

His 2d and 3d epistles were omitted in the Peshito, [2] were not established as late as at the close of the second century, [3] and were doubted by Eusebius himself. Even as late as 1562, when Ignatius, Patriarch of Antioch, hearing of the advantages of printing, sent a certain priest of Mesopotamia into Europe, with a copy of the Syriac Testa-

(1) Tertullian, de Præs., c. 36.

(2) Westcott, Hist. Canon, p. 221.

(3) Ibid., p. 297.

ment to be printed, it lacked the 2d Epistle of Peter, 2d and 3d John, Jude, and Revelation.[1]

THE APOCALYPSE, OR REVELATION, ascribed to John, seems to have been one of many productions of the kind which appeared early in the second century. It is similar to the Revelation of Cerinthus, and may have emanated from the same source.

It was omitted from the Peshito Version; from the Catalogue of Cyril of Jerusalem; from that of Gregory Nazianzen; and Davidson thinks it was not in the collection of New Testament books made by Eusebius for the use of the churches, by order of Constantine.[2]

It was not established at the close of the second century,[3] and was not in the Syriac Testament, sent to be printed in 1562.

But the most remarkable circumstance is the fact that it was rejected by the very churches to whom it was addressed.

In the Council of Laodicea, A. D. 365, consisting of 32 bishops, from the different Asiatic churches, by the 60th canon, it was solemnly decreed what should be the canonical books of the New Testament. The Apocalypse was omitted.[4]

Eusebius argues against it, and thinks it was written by John the Presbyter, or Elder, who lived in the second century.[5]

After all this evidence, it would seem superflu-

(1) Jones, vol. 1, p. 87.
(2) Canon, p. 118.
(3) Westcott.
(4) Landon's Manual of Councils, pp. 284 to 287.
(5) Ecc. Hist., 3. 39. Also, 7. 25. The argument is credited to Dionysius.

ous to add, that the church at Thyatira was not founded until after the death of the Apostle John.

THE GOSPEL ACCORDING TO JOHN.—The Rev. Dr. Davidson, who is considered such high authority that he was employed to write the article on the Canon for the new edition of the Encyclopedia Britannica, says:

"Its existence [the Gospel of John] before 140 A. D., is incapable either of decisive or probable showing." And again: "The Johannine authorship has receded before the tide of modern criticism; and although the tide is arbitrary at times, it is here irresistible." [1]

THE JAMESES.

Two apostles are mentioned by the name of James; one, the son of Zebedee, and brother of John, also called James the Elder; and the other, James the son of Alphæus, who was called James the Less, and James the Just. But whether the latter James was the same with the brother of the Lord, commentators have not been able to decide. This, the great church historian, Neander, pronounces the most difficult question in apostolic history.

James, the brother of Jesus, is a historic personage. An account of his death is given, with full particulars, by Josephus. Some evangelical writers have been inclined to let this passage go with the other, as a forgery. But there does not appear to be any good reason to deny its authenticity. The account is as follows:

(1) Canon of the Bible, by Samuel Davidson, D. D., LL. D., London, 1877, p. 99. John not written before 150. See Davidson's Int. N. T.

"Festus was now dead, and Albinus was but upon the road; [hav-
ing been appointed procurator of Judæa]; so he [Ananus, who had
just been appointed high priest], assembled the Sanhedrim of judges
and brought before them the brother of Jesus, who was called
Christ, whose name was James, and some of his companions ; and
when he had formed an accusation against them, as breakers of the
law, he delivered them to be stoned."—[Antiq. bk. 20, ch. 9.

The historian then proceeds to relate, that some
of the citizens condemned the proceeding, and went
to meet Albinus, who was returning from Alexandria; that they complained to him of Ananus, and
claimed that he had no right to assemble the Sanhedrim without Albinus' consent; that Albinus,
taking the same view of the matter, wrote a severe
letter of reproof to Ananus, and soon after, had the
high-priesthood taken from him.   Now here is a
network of historical facts and incidents connected
with the customs and ecclesiastical polity of the
Jews, which forbids the supposition of the whole
account being a forgery. And if the words relating
to Christ are to be stricken out, there must be some
good reason given for it. We do not see any.
There is nothing inconsistent in the language.   Josephus is not here, as in the other passage, made
to declare that Jesus is the Christ. He is spoken
of as "Jesus who was called Christ," to distinguish him from other Jews by the name of Jesus.

EPISTLE OF JAMES.—Commentators think this
epistle was written by James the son of Zebedee,
according to the subscription of the Syriac Version;
or James the son of Alpheus, [1] or James the brother
of the Lord, [2] or an unknown James, which was

(1.) Dr. Davidson, Introduction to N. T., i. 385, supports 2d or 3d hypothesis.
(2.) Alford, Gr. Test. 4. 28, supported by Eusebius.

Luther's opinion. As the Epistle maintains its place among the writings of the New Testament, we must conclude that upon the question of its inspiration, it is immaterial by whom it was written.

THE JUDASES AND THE OTHER APOSTLES.—There were two apostles by the name of Judas. The one, called Thaddæus, the other, Judas Iscariot. Whether the one called Thaddæus, and at other times Lebbæus, was also the Lord's brother, here again the learned cannot agree; nor whether he was the author of the Epistle of Jude. This epistle was not in the Peshito, nor in the Syriac Version of 1562. It was rejected by Norton [1] and had been long before by Michaelis. [2] This was one of the seven books which were for a long time discredited by the fathers. The others were 2d Peter, 2d and 3d John, James, Hebrews and Revelation.

It is scarcely worth while to attempt to complete a history of the apostles. The whole subject is involved in obscurity. After, with much difficulty, we have settled upon eleven apostles, the twelfth, in the synoptic gospels was Bartholomew, while in John it was Nathanael.

(1.) Vol. 2, p. 162.
(2.) Vol. 1, p. 291.

THE APOSTOLIC FATHERS.
A. D. 80 TO A. D. 120.

CHAPTER III.

CLEMENT OF ROME, IGNATIUS, AND POLYCARP.

CLEMENT. A. D. 97.—No grander character appears in Christian history, than Clement of Rome.

Whether we look at his First Epistle to the Corinthians, generally considered to be genuine, or at the numerous other writings attributed to him, and the recorded traditions concerning his life and teachings, we find, in either case, one of the highest and noblest types of Christian character. His first Epistle, written about A. D. 97, will compare favorably with the Epistles of Paul.

The great and absorbing question connected with this, the first authentic Christian writing outside the gospels, and subsequent to the New Testament Epistles, is, whether any of the gospels are recognized in it, and which?

There are some passages claimed as parallel, but there is no mention of any gospel by name. Of the supposed parallel passages, some have a similarity of language, while the idea is different; in others, the same or a similar meaning is conveyed in different language.

When these are eliminated, it will be found, that while there are, in Clement, twenty passages parallel to similar ones in the N. T. Epistles, there are but five parallel to any in the canonical gospels. But these do not by any means indicate that these gospels were then in existence. The passages all relate to the sayings of Christ, which were preserved by tradition, as well as in older gospels. Four of the parallelisms are in Matthew, and no doubt were in the Oracles, or other collections of sayings, to which Clement had access. The other is in Luke, 6th chapter, vv. 36 to 38. That also is a saying of Christ, which in Clement differs considerably from Luke, although Clement professes to give the very "words of the Lord Jesus, which he spake."— [Clem. Ep. ch. 13.

Tischendorf concludes that Clement's Epistle does not furnish proof of the existence of the four gospels at that time.[1]

In connection with the Epistle of Clement, there is a circumstance worthy of notice.

In the 17th chapter of Luke, between the 1st and 2d verses, the words elsewhere occurring in the gospels, "it had been good for that man if he had not been born," are wanting. Now these very words were in the Gospel of Marcion, in the same connection as they would be if between verses 1st and 2d, of 17th Luke. They were also used in a similar connection, by Clement, in the 46th chapter

(1.) Origin of the Four Gospels, p. 52.

of his Epistle, long before the time of Marcion. If then, as is claimed, Marcion's Gospel is nothing but a corruption of Luke, how did it happen, that Marcion should interpolate a sentence precisely in the same connection in which it had been used by Clement? Is it not more probable that Clement and Marcion were using in common an ancient gospel, in which that sentence occurred, and that the author of Luke either omitted the sentence, or made use of a different version of the same ancient gospel? It is true, these or similar words occur in Mark and Matthew, but not in the same connection as in Marcion. In Clement they are in the same connection.

The authorities are somewhat conflicting, as to the time when Clement was Bishop, but it is now pretty generally agreed that he wrote his Epistle about A. D. 97. He is said to have lived to the year 100.[1]

Besides his First Epistle to the Corinthians, there are several volumes of writings attributed to Clement. There is a Second Epistle to the Corinthians; the Epistle to James, giving an account of his ordination by Peter; two Epistles in praise of Virginity; the Canons and Apostolic Constitutions, and the Clementines, so called, consisting of the Epitome, the Homilies and the Recognitions.

The Recognitions is a religious romance of much interest, throwing light upon the manners and customs of the times, and upon the religious views and practices of the early Christians, and especially illustrating the prevailing rage for miracles.

(2.) Mosheim, vol. 1, p. 96; 2d ed. note.

There is but little doubt that portions of it, at least, were written in the second century; the evidences which have been detected of a later date, being in the interpolations.   The Latin translator, Rufinus, (A. D. 410), is the same who is generally believed to have taken such unwarrantable liberties with the text of Origen.

Origen referred to the Recognitions, A. D. 230.

Clement commences, in the Recognitions, by stating that he was born in the city of Rome, and was, from his early youth, given to meditating upon serious subjects; upon the nature of life, whether there was pre-existence, and would be immortality, &c.   While engaged in these reflections, a report reached him, which took its rise in the regions of the east, in the reign of Tiberius Cæsar.   He speaks of the miracles of Christ.   These reports became confirmed.   About this time, Barnabas came to Rome to preach; and he being derided by the people, and a tumult having arisen, Clement, who was a person of distinction, interfered in behalf of Barnabas.   He becomes interested, and resolves to return with him to the east.   Barnabas sails, and Clement, as soon afterwards as he can arrange his affairs.

Arriving at Cæsarea, Barnabas presents Clement to Peter, who receives him joyfully, and running up to him, kisses him.   Peter is preparing for a debate with Simon Magus.   (For an account of this discussion, see chapter 8.)

After a long stay, and meeting with many incidents, Clement recognizes in two of the disciples of

Peter, Niceta and Aquila, two brothers of Clement, who, with their mother, had gone to a distant country, in their boyhood, and whom he had never heard of since. He also recognizes, in an old woman, and an old man, who are unknown to each other, and whom Clement meets at different times, his mother and his father; neither of whom he had seen since his boyhood. These are the "Recognitions," which give title to the book.

DOCTRINES.—Turning again to the First Epistle of Clement to the Corinthians, which, out of deference to the learned, is the only one of the writings attributed to him which can be recognized as genuine, let us see what it contains.

Though it is a long epistle, covering more than forty octavo pages, and is full of doctrinal allusions, we look in vain for any trace of the immaculate or miraculous conception of Jesus, or of his miracles, or of his material resurrection.

His views of the resurrection are given in the 24th chapter, in beautiful language, similar to that used by Paul, in his letter to the Corinthians. He compares the burial of the body, to the sowing of fruit in the earth.

"The sower goes forth and casts it into the ground; and the seed being thus scattered, though dry and naked when it fell upon the earth, is gradually dissolved. Then out of its dissolution, the mighty power of the province of the Lord, raises it up again," &c.

He refers to the phenix; a bird which was reported to live to a great age; and says, when its days are fulfilled, it builds its nest, and lies down and dies, and when its flesh has decayed, a new bird arises in its place.

It is difficult to believe, that Clement, when he wrote these words, or Paul, when he declared, "It is sown in corruption, it is raised in incorruption," "it is sown a natural body, it is raised a spiritual body," had before him a gospel in which it was recorded, that Jesus expressly denied being a spirit, after his resurrection, and called for meat, that he might demonstrate to his disciples, that he had a material body like theirs.

The spiritualism of Paul and Clement was too refined for the gross conceptions of the second century, which would be satisfied with nothing less than the resurrection of the very crucified body of Jesus. Gospels were accordingly constructed, containing accounts of such a resurrection, related with great circumstantiality.

In the 40th chapter, Clement recognizes the rites and ceremonies of the Jewish worship, as still subsisting in his day, apparently even in the Christian church.

A large part of this epistle relates to those stirring up sedition and schism in the church. By the acts of these, the large-hearted father was deeply grieved.

After reminding them of the time when they were united and harmonious, in the following beautiful and affecting words,

"Every kind of faction and schism was abominable in your sight; ye mourned over the transgressions of your neighbors; their deficiencies you deemed your own;"

He refers to those who, "through pride and sedition, have become the leaders of a detestable emulation." But so far from expressing feelings of hatred toward them, he says in the same paragraph, "Let us be kind to one another, after the pattern of the tender mercy and benignity of our Creator." After citing many examples of humility and long suffering from the Old Testament, he calls upon his brethren to reflect, how free from wrath God is, toward all his creation.—[ch. 19.

Illustrating his subject by the peace and harmony of the universe, he says :

"The heavens, revolving under his government, are subject to him in peace. Day and night run the course appointed by him, in no wise hindering each other. The sun and moon, with the companies of the stars, roll in harmony, according to his command, within their prescribed limits, and without any deviation. The fruitful earth, according to his will, brings forth food in abundance," &c. "The vast, immeasurable sea, gathered together by his working, into various basins, never passes beyond the bounds placed around it, but does as he has commanded."

"Those," said he, "who have been the leaders of sedition and disagreement, ought to have respect to the common hope."

He closes with this sublime benediction :

"May God, who seeth all things, and who is the ruler of all spirits, and the Lord of all flesh,—who chose our Lord Jesus Christ, and us through him, to be a peculiar people,—grant to every soul that calleth upon his glorious and holy name, faith, fear, patience, long-suffering, self-control, purity and sobriety; to the well pleasing of his name, through our High Priest and Protector, Jesus Christ, by whom be to Him glory, and majesty, and power, and honor, both now and forevermore, Amen."

IGNATIUS. A. D. 115.—The personal history of Ignatius is so complicated with that of his epistles, that they cannot be separated.

Two hundred years ago, there were fifteen epistles in circulation, ascribed to Ignatius, who was Bishop of Antioch, about the commencement of the second century.

Scholars soon decided that eight of them were spurious. The other seven, being those addressed to the Ephesians, Magnesians, Trallians, Romans, Philadelphians and Smyrnæans, and to Polycarp, appeared in two forms; one very much longer than the other, and in some places, containing whole pages not in the shorter form. Internal and other evidence caused the rejection of the long form, or long recension, and the learned settled down upon the short recension, or the Vossian Epistles, as they were named, from Vossius, their publisher, as the genuine writings of Ignatius; not, however, without some doubt expressed, as to the genuineness even of these.

Thus matters stood until 1845; when Dr. Cureton, who had charge of the Syriac department of the British Museum, published three Syriac Epistles of Ignatius, which had been discovered three years previous, having been procured by Archdeacon Tattam, from the monastery of St. Mary Deipara, in the desert of Nitria, in Egypt.

Dr. Cureton, in an able treatise, maintained that these were the only genuine epistles of Ignatius. They were the Epistles to the Ephesians, to the

Romans, and to Polycarp ; all in shorter form than in the Vossian Letters.

For a number of years, the opinion of Dr. Cureton gained ground, and promised fair to become universal. But of late, the investigations of German scholars have resulted in raising grave doubts as to the integrity of any of the epistles. In England, the subject has undergone an animated discussion, and has been made the occasion of exhaustive research, resulting in very able treatises on both sides of the question.

The subject was opened by the author of "Supernatural Religion." After reviewing the arguments against the accepted statements of the fathers, that Ignatius was sent from Antioch to Rome to be martyred, statements upon which the genuineness of the letters in any shape depends, since in every form they purport to be written on such a journey, the author says :

" This conclusion, irresistible in itself, is, however, confirmed by facts arrived at from a totally different point of view. It has been demonstrated that Ignatius was not sent to Rome at all, but suffered martyrdom in Antioch itself on the 20th of December, A. D. 115; when he was condemned to be cast to wild beasts in the amphitheater, in consequence of the fanatical excitement produced by the earthquake which took place on the 13th of that month."—[*Sup. Rel. vol. 1, p. 268.*

The writer refers to a number of authorities, all German, except Dr. Davidson.

This statement was subjected to the most searching criticism, by Mr. Westcott, in the Preface to the 4th edition of his work on the Canon, and by Dr. Lightfoot, in an article on the Ignatian Epistles, published in the Contemporary Review for February, 1875. Also in a milder and more liberal style, by Mr. Sanday, in "The Gospels in the Second Century."

The criticisms of Lightfoot, Westcott and others, were replied to with great ability, in over fifty pages of the Preface to the sixth edition of, Supernatural Religion.

The argument, briefly stated, on both sides, is as follows :

AGAINST THE MARTYRDOM AT ROME, AND AGAINST THE GENUINENESS OF ANY OF THE EPISTLES.—It is shown that during the winter of 115–116, the Emperor Trajan, being engaged in war with the Parthians, was in Antioch. If, therefore, he condemned Ignatius to martyrdom, he would be more likely to do it there, where they both were. Sending him to Rome would be an additional act of cruelty, not in accordance with the character of Trajan, who was a mild prince, under whose reign but one other instance of martyrdom is recorded, and that not well established. Ignatius, according to the account, was sent by a long and difficult land route, instead of the shorter and easier route by sea ; which is improbable. Deputations of Christians have access to him, and accompany him, though he represents himself as guarded strictly by ten leopards. (Roman soldiers.) He is represented as being permitted to write long letters, advocating the very doctrines for which he is condemned. The epistles do not contain the last exhortations and farewell words that might be expected ; but "are filled with ad-

vanced views of church government, and the dignity
of the episcopate.'' There is no instance recorded,
even during the persecutions under Marcus Aurelius,
in which any one was sent to Rome, to be cast to
wild beasts ; although such executions frequently
took place in Syria. Again, an earthquake occurred
in Antioch, on the 13th of December, A. D. 115,
which caused great consternation. This was a week
before the martyrdom. It is probable that Ignatius
fell a victim to the superstitious feeling which resulted from it. His remains were afterward known
to be at Antioch, said to have been brought from
Rome, but they were probably there all the time.

These arguments are endorsed by Davidson in
England, and in Germany, by Volkmar, Bauer,
Scholten and Hilgenfeld. Volkmar also adds the
authority of an ancient writer, John Malalas, about
A. D. 600, who lived at Antioch, and would there-
fore, be likely to know.

For the Martyrdom at Rome, and the Genuineness of the Cureton (the three Syriac) Epistles.
—The unbroken testimony of the fathers for nearly
five hundred years. If Malalas lived at Antioch,
so did Chrysostom and Evagrius, both earlier than
Malalas, and both of whom state the martyrdom
was at Rome. Besides, Malalas is shown to be entirely unreliable on several other subjects. Many
reasons may have operated on the mind of Trajan,
to induce him to send Ignatius to Rome, which
cannot be judged of at this late day. Other instances
are shown, where Christians, when in imprisonment,

had been permitted to see their friends, and communicate with them. It is conceded that Ignatius suffered martyrdom, by order of Trajan. Arguments therefore go for naught, which are based upon the clemency of Trajan, or on the supposed fact that there were no other martyrdoms. The objection that he was permitted to write long letters, is removed, since it is generally conceded, that not more than the three short letters, according to Syriac version, are genuine. But little can be inferred from the contents of the letters. The martyr wished to improve that opportunity to give advice and instruction which would be of lasting benefit. The connection between his execution and the earthquake, is merely speculation. Furthermore,—and these two considerations are probably the strongest of all—First, the epistles are referred to in such a way in the Epistle of Polycarp, as to require a complicated double forgery, if the Ignatian letters are not genuine; and secondly, the Epistles of Ignatius are quoted by Origen, A. D. 230, and still earlier, by Irenæus, A. D. 190; both quotations being found in the Cureton Epistles.

Such arguments are urged by Drs. Westcott, Lightfoot and others in England, and in Germany, by Bleek, Guericke and Mayerhoff.

In our judgment, the scales turn on the side of the martyrdom at Rome, and the authenticity of the Cureton Epistles.

Dr. Lightfoot, while he accepts these epistles as genuine, states that the Vossian letters are a production of not later than the middle of the second century, and desires the question of genuineness to remain an open one. But do not the Cureton letters, if genuine, exclude any longer form of the same epistles? Besides, that question was supposed to have been settled by Lipsius, whose opinion Dr. Lightfoot himself had indorsed, before writing this article for the Contemporary Review. Lipsius had come to the conclusion that the Vossian letters were an interpolation ; that is, a forgery as to four, and an interpolation as to the other three ; and that they were written about A. D. 140.

THE CURETON EPISTLES.—They are written in an affectionate and fatherly spirit, and the sentiments and views of the writer are expressed in language at once simple and dignified.

When referring to those making trouble in the church, he does so in the following words :

"Bear with all men, even as our Lord beareth with thee." (Addressed to Polycarp.) "If thou lovest the good disciples only, thou hast no grace; rather subdue those that are evil by gentleness." "Let not those who seem to be somewhat, and teach strange doc-trines, strike thee with apprehension." "More especially is it fitting, that we should bear everything, for the sake of God, that he also may bear us."

In the Epistle to the Romans, the condemned martyr looks joyfully forward to the time when he shall be offered up, as a testimony to the faith. He is even apprehensive, lest the brethren should interfere.

"Ye cannot," said he, "give me any thing more precious than this, that I should be sacrificed to God, while the altar is ready." Again: "I am the wheat of God, and by the teeth of the beasts I shall be ground, that I may be found the pure bread of God." (Quoted, with a slight variation, by Irenæus, adv. Hær., 5. 28.)

The zeal and enthusiasm of Ignatius, in contemplation of his martyrdom, rose to the height of fanaticism. His mind even dwelt with delight upon the details of his sufferings.

"Fire and the cross, and the beasts that are prepared, cutting off of the limbs, and scattering of the bones, and crushing of the whole body, harsh torments of the devil, let them come upon me, but only let me be accounted worthy of Jesus Christ."

He coveted and earnestly desired the glory of martyrdom, and feared the brethren at Rome, whom he was addressing, might interfere in his behalf, before his arrival.

THE IMMACULATE CONCEPTION.

DOCTRINE.—In the Epistle of Ignatius to the Ephesians, there is, apparently, an obscure reference to the immaculate conception of Jesus; the first intimation of such a doctrine, which we have been able to find in history.

It is in these words:

"There was concealed from the ruler of this world, the virginity of Mary, and the birth of our Lord, and the three renowned mysteries, which were done in the tranquility of God, from the Star."

This, at first, even in connection with what follows, is not very clear. There appears to be a hidden meaning, not easily fathomed.

But if it be remembered, that Ignatius was Bishop of Antioch, in Syria, a country imbued with the religious and mythological ideas of Persia, that he must be supposed to have been familiar with the two principles, one of good, and the other of evil, and of their conflict through the ages; and also that Zoroaster had been immaculately conceived by a ray

from the divine reason ; had been taken to heaven
by lightning, and there enthroned as a living star ;
if we suppose these thoughts and images to be blended with his Christian convictions, giving his religious views a tinge of that Gnosticism then commencing to prevail so extensively in the church, the
paragraph cited may be read with what follows
more intelligibly.

"There was concealed from the ruler of this world, the virginity of
Mary, and the birth of our Lord, and the three renowned mysteries,
which were done in the tranquility of God, from the Star." Then the
following: "And here, at the manifestation of the Son, magic began
to be destroyed, and all bonds were loosed; and the ancient kingdom
and the error of evil were destroyed."

The ancient struggle is at an end ; the principle
of good has triumphed ; and this has come from the
influence of the living Star.   The Gospel of the Infancy, which was published soon afterward, and
which Ignatius may have seen, states that the magi
came to Bethlehem, guided by a star, in accordance
with the prophecy of Zoroaster.

EVIDENCE AS TO THE FOUR GOSPELS.—There is but
one passage in the Cureton Epistles, which can be
cited, even as apparent evidence of the existence of
either of the four gospels.

"Be thou wise as the serpent in every thing, and
harmless, as to those things which are requisite, as
the dove."   No source is indicated, whence this is
taken.   It is one of the sayings of Jesus, which
were preserved in various forms, both by tradition,
and in the older gospels.   It is not much relied on
as evidence.   Rev. Mr. Sanday, after citing the

passage, from the Epistle of Ignatius to Polycarp, and thinking it ought to be referred to the similar passage in Matthew 10.16, adds:

"It is however, possible, that Ignatius may be quoting, not directly from our gospel, but from one of the original documents, (such as Ewald's hypothetical Spruch-Sammlung), out of which our gospel was composed; though it is somewhat remarkable that this particular sentence is wanting in the parallel passage in St. Luke."—[*Gospels in the Second Century*, *p. 78*.

Ignatius had been forty years bishop of Antioch, and was said to be 86 years old at the time of his death.

" THE MARTRYDOM OF IGNATIUS."—This purports to have been written soon after the martyrdom, by some persons who accompanied Ignatius to Rome.

Many have expressed doubts as to its authenticity; others have rejected it altogether. It is unnecessary to decide. The document has but little historic value, since the martyrdom is generally admitted.

POLYCARP. A. D. 116.—It is difficult to understand how the Ante-Nicene editors and some other writers can concede the genuineness of the Epistle of Polycarp to the Philippians, and still claim that it cannot be dated earlier than the middle of the second century. If there is any portion of it that belongs to that period, it must be an interpolation. The original epistle, if genuine, was written very soon after the martyrdom of Ignatius. This will become manifest, by comparing this letter with the one from Ignatius to Polycarp.

In that letter, Ignatius says, " I salute him who
is reckoned worthy to go to Antioch, in my stead,
as I directed thee." This can only become intel-
ligible by reference to the 13th chapter of the Epistle of Polycarp to the Philippians. It must be borne
in mind that Smyrna, the residence of Polycarp,
was southeast of Philippi, in Macedonia, the place
to which his letter was directed; that Ignatius had
passed through Macedonia, on his way to Rome, and
that Antioch, whence he started, was a long way
southeast of Smyrna. Polycarp, writing from
Smyrna to the Philippians, says: " Both you and
Ignatius wrote to me, that if any one went into
Syria, he should carry your letter with him." He
proceeds to say, in substance, that he will send the
letter, if he has an opportunity. Again, same
chapter (13), he says: "Any more certain information you may have obtained, both respecting
Ignatius himself, and those with him, have the
goodness to make known to us."

He refers to Ignatius in language implying that
he had proceeded, with his friends, on his journey
to Rome. Nothing can be plainer, than if the letter is genuine, it was written after Ignatius had
gone to Rome to suffer martyrdom, but before information of the particulars had been sent to
Smyrna.

It has been objected, that in ch. 9, he spoke of
Ignatius as having already suffered martyrdom,
while afterward, he asked for information of Ignatius and "those with him." The latter portion has
been thought to be an interpolation. But we do not

think the two passages irreconcilable. Ignatius had gone to Rome as a martyr, and Polycarp believed him to have suffered when he wrote; and inquired after his companions, and for the particulars of the martyrdom.

Upon the question of the genuineness of this Epistle, also, there has been considerable discussion. But it was expressly referred to, about the year 190, by Irenæus, who in his youth had known Polycarp personally. Polycarp lived till 155.

EVIDENCE AS TO THE FOUR GOSPELS.—The passages claimed as parallel, are all sayings of Christ, somewhat similar to those in the canonical gospels, but not ascribed to any definite source. No mention is made of either of the Gospels Luke, Mark, John or Matthew, by Clement, Ignatius or Polycarp.

One of the sayings of Jesus quoted by Polycarp, is precisely like one quoted by Clement; but is not in any one of the four gospels. It is as follows: " Be pitiful, that ye may be pitied." In Clement, word for word the same. Again : Clement ; " Forgive, that it may be forgiven you." Polycarp ; " Forgive, and it shall be forgiven you." The nearest to which in the canonical gospels, is, "For if ye forgive men their trespasses," &c.

These circumstances and some others struck the mind of the Rev. Mr. Sanday with so much force, that he admitted the passages might have been derived from other collections.[1]

(1.) Gospels in the Second Century, p. 87.

He concludes, that if the apostolic fathers did not make use of the gospels, they had writings closely resembling them.   That is true, so far as the sayings of Christ are concerned.   But in other respects, they were widely different.   The sayings of Jesus had become so extensively known among his disciples, and had been preserved in so many different ways, that they maintained, for the most part, a substantial identity, in whatever writing contained.

Perhaps the most satisfactory solution of the question of the evidence of the apostolic fathers, was found by Dr. Less, a German evangelical scholar, who wrote about the year 1770.   He was author of a celebrated work, written to establish the "authenticity, uncorrupted preservation, and credibility of the New Testament."   He was stimulated to investigate the question, by a remark of Lord Bolingbroke.   In his Letters on the Study of History, Bolingbroke had exposed a want of judgment in "those who attempt to vindicate the antiquity of the sacred writings by examples drawn from the fathers of the first century, with a design to prove that these fathers had read the gospels; though the instances alleged amounted to no demonstration."

Whereupon Dr. Less gave the subject a very careful and thorough examination.   The result is given by Bishop Marsh, in a note to Michaelis, as follows:

"From the EPISTLE OF BARNABAS, no inference can be adduced that he had read any part of the New Testament.

"From the GENERAL EPISTLE, as it is called, of CLEMENT OF ROME, it may be inferred, that Clement had read the First Epistle of the Corinthians.

"From the SHEPHERD OF HERMAS, no inference whatever can be drawn.

"From the EPISTLE OF IGNATIUS, it may be concluded that he had read St. Paul's Epistle to the Ephesians, and that there existed in his time, evangelical writings, though it cannot be shown that he quoted from them. (This investigation was made long before the discovery of the Cureton Epistles, and the remark of Dr. Less was founded upon the Vossian Letters, which were more voluminous, and included four spurious letters ascribed to Ignatius.)

"From POLYCARP'S EPISTLE TO THE PHILIPPIANS, it appears that he had heard of St. Paul's Epistle to that community, and that he quotes a passage which is in the First Epistle to the Corinthians, and another which is in the Epistle to the Ephesians; but no positive conclusion can be drawn, with respect to any other Epistle, or any of the Four Gospels."—[*Michaelis by Marsh, vol. 1, p. 354, citing Less, Gesch. der Religion, pp. 503-537, ed'n 1786.*

As the result of this analysis, including, besides the apostolic fathers proper, Barnabas and Hermas, and extending to about the middle of the second century, no evidence of the four gospels was seen, in the writings of the apostolic fathers, by this eminent German theologian. Subsequent English and American ecclesiastical writers have discovered much, as they suppose, which escaped his careful scrutiny.

All three of the apostolic fathers mentioned Paul expressly, and referred to his writings.

Clement, in writing to the Corinthians, referred to Paul's Letter to them, and Polycarp, in his Letter to the Philippians, spoke of Paul's Epistle to that Church.

There has been an attempt made to make Polycarp a witness for the four gospels, in another man-

ner. Feuardentius, in his note to Irenæus, 3. 3,
published, with some other fragments, what purported to be a fragment of Polycarp, out of a very
ancient manuscript of Victor Capuanus' catena
upon the four evangelists, wherein Polycarp mentioned each by name; "which catena," says Feuardentius, "he there promises to publish ; but whether
he did or no, I know not."   Victor Capuanus lived,
A. D. 480, according to this writer.   Grynæus
places him at A. D. 455 : others a hundred years
later.

This testimony may be stated thus : Feuardentius
says, that Capuanus had, in 480, a manuscript,
showing that Polycarp, more than 300 years previous, mentioned the four gospels.

Westcott prudently abandons this evidence, sig-
nificantly asking, "Is anything known of the MS.
catena, from which it was taken?"[1]

Polycarp was for many years, Bishop of Smyrna,
and was martyred, A. D. 155.

He was a devoted Christian, and an able expounder of the faith.   In his treatment of heretics,
he traveled in the footsteps of Clement and Ignatius.

Speaking of Valens, who had been a presbyter,
but who had departed from the faith, he says :

"I am deeply grieved, therefore, brethren, for him and for his wife;
to whom may the Lord grant true repentance ! And be ye, then,
moderate in this matter, and do not count such as enemies, but call
them back as suffering and straying members, that ye may save your
whole body."—[Ch. 11.

(1) Canon, p. 36.

RECAPITULATION.

The apostolic fathers make no mention of the miracles of Jesus, nor do they refer to any of the circumstances connected with the alleged material resurrection.

Upon that subject, Clement holds the same views with Paul, and illustrates them in an impressive and beautiful manner.

Ignatius, A. D. 115, appears to allude, in a mysterious way, to the immaculate conception of Jesus; the first time we find it mentioned in history.

No reference is made to either of the four gospels, nor to the Acts of the Apostles, nor are there any quotations except such as evangelical writers concede may have been taken from other sources.

"THE MARTYRDOM OF POLYCARP." — This was doubtless one of the earliest of the martyria. Its genuineness has been denied; but the question is of little importance, as the document contains nothing of much historical value, in the way of fact or doctrine.

CHAPTER IV.

THE LOST GOSPELS OF THE SECOND CENTURY.

GOSPEL ACCORDING TO THE HEBREWS.

This is the most celebrated of all the ancient gospels. It made its first appearance early in the second century; probably not later than 125, and possibly five or even ten years sooner.

As this gospel, in various forms, and under different titles, was the one most in use among the Christians of the second century, we shall give all the citations of it by the fathers, and all the fragments of the gospel which they have preserved.

1. HEGESIPPUS; A. D. 185. According to Eusebius, Ecclesiastical History, bk. 4, ch. 22.

Eusebius here says of Hegesippus,

" He has also written (laid down) some things concerning the Gospel according to the Hebrews and Syrians, as also concerning the Hebrew language, by which he evidences that he was converted from Judaism to Christianity."

It may be mentioned in passing, that this is the principal testimony relied upon to show that there was a Syriac Version of the canonical gospels in the second century. But so far from its being any evidence of the fact, Eusebius was not referring at all to the canonical gospels, or either of them, but to the Gospel of the Hebrews.   He calls it the Gospel according to the Hebrews and Syrians ; by which he evidently means, that it was used by the Jews in Syria, as elsewhere.

This view is confirmed by the statement of Jerome, which will appear presently, that the Gospel of the Hebrews was written "in the Chaldee and Syriac languages."   It appears it was used by the Nazarenes residing in Berea, Syria ; hence it was translated into Syriac.

2. CLEMENT OF ALEXANDRIA ; A. D. 200. Stromata, bk. 2, ch. 9.

"And it is written in the Gospel according to the Hebrews, 'He who wonders shall reign, and he who reigns shall be at rest.'"

3. ORIGEN ; A. D. 230.   Comm. in Joan. :

"But if any one will receive the Gospel according to the Hebrews, in which our Savior says, 'The Holy Ghost, my mother, lately took me by one of my hairs, and bore me to the great mountain Tabor,'" &c.

From the same.   Fragment of the gospel, preserved in Hom. 8, in Matt. tom. 3, p. 21 :

"But let us treat this place a little otherwise: It is written in a certain gospel, which is entitled, 'according to the Hebrews,' (if any one be pleased to receive it, not as of any authority, but only for illustration) of the present question."

Then comes the following account of the colloquy between Jesus and the rich man, which the reader can compare with Matt. 19. 16–24. As he does so, he may wonder at its being pronounced by Origen, "not of any authority," since it is in spirit the same as the account in Matthew, and is somewhat more simple and natural.

There is reason to believe that the clause in brackets is one of the many interpolations to which it is well known the writings of Origen have been subjected. In the same sentence he himself speaks of it as a gospel; not as a book called "the Gospel according to the Hebrews," but as a gospel, "entitled according to the Hebrews." The phrase "it is written," used by the fathers, is generally understood to apply to writings considered scriptural. Origen says, "It is written in a certain gospel." It will be seen also directly, that Jerome speaks of this gospel as "one which Origen often used."

The following is the narrative.

"Another rich man said unto him, 'Master, what good thing shall I do that I may live?' He said unto him, 'O man, fulfil the law, and the prophets.' And he answered him, 'I have done so.' Then said he unto him, 'Go sell all thou hast, and give to the poor; and come, follow me.'

"Then the rich man began to smite his head, and it pleased him not. And the Lord said unto him, 'How sayest thou, I have fulfilled the law and the prophets, when it is written, in the law, Thou shalt love thy neighbor as thyself? And lo, many of thy brethren, sons of Abraham, are covered with filth, and dying of hunger, and thy house is full of many good things, and nothing therefrom goeth forth at any time unto them.'"

"And turning himself about, he said unto Simon, his disciple, sitting near him, 'Simon, son of Jonas, it is easier for a camel to go through the eye of a needle, than for a rich man to enter into the kingdom of heaven.'"

Rev. S. Baring-Gould, after comparing this with the corresponding passage in Matthew, says:

"The comparison of these two accounts is not favorable to that in the canonical gospel. It is difficult to understand how a Jew could have asked, as did the rich young man, (according to Matthew's Gospel), what commandments he ought to keep, in order to enter into life. The decalogue was known by heart to every Jew. Moreover, the narrative in the lost gospel is more connected than in the canonical gospel."

To which may be added, that the account is considerably shorter than in the Gospel of Matthew, or Mark ; indicating, according to a principle which will be frequently adverted to as we proceed, that it was first written. The narrative in Luke is of about the same length with that in the Hebrews.

4. EUSEBIUS ; A. D. 325. Ecc. Hist. bk. 3, ch. 25.

In enumerating the apocryphal books, he adds :

"In this number, some have placed the Gospel according to the Hebrews; with which they of the Jews, who profess Christianity, are very much delighted."

Again, speaking of the Ebionites ; ib. ch. 27 :

"They made use only of that which is called the Gospel according to the Hebrews; very little esteeming any other."

Again, speaking of Papias ; ch. 39 :

"He mentions another history, concerning a woman accused of many crimes before our Lord, which is contained in the Gospel according to the Hebrews."

5. EPIPHANIUS ; A. D. 385. Hæres. 29, sec. 9 :

"They (the Nazarenes) have the Gospel of Matthew most entire in the Hebrew language, among them: for this truly is preserved among them; as it was at first in Hebrew characters. But I know not whether they have taken away the genealogy from Abraham to Christ."

Again, against Heresies, 30 : (Ebionites.)

"They (the Ebionites) also receive the Gospel according to Matthew. For this, both they and the Cerinthians make use of, and no other. They call it the Gospel according to the Hebrews; for the truth is, that Matthew is the only one of the New Testament writers who published his Gospel and preaching in the Hebrew language and Hebrew characters."

Again ; in Sec. 13 :

"In the gospel which they (the Ebionites) have called the Gospel according to Matthew, which is not entire and perfect, but corrupted and curtailed, and which they call the Hebrew Gospel, it is written:

"There was a certain man called Jesus; and he being about thirty years of age, made choice of us. (This was called also the Gospel of the Twelve Apostles.) And coming to Capernaum, he entered into the house of Simon, called Peter, and opening his mouth, said: When I passed by the Lake of Tiberias, I chose John and James, the sons of Zebedee, and Simon and Andrew, and Thaddeus, and Simon Zelotes, and Judas Iscariot; and thee, Matthew, sitting at the receipt of custom, I called, and thou didst follow me. I will, therefore, that ye be my twelve apostles, for a testimony to Israel. And John the Baptist was baptizing, and the Pharisees went out to him, and were baptized, and all Jerusalem.

"'And John had his garment of camel's hair, and a leathern girdle about his loins, and his meat (according to that gospel) was wild honey, the taste of which was like manna, or as cakes made with honey and oil.' Thus they change the true account into a falsehood, and for locusts, put cakes made with oil and honey.

"The beginning of their gospel was this: 'It came to pass, in the days of Herod, King of Judæa, that John came baptizing with the baptism of repentance, in the River Jordan, who was reported to be of the family of Aaron, the high priest, the son of Zacharias and Elizabeth; and all people went out after him.'

"And after several other things, it is said in this gospel: 'The people being baptized, Jesus also went, and was baptized by John; and as he ascended out of the water, the heavens were opened, and he saw the Holy Spirit of God in the form of a dove, descending and entering into him; and a voice was made, (*egeneto*), from heaven, saying: Thou art my beloved Son, in whom I am well pleased; and then another, I have this day begotten thee; and suddenly there shone around the place a great light; which when John saw, (says this gospel), he said to him, Who art thou, Lord? and then another voice from heaven came to him, 'This is my beloved Son, in whom I am well pleased.' Hereupon, (according to this gospel), John fell down before him, and said, 'O Lord, I pray thee, baptize me;' but he hindered him saying, that it is so fit, that all things should be fulfilled. See how their false doctrine appears everywhere, how all things are imperfect, disordered and without truth or order.

"So also Cerinthus and Carpocrates, using the same gospel of theirs, would prove from the beginning of that Gospel according to St. Matthew, viz., by the genealogy, that 'Christ proceeded from the seed of Joseph and Mary.' But they (the Ebionites) have quite other sentiments; for they have taken away the genealogy from Matthew, and accordingly begin their gospel, as I have above said, with these words: It came to pass, in the days of Herod, King of Judæa, &c."

Again, Epiphanius says, sec. 16 :

"They (the Ebionites) do not say that he, (Christ), was begotten of the Father, but made as one of the angels; but being greater than they, he has dominion over them, and all the works of the Almighty; and that he came and taught that which is contained in their gospel, viz., 'I came to abolish sacrifices; and unless ye cease to offer sacrifices, the wrath (of God) shall not cease from you.' And such as these are their tenets."

Epiphanius also tells us,[1] that a certain Jew, called Joseph, found in a cell at Tiberias, in the time of Constantine, the Hebrew Gospel ascribed to Matthew. Not much confidence has been placed in this statement by subsequent writers.

6. JEROME ; A.D. 400. Catal. Vir. Illust. in Matt.

"Matthew, also called Levi, who became from a publican an apostle, was the first who composed a gospel of Christ; and, for the sake of those who believed in Christ from among the Jews, wrote it in the Hebrew language and letters; but it is uncertain who it was who translated it into Greek. Moreover the Hebrew (copy) itself is to this time preserved in the library of Cæsarea, which Pamphilus the martyr, with much diligence, collected. The Nazarenes who live in Berea, a city of Syria, and make use of this volume, granted me the favor of writing it out; in which (gospel), there is this observable, that

(1.) Hæres. 30, Ebion. sec. 6.

wherever the evangelist either cites, himself, or introduces our Savior
as citing, any passage out of the Old Testament, he does not follow
the translation of the LXX, but the Hebrew copies; of which there
are these two instances, to wit: 'out of Egypt have I called my Son;'
and 'he shall be called a Nazarene.'"

[NOTE.—If this statement of Jerome, who is not very reliable, could
be depended upon, there was a version of the Old Testament then in
circulation, containing the latter passage; a passage which, it has been
often asserted, was not in the Old Testament; and which is not now
to be found in that volume.]

Again, same work, Life of James ; after relating
various wonderful things concerning James, he says :

"The gospel also, which is called 'according to the Hebrews,' and
which I translated into Greek and Latin, and which Origen often used,
relates that after our Savior's resurrection, when our Lord had given
the linen cloth to the priest's servant, he went to James, and appeared
to him; for James had sworn that he would not eat bread, from that
hour in which he drank the cup of the Lord, till he should see the
Lord risen from the dead. And a little after, the Lord said, 'Bring
the table and the bread;' and then it is added, he took the bread and
blessed it, and brake it, and gave it to James the Just, and said
to him, 'My brother, eat thy bread; for the Son of man is risen from
the dead.'"

This appearance is not related in the canonical
gospels ; but an appearance to James is mentioned
by Paul, 1 Cor. 15. 7 ; which would indicate that
the Gospel of the Hebrews contained the oldest
traditions.

Again ; JEROME, adv. Pelag. 1. 3, in prin.

"In the Gospel according to the Hebrews, which is written in the
Chaldee and Syriac languages, which the Nazarenes use, that according to the Twelve Apostles; or as most think, according to Matthew;
which is in the library of Cæserea, there is the following history:

" 'Behold, the mother and brethren of Christ spake to him: John the
Baptist baptizeth, for the remission of sins; let us go and be baptized
of him. He said to them, In what have I sinned, that I have need to
go and be baptized by him? unless my saying this proceeds, perhaps,
from ignorance?'

"And in the same volume it is said, 'If thy brother offend thee by any word, and make thee satisfaction, though it be seven times in a day, thou must forgive him.' Simon, his disciple, said to him, 'What! Seven times in a day?' The Lord answered and said unto him, 'I tell thee also, even till seventy times seven.' "

Again, Jerome, Lib. 4, Comm. in Isai. c. 11.

"According to this gospel, which is written in the Hebrew language and read by the Nazarenes, the whole fountain of the Holy Ghost descended upon him. Besides, in that gospel just mentioned, we find these things written:

" 'It came to pass, when the Lord ascended from the water, the whole fountain of the Holy Ghost descended, and rested upon him, and said to him, 'My Son, among all the prophets, I was waiting for thy coming, that I might rest upon thee; for thou art my rest; thou art my first begotten Son, who shall reign to everlasting ages.' "

And again, in Lib. 11, Comm. in Isai. 40, 11:

"But it is written in the Gospel according to the Hebrews, which the Nazarenes read, 'The Lord said, The Holy Ghost, my mother, just now laid hold on me.' "

By the same, in Lib. 2, Comm. in Mic. 7. 6:

"Whoever reads the book of Canticles, and will understand, by the spouse of the Soul, the word of God, and will believe the gospel which is entitled, 'The Gospel according to the Hebrews,' which I lately translated, in which our Savior is introduced, saying, 'Just now my mother, the Holy Ghost, laid hold on me by one of my hairs,' will not scruple to say, the Word of God was born of the Spirit, and the soul, which is the spouse of the Word, has the Holy Ghost for its mother-in-law, who, in the Hebrew language, is expressed in the feminine gender."

The same in Lib. 6, Comm. Ezek. 18. 7:

"In that which is entitled, 'The Gospel according to the Hebrews,' it is reckoned among the chief of crimes, for a person to make sorrowful the heart of his brother."

Again; Jerome, Lib. 1, Comm. in Matt. 6. 11:

"In the gospel entitled, 'according to the Hebrews,' I find, instead of supersubstantial bread,' 'mahar;' which signifies the morrow; so, the sense is, 'Give us this day, the bread necessary for the morrow;' i. e., for the future."

Again, the same. Lib.2, Comm. in Matt. 12. 13.

"In the Gospel which the Nazarenes and Ebionites use, (which I lately translated out of Hebrew into Greek, and which is by most esteemed the authentic Gospel of Matthew), the man who had the withered hand, is said to be a mason, and prayed for relief in the following words:

"'I was a mason, who got my livelihood by my hands; I beseech thee, Jesus, that thou wouldst restore to me my strength, that I may no longer thus scandalously beg my bread.' "

And again, in Lib. 4, Comm. in Matt. 23.

"In the gospel which the Nazarenes use, for the son of Barachias, I find written, 'The son of Joiada.' "

The following extracts also are from Jerome:

From Lib. 4, Comm. in Matt. 27. 16:

"In the gospel entitled, 'according to the Hebrews.' he (Barabbas), is interpreted, The son of their master, who was condemned for sedition and murder."

Same book:

"In the gospel which I have often mentioned, we read, that a lintel of the temple, of immense size, was broken and rent." (At the time of the crucifixion.)

From Epistle ad. Hedib. ch. 8.

"In that gospel which is written in Hebrew letters, we read, not that that the vail of the temple was rent, but that a lintel (or beam) of a prodigious size fell down."

From lib. 3, Comm. in Ep. ad. Eph. c. 5, v. 4:

"In the Hebrew Gospel, we read, that our Lord said to his disciples, 'Be ye never cheerful, unless when you can see your brother in love.'"

From Præf. lib. 18, Comm. in Isai.:

"For when the apostles supposed him to be a spirit, or according to the Gospel which the Nazarenes received, an incorporeal demon, he said to them, 'Why are ye troubled,' &c."

And in De Vir. Ill. c. 16, in Ig., he bears the following testimony to the source whence Ignatius was supposed to have taken the quotation, concerning the conversation between Jesus and his disciples, after the resurrection.

"In the epistle to the Smyrnæans, (which, in the time of Jerome, and until lately, was thought to have been written by Ignatius,) he (Ignatius) takes a testimony from the Gospel which I lately translated, as spoken by Christ; he says, I saw Christ in the flesh after the resurrection, and believe that it was he; and when he came to Peter, and to those who were with Peter, he said unto them, Behold, feel me, and see that I am not an incorporeal spirit; and presently they touched and believed. "

Such are the testimonies of the fathers concerning this famous gospel, and the fragments of it which they have preserved for our inspection.

It may be added, that it was not condemned in the decree of Gelasius, A. D. 494.

There has been much diversity of opinion, and a good deal of learning brought to bear upon the question whether the Gospel according to the Hebrews was written by Matthew; and if not, whether Matthew wrote a Gospel in Hebrew.

It will be seen by the foregoing extracts, that Epiphanius and Jerome are very explicit in asserting that this was the Gospel of Matthew.

The readiness with which these statements are set aside by able modern writers, may be regarded as an instructive commentary upon the degree of credit and authority to which the fathers are entitled, on questions requiring for their decision an educated and critical judgment.

It will be noticed hereafter, that Jerome asserts, with the same positiveness, that the Gospel of the Infancy, which he translated from memory, and a portion of which translation has since been called the Gospel of the Birth of Mary, was written also by Matthew. In that case, he went so far as to say, it was in Matthew's own handwriting. (See chapter 17.)

That the Gospel of the Hebrews was Matthew's Hebrew Gospel, was the opinion of Dupin,[1] and Father Simon.[2] Beausobre considered it, whether written by Matthew or not, very ancient, and of very high authority.

Dr. Niemeyer thought this gospel, "the fountain from which other writings of this sort, have derived their origin ; as streams from a spring." Baronius said, "The present Greek text of St. Matthew is of no value or authority, unless it were to be compared with the Hebrew Gospel of the Nazarenes, which is the true original."[3]

Michaelis [A. D. 1777], examined the question critically. After citing Father Simon, Dr. Mill, and other writers, and admitting frankly that the Nazarenes knew nothing of the Greek gospels, he considers whether in the gospel of the Nazarenes, like that of the Ebionites, the first two chapters of Matthew were wanting. He examines Jerome's references to the gospel which he had translated, and comes to the conclusion, that while there is no

(1.) History of the Canon, vol. 2, c. 2, 3.
(2.) Crit. Hist. N. T., Pt. 1, ch. 7, 9.
(3.) Annal. ad. Am. Ct. 34, num. 175.

trace of the first chapter of Matthew, it probably contained the second chapter.   He does not speak with much confidence, however, and says, "at different times, I have entertained different opinions on this subject."

The difficulty experienced by this eminent scholar, appears to have been easily surmounted by more modern writers, some of whom do not hesitate to assert, in the most positive manner, that the references of Jerome prove that the gospel which he translated contained both chapters.

Michaelis finally concludes, upon the main question, that if the Gospel of the Hebrews was originally the Hebrew Gospel of Matthew, it received various additions among the Nazarenes, after it had been translated into Greek.[1]

Bishop Marsh, assuming that the Gospel of Matthew was a translation from the Hebrew, thinks the first two chapters may not have been in the original, and that the Greek translator prefixed a translation of some other Chaldee document, containing an account of the birth of Christ.[2]

Stroth, (1780), whose essay on the subject was printed in Eichhorn's Repertorium, contended that the Gospel of the Hebrews was used by Justin Martyr ; an opinion which many others have since adopted.

(1.) Vol. 3, p. 169.
(2.) Notes to Michaelis. vol. 3, pt. 2, p. 139.

Bishop Marsh, referring to this theory of Stroth, and to the reasons given, which had been favorably referred to by Dr. Rosenmueller (A. D. 1800), says, "It is true that if the force of these arguments be admitted, and they seem really convincing, we cannot produce Justin as an evidence of the four gospels."[1]

Norton thinks the Gospel of the Hebrews should not be considered apocryphal, and says, in its primitive form it was probably the Hebrew original of Matthew.[2]

Toland says the Gospel of the Hebrews was publicly read in the Nazarene and Ebionite churches as authentic, "for above 300 years;" and was "alleged as a true gospel" by Papias, Ignatius, Clemens Alexandrinus, Justin Martyr, Hegesippus and others. Tischendorf finds that it was probably used by Justin, by the author of the Clementines, and by Tatian and Hegesippus.[3]

From the views of these writers, after comparing them carefully with the testimony of the fathers, in the foregoing pages, we may, perhaps, elicit the truth, and state it in a few simple propositions.

1. The Gospel of the Hebrews was an ancient gospel, and nearly the only one in use among the Jewish Christians, in the first ages of the Church. It was also extensively used by others, and was of high authority with the fathers.

(1,) Notes to Michaelis, vol. 1, p. 361.
(2.) Genuineness of the Gospels, vol. 1, pp. 214, 225.
(3.) Origin of the Four Gospels, p. 78.

2.   It was universally attributed to Matthew.

3.   There was no other Gospel of Matthew at that time. (First half of second century.) The Hebrew Gospel of Matthew so much talked about, other than the Gospel of the Hebrews, is a myth, so far as there is any historical evidence.

4.   The Greek Gospel of Matthew was a subsequent production, and either originally appeared in the Greek language, or was a translation of the Gospel of the Hebrews, with extensive changes and additions.   There is reason to believe it to have been an original compilation, based upon the Oracles of Christ, but containing, in whole, or in part, a number of other manuscripts.

The arguments used to prove that Matthew's Gospel was originally in Hebrew, all run in a circle.   They assume that the Greek gospel is in some way from Matthew, and is therefore authoritative. The reasoning then runs smoothly, and ends in proving a Hebrew Matthew, a document of the existence of which no mention is made in history ; if we except a vague tradition never yet traced to its source.

As a specimen of this reasoning, we may refer to the argument of Jones, contained in three propositions :

1.   The Greek gospel contains all that Matthew ever wrote ; else it would not be a complete revelation of the divine will, so far as Matthew is concerned.

2. It differed from the Gospel of the Hebrews.

3. Therefore the latter was not written by Matthew.

The corollary would be, that there was a Gospel of Matthew in Hebrew, different from the Gospel of the Hebrews.

BY WHOM AND WHEN WRITTEN.—It will be safe to accept the almost unanimous opinion of theological writers, that the Hebrew Gospel used by the Nazarenes and Ebionites, was not written by Matthew. The author is unknown.

It was a compilation made for the use of the Jewish Christians, from the gospels and gospel documents then in circulation; the manuscripts principally used appearing to be, the Oracles or Sayings of Christ, and the Gospel, Preaching and Doctrine of Peter. The Oracles probably constituted the principal basis, and as they had been attributed to Matthew, that circumstance is sufficient to account for the association of the apostle's name with this gospel.

The exact time when it was written can only be a matter of conjecture. It could not have been later than the first quarter of the second century.

Jerome supposed it to have been written before the epistles of Ignatius. But this was because he thought Ignatius had referred to it in his epistle to the Smyrnæans; a document of which Ignatius was not the author.

DOCTRINES.—There is no sufficient evidence that this gospel contained the doctrine of the immaculate conception of Jesus. On the contrary, it is well understood that the earlier Jewish Christians did not believe in it.

The miracles of Christ now first begin to be heard of, and as might be expected, the first mentioned are those relating to the healing of the sick and deformed. The more wonderful and startling, such as turning water into wine, and raising to life a human body in a state of decomposition, are not met with until some time afterward.

The doctrine of the resurrection of Christ in a material body, now for the first time appeared, and was stoutly maintained by the fathers afterward.

CHAPTER V.

GOSPEL ACCORDING TO THE EGYPTIANS.

This is universally conceded to have been a very ancient gospel. The learned Dr. Lardner thinks it was not written until the second century.[1]

Clement of Alexandria (A. D. 200) mentions it in various places, and gives several fragments from it:

1. From Stromata, bk. 3, ch. 6.

"When Salome asked our Lord, 'How long death should prevail,' (not as though life were an evil, or the creation an evil), he answered, 'As long as ye women do bring forth children.'"

From what follows, it will be seen that this passage was in the Gospel of the Egyptians. The fact that the gospel is not cited by name in this place, becomes, after we know the quotation was taken from that book, a very strong indorsement of it; since it is asserted that Jesus said what he was reported to have said, in the Gospel of the Egyptians.

2. From the same, ch. 9.

"But they who oppose the established order of God, by their spurious pretences to celibacy, cite those things which our Saviour spake to

[1] Works, vol. 3, p. 204.

Salome, which I just before mentioned. They are, I think, in the Gospel according to the Egyptians; for they say that our Savior himself said, 'I am come to destroy the works of the woman; that is, the works of female concupiscence, generation and corruption.'

"Afterward, Salome asked him how long it should be that death should prevail against men? And he answered, While ye women bring forth children.

"Hereupon she said, 'Then I have done well in bearing no children, seeing there is no necessity of generation.' To which our Lord replied, 'Feed upon every herb, but that which is bitter, eat not.' "

3.   From the same, ch. 13.

"Wherefore Cassianus saith, that when Salome asked, when the things should be known concerning which she inquired, our Lord answered, 'When you shall despise the covering of your nakedness, and when two shall become one, and the male with the female, neither male nor female.' First, (I observe) we have not this saying in the four gospels given to us, but in that according to the Egyptians."

This passage, quoted from the Gospel of the Egyptians, may be found in similar language in the second Epistle to the Corinthians, formerly attributed to Clement of Rome, but which is now thought to have been written not earlier than A. D. 150.

The next author who refers to this gospel, is Origen; (A. D. 230.) In his Homily on the Gospel of Luke, ch. 1. v. 1, he says:

"The church has four gospels, the heretics many; among which is that according to the Egyptians, that according to the Twelve Apostles," &c. (This according to the Latin translator of Origen.)

The next is Jerome; Præf. in Com. in Matt. :

"The evangelist Luke declares that there were many who wrote gospels, when he says, 'Forasmuch as many,' &c. &c. (ch, 1, v. 1,) which being published by various authors, gave birth to several heresies; such as that according to the Egyptians, and Thomas, and

Matthias, and Bartholomew, that of the Twelve Apostles, and Basilides, and Apelles, and others, which it would be tedious to enumerate; in relation to these it will be enough at present to say, that there
have been certain men who endeavored, without the spirit and grace
of God, rather to set forth some sort of account, than to publish a
true history."

It will be seen that Jerome admits that not only
the Gospel of Basilides, composed about A. D. 125,
and other gospels, admitted to have been first published in the second century, were written before
that of Luke, but even the Gospel of Apelles also,
which was written not earlier than A. D. 160.

That the Gospel of the Egyptians was one of
those referred to in Luke's preface, was the opinion
of Origen, Theophylact and others of the ancients,
and among the moderns the same view has been
expressed by Grotius, Dr. Grabe, Erasmus, and
many others.

Epiphanius speaks of this gospel,[1] and thus refers
to one of its doctrines :

"They (the Sabellians) make use of all the Scriptures, both of the
Old and New Testament, but principally of some certain passages,
which they pick out according to their own corrupt and preposterous
sentiments. But the whole of their errors and the main strength of
their heterodoxy they have from some apocryphal books, but principally from that which is called the 'Gospel of the Egyptians;' which
is a name some have given it: for in that, many things are proposed
in a hidden, mysterious manner, as by our Savior, as though he had
said to his disciples, that the Father was the same person, the Son the
same person, and the Holy Ghost the same person."

The learned Dr. Grabe[2] has a long dissertation
concerning this gospel, the substance of which is,

(1.) Hæres. 62. 2.
(2.) Spiceleg. Patr. tom. 1, pp. 13 to 34.

that it was composed by some Christians in Egypt ; that it was published before either of the canonical gospels, and that Clement of Alexandria did not reject it, but endeavored rather to explain it ; which he would not have done, had he considered it the work of a heretic.

Dr. Mill [1] thinks this and the Gospel of the Hebrews were composed before either of our canonical gospels, and that the authors of it were probably Essenes, who received the Christian doctrine from the preaching of Mark at Alexandria.

Mr. Whiston says :

"The Therapeutæ mentioned by Philo seem to have been those first Christian ascetics, who were converted from the Jews, chiefly in Egypt, soon after our Saviour's passion, before the coming of Mark thither, and to have both imperfectly understood and practiced the Christian religion. Eusebius, Epiphanius and Jerome plainly take them for Christians, and their sacred, ancient, mystical books are by Eusebius supposed to be the gospels and epistles of the New Testament. The modern critics are entirely puzzled about these Therapeutæ, and yet are not willing commonly to believe them Christians. And indeed Eusebius' opinion, that their ancient allegorical books were our gospels and epistles, is liable to great exceptions, since they are not allegorical in their nature, nor were they published any considerable time before Philo's own writings; so that upon the whole, I believe, it is more reasonable to say, these Therapeutæ were those first Christian ascetics, who had gotten very imperfect accounts of Christianity, and were guided by the Gospel according to the Egyptians, which we know by the fragments remaining, was a gospel sufficiently mystical and allegorical, according to the genius of that nation."—[*Essay on Const.* 1. 37.

The statement of Eusebius,[2] that the Therapeutæ of Egypt became Christians, (though not in the first century), may be accepted. It is supported by Epiphanius and Jerome, and by the historical

(1.) Prolegom. in N. T. sec. 35 to 38, and sec. 50.
(2.) Ecc. Hist. 2. 16, 17.

fact, that the Christian monkish system had its
origin in Egypt.

How far the Therapeutæ of Egypt and the Essenes of Palestine may be identified as one and the
same class or sect, is a question which has been
much discussed.   Their beliefs and practices were
similar ; they both had, anterior to the Christian
system, many of its peculiar doctrines, and the
members became easy converts to the new religion,
and were among the first Christian disciples.

A full account of the Essenes will be found in
the writings of Josephus.

Jerome says, in his life of Mark,

"He went with his gospel into Egypt, and there constituted a
church; that he was so remarkable in the abstemiousness of his life,
that he obliged all his converts to follow his example; insomuch that
Philo, the most eloquent of all the Jewish writers, when he saw the
first church at Alexandria still observing the Jewish customs, thought
it would be to the honor of his nation to write a book concerning
their way of life; and as Luke says the Christians at Jerusalem had
all things common, so he relates that it was at Alexandria, under
Mark's instructions."—[*Catal. Vir. Illust. in Marco.*

And again, in his life of Philo, he says, he places
Philo among the church writers, because,

"By writing a book concerning the first church of Mark at Alexandria, he has said much in commendation of the Christians. He not
only mentions such as were there, but in many other provinces; and
calls their places of abode monasteries; from whence it appears, that
the first Christians, who believed there on Christ, were such as the
monks now pretend and desire to be; to wit, to have all things common," &c.—[*Catal. Vir. Illust. in Philone.*

This is a good illustration of the careless writing
of the fathers, and of their readiness to supply,
from their own imaginations, what is wanting in
historical data.   Philo, though he writes of the

Therapeutæ, and of their mode of life, says nothing of any church of Mark at Alexandria, or of any other church, nor does he once mention the Christians in that connection, if indeed in any other.

There is, in fact, no historical evidence, at all reliable, that any Christian church was founded in Egypt in the first century. The first reliable information upon the subject, is in the letter of Hadrian to Servianus, husband of Paulina, the Emperor's sister. Servianus was consul, A. D. 134. The letter is preserved by Vopiscus, who wrote about the year 300, and who took it from the books of Phlegon, the historian, who was a freedman of Hadrian. From this epistle it appears, that the religion of the Christians was so crude that Christ and Serapis were worshiped indiscriminately; from which we may reasonably infer that the Christian religion had not long been established in that country.

The testimony of Epiphanius is as follows:

"They who believed on Christ were called Jessæi, (or Essenes), before they were called Christians, either because Jesse was the father of David, or from Jesus, the name of our Lord, because they were his disciples, and derived their constitution from him, or from the signification of the name Jesus, which in Hebrew signifies the same as Therapeutes, (the name by which Philo calls them), i. e. a Savior or physician."—[*Hæres.* 29. 4.

Who this Mark or Marcus was, who established the first Christian church at Alexandria, is uncertain; possibly it was the same who wrote the Gospel of Mark, in the second century.

That it was not Mark, the associate of Peter, who wrote the Preaching, and perhaps the Gospel, of Peter, is manifest from the fact, that in this first church in Egypt the ascetic system among the

Christians had its origin; and that system, as we learn from other sources, originated not earlier than the second half of the second century.[1]

Jerome also witnesses that it was not earlier than that, in the following passage :

"It has often been a question, from whom the desert way of life of the monks, derives its original. Some derive it as far as from Elijah and John.

"Others, which is the prevailing opinion, from Antonius; which is in part true; for he was not so much the first in this way of life, as the means of propagating it; for Amathas and Macarius, two disciples of Antonius, affirm, that one Paul of Thebais, (in Egypt), was the chief author of this matter; which I also assent to."—[*In Vita Paul, Eremit. par.* 3, *tr.* 8. *De Vit. Con. Ep.* 37.

Antonius and Paul of Thebais are thought to have lived in the third century. However that may be, it is manifest, from all the evidence, that the ascetic system of the Christian monks cannot be traced back further than the latter half of the second century. Baring-Gould thinks the Gospel of the Egyptians was related to that of Mark, and that it was composed at the beginning of the second century. He classes it among the Petrine Gospels.[2]

It was no doubt older than Mark, and this, as has been shown, is the opinion of eminent Christian writers.

Davidson says[3] it was classed by Origen with the Gospel of the Hebrews, as inauthentic.

Norton[4] thinks it was not a historical, but a doctrinal book.

(1.) Consult Serarius, Sozomen and Spanheim.
(2.) Lost and Hostile Gospels, pp. 117, 123.
(3.) Canon, p. 115.
(4.) Vol. 3, p. 243.

This gospel was not condemned in the famous decree of Pope Gelasius.

As has been already seen, the decree did not include either of the first century gospels; the Gospel of Paul, the Gospel of Peter, the Oracles of Matthew; neither did it touch the Gospel of the Hebrews.

Jones objects to the Gospel according to the Egyptians, that it contradicts the canonical gospels, in representing Salome to be a single woman. But it will be found, upon examination, that the objection is hastily made. Matt. 27. 56, and Mark 15. 40, are cited to show that Salome was the mother of Zebedee's children; assuming that the third woman spoken of in each place, as present at the crucifixion, was the same. But this may or may not have been the case. It is stated, both in Mark and Matthew, that many women were there. Because each historian mentions two of the number alike, it by no means follows, that the third was also the same.

If Salome had been the mother of the two apostles, James and John, she would doubtless have been so designated, wherever spoken of.

Before leaving the Gospel of the Egyptians, it will be necessary to notice a mistranslation of Jones, made for the purpose of bringing this gospel into disrepute.

He makes Clement of Alexandria say, Strom. 3, ch. 9,

"The things which follow, spoken to Salome, they cite, who had rather follow any thing, than the true canon of the gospel," &c. —[*Jones, vol.* 1, *page* 208.

The inference would be that Clement considered the Egytian Gospel an uncanonical book.

The Greek used by Clement is,

"Epipherousin hoi panta mallon ee to kata teen aleetheian euanggeliko stoikeesantes kanoni, phamenees gar autees," etc.

" They cite, who rather follow anything, than what is according to the truth, in the gospel rule."

The Greek word kanon meant, literally, a rule of measurement; hence, secondarily, a moral rule. It was not used, as applied to the collection of New Testament books, until the fourth century; while Clement wrote at the close of the second.

WHEN AND BY WHOM WRITTEN. The original of this gospel may have been in use among the Therapeutæ of Egypt, a long time before the introduction of Christianity, the passages relating to Christ being afterward added. Or it may have been written in another country, and brought into Egypt, with the Christian religion. In either case it may be dated as early as A. D. 110 to 115.

DOCTRINES. We find no evidence that this gospel contained the doctrine of the immaculate conception or of the material resurrection, or made any allusion to the miracles of Christ.

RECAPITULATION.

The Gospel of the Egyptians was very ancient; written early in the second century; is mentioned in several places, and fragments given by Clement of Alexandria, A. D. 200, who emphatically indorses it, although Jones disingenuously attempts to prove otherwise. The gospel taught abstemiousness and celibacy and gave countenance to the Sabellian form of the doctrine of the unity

of the Godhead.   According to Jerome, Origen and
Theophylact of the ancients, and Grotius, Erasmus,
Dr. Grabe, Dr. Mill, and others of the moderns, it
was written before the Gospel of Luke, and in the
opinion of Drs. Grabe and Mill, and other eminent
theologians, before either of the canonical gospels.
Was not condemned in the decree of Gelasius.   The
objection as to Salome shown to be untenable.   The
gospel probably written more than fifty years before the introduction of Christianity into Egypt;
the Christian religion having probably been introduced at the same time with Mark's gospel, and
with the establishment of the monkish system;
toward the close of the second century.

The story of Joseph and Mary appears not to
have been known when this gospel was written.
Neither is any thing said, so far as we have information of its contents, of the miracles of Christ, or
of the material resurrection.

CHAPTER VI.

LOST GOSPELS OF THE SECOND CENTURY.—Concluded.

OTHER LOST GOSPELS.

GOSPEL OF PERFECTION—GOSPEL OF ANDREW—OF BAR-
THOLOMEW—OF PHILIP—THE SYRIAC GOSPEL—GOSPEL OF
EVE—THE GOSPEL OF MATTHIAS—OF JUDAS—OTHER GOSPELS
AND UNCANONICAL WRITINGS.

THE GOSPEL OF PERFECTION.—Epiphanius alludes
to this gospel in the following manner :

But others of them (the Gnostics) produce a certain spurious and
suppositious work, to which work they have given the name of the
Gospel of Perfection; which really is no gospel, but the perfection of
sorrow; for all the perfection of death is contained in that product of
the devil."—[*Adv. Hæres.* 26. 2.

Baring-Gould classes this as a Pauline gospel.
It was regarded as sacred by the Ophites. Bauer
thinks it the same as the Gospel of Eve. But they
are distinguished by Epiphanius. Norton says, if
it ever existed, it was not a historical work.[1]

The doubt expressed by Norton, as to the existence of this gospel, might well be indulged, if it
depended only upon the assertions of Epiphanius.
But it is expressly mentioned in the Gospel of the
Infancy, one of the oldest pre-canonical gospels
which have been preserved.

(1) Genuineness of the Gospels, vol. 3, p. 222.

In that gospel, after a lengthy account of the miracles performed by Christ while a child in Egypt, it is added :

"And the Lord Jesus did many miracles in Egypt, which are neither to be found in the Gospel of the Infancy, nor in the Gospel of Perfection."—[*Infancy, ch. 25.*

Camerarius supposed that Basilides and other Gnostics used this gospel, and that it was the same with the Gospel of Philip.[1] But Epiphanius distinguishes between them. (See Gospel of Philip.)

GOSPEL OF ANDREW.—There are no fragments extant of the Gospel of Andrew, and but little is known of it beyond the fact, that it was condemned as apocryphal in the decree of Pope Gelasius, A. D. 494.   In some copies of the decree, however, it was not mentioned.

The Gospel of Andrew is considered by Jones and others to have been one of the "many" referred to in the preface of Luke.   It is thought to have been alluded to by Augustine (A. D. 420), in his Prol. in Matthæum.

GOSPEL OF BARTHOLOMEW.—Strauss refers to the Gospel of Bartholomew as one of those "always current," quoted by heretics and sometimes by orthodox.[2]

No fragments are extant.   It was pronounced apocryphal by the decree of Gelasius.   Was counted by Jerome, Venerable Bede and others, among those referred to in Luke.

(1.) Fabricius, Codex. Apoc. vol. 1, p. 373. Note.
(2.) New Life of Jesus, vol. 1, p. 56.

Some have thought it the same as the Hebrew Gospel of the Nazarenes ; but Jerome, who saw and read the Gospel of the Nazarenes, spoke of the Gospel of Bartholomew as distinct from it.

It was reported that Pantænus, when sent to India to preach the gospel, found that Bartholomew had preached there before him, and had left the Gospel of Matthew in Hebrew ; and Jerome says he brought it back with him to Alexandria. This has been thought to be the same as the Gospel of Bartholomew. The subject is involved in much confusion and uncertainty.

Nicephorus says, Bartholomew, while in India, dictated the Gospel of Matthew to them out of his memory, and did not take it along with him.[1]

Monsieur Daille supposed the Gospel of Bartholomew was forged, a short time before Gelasius.[2]

GOSPEL OF PHILIP.—The following notice of this gospel, and fragment of its contents, is taken from Epiphanius on Heresies, ch. 25, sec. 13.

"They (the Gnostics) laugh at the conduct of the monks, and those who profess chastity and virginity, as submitting to unnecessary hardships. They produce a forged gospel, under the name of the holy Apostle Philip; in which it is written:

" 'The Lord hath revealed to me what the soul must say when it ascends into heaven, and what answer it must make to each of the celestial powers: I knew myself and gathered; recollected myself on all sides, and did not raise children for the devil, (Archon, prince of this world), but extirpated all his principles, and I have gathered myself together, the scattered members; and I know who thou art, for I am one of the celestial number. And thus,' says that book, 'she is set at liberty.' But it adds, that if the soul be found to have propagated children, it is obliged to stay below, till she shall be able to receive and bring those children to herself."

(1.) Ecc. Hist, 1, 4, c, 3, 2.
(2.) De Pseud. Dion. Areop. c. 27.

It is not safe to place reliance upon these accounts.

Norton says, " Epiphanius is a writer as deficient in plausibility, as in decency and veracity." [1] He was fond of indulging in obscenity, when treating of the doctrines and practices of heretics.[2]

Dupin supposes the Gospel of Philip was made use of by Basilides and Apelles, and by the Ebionites.[3]

If Epiphanius is to be at all relied upon, there could have been but little affinity between the Gospel of Philip and that of the Hebrews, or Nazarenes.

The Gospel according to Philip is mentioned by Timotheus,[4] as one of the new books which the impious Manichæus, inspired by the devil, had made. It is one of the Pauline gospels of Baring-Gould. Philip, like Paul, is said to have been an apostle of the Gentiles.

"This Gospel," says Baring-Gould, "belongs to the same category as those of Perfection, and of Eve, and belonged, if not to the Ophites, to an analogous sect, perhaps that of the Prodicians."—[*Lost and Hostile Gospels, p. 293.*

THE SYRIAC GOSPEL.—This was probably nothing but the Gospel of the Hebrews in the Syriac language. It is said to have been used by Hegesippus, the first church historian, A. D. 185.

GOSPEL OF EVE,—Is another of the gospels of Epiphanius. The following extract is from his famous work against heresies.

(1.) Genuineness of the Gospels, by Andrews Norton, 1837, vol. 2, p. 211.
(2.) See his work, adv. Hær. 26. 5,
(3.) History of the Canon, vol. 2.
(4.) In Epist. &c. p. 117.

"Some of these, (the Gnostics), do produce a certain spurious and forged writing which they call the Gospel of Perfection;—others have the impudence to produce one called the Gospel of Eve;—for under her name, as reported to have received great discoveries, revealed to her in her discourse with the serpent, they propagate their principles.

"But as the discourses of a person in drink, pretending to give advice, are according to his giddy fancy, not equal, but some of them merry, others melancholy, so are the wicked principles of these impostors. For they are led away with certain ridiculous testimonies and visions, which are in that gospel which they make use of. They produce such as the following:

"'I stood upon a very high mountain, and saw one man very tall and another short. And I heard a voice, as it were of thunder; upon which I went nearer to hear; and he spake to me saying, I am thou, and thou art I; and again, I am thou and thou art I; and where thou art, there am I; and I am in all places, and in everything; and wheresoever thou wilt, thou shalt find me, and in finding me thou findest thyself.' Behold the doctrine of devils."—[46, 47.

Other pretended quotations are made from this gospel, which can scarcely be given in English.[1]

Baring-Gould dignifies this doubtful production with a place among his Pauline gospels.[2] He thinks it was used by Marcus the Valentinian, and says it contained the Alpha Beta story of the childhood of Christ, to be found in some of the extant gospels.

GOSPEL OF MATTHIAS.—There are no fragments of the Gospel of Matthias extant. It was well known by the ancients, having been referred to by Origen, Eusebius, Ambrose and Jerome, and in some copies of the decree of Gelasius.

Origen calls it a gospel of the heretics.[3]

Jerome and Erasmus include it among those

(1.) See the Greek text of Epiphanius. adv. Hær. ch. 26, sec. 2, 3, and 5.

(2.) Lost and Hostile Gospels, p. 287.

(3.) Homil. in Luc. 1. in init.

which they think were written before Luke. So also Origen. Venerable Bede was of the same opinion. Dr. Grabe and Dr. Mill think it the same as the Traditions of Matthias.

GOSPEL OF JUDAS ISCARIOT.—Judas also had his gospel.

It is mentioned by Irenæus as follows :

"But there are other heretics who say Cain (was delivered) by a heavenly power, and who acknowledge Esau, Corah and the Sodomites, as their pattern; who, though they were fought against by the Creator, yet received no damage thereby; for Wisdom took from them whatever belonged to it. These things, they say, Judas, who betrayed Christ, carefully obtained the knowledge of; and as he was the only one of the apostles who knew the truth, he accomplished the mystery of betraying Christ. By him (Judas) they say, all things in heaven and earth were dissolved; and according to their views, they produce a certain forgery, which they call the Gospel of Judas."—[*Adv. Hær.* 1 31. 1.

Epiphanius says :

"They will have him to be their relation, and esteem him to have obtained extraordinary knowledge; inasmuch as they produce a certain book under his name, which they call the Gospel of Judas."—[*Adv. Hær.* 38. 1.

Mr. Toland having spoken of the gospel with some respect, Jones becomes indignant, and calls those who use it, "a set of impious, beastly, profane wretches." He must have accepted the statements of Epiphanius concerning them, which, by more moderate writers, are rejected as malicious slanders. Dr. Lardner refers to some of his stories concerning the heretics, as "fictions of Epiphanius."[1]

(1.) Vol 4, p. 397.

Theodoret speaks of this gospel.[1] Baring-Gould
makes it a Pauline gospel.[2] He thinks it was composed by the Cainites.

Not a fragment has been preserved, outside of the
writings of Irenæus and Epiphanius.

OTHER LOST GOSPELS.

The following, mentioned by various writers, are
not included in the foregoing list, for reasons which
will be given.

GOSPEL OF APELLES.—This and some others will
be treated of in connection with the persons to whom
they are attributed. (See Apelles.)

THE GOSPEL OF BARNABAS does not appear to belong to the second century.

It is first expressly mentioned in the decree of
Gelasius, A. D. 494. It has been supposed, however, by some, that Clement of Alexandria alluded
to it, when, commenting on Psalms, 118. 19, 20, he
says :

"Barnabas, expounding this saying of the prophet, thus reasons:
" 'Although there are many gates opened, righteousness is the gate
which is in Christ, at which all they that enter shall be blessed.' "—
[*Stromata.* 6, 8.

But as this passage is not in the Epistle of Barnabas, but is in the first Epistle of Clement of Rome
to the Corinthians, it has been thought by Dr. Grabe
and others, that Clement of Alexandria made a mistake in the citation. Either that, or both Clements
took the passage from the Gospel of Barnabas.

(1.) Lib. I, Hær. F. c. 15.
(2.) Page 305.

Dr. Grabe found also, in an ancient manuscript, another citation, as follows :

"Barnabas the apostle saith, 'He who prevails in unlawful contests, is so much the more unhappy, because he goes away, having more sin.' "

Dr. Grabe was inclined to think this came from the Gospel of Barnabas.   Others were of the opinion that it was in the lost portion of the Epistle of Barnabas.   Since the discovery of the entire manuscript of the Epistle by Tischendorf, as it is found not to contain this passage, more weight is now to be given to the conjecture of Dr. Grabe.

Mr. Toland, in the "Nazarenus," says that he saw this passage in substance, in an Italian manuscript, in Holland, entitled "The True Gospel of Jesus called Christ, a new Prophet sent by God to the world, according to the relation of Barnabas his Apostle."   This is supposed to have been a Mohammedan imposture, as Mohammed is, in several places, expressly named as the Paraclete, or promised Comforter.

There is a hypothetical history of the Gospel of Barnabas, which may be worthy of attention.

It is related by Theodorus Lector, Suidas, Nicephorus and others, that, in the reign of the Emperor Zeno, the remains of Barnabas, the apostle and companion of Paul, were found in Cyprus, under a tree, and upon the breast the Gospel of Matthew in Barnabas' own hand-writing.   The book was carried to the emperor, and was very highly esteemed by him, and put under a crown in his palace.   There is a historical incident connected with this story,

which gives it an air of probability. It is stated
that on account of the honor which attached to Cyprus, by virtue of this discovery, the inhabitants,
by means of it, prevailed in their contest with the
Bishop of Antioch, so that their metropolis had an
independent bishop, not subject to the jurisdiction
of Antioch.

The hypothesis was, that this book, thus found
on the breast of Barnabas, was an interpolated and
corrupted Gospel of Matthew, and was henceforth
called the Gospel of Barnabas.

According to this, one of the gospels became so
corrupted and interpolated by being copied by an
apostle, that it became necessary for the head of the
church to pronounce it apocryphal.

GOSPEL OR HARMONY OF BASILIDES.—(See Basilides.)

THE CLEMENTINE GOSPEL occupies a conspicuous
place in the work of Baring-Gould. He appears to
be the only writer who has given this name to the
gospel or gospels used in the Clementines. It is
commonly supposed that the principal gospel made
use of in these works, was that of the Hebrews.

GOSPEL OF CERINTHUS.—(See Cerinthus.)

ACCOUNTS OR GENEALOGIES OF THE DESPOSYNI.—
The Desposyni is the term made use of by Eusebius,
to designate those relatives of Christ, who were supposed to keep family records and genealogies. Fabricius has the above title in his list of gospels.

DESCENT FROM THE CROSS, BY JOHN.—One of the many apocryphal writings of uncertain origin, sometimes classed among the gospels.

GOSPEL OF THE ENCRATITES.—Fabricius and others have inferred that Epiphanius ascribed a gospel to to the sect of the Encratites. It is more probable, however, that he referred to the Gospel of Tatian.[1]

THE ETERNAL GOSPEL.—The idea of the Eternal Gospel, was taken from Revelation, 14, 6. It was thought John had promised an eternal gospel ; and none having appeared, one was accordingly brought to light, as late as the 13th century ; attributed by some to John of Parma.

GOSPEL OF THE GNOSTICS is a term sometimes used. The Gnostics had various gospels. Epiphanius speaks of their writing " The Revelations of Adam, and other false gospels."

FALSE GOSPELS OF HESYCHIUS.—This phrase is found in the decree of Pope Gelasius, wherein certain gospels are condemned by that title. What they were, is uncertain. Jerome speaks of "those books which go under the names of Lucian and Hesychius, and are esteemed through the perverse humors of some." [2]

THE BOOK OF THE HELKESAITES is spoken of by Epiphanius and Eusebius. The Helkesaites affirmed, that the book had fallen down from heaven ; and that they who believed and observed it, should obtain the pardon of their sins.

(1.) See Epiph. Hæres. bk. 30, 13, also bks. 46 and 47.
(2.) Praefat. in Ev. ad. Damas.

Epiphanius says, it described Christ as a power, whose height was twenty-four schœna, or Egyptian leagues, or about sixty-six miles ; his breadth twenty-four miles and his thickness in proportion.   His limbs and feet were correspondingly large.   Also, that according to this book, the Holy Ghost was of the female sex, and like Christ, reaching above the clouds, and standing between two mountains.

GOSPEL OF JUSTIN.—Renan employs this term in referring to the gospel principally used by Justin Martyr.   This is supposed to have been the Gospel of the Hebrews, or the Gospel of Peter, which may have been nearly the same.

GOSPEL OF JAMES THE LESS.—This is spoken of by some writers, but appears to be none other than the Protevangelion, which will be fully considered in a subsequent chapter.

GOSPEL OF JUDE.—The same as the Gospel of Judas Iscariot.

GOSPEL OF THE LORD.—One of the Lost Gospels of Rev. S. Baring-Gould.   He says the Gospel of the Lord was used by Marcion, and apparently before him by Cerdo.   It may, however, be affirmed with much confidence, that Marcion's Gospel was not used before his time ; since Marcion is universally conceded to have been the author or compiler of it.   But as this consisted of a collection of numerous manuscripts, it is possible that Cerdo may have used a collection, consisting of a portion of the same manuscripts.

GOSPEL OF LUCIUS.—Such a title is to be seen in the list of Fabricius, but it appears to be one of the books designated as the

FALSE GOSPELS OF LUCIANUS.—These were pronounced apocryphal in the decree of Gelasius; but as in the case of the False Gospels of Hesychius, they are not described with sufficient certainty to enable us to identify them.

GOSPEL OF LIFE.—This is mentioned by Fabricius, citing Photius, Cod. 85; also Timotheus, Presb. C., Politanus, in Epist. &c., p. 117, who says: "The impious Manichæans, following him (Manes), and inspired by the devil, make new books, such as, (1.) Evangelium Vivum," etc.

THE LEGAL PRIESTHOOD OF CHRIST is an obscure book, sometimes spoken of as a gospel. But little is known of its contents.

GOSPEL OF LONGINUS.—Nothing definitely known concerning it. Probably not of the second century.

GOSPEL OF MANES.—(Third century.)

GOSPEL OF MARCION.—(See Marcion.)

MEMORABILIA OF JUSTIN.— No gospel, though sometimes alluded to as such. Same as the "Memoirs," so often referred to by Justin.

MIDWIFE OF OUR SAVIOR.—Condemned by Gelasius, which appears to be all that is known of it.

MANICHEE GOSPEL.—(See Gospel of Manes.)

GOSPEL OF MERINTHUS. — Merinthus was only another name for Cerinthus.

PASSING OF ST. MARY, by St. John.   In the list of Fabricius.   But little is known of it.

PERSIAN HISTORY OF CHRIST. — Written by Jerome Xaverius, from the Persian, A. D. 1600.

GOSPEL OF SCYTHIANUS.—Nothing known relating to it.

GOSPEL OF SIMONIDES, or of the Simonians. — (See Simon Magus.)

GOSPEL OF THADDÆUS.—Rejected by Gelasius.

GOSPEL OF TATIAN.—(See TATIAN.)

GOSPEL OF TRUTH.—(See VALENTINUS.)

OTHER UNCANONICAL WRITINGS OF THE SECOND CEN-TURY.

Besides the foregoing gospels, there appeared in the second century, a large number of other writings relating to Christ and his apostles ; Acts, Epistles, Revelations, etc.   Fabricius gives a list, alphabetically arranged, of Apocryphal Acts of the Apostles, 36 in number ; among which are the Acts of Peter, Acts of Peter and Andrew, Acts of John, Acts of St Mary, etc.

Then there was the Apocalypse of Peter, Apocalypse of John, (another), Apocalypse of Paul, Bartholomew, etc.

These were subsequently called apocryphal ; a term, meaning, at first, only hidden ; but which, afterward, when the books had been for some time laid aside and disused, came to be looked upon as a term of reproach.

CHAPTER VII.

THE AGE OF MIRACLES.

APOLLONIUS OF TYANA.

Apollonius Tyaneus, one of the most remarkable characters of history, was born two years before the commencement of the Christian era. He lived a hundred years, witnessed the reign of a dozen Roman emperors, and during his long and brilliant career, sustained the role of a philosopher, teacher, traveler, religious reformer and worker of miracles.

The most of our information concerning him is derived from his biography, written in Greek, by Flavius Philostratus, in the year 210. It was composed at the request of the beautiful and gifted Julia Domna, wife of the Emperor Septimius Severus.

As soon as Julia was made empress, she gathered around her the finest intellects and the greatest orators of the day. Among them were Dion Cassius, the historian, the eminent lawyers, Paulus, Papinian and Ulpian, and the learned sophist and scholar, Philostratus. It was under such auspices that the life of Apollonius was written. The work has attracted much attention, and has been translated into various languages.

In England in 1680, Charles Blount, the deist, commenced a translation, and had proceeded as far as the first two books, which he published with extensive notes, when he seems to have become alarmed at the opposition of the ecclesiastics of his day, and did not further prosecute the work.

In his preface, Blount refers, in his quaint manner, to the supposed opposition of the book of Philostratus to the Christian Scriptures. "Philostratus does not," says he, "anywhere so much as mention the name of Christ; and if one heathen writer, Hierocles, did make an ill use of this history, by comparing Apollonius to Christ, what is that to Philostratus? Now as to myself," he continues, "I am so far from comparing him to our blessed Savior, or from giving credit to any new miracles, that my daily request to God is, to give me faith enough to believe the old."

In the year 1809, the Rev. Edward Berwick, Vicar of Leixslip, in Ireland, translated the whole eight books of Philostratus; the celebrated Lardner having in the mean time given his opinion, that the work was not intended to antagonize the New Testament.

Let us now open this celebrated book of Philostratus, and take a brief survey of its contents.

He commences by giving an account of the materials from which the work was composed; stating that he obtained them from the different cities and temples, from tradition, and from the epistles of

Apollonius, "addressed to kings, and sophists, and philosophers; to Elians, Delphians, Indians and Egyptians." Also that he had made use of the book of Maximus the Ægæan, the biography written by Damis the Assyrian, who had accompanied Apollonius in his travels, and a work written by one Meragenes.

The following is an epitome of the biography, as given by Philostratus.

LIFE OF APOLLONIUS.

Apollonius was born at Tyana, a town founded by Greeks, in Cappadocia.

Before his birth, Proteus, an Egyptian god, appeared to his mother. She asked the god, whom she should bring forth. To which he replied, " Thou shalt bring forth me." Apollonius was born in a meadow, under a temple since dedicated to him. When his mother was near the time of her delivery, she was warned in a dream to go and gather flowers in a meadow. When she came there, while her maidens were dispersed up and down, employed in their several amusements, she fell asleep on the grass. While thus situated, a flock of swans that was feeding in the meadow, formed a chorus around her, and clapping their wings, as their custom is, sang in unison, while the air was fanned by a gentle zephyr. At the same time, her son was born. The natives of the place affirm that at the instant of his birth, a thunderbolt, which seemed ready to fall upon the ground, rose aloft, and suddenly disappeared.

All the people of the country said he was the son of Jupiter; but he constantly called himself the son of Apollonius.

As he grew up, he gave signs of great strength of memory, and persevering application.

The eyes of all were attracted by his beauty.

His youth was spent, partly in Tarsus, and partly in Ægæ, where he enjoyed the conversation of Plato, Chrysippus and Aristotle. He was an enthusiastic admirer and devoted follower of Pythagoras. He declined eating anything that had life, living exclusively on fruits, and other productions of the earth. His fame was spread far and near. While in his youth, he lost his parents, and buried them in his native town, Tyana. He resolved never to marry.

As a true disciple of Pythagoras, he maintained silence for five years. Opposes hot baths. Wherever he goes he reforms religious worship.

His probationary term of silence having expired, he resolves to travel to India, and visit the Brahmins and Germanes, and converse with the magi inhabiting Babylon and Susa; saying it was his duty to go where wisdom and his guardian angel led him. While on this journey, he acquired from the Arabians a knowledge of the language of animals; an art for which others of the ancients were celebrated; Melampus, Teresius, and Thales Milesius.

Entering the territories of Babylon, he had an interview with the satrap. He continued his journey, interpreting to Damis, his companion, dreams and visions, by the way. Then we have an account of Babylon, with its royal mansions, covered with brass, and the apartments and porticos, adorned with silver, with tapestry of gold, and with beaten gold.

Apollonius enters the king's palace, conversing with Damis, and not noticing at all the splendid things surrounding him. He was received with honor by the king, Bardanes, who invited him to join in the sacrifice he was then preparing, of a white horse of the Nisæan plains, to be offered to the sun, adorned as if in a solemn procession. Apollonius declined; but sacrificed to the sun with frankincense, and then retired; lest he should be made a partaker in the shedding of blood.

He visits India, and is well received by Phraotes, the king. He is offered money by both these kings, but refuses to receive it.

We must not omit to mention, that while on this journey to India, Damis, the companion of Apollonius, saw on Mt. Caucasus, the very chains with which Prometheus had been bound.

They arrive at the wonderful hill occupied by the Brahmins. The sages communicate freely with Apollonius, who participates in their ablutions and ceremonies. Philostratus relates, that when, with staves uplifted, the Brahmins struck the earth all together, they made it heave and swell like waves of the sea, and they themselves were elevated to the height of almost two cubits above it. There they would dance awhile in chorus, and then descend together. Iarchus, the chief of the Brahmins, declares that Apollonius was, in a previous life, a pilot of an Egyptian vessel. Apollonius admits it to be true, and gives some account of his life as a pilot.

Then comes a feast, given by the king and Brahmins. Four Pythian tripods, like those described in Homer, came forward of their own accord. Then advanced cupbearers of black brass, like the Ganymedes and Pelops of the Greeks. The earth strewed under them herbs, softer than beds. Bread and fruits, and the vegetables of the season, together with the dainties used at second courses, came of themselves, each in order, better dressed than they could be by our cooks. The cupbearers of brass mixed the wine and the water for the company, which they presented, in small cups, to every guest.

Iarchus cures the lame, and the blind, and performs many other miracles.

Apollonius returns home by going south to the sea, thence by vessel, up the Euphrates to Babylon, thence, by way of Antioch, to Cyprus and Paphos.

He goes to Ephesus. People flock about him. Certain prophecies from the oracles at Coryphon, Didyme and Pergamos, in his favor, spread abroad. Ambassadors come to him from several cities. He predicts the plague, and tells what is going on at a distance.

The plague raging at Ephesus, ambassadors were sent to him at Smyrna, entreating him to come to their assistance. Apollonius said, "I think the journey is not to be delayed." No sooner had he uttered these words, than he was at Ephesus. There he put an end to the plague, by having the people stone a demon, which took various forms.

He travels through Greece. At Athens, casts out an evil spirit from a youth. As soon as Apollonius fixed his eyes upon him, the demon broke out into the most angry and horrid expressions, and then swore he would depart out of the youth. Apollonius rebuked him, commanded him to come out, and told him to give a visible sign. Immediately the demon cried out, "I will make that statue tremble;" to which he pointed, standing in a royal portico. Whereupon the statue first began to shake, then totter, and finally tumbled down.

Apollonius visits the temples of Greece, and reforms their religious rites and ceremonies.

At Corinth, Menippus, one of his disciples, a young Lycian, was in love with a beautiful and intelligent woman, whom he was soon to marry. Apollonius goes as a guest to the wedding. When everything is ready, Apollonius announces that the woman is one of the Empusæ, who pass under the name of Lamiæ and Larvæ. Upon this announcement, everything vanished into thin air; the gold and silver vessels, cupbearers and cooks, and the whole domestic apparatus. Whereupon the phantom, appearing as if in tears, begged not to be tormented, nor forced to make a confession. But Apollonius was peremptory, and she confessed to being an Empusa, and that she had pampered Menippus with rich dainties, for the express purpose of devouring him. Philostratus says, "I have been necessarily induced to mention this transaction, as it was one of the most celebrated performances by Apollonius, and as it happened in the center of Greece, many were acquainted with it."

Having traveled all over Greece, he next went to Rome. As Nero was persecuting philosophers, his companions became frightened, and nearly all left him. At Rome, he was accused of treason. The accuser came forward, holding in his hand a roll, on which had been written the accusation. When the roll was unfolded, lo and behold, neither letter nor character was to be seen.

A girl, when about to be married, "seemingly died," says the biographer, and the funeral procession was on its way to bury her. She was of a consular family, and all Rome condoled with the young husband. Apollonius, meeting the procession, said to the attendants, "Set down the bier, and I will dry up the tears which you are shedding for the maid." He touched the young woman, and uttering a few words over her, in a low tone of voice, he wakened her from that death with which she seemed to be overcome. The relatives of the girl presented him with a hundred and fifty thousand drachmas, which he settled upon the bride, as a marriage portion.

"It is difficult to me," adds Philostratus, "as it was to all who were present, to ascertain whether Apollonius discovered the vital spark, which had escaped the faculty, (for it was raining at the time, which caused a vapor to rise from her face), or whether he cherished and brought back her soul, which to all appearances was extinct."

Apollonius visits Spain and Africa, and thence returns to Italy and Sicily. At Syracuse he makes a prediction, concerning the three emperors which Rome was soon to have, which was fully verified in Galba, Vitellius and Otho. He again travels through Greece. Leaving one vessel, and taking another, the one he leaves is shipwrecked. He goes to Egypt. Arriving at Alexandria, he declares a convicted man innocent. A further examination proves him to be so, and his life is saved.

At Alexandria, he has an interview with Vespasian, who, on his way to Rome from Judea, where he had been carrying on the Jewish war, goes to Egypt on purpose to visit Apollonius.

While Apollonius was in this part of Egypt, a tame lion coming up to him, and paying him special attention, Apollonius stated to the people, that the lion wanted him to tell them by what human soul he was inhabited. He tells them it is the soul of Amasis, who was formerly king of Egypt, in the district of Sais. The moment the lion heard this, he roared in a piteous strain, crouching on his knees, and at the same time, bursting into tears. The lion was then dressed in collars and garlands, and sent into the interior parts of Egypt, accompanied all the way with the sound of flutes, and the singing of hymns.

Journeying into the interior of Ethiopia, Apollonius visits the gymnosophists. To show they could perform wonders as well as the Brahmins, Thespesion, their leader, said to an elm tree near the one under which they were sitting, "Salute Apollonius, O tree." No sooner were the words uttered, than the tree saluted him; speaking in a voice which was articulate, and resembled that of a woman.

Titus, having been declared emperor of Rome, requested Apollonius to meet him at Argos. On his arrival, Titus embraced him, and said he had a letter from his father, Vespasian, wherein he said, he considered that Apollonius was his benefactor, to whom they were under many obligations.

Apollonius again travels through Greece and Italy. In the Hellespont, he drove out the wandering Egyptians and Chaldeans, who, for their own gain, operating on the fears of the people, who were dreading earthquakes, were collecting money, on pretense of making costly sacrifices.

He now took up his residence at the grove of Smyrna, on the banks of the Meles, where he discoursed of fate and necessity. Knowing that Nerva was to succeed Domitian, he spoke of it as a matter of public notoriety; and showed that tyrants themselves were unable to resist the decrees of fate.

Some of his expressions having been repeated to Domitian, Apollonius was cited to appear before him. Before receiving the summons, however, he was apprised of it by his guardian spirit, and started at once for Italy. Arriving at Rome, he is brought before the emperor, and is accused, with great violence, of being an enchanter. Is taken to prison. Discourses encouragingly to his fellow prisoners.

Being brought before the emperor, he talks with so much boldness, that Domitian orders his hair and beard to be cut off, and that he be sent back to prison, loaded with chains, and be cast among the vilest felons. He was now nearly a hundred years old.

Damis, who was also in prison, asked him when he would be at liberty. "To-morrow," answered Apollonius, "if it depends on the judge; this instant, if it depends on myself." Saying this, he drew his leg out of the fetters, and said to Damis, "You see the liberty I enjoy." He then put his leg in the fetters again.

He goes to the tribunal, to make his defense. Domitian perused the indictment, sometimes in great wrath, sometimes with more composure. "I think," says Philostratus, "we may represent Domitian to our minds, as a man highly incensed at the laws, for ever having suffered such things as tribunals to be constructed. Apollonius was required to enter the tribunal, free from amulet, book or charm, or any writing whatever. As he went into the room, he did not once look at the emperor. He was commanded to look at Domitian, as the god of men. Apollonius lifted his eyes to the vaulted arch of the court, and by his gesture showed that they were turned to Jupiter. The water was then measured into the clepsydra, the dropping from which was to measure the time of his defense.

There were four articles of accusation.

The accuser thus began: "What is the reason, Apollonius, you do not wear the same kind of garments as other men?"

"Because," replied he, "the earth, which supplies me with food, supplies me also with raiment; and by wearing garments derived from it, I offer no injury to miserable animals."

2. "Why do men call you a god?"

"Because," said he, "every man that is good, is entitled to the appellation."

3. How could he fortell the plague at Ephesus? Answer, "By living on a lighter diet than other men."

4. "Tell me, Apollonius," said the accuser, "on whose account you sacrificed a boy on the day you left your house and went into the country?" "If it can be proved," replied Apollonius, "that I left my house on the day alluded to, I will grant my being in the country, and offering the sacrifice in question; but it shall require persons of both credit and character to substantiate the fact." Thereupon a shout of applause arose from the spectators; and Domitian himself, being affected by the strength and ingenuity of his answers, said, "I acquit you of the crimes laid to your charge, but here you shall stay until I have had some private conversation with you."

Apollonius replied, "You can detain my body, but not my soul; and I will add, not even my body; for as Homer says,

'Not even thy deadly spear can slay me
Because I am not mortal.'"

While uttering these words, he vanished from the tribunal.

Damis had gone to Puteoli, where he and Demetrius the philosopher, a friend of Apollonius, were on that day, musing and walking together, on the seashore, celebrated by the story of Calypso.

They had little or no hope of ever seeing Apollonius again. Tired with their walk, they sat down in a Nymphæum, a building adorned with statues of the nymphs, wherein was a cistern of white marble, containing a living spring of water, which never rose above, and was never drawn below its margin. They were talking listlessly, while sorrow filled their hearts, when suddenly Apollonius appeared before them. It was on the same day of the trial, though Puteoli was more than three days journey from Rome. Demetrius wished to know if he was alive. Apollonius stretched out his hand, and commanded him to take it, to assure himself that he was still living.

He returned to Greece, and traveled through all the cities, teaching the crowds who flocked to see him.

While Domitian was being assassinated at Rome, by Stephanus, Apollonius was walking and talking, disputing among the trees, in one of the xystas of Ephesus. It was about mid-day. Suddenly Apollonius let his voice fall, as if alarmed at something. He then went on, conversing in a lower tone. Then became quite silent. Soon after, fixing his eyes steadfastly on the earth, and advancing three or four steps, he cried out, "Strike the tyrant; strike;" as if actually witnessing some occurrence.

All Ephesus was astonished at what was heard, there being a large concourse present. But Apollonius, after stopping some time, cried out, "Keep up your spirits, O Ephesians, for this day the tyrant is killed. And why do I say this day? At this very moment, while the words are in my mouth, I swear it by Minerva, the deed is done." Then he remained silent.

This is the account of Philostratus. The same transaction is related by Dion Cassius, with such variation of details as is supposed to strengthen statements of that kind. That author's account is as follows:

On the very day—nay, the moment Domitian was assassinated, as it was afterward known upon a most exact search into the matter, Apollonius Tyaneus got up, whether it was in the city of Ephesus or elsewhere, upon a very high stone, and calling the people together, cried out with a loud voice, "Courage, Stephanus, courage! strike the murderer. Thou hast struck him; thou hast wounded him; thou hast killed him." "As incredible as the fact seems to be," says the historian, "it is no less true."—[Manning's Dion Cassius, vol. 2, p 92.

This testimony of Dion Cassius is more important from the fact that he was no admirer of Apollonius, but, in another part of his history, puts him down as an impostor and a magician. He complains of Caracalla, that he was such a favorer of impostors and magicians, that he paid great honors to the memory of Apollonius of Cappadocia, and raised a monument to him.—[Dion Cassius, vol. 2, p. 327.

Baronius supposes the assassination of Domitian to have been communicated to Apollonius, by a demon.

The time was now approaching which was to terminate the career of this remarkable man. Nerva having sent a letter to the philosopher, requesting him to come to Rome and give him his advice, Apollonius replied as follows:

"We will converse together, O emperor, during a long time, where we will neither command others, nor will others command us."

This letter was afterward construed to mean, that Apollonius was about to leave this world, and that Nerva's reign was to be short.

"Here," says Philostratus, "ends the history of Apollonius the Tyanean, as written by Damis the Assyrian. Concerning the manner of his death," he continues, "if he did die," various are the accounts.

"Some say he died at Ephesus, waited on by two handmaids, to one of whom he gave her freedom, forseeing it would be better for the other to remain where she was.

"Some say he entered the temple of Minerva at Lindus, and there disappeared."

Others affirm that his exit was made at Crete, in a still more extraordinary way. The temple of Dictyma, at Crete, was under the protection of dogs, who took care of the riches laid up in it. When Apollonius entered the temple, the dogs did not bark at him as they did at others, but received him with fawning affection. The priests who had the care of the temple, seeing this, seized Apollonius, and bound him; thinking him a magician, or a robber. About midnight, he freed himself from his chains, and called the priests, to show that he did nothing in secret. Then, going to the gates of the temple, he found them open. As soon as he entered them, they shut of themselves, as they had been before, and the temple resounded with the singing of many virgins; the burden of whose song was, "Leave the earth; come to heaven; come, come!"

After his death, he appeared at Tyana, to a young man who had doubted the immortality of the soul, and discoursed with him upon the subject. The young man cried out, "I believe you now." He had often requested Apollonius to appear to him, and he finally did so.

Here ends the history by Philostratus. Suidas and Eudocia inform us that a life of Apollonius was written also, by one Soterichus Oasites.

For several centuries after his death Apollonius was worshiped as a god, in many parts of the world. Not only did Caracalla build him a temple, but Alexander Severus held him in such esteem that he had his statue in his private closet. On account of Apollonius, Tyana was held sacred, and exempted from the jurisdiction of governors sent from Rome.

Roman emperors have not refused him the same honors as were paid to themselves; and Gibbon relates that when Aurelian took the town of Tyana, "a superstitious reverence induced him to treat with lenity the countrymen of Apollonius the philosopher."

M. Bayle remarks that Apollonius was worshiped in the beginning of the fourth century, under the name of Hercules, and refers to Vopiscus, Eusebius and Marcellinus, to show that the people of Tyana had not left off the worship of Apollonius in the beginning of the fourth century. His image was set up in many temples. Roman emperors encouraged it.

Lampridius states that Christ was really worshiped by some of the later heathen emperors, together with Abraham, Orpheus, and Apollonius; these being all looked upon as holy men, and tutelary genii.[1]

Albert Reville says, "The universal respect in which he was held by the whole pagan world, testi-

(1.) Lamp. Life of Alex. Severus.

fied to the deep impression which the life of this
supernatural being had left indelibly fixed in their
minds; an impression which caused one of his
contemporaries to exclaim, 'We have a god living
among us.' "—["Pagan Christ," etc., by Albert
Reville, London, 1866, p. 39.

Eunapius, who wrote at the beginning of the
fifth century, says of him, that he was not so much
of a philosopher, as something between a god and
a man, and that Philostratus ought to have entitled his history, "The Descent of a God upon
Earth."[1]

Sidonius Apollinaris, (A. D. 475), praises the
morals and philosophy of Apollonius, without
speaking of his miracles. In the 8th book, 3d
epistle to Leon, counselor to the king of the Goths,
he delivers a glowing eulogium upon Apollonius;
speaks of his disdain for riches and ostentatious
display; of his love for science, his frugality, his
gravity, sincerity and uprightness of character, his
abstinence from animal food, etc., and closes as
follows: "In one word, to say the truth, I do not
know as there is, in all antiquity, the life of a philosopher equal to this one; and I am very certain
that such a one cannot be found in this age."[2]

Notwithstanding all this evidence of the high esteem in which he was held by the ancients, the
historian Froude, on the strength of a sentence or
two of Lucian, in a letter to Celsus, would place
him on a level with the impostor, Alexander Abonotichus, of the second century.

(1.) Life of Apollonius, by M. le Nain de Tillemont, page 42.
(2.) History of Apollonius, by Dupin, Paris, 1705, Pref. p. 16.

That such a classification would do great injustice to Apollonius, is manifest from his epistles, which are still extant.[1]

They are addressed to individuals, to societies, to philosophers, to kings and emperors.

These writings show him to have been a man of learning, with a consummate knowledge of human nature, imbued with the noblest sentiments, and with the principles of a profound philosophy.

In his letter to Hestiæus, he says:

"The truth is not concealed from us, how beautiful it is to have all the earth for one's country, and all men for brothers and friends; and that those who derive their origin from God, are all endowed with one and the same nature and with a community of reason and affections; and that wheresoever any one may be, or in whatever manner born, whether barbarian or Greek, he is still a man. But the claims of kindred cannot be evaded, and one recalls to himself whatever is properly his own. Thus the Ulysses of Homer, as they say, did not prefer immortality, even when offered by the goddess."

In the epistle to Valerius, we have the doctrine of the indestructibility of matter:

"There is no death of any thing, except in appearance; and so, also, there is no birth of any thing, except in appearance. That which passes over from essence into nature, seems to be birth, and what passes over from nature into essence, seems, in like manner, to be death; though nothing really is originated, and nothing ever perishes; but only now comes into sight, and now vanishes. It appears, by reason of the density of matter, and disappears by reason of the tenuity of essence; but is always the same, differing only in motion and condition."

In the next paragraph, enlarging upon the same idea, he closes by saying, "no thing is ever created or destroyed." Again:

(1.) They may be seen in the original Greek, in the Library of Congress.

"By what other name, then, than First Essence, shall this rightly be called? These things are done and permitted by the Eternal God, who becomes all, in all, and through all, and who, *if he were to clothe himself in names and forms, would suffer loss and damage in his own nature.*"

To a brother, who had lost his wife, he writes:

"It is destined, that whatever has come to perfection, must pass away. Let not, therefore, the loss of your wife, in the ripeness of age, shock you, and not, because something is called death, consider life better than it, since life is considered inferior, by every wise person.

"If there had been anything to be reprehended in your late wife, you might reasonably be cast down. But she was always esteemed by us, was always loving to her husband, and everything to be desired."

He closes the letter with these affecting words:

"For tears have I not been able to write more, and more than this I have not thought necessary."

As to the miracles ascribed to Apollonius, the most of them were probably the invention of the second century. There is little doubt, however, that he possessed some extraordinary faculty, which he exercised in such a way as to establish and maintain an influence over his fellow men, beyond what he could otherwise attain.

Perhaps the highest tribute paid to Apollonius, was by the emperor Titus. The philosopher having written him, soon after his accession, counseling moderation in his government, Titus replied as follows:

"In my own name, and in the name of my country, I give you thanks; and will be mindful of those things. I have indeed taken Jerusalem, but you have captured me."

The miracles of Apollonius were extensively believed in the second century, and for hundreds of years afterward; and by Christians as well as others. As late as the fourth century, when Hierocles had drawn a parallel between Apollonius and Christ, Eusebius, who thought it necessary to make an elaborate reply, did not deny the performance of miracles by Apollonius, but attributed them to sorcery.

Tillemont thought he had the assistance of Satan.

"The devil," said he, "may know the history of past ages," etc., "and he may know what men are doing, in very distant places. And what he knew, he might discover to Apollonius." Reville is of the opinion, that Apollonius practiced what this writer calls "theurgy;" a sort of compromise between imposture and the display of miraculous power.

The difficulty in placing a proper estimate upon such a character, at this distance of time, is great. But it may safely be asserted, that Apollonius was a man possessed of many elements of greatness; that he was a man of much learning and great ability; and whatever may have been his weaknesses, he was endowed with a certain grandeur of soul, which at once commands our respect and admiration.

CHAPTER VIII.

THE AGE OF MIRACLES.—Continued.

Simon Magus.

Simon Magus was another miracle worker, who lived in the first, and whose miracles were written up in the second century.

Simon was the prince of heretics. His miracles were notorious, and admitted by all. By orthodox Christians they were attributed to magic, or to the machinations of Satan. At a later day, it has been supposed they might be accounted for on scientific principles.

Dr. Westcott says, "It would be interesting to inquire how far the magic arts universally attributed to Simon and his followers, admit of a physical explanation. In his school, if anywhere, we should look for an advanced knowledge of nature."[1]

Mosheim is not willing to class Simon among the heretics, since that would be impliedly admitting that he was a Christian ; but he concedes that "nearly all the ancient and modern writers make

---

(1.) History of the Canon, p. 249, Note.

him to have been the head, the father and the ring-leader of the whole heretical camp." [1]

This conspicuous position makes his opinions of some importance.

Theodoret, (A. D. 430), says that he denied that there was but one principle. He asserted two, and held that there was another maker of this world. This was the Demi-Ourgos, who was under the control of the Supreme God, who presided over the whole universe.[2]— This doctrine was extensively believed in by the Gnostics of the second century.[3] In his system, the third power in the trinity was a woman.[4] For this his followers had the authority of the Gospel of the Hebrews.

Simon held that matter was eternal, and that an evil deity presided over it.[5] He was educated at Alexandria.[6] His followers became so numerous that they were spread over the whole world, and in Rome, in the reign of Claudius, a statue was erected in his honor.[7]

In the 8th chapter of the Acts of the Apostles, we have a glimpse of Simon, who had bewitched the people, insomuch that they all gave him heed, "from the least to the greatest, saying, 'This man is the great power of God.' " [Acts. 8, 9, 10.]

(1,) Mosheim, vol. 1, p. 92,

(2.) Hæret. Fab. 4. 188.

(3.) See Dr. Lardner's Works, vol, 4, p. 511.

(4.) Fabricius, Codex Apoc. vol, 1, p. 362. Note.

(5.) Mosheim, Ecc. Hist. vol. 1, p. 93.

(6.) Clementine Homilies, 2. 22.

(7.) Justin Martyr, 1st Apology, 26. 56; Irenæus, v. Hær. 1. 23.

In the Recognitions, attributed to Clement of Rome, and a portion of which, at least, was written about the same time with the Acts, there is a fuller account of this wonderful man. As in the Acts of the Apostles, so in the Recognitions, he appears as the great antagonist of Peter.

The reader may be introduced to Peter at Cæsarea, where he is preparing for a discussion with Simon Magus.

"When the day dawned, which had been fixed for the discussion with Simon, Peter, rising at the first cock-crowing, aroused us also; for we were sleeping in the same apartment, thirteen of us all; of whom, next to Peter, Zaccheus was first, then Sophonius, etc. After these, I (Clement) and Nicodemus, then Niceta and Aquila, who had formerly been disciples of Simon, and were converted to Christ, under the teachings of Zaccheus. Of the women, there was no one present."
—[Recognitions, book 2, chapter 1.

Peter then tells them that he has formed the habit of waking in the middle of the night, and lying awake till morning, recalling and arranging in his memory the words of the Lord.

The conversation turning on the coming discussion, Peter wishes to know what kind of a person Simon is. Niceta thinks he will prove to be a formidable antagonist. Aquila gives a full history of Simon, from which it appears, that his father was Antonius, and his mother Rachel. By nation he was a Samaritan, of the Gettones. His profession was that of a magician, yet exceedingly well trained in Greek literature; desirous of glory, and boasting above all the human race.

"So that he wishes to be an exalted person, who is above God the Creator, and to be thought to be the Christ, and to be called 'the Standing one.' He uses this name, as implying that he can never be dissolved; asserting that his flesh is so compacted by the power of his divinity, that it can endure to eternity."—[Ibid. chs. 3 to 7.

Simon had been a disciple of Dositheus, and became one of the thirty. Aquila proceeds with his story :

"But not long after, he fell in love with that woman whom they call Luna, and he confided all things to us as his friends; how he was a magician, and how he loved Luna, and how, being desirous of glory, he was unwilling to obtain her ingloriously;" but was waiting patiently, when he could have her honorably.

"Yet so if we also would conspire with him, in the accomplishment of his desires.

"Meantime, at the outset, as soon as he was reckoned among the thirty disciples of Dositheus, he began to depreciate Dositheus himself, saying that he did not teach purely or perfectly, and that this was the result, not of ill intention but of ignorance. Dositheus, when he saw that Simon was depreciating him, fearing lest his reputation among men might become obscured, (for he himself was supposed to be the Standing-one), moved with rage, when they met as usual at the school, seized a rod and began to beat Simon; but suddenly the rod seemed to pass through his body, as if it had been smoke. On which Dositheus, being astonished said to him, 'Tell me if thou art the Standing one; that I may adore thee.' And when Simon assured him that he was, Dositheus, perceiving he himself was not the Standing one, fell down and worshiped him, and gave up his own place as chief to Simon, ordering all the rank of thirty men to obey him; himself taking the inferior place which Simon formerly occupied. Not long after this he died.

"After the death of Dositheus, Simon took Luna to himself, and with her he still goes about, as you see, deceiving multitudes, and asserting that he himself is a certain power, which is above God, the Creator, while Luna, who is with him, has been brought down from the higher heavens. That she is Wisdom, the mother of all things; 'for whom,' says he, 'the Greeks and barbarians, contending, were able, in some measure, to see an image of her; but of herself, as the dweller with the first and only God, they were wholly ignorant."

He then proceeds to relate a miracle which he (Aquila) once saw ; Luna being in the tower, and looking out of all the windows of the tower at the same time.

Peter evidently believes what Aquila had related, for he says, ''It has been permitted to the wicked one, to use those arts by which the affections of every one toward the true father may be proved.'' [Bk. 2, chs. 9–18.

THE DISCUSSION.

CHAPTER 19.—Zaccheus enters, saying it is time the disputation commenced, for a great crowd, collected in the court of the house, was awaiting him. Then Peter, having prayed with the brethren, went forth to the court of the house, and when he saw the multitude all looking intently on him, in profound silence, and Simon, "standing like a standard bearer in the midst of them," he commenced:

First he invoked a peaceable discussion. But Simon at once retorted, that Christ said, he came, not to send peace but a sword. Peter replies in the words of Jesus, " Blessed are the peace-makers." Simon continues to comment upon the inconsistency of Christ, if he came not to bring peace, enjoining upon others to keep it.—[Chs. 19 to 27.

Simon announces his position. " I say," said he, " that there are many gods, and that there is one, incomprehensible and unknown to all; that he is the God of all these gods. He then argues for polytheism; saying to Peter, that he will prove it from his own scriptures. He cites Genesis, 3. 5: " On the day ye eat of the tree of knowledge, of good and evil, ye shall be as gods." Also, Gen. 3. 22: " Behold, Adam is become as one of us." Also Gen. 1. 26: " Let us make man after our own image and likeness;" and Gen. 3. 22: " Let us drive him out." Also, Gen. 11. 7: " Come, let us go down, and confound their language;" and Exodus, 22. 28: " Thou shalt not curse the gods," etc. "One of these," says Simon, "was chosen by lot, that he might be the god of the Jews."

" But," says he, "it is not of him that I speak; but of that God who is also his God, whom even the Jews themselves do not know. For he is not their God, but the God of those who know him."

Peter has a long disquisition on God, to which Simon replies, that he would refute him from the words of his master, who said no one knew the Father but the Son, and he to whom the Son should reveal him. Yet the god of the Jews was known to Adam, to Enoch, to Noah, to Abraham, Isaac and Jacob, and to Moses.—[Chs. 38 to 47.

"Remember," Simon urges, "that you said that God has a son; which is doing him wrong; for how can he have a son, unless he is subject to passions, like men or animals? My opinion is, that there is a certain power of the Universe, an ineffable light, whose greatness is to be held to be incomprehensible; of which power, even the maker of the world is ignorant, and Moses the lawgiver, and Jesus, your master."—[Ch. 49.

The reasoning of Simon: That there is one God, who is better than all, from whom all that is, took its beginning; that he must be perfect. That the god who created the world, shows many signs of imperfection. There must, therefore, be a God over him. He argues the imperfection of the god who made the world and man, thus: The many evils in the world which are not corrected, show that its creator is powerless, if he cannot correct what is done amiss; or else, if he does not wish to remove the evils, then he is himself evil; but if he neither can nor will, then he is neither powerful nor good.—[Chs. 53, 54.

The disputation was closed for the day.

The audience, of whom there were about 3,000, divided, about one-third going away with Simon, and the rest staying with Peter.

Book 3. The debate is re-commenced next day, and is continued two days longer.—[Chs. 1 to 69. Ante-Nic. Ch. Lib. vol. 3, pp. 240 to 265.

The second day there is some acrimony in the discussion, and some difference as to the questions to be debated.

They discuss the nature of evil, free will, the power of God, etc.

CH. 23.—Simon says, "What I wish to know is this: If what God wishes to be, is; and what he does not wish to be, is not?" The purport of the answer of Peter is, that some actions depend upon the will of man.

The discussion closed for the day; Simon calling upon Peter each day to show him whether the soul was immortal.

Third day. Simon pressing for evidence of the immortality of the soul, Peter argues in favor of it, because of the necessity of having a day of judgment; since men do not get their deserts in this world.

Simon claims that Peter cannot assert that the soul is immortal, and that he knows if it be proved to be mortal, his religion will fall.

"But Peter, when he heard him speaking thus, grinding his teeth, and rubbing his forehead with his hand, and sighing with a profound grief, said: 'Armed with the cunning of the old serpent, you stand forth to deceive souls.' "—[Ch. 42.

CH. 44.—Peter having offered to prove to Simon, in one sentence, that the soul is immortal, asks him, which is the best evidence, hearing or seeing? Simon answers seeing. Peter then tells him to go to his (Simon's) own house, and entering the inner bed-chamber, he would see an image, containing the figure of a murdered boy, clothed in purple.

Simon hearing this, was smitten in his conscience, changed color, and became bloodless. He then proposed to become a convert; thinking Peter possessed the power of divination. Peter disabused him and admitted that he had only stated what he had been informed of, and spake "what he knew, and not what he foreknew."

Thereupon Simon, seeing himself betrayed, went from one extreme to another, and becoming fairly furious with anger, burst forth as follows:

"I stood by and spoke with you in my goodness, and bore patiently with you. But now, I shall show you the power of my divinity, so that you shall quickly fall down and worship me. I am the first power, who am always, and without beginning. But having entered into the womb of Rachel, I was born of her as a man, that I might be visible to men. I have flown through the air; I have mixed with fire, and been made one body with it; I have made statues to move; I have animated lifeless things; I have made stones bread; I have flown from mountain to mountain; I have moved from place to place, upheld by angels' hands, and have lighted on the earth. Not only have I done these things, but even now I am able to do them; that by facts I may prove to all, that I am the Son of God, enduring to eternity, and that I can make those who believe on me, endure in like manner forever. But your words are all vain; nor can you perform any real works. (Such as I have mentioned.) He also who sent you is a magician, who yet could not deliver himself from the suffering of the cross."

To this speech Peter answered,

"Do not meddle with the things that belong to others; for that you are a magician, you have confessed and made manifest, by the deeds that you have done."

At this point in the proceedings, the historian relates, that Simon endeavored to make a riot, and the people, in indignation, cast him from the court, and drove him forth from the gate of the house. It does not appear, however, that Peter denied the truth of what Simon asserted, or that he challenged him to a proof of his miraculous powers.

After Simon and his friends had gone, Peter explained to those remaining, his reference to the image of the murdered boy; Simon had been deluded by demons, and he had persuaded himself that he had the soul of a murdered boy, ministering to him, in whatever office he pleased to employ it.

Peter then pronounced a benediction, and dismissed the multitude, and thus ended this most remarkable discussion.—[Chs. 48 to 50.

The next morning, Niceta said to Peter, he desired to learn how Simon, who was the enemy of God, was able to do such wonderful things. "For indeed," says Niceta, "he told no lie in his declaration of what he had done." (Niceta had been one of Simon's disciples.) Peter undertakes to explain how Simon "is able to do so great marvels." Simon, he said, was a magician.

Niceta asked, "In what respect do they sin, who believe Simon, since they see him do so great marvels? Or is it not marvelous to fly through the air, to be so mixed with fire as to become one body with it, to make statues walk, etc. Yea," says Niceta, "he has also been seen to make bread of stones. But if he sins who believes those who do signs, how shall it appear that he also does not sin, who has believed our Lord, for his signs and works of power?"—[Chs. 52 to 57.

Peter replies, that if a man believes him who comes first, showing signs, he must of necessity, for the same reason, believe him who comes second. When he believes the second one, he will learn from him that he ought not to believe the first, who comes of evil.—[Chs. 58 to 62.

After the disscussion, Simon sets out for Rome, and Peter resolves to follow him.—[Chs. 63 to 65.

Following Simon Magus to Rome, we learn that he there lost his life. In the Encyclopedia Americana it is stated that he perished in an aeronautic expedition; giving as authority, Eusebius and Suetonius. Suetonius in relating the cruel sports and games which Nero instituted for his own diversion, merely says, "Icarus fell, splashed with blood." From which the reader may infer, only, that Nero had compelled some one to attempt the flight of Icarus. The story is to be traced to "THE ACTS OF PETER AND PAUL."

From that book, we take the following:

"When, consequently, the people were making a seditious murmuring, Simon, moved with zeal, roused himself, and began to say many evil things about Peter; saying that he was a wizard and a cheat. And they believed Simon, wondering at his miracles. For he made a brazen serpent move itself, and stone statues to laugh, and move themselves, and himself to run, and suddenly to be raised into the air. As a set-off to this, Peter healed the sick by a word, by praying made the blind to see, and put demons to flight by a command. Sometimes, he even raised the dead. Those who adhered to Simon, strongly affirmed Peter to be a magician."

The matter coming to the ears of Nero, he ordered Simon the Magian to be brought before him.

And he, coming in, stood before him, and began suddenly to assume different forms; so that on a sudden he became a child, and after a little an old man, and at other times a young man. For he changed himself both in face and stature, into different forms, and was in a frenzy, having the devil as his servant.

"And Nero, beholding this, supposed him to be truly the Son of God. But the apostle Peter showed him to be both a liar and a wizard."

After considerable conversation, Nero says :

"Art thou not afraid, Peter, of Simon, who confirms his godhead by his deeds?"

Peter replies, that Simon does not know the hidden thoughts of men.

Nero said, "Do you mean me to believe, that Simon does not know these things, who both raised a dead man, and presented himself the third day after he had been beheaded, and who has done whatever he said he would do?"

Peter said, "But he did not do it before me." Nero said, "But he did all these things before me. For assuredly, he ordered angels to come to him, and they came." Peter still demanded that Simon should tell what was in his thoughts. Simon made the same challenge to Peter. Peter then demanded of Simon, to know what he, Peter, had just done in secret. For, having taken a barley-loaf, he had broken it, and hid it in his sleeves.

"Then Simon, enraged that he was not able to tell the secret of the apostle, cried out, saying: 'Let great dogs come forth, and eat him up, before Cæsar.' And suddenly there appeared great dogs, which rushed at Peter. But he, stretching forth his hands to pray, showed to the dogs the loaf which he had blessed, and the dogs, seeing it, no longer appeared.

"Simon said, 'Dost thou believe, O Good Emperor, that I, who was dead and rose again, am a magician?'"

[The writer of the Acts of Peter and Paul here explains how Nero had been deceived by Simon; stating, that as Simon was to be beheaded, he had requested that it be done in a dark place; and when the executioner came, and was about to strike the blow, Simon turned himself into a ram. He so remained until the ram's head was taken off, when be became himself again. On the third day, he appeared, as if risen from the dead.]

Then followed a conversation in which Nero, Simon, Peter, and Paul also, who was present, participated.

Nero, not being able to satisfy himself, says: "The three of you show that your reasoning is uncertain; and thus in all things you have made me doubt, so that I find I can give credit to none of you."

Simon now proposes to Nero, that if he will build a high wooden tower, he will go to the top, and thence fly through the air, attended by his angels; and thus give open evidence of his divinity.

Nero agrees to the proposal, and the next day builds the tower. Simon goes upon it, and commences flying in the air, attended by his angels. Peter, looking steadfastly at him, prays to the Lord to stop him. His prayer is answered, and Simon falls headlong, in a place called Sacra Via, or Holy Way, and perishes.[1]

This, no doubt, was the aeronautic expedition, alluded to by the encyclopedic compiler, and to which he supposed Suetonius to refer, when "Icarus fell splashed with blood."

Simon Magus also had his gospel. It was called "The Great Announcement," and consisted of the revelations which, as he claimed, had been communicated to him from the Supreme God. It was sometimes called the Gospel of Simonides; also, the Gospel of the Simonians.

(1.) Ante-Nicene Ch. Lib. vol. 16, pp. 263 to 273.

CHAPTER IX.

THE AGE OF MIRACLES—Concluded.

OTHER MIRACLES AND MIRACLE-WORKERS.

ALEXANDER ABONOTICHUS — APULEIUS — ANTINOUS—JEW-ISH SUPERSTITIONS—MIRACLES OF THE FATHERS—THE THUNDERING LEGION—CHANGE OF WATER INTO OIL, ETC.—THE MIRACLES OF THE NEW TESTAMENT.

ALEXANDER ABONOTICHUS.—The satirist, Lucian, at the request of Celsus, wrote an account of this celebrated imposter. The following is a condensed statement of it, as reproduced by the historian, Froude :

Alexander was born at Abonotichus, a small town on the south shore of the Black Sea, early in the second century. The boy was of unusual beauty. He was taken up by a doctor, who had been a disciple of Apollonius. Alexander's master was a magician, and he himself became an apt pupil.

At the age of twenty, when his master died, he set up for himself. He started for Byzantium, the great mart of ancient commerce. Here he became acquainted with one Coconas, by whom he was introduced to a wealthy Macedonian lady. She fell in love with him, and took him and his friend with her, to her country seat at Pella. Here the two friends laid plans for the future. They purchased a large, tame snake; took it with them when they left Pella, and by the aid of the serpent, made a business of fortune-telling.

They repaired to Abonotichus. From Chalcedon they brought some brass plates, which had been discovered buried, and which bore an inscription, that Apollo and Esculapius were about to appear at Pontus. The people of Abonotichus commenced building a temple for Alexander, who now soon acquired great reputation and renown.

Lucian describes him as he then appeared; tall, majestic, extremely handsome—hair long and flowing, complexion fair, a moderate beard, partly his own and partly false, but the imitation excellent; eyes large and lustrous, and voice sweet and limpid. "As to his character," says he, "God grant that I may never meet with such another. His cunning was wonderful, his dexterity matchless. His eagerness for knowledge, his capacity for learning and power of memory, were equally extraordinary."

He made for the serpent a human face, of linen, which was painted in an ingenious manner, and so arranged that the mouth would open and shut, and this was the face of Esculapius. From it he delivered oracles and spoke in unknown tongues.

The temple was finished, the god was formally established in it, and the oracles became a permanent institution. People flocked from all parts of Asia Minor, to consult them. Immense treasures flowed into the coffers of Alexander.

"The air was full of miracles. The sick were healed; the dead were raised to life." The Christians considered him a missionary of the devil.

Among his dupes was Rutelian, a senator, in high favor with the emperor.

There was a girl, said to be the daughter of Selene, the moon, and Alexander. She is declared to be destined for Rutelian, and the marriage is celebrated with great pomp and splendor.

Lucian himself visited Alexander and endeavored to expose him. He frankly admits that the attempt was a complete failure. When the prophet gave him his hand to kiss, Lucian bit it to the bone. For this, he came near paying the forfeit of his life. Alexander, concealing his pain and mortification, treated Lucian with the utmost courtesy and kindness, and gave him a vessel for his return home. The commander was secretly instructed to throw him overboard. This he

was too humane to do, but told Lucian he should be obliged to put
him ashore, which he did; and Lucian found himself in Bithynia, a
long way from home.

He returned, a wiser man, and the prophet continued to flourish.
The emperor bestowed distinctions upon him. He lived to be an old
man, and died in the acme of his fame.

APULEIUS.—Some of the early writers speak of
Apuleius as a worker of miracles. He was a pagan
philosopher of the Platonic school, born at Madau-
ra, in Africa.

He lived about A. D. 150. He was distinguished
for his eloquence, and stood high as a Latin writer.
Having married a rich widow in Tripoli, he was
prosecuted by his relations, on a charge that he had,
in his courtship, made use of magical arts. He de-
fended himself on that occasion, by an 'Apology,'
which is still extant. There has also come down to
us, another of his works, entitled, "Metamorpho-
sis, or the Golden Ass;" supposed to have been a
satire on the wealthy debauchees of his time. Lactantius, referring to what Hierocles had asserted,
that Apollonius was greater than Christ, because he
rescued himself from Domitian, while Christ was
put to death, says it is somewhat strange that writers should pass over Apuleius, "of whom many
wonderful things are commonly said." [1]

ANTINOUS was a beautiful youth, a favorite of the
Emperor Hadrian. He was born in Bithynia.
He accompanied Hadrian to Egypt, and was drowned
in the Nile, A. D. 132. A city called Antino-opolis,
was built by the emperor, near the spot where he

(1.) Lact. Inst. lib. 5, ch. 3.

perished, and countless statues were erected in his honor. Some of them still exist, and are remarkable for their beauty.

Justin Martyr says he was worshiped as a god.[1]

Origen says there were miracles wrought in many places,[2] and Celsus mentions, as miracle-workers, Esculapius, Aristeas of Proconnesus, and Cleomedes of Astypalæa.

JEWISH SUPERSTITIONS.

The Jews were ever exceedingly superstitious. The miracles of the Old Testament are familiar to the reader. These were supplemented by an innumerable multitude of angels and demons of every description.

The casting out of demons was familiar to the Jews, long before the coming of Christ. In the Book of Tobit, the angel Raphael directs fumigation with the heart and liver of a fish, in order to drive a demon out of a man or woman, so that it will never return. The demon Asmodeus was in love with Sara, the daughter of Raguel, and had strangled seven men who were going to marry her; but by the process mentioned above, he was driven out, and flew into Egypt, where he was bound by the angel.—[Book of Tobit, 6. 7; 8. 7; 6. 14, etc.

In the Book of Enoch, the names of twenty-one angels are given, who had fallen, through love for the daughters of men. The offspring of these were giants, whose height was 3,000 ells. From these come the evil demons of earth.

Raphael was the angel who presided over the spirits of men. Uriel was the angel of thunder, earthquakes, etc. There were spirits controlling the winds and the lightning, others over the seas, and still others over hail, snow, frost, etc., etc.—[Book of Enoch, ch. 69; chs. 7, 8, 9, 34, etc.

The Jews believed the stars were animated beings.—[Gfroerer, das Jahrhundert des Heils, 1, p. 362.

Enoch saw seven stars bound together, and he inquired of the angel, on account of what sin they were bound. Uriel replied, they were

(1.) 1st Apology, ch. 29.
(2.) Contra Celsum, 3, 3.

stars which had transgressed the commands of the highest God, and they were thus bound till ten thousand worlds, the number of days of their transgression, should be accomplished.—[Chs. 21 and 18.

The targums are full of similar views, concerning the stars and other heavenly bodies.

The multitude of angels was innumerable.

Each angel had a particular duty to perform. Michael was angel over water, Jehuel over fire, Jechiel over wild beasts, and Anpiel over birds. Hariel was appointed over cattle, Messannahel over reptiles, Deliel over fish, and Samniel over created things moving in the waters, and over the face of the earth. Ruchiel was set over the winds, Gabriel over thunder and fire, and over the ripening of fruit. Nuriel over hail, Makturiel over rocks, Alpiel over fruit-bearing trees, Saroel over those which do not bear fruit, and Sandalfon over the human race. Under each of these were subordinate angels.— [Sanhed. 95. 2; Eisenmenger, Entd. Jud. 2. 378. Sup. Relig. vol. 1, p. 108.

The demons were equally as numerous. They were in the air, on earth, in the bodies of men and animals, and even at the bottom of the sea. They were the offspring of the fallen angels who loved the daughters of men.—[Eisenmenger, Ent. Jud. 1. 380; 2. 437.

"Their number is infinite. The earth is so full of them, that if man had power to see, he could not exist, on account of them. There are more demons than men, and they are about as close as the earth thrown up out of a newly made grave."

It was stated that each man had 10,000 demons at his right hand, and 1,000 on his left. "He who wishes to discover these spirits, must take sifted ashes, and strew them about his bed, and in the morning he will perceive their footprints upon them, like a cock's tread. If any one wishes to see them, he must take the afterbirth of a black cat, which has been littered by a first born black cat, whose mother was also a first birth, burn and reduce it to powder, and put some of it in his eyes, and he will see them."—[Bab. Beracoth. 6. 1.

The casting out of demons, was an important feature in the Jewish theological system. Dr. Lightfoot says, "There was hardly any people in the whole world, that more used, or were more fond of amulets, charms, mutterings, exorcisms, and all kinds of enchantments." —[Lightfoot, Horæ Heb. et. Talm. Works, 11. p. 299.

Josephus states, that among other gifts, God gave to Solomon knowledge of the way to expel demons. Josephus himself had seen a countryman of his own, named Eleazar, release people possessed of devils, in the presence of the Emperor Vespasian and his sons, and his army. He put a ring, containing one of the roots prescribed by Solomon, to the nose of the demoniac, and drew the demon out by his nostrils, and in the name of Solomon and reciting one of his incantations, he adjured him to return no more.—[Antiquities of the Jews, bk. 8, ch. 2, sec. 5.

MIRACLES OF THE FATHERS.—These commence about the middle of the second century. More than a hundred years ago, Rev. Dr. Middleton, in his "Free Enquiry into the Miraculous Powers of the Christian church," called attention to the fact, that in the writings of the apostolic fathers, (referring to those who had written previous to about A. D. 150,) there was not the least pretense to the possession of extraordinary gifts, nor to any standing power of working miracles; and showed that the claim in the second century, was first set up about the time of Justin Martyr.

"Here, then," said he, "we have an interval of about half a century, the earliest and purest of all Christian antiquity, after the days of the apostles, in which we find not the least reference to any standing power of working miracles."[1]

In the writings of Justin Martyr, (A. D. 150 to 160), the claim to miraculous power was put forth with much distinctness. He says:

"There are prophetical gifts among us at this day, and both men and women are endued with extraordinary powers by the spirit of God."[2]

He frequently appeals to what he says every one might see with his own eyes, in every part of the

(1.) Middleton's Miscellaneous Works, vol. 1, p. 8.
(2.) Dialogue, chapter 88.

world, and particularly in Rome, in the case of persons possessed with devils, "who were cured and set free, and the devils themselves baffled and driven away, by the Christians adjuring and exorcising them in the name of Jesus, when all other exorcists and enchanters had tried in vain to help them."[1]

Justin says the angels to whom God had committed the care of mankind, had been led away by love of the daughters of men, and begat children, who are the demons, who have corrupted the human race.[2]

He thinks demoniacs are possessed and tortured by the souls of the wicked dead.[3]

Irenæus (A. D. 190 to 200), affirms, that "all who are truly disciples of Jesus, receiving grace from him, wrought miracles in his name, for the good of mankind, according to the gift which each man had received. Some cast out devils, so that those from whom they were ejected, often turned believers, and continued in the church. Others had the knowledge of future events, visions, and prophetical sayings. Others healed the sick by the imposition of hands. Even the dead had been raised, and lived afterward many years among them. It was impossible to reckon up all the mighty works which the church performed, every day, to the benefit of nations."—[Adv. Hær. lib. 2, ch. 32.

And in regard to raising from the dead, he declares it to have been "frequently performed on necessary occasions, when by great fasting, and the joint supplication of the church of that place, the spirit of the dead person returned into him, and the man was given back to the prayers of the saints."—[Adv. Hær. 2. 31.

Again: "We have many," says he, "in the church, endued with prophetic gifts; speaking with all kinds of tongues, laying open the secrets of men, for the public good."—[Ibid. 5. 6.

(1.) Apology, 2, 6.
(2.) Apol. 2. 5.   Ibid. 1, 5, 14.
(3.) Ibid. 1. 18.

Clement of Alexandria (A. D. 200) says presiding angels were distributed over nations and cities ; that the Son gave philosophy to the Greeks, by means of the inferior angels ; and argued that it was absurd to attribute it to the devil.[1]

Tertullian (A. D. 200 to 210) calls upon the heathen magistrates to "summon before their tribunal any person possessed with a devil; and if the evil spirit, when exorcised by any Christian whatsoever, did not own himself to be a devil, as truly, as in other places he would falsely call himself a god, not daring to tell a lie to a Christian, that then they should take the life of that Christian."—[Apology, ch. 23.

Again: "There is a sister among us, endued with the gifts of revelations, which she suffers in the church, during the time of divine service, by an ecstasy, in the spirit. She converses with angels, and sometimes also with the Lord; sees and hears mysteries; and knows the hearts of some, and prescribes medicines to those who want them."—[De Anima, sec. 9.

He has a disquisition concerning angels and demons, in which he enters into minute details.[2]

He gives the case of a woman who went to a theater, and came back possessed by a demon ; and on being cast out, the evil spirit said he had a right to act as he did, having found her within his limits.[3]

Origen (A. D. 230) was of the opinion that certain demons, offspring of the Titans or giants, who haunt the grosser parts of bodies and the unclean places of the earth, had the power of divining the future.[4]

After fully discussing the question, and citing many passages of scripture, he comes to the conclu-

(1.) Stromata, 6. 17.
(2.) Apol. sec. 22; Ad. Scapulam, sec. 2.
(3.) De Spectaculis, sec. 26.
(4.) Contra Celsum, 4. 92; 8. 11.

sion that the sun, moon and stars are living, rational beings.[1]

He says many could heal the sick, by invoking the name of God over them, and of Jesus, with a recital of some story of his life. "I myself," says he, "have seen many so healed in difficult cases ; loss of senses, madness, and innumerable other evils, which neither men nor devils could cure." [2]

Theophilus, Bishop of Antioch (A. D. 180), says that evil and seducing spirits were exorcised and cast out in his day.[3]

Minucius Felix, (3d century), addressing himself to his heathen friend, in his Dialogue of "Octavius," says, "The greatest part of you know what confessions the demons make, concerning themselves, as oft as they are expelled by us, out of the bodies of men, by the torture of our words, and the fire of our speech. Saturn himself, and Serapis, and Jupiter, and the rest of them, whom you worship, constrained by the pain which they feel, confess what they are."—[Minuc. Octav. p. 23, ch. 27.

Cyprian (A. D. 250), Arnobius (A. D. 303), and Lactantius (A. D. 310), all give testimony in similar language, to the casting out of devils and evil spirits by the Christians.[4]

Eusebius had similar views.[5]

Tertullian relates that a woman, whom he knew, a member of the church, after having died, while the presbyter was praying for her, removed her

---

(1.)   De Principiis, 1. 7, sec. 3; Contra Cels. 5. 10, 11.

(2.)   Ibid. lib. 3, ch. 24.

(3.)   Ad Autolycum.

(4.)   Cyprian, Epist.; Arnobius, lib. 1. 46; Lactantius, Divin. Inst. l. 2, c. 16.

(5.)   Præp. Evang., 5. 2.

hands from her sides, and folded them in the attitude of supplication.[1]

Even the great Augustine relates a number of most astounding miracles, which were performed in the church, in his immediate neighborhood.[2]

THE THUNDERING LEGION.—Eusebius quotes from a lost work of Claudius Apollinaris, his account of a remarkable answer to prayer, received, about A. D. 175, by the Christian soldiers of the Emperor Marcus Aurelius, in his war with the Quadri. Tertullian, writing about A. D. 200, in a public apology, also urges the same fact.

The incident referred to was this:

"It is said, that when Marcus Aurelius Cæsar was forming his troops in order of battle, against the Germans and Sarmatians, he was reduced to extremities, by a failure of water."

Thereupon, in answer to the prayers of the Christian soldiers of the Melitine Legion, so called, there came thunderbolts, which caused the enemy's flight and overthrow. And upon the emperor's army, a rain, "which restored it entirely, when it was all but perishing by thirst."—[Euseb. Ecc. Hist., 5. 5.

This circumstance we mention, not because there is any miracle connected with it, even in appearance ; since there is nothing miraculous in a sudden shower, or in a superstitious people being frightened by thunderbolts ; but because of the great prominence which has been given to it, in what might be called miraculous literature.

Much has been written about it. Dion Cassius attributes the occurrence and the preservation of the army to an Egyptian magician by the name of

(1.) De Anima, sec.51. (2.) De Civ. Dei, 22. 8.

Amuphis. Julius Capitolinus attributes it to the emperor's prayers. Themistius the same. Baronius, Moyle, Scaliger, Valesius and other have written about it; and more recently, the late Cardinal Newman devoted fourteen pages to it, at the close of which, he concludes it to have been a very noted miracle.[1]

There was, no doubt, an occurrence of the kind; the army, when in dire extremity, having been relieved by a sudden fall of rain. This we learn from Dion Cassius and other heathen writers, and from a sculpture of the celebrated Antonine Column at Rome, where is a figure of Jupiter Pluvius, scattering lightning and rain, the enemy and their horses lying prostrate, and the Romans, sword in hand, rushing upon them.

We hear nothing of any connection of Christians in the transaction, except from Tertullian and Eusebius, and those who copied from them.

As to the Christian legion, called, according to Eusebius, the Melitine Legion, which he represents as afterward remaining intact, Moyle says there were few or no Christians in the army; and adds, "I would as soon believe my Lord Marlborough had a whole regiment of Quakers in his army, as that Antoninus had a whole legion of Christians in his."[2]

Then, as to the name "Thundering," applied to the Melitine Legion, which Eusebius makes Apollinaris say the emperor gave to it on account of this transaction, the fact is, that one of the Roman legions had that name, from the time of Augustus Cæsar.

TURNING WATER INTO OIL.—Narcissus, Bishop of Jerusalem, when oil failed for lamps, at the vigil of Easter, sent the persons who had the care of them, to the neighboring well for water. When they brought it, he prayed over it, and it was changed into oil. At least, so says Eusebius.[1] Narcissus was made bishop about 180.

This reported miracle has been the occasion of learned disquisitions by Dodwell, Jortin and many others. Newman devotes several pages to it, and closes by saying, that while he cannot say positively that he believes it, yet he has no doubt about it.[2]

From the list of noted miracles discussed by Dr. Newman, those two have been mentioned, because they are said to have occurred in the second century.

It is a significant fact, that they both come, either originally, or with important accessions, from Eusebius.

APOCRYPHAL WRITINGS.

From the middle of the second century, and even earlier, the Christian world was flooded with anonymous writings of a religious character, filled with miracles of every description. There was a morbid demand for that kind of literature. At a later day, these writings were styled apocryphal.

(1.) Ecclesiastical Hist., 6. 9.   (2.) Essays on Miracles, p. 259.

There were gospels, acts, revelations, epistles, etc., etc.

The Revelation of Moses gives a long history of Adam and Eve. The Revelation of Esdra resembles somewhat the Apocalypse of John. The Revelation of Paul is of the same sort, relating, at great length, the wonderful things revealed to Paul, when he went up to the third heaven, and was caught up into paradise, and heard unspeakable words. [2d Cor. 12. 4.] There is another Revelation of John, the Book of John concerning the Falling Asleep of Mary, the Passing [Translation] of Mary, etc.

The Acts of Peter and Paul, the Acts of Paul and Thecla, and the story of Perpetua, have already been mentioned.

The Acts of Barnabas relate the journeyings, the miracles and martyrdom of that apostle.

Finding a town, called Curium, was very wicked, he rebuked it, and the western part fell, "so that many were wounded, and many of them also died."

THE ACTS OF PHILIP.—Nicanora, wife of the proconsul of Hierapolis, having been converted and healed of her sickness by the preaching of Philip, her husband was so enraged, that he caused them both, with Bartholomew, to be scourged, and the two apostles to be hanged, Philip head downward. In this position, Philip has a long conversation with Bartholomew, and preaches a discourse to those standing about. When Mariamne was stripped, her body was changed, and became a glass chest filled with light.

THE ACTS AND MARTYRDOM OF ANDREW.—Andrew has a discussion with Ægeates, the proconsul. Ægeates, becoming very angry, has Andrew crucified. Afterward, he was himself tormented by the devil, and came to a violent death.

Besides these, there were the Acts of Andrew and Matthias, in the City of the Man-Eater, the Acts of Peter and Andrew, the Acts and Martyrdom of St. Matthew, the Acts of the Holy Apostle Thomas, and many others.—Fabricius has a list of Apocryphal Acts, 36 in number. Some of them are written very much in the style of the Acts of the Apostles.

ACTS OF PAUL.—Dr. Lardner thinks that Origen referred to a book entitled "The Acts of Paul."—De Principiis, 1, 2, T. 1, p. 54.

THE MIRACLES OF THE NEW TESTAMENT.

When we turn to the miracles of the New Testament, we instinctively feel like making them an exception to the mass of wonders of that age. How much of this feeling may be owing to education and association, we will not stop to inquire; and perhaps it would not be found easy to determine.

The fact, however, cannot be ignored, that there is no evidence showing that either of the five books in which these miracles are recorded, was written until nearly one hundred and fifty years after the transactions are said to have occurred. How much earlier the manuscripts existed from which these books were compiled, is not known. None of them can be clearly traced to the first century.

There are other important considerations. A number of these miracles consist in casting out demons from human beings. But the doctrine of demons is a doctrine of the past. It is now recognized and admitted, that from the beginning, the demons have existed only subjectively, as forms of doctrine and belief. What then becomes of this class of miracles?

If, without irreverence, we carefully examine even the most imposing class of New Testament miracles, looking upon them at the same time as violations of known laws of nature (without which a miracle loses its force and meaning), we meet with very serious obstacles in the way of giving them implicit credence.

In the case of Jairus' daughter, we have but to take the explicit language of Jesus himself, "The maid is not dead, but sleepeth."

There are two other reported cases of raising from the dead, in the canonical gospels. The raising of the son of the widow of Nain, is found only in the compilation of Luke. The authorship of the manuscript containing it, and the time when it was written, are involved in obscurity.

The raising of Lazarus, and the turning of water into wine, the two transactions most plainly contravening the laws of nature, are only related in the Gospel of John; the author of that work having probably taken them from the Acts of Pilate.

Why do the other canonical gospels contain no mention of those stupendous miracles?

How can the belief in miracles be of any importance in the Christian system? If the doctrines and precepts of the Christian religion are adapted to the nature of man, and in harmony with the divine economy of the universe, they will stand, through all time. If not, they will fall. The changing of one element or substance into another, or even the raising of a person from the dead, cannot make wrong right, or change the truth into falsehood.

This great truth was all but comprehended by Tertullian, intellectually the most vigorous of all the early fathers. He declared that the proof of the Christian religion by miracles, was inconclusive; "because," said he, "Jesus Christ has assured his disciples that some would arise, who should work false miracles."—[Adv. Marcion, 3. 3.

Archbishop Trench falls into the same line of argument:

"A miracle does not prove the truth of a doctrine, or the divine mission of him that brings it to pass. The doctrine must first commend itself to the conscience as being *good*, and only then can the miracle seal it as *divine.*—[Notes on the Miracles of our Lord, 8th Ed. 1866, p. 25.

The same view is taken by Mozley and others. But if the doctrine has received the sanction of the conscience as good, is it not already divine? And what need of the miracle afterward?

THIRD PERIOD.

CHAPTER X.

THE THREE APOCRYPHAL GOSPELS.

THE PROTEVANGELION.

Of the extant gospels of the second century, the three most ancient are, the Protevangelion, or Book of James, the Gospel of the Infancy, and the Acts of Pilate, or Gospel of Nicodemus.

The Protevangelion was attributed to the apostle James, and was called by Origen, "The Book of James."

It is generally considered one of the oldest gospels of the second century; probably appearing about the third decade. The name, "First Gospel," would indicate it to be the first of certain writings of the kind.

The following is an abstract of its contents:

THE PROTEVANGELION.

CHAPTER 1.—An account of Joachim, and of the refusal of his offerings in the temple, which were despised, because he had no children.

CHAPS. 2 and 3.—Anna, the wife of Joachim, mourns her barrenness, and has a conversation upon the subject with her maid, Judith.

CHAPS. 4 to 7.—The angel announces to Anna that she is to have a child.

She brings forth a daughter, and calls her name Mary.

When Mary was nine months old, she walked nine steps. When she was a year old, Joachim gave a great feast to the priests, scribes, elders, and all the people of Israel.

When she was three years old, they took her to the temple, accompanied by the daughters of the Hebrews, carrying lamps.

CHAPS. 8 and 9.—She continued in the temple, and received her food from the hand of an angel. When she was twelve years old, the priests met in consultation, to determine what to do with her. Zacharias, the high priest, consulting the Lord, was told to summon the widowers with their rods, etc. The priest took the rods, and went into the temple to pray. After finishing his prayer, he came out and distributed the rods.

"The last rod was taken by Joseph, and behold, a dove proceeded out of the rod, and flew upon the head of Joseph." The high priest then designated Joseph as the one to take the virgin.

"But Joseph refused, saying: 'I am an old man, and have children; but she is young, and I fear lest I should appear ridiculous in Israel.'" The priest insisting, Joseph took her to his house, and then went away, to mind his trade of building.

CHAP. 10.—Mary selected by the priests to spin the true purple, for a new vail for the temple.

CHAP. 11.—The announcement to Mary by the angel. Similar to Luke.

CHAP. 12.—Mary visits her cousin Elizabeth. Similar to the account in Luke. She is now 14 years old.

CHAPS. 13 and 14.—Joseph, returning from building houses abroad, found the virgin with child, and reproached her. Mary protested her innocence, saying, she knew not how it had occurred.

Joseph was about to put her away, when an angel appeared, and dissuaded him from it. Joseph then took the virgin, glorifying God.

CHAPS. 15 and 16.—Joseph and Mary were brought before the priest, accused of having violated her virginity; Joseph having taken her merely to keep as a virgin.

Joseph was required to drink holy water, which he did, unharmed. He was then acquitted.

CHAPS. 17 and 18.—Joseph and Mary went to Bethlehem to be taxed. As Mary's time drew near, they were obliged to stop, three miles from Bethlehem.

Mary was taken into a cave, and left, with Joseph's sons, while Joseph went to Bethlehem after a midwife. On the way, he saw various prodigies. Fowls of the air, stopping in the midst of their flight; people sitting before a table at dinner, their hands on the table motionless; sheep standing still, the shepherd with his hand raised to smite them, his hand remaining motionless; kids with their mouths to the water, but not drinking.

CHAPS. 19 and 20.—Joseph met a mid-wife. As they approached the cave, a bright cloud overshadowed it, and going in, they found Jesus was born. Salome came to the cave, and desiring proof that Mary was a virgin, proof was vouchsafed. But as a result, Salome's hand immediately withered. She prayed to the Lord; an angel appeared, and told her to take the child, and her hand would be restored. She took the child, and her hand was made whole.

CHAP. 21.—Wise men came from the east to Bethlehem, inquiring for the King of the Jews. The interview between Herod and the wise men. Similar to Matthew.

CHAPS. 22 to 24.—Herod having issued his order for the slaughter of the children, "Mary, hearing that the children were to be killed, being under much fear, took the child, and wrapped him up in swaddling cloths, and laid him in an ox-manger, because there was no room for them in the inn."

Elizabeth, hearing that her son John was to be searched for, took him, and went up into the mountains. There a mountain opened and received them. Zacharias, because he would not disclose the hiding place of his son John, was murdered in the entrance of the temple. When Zacharias was killed, "the roofs of the temple howled, and were rent from the top to the bottom, and his blood was congealed to stone."

CHAP. 25.—CONCLUSION. "I, James, wrote this history in Jerusalem; and when the disturbance was, I retired into a desert place, until the death of Herod. And the disturbance ceased at Jerusalem."

OPINIONS OF THE FATHERS.

The account in the Protevangelion, of the murder of Zacharias, father of John the Baptist, was generally accredited by the fathers. It is mentioned and endorsed by Tertullian,[1] by Origen,[2] by Epipha-

(1.) Scorpiac, adv. Gnost., c. 8.
(2.) Hom.26, Matt. 23, fol, 49.

nius,[1] by Theophylact,[2] and others.

The Protevangelion says, Zacharias was killed at the entrance of the temple, and his blood was hardened into stone.—(Ch. 24.)

Tertullian says, Zacharias was killed between the altar and the temple, and the drops of his blood made indelible impressions on the stones.

As has been already mentioned, the circumstance of Joseph being an old man when Mary was betrothed to him, and having had children by a former wife, was accredited by the fathers generally. The Protevangelion was here supported by the Gospel of Peter.

Origen, it is true, only refers to it as believed by some, but others adopt it implicitly. Eusebius says James was called the brother of Christ, because he was also called the son of Joseph.[3] Epiphanius says the same,[4] and in another place, that Joseph was about fourscore years old when he married Mary ; and had six children before that time, by a former wife ;[5] and again, writing against a sect which denied the perpetual virginity of Mary, he says :

"Joseph was very old when he married Mary, and had been many years a widower; that he was the brother of Cleophas, the son of James, surnamed Panther; that he had his first wife of the tribe of Judah, and by her six children, to wit, four sons and two daughters. His eldest son was James, surnamed Oblias, [this probably taken from

(1.) De Vit. Prophet. vol. 2, p. 250, (attributed to Epiphanius.)
(2.) In Matt.
(3.) Ecc. Hist., 2. 1.
(4.) Hæres. 29; Naz. sec. 3, 4.
(5.) Hæres. 51; Alogor. sec. 10.

Eusebius, Ecc. Hist. 2. 23], that he begat him when he was about forty years old; after him he had another son named Jose, then Simeon and Judas, and then his two daughters Mary and Salome: after his wife's death, he continued many years a widower, and about fourscore years old, married Mary."—[Epiph. Hæres., 78, sec. 8.

So also was the account in the Protevangelion accepted as true by Hilary,[1] by Chrysostom (A. D. 407), Cyril (A. D. 375), by Euthymius and Theophylact, and generally, as Bishop Pearson says,[2] by all the Latin fathers till Ambrose (A. D. 390), and the Greek fathers afterward.

Epiphanius refers, also, to the death of Zacharias, but there is a wide departure from the account in the Protevangelion.

"It was," he says, "the occasion of the death of Zacharias in the temple, that when he had seen a vision, he through surprise was willing to disclose it, and his mouth was stopped. That which he saw, was at the time of offering incense; and it was a man standing in the form of an ass.

"When he had gone out, and had a mind to speak thus to the people, 'Wo unto you, whom do ye worship?' he who had appeared to him in the temple, took away the use of his speech. Afterward, when he recovered it, and was able to speak, he declared this to the Jews, and they slew him. They add, that on this very account, the high priest was appointed by their lawgiver to carry little bells, that whensoever he went into the temple to sacrifice, he whom they worshipped, hearing the noise of the bells, might have time enough to hide himself, and not be caught in that ugly shape and figure."—[Epiph. Hær., 79. 5.

That Mary, at three years of age, was taken to the temple, and remained there eleven years, was received as true by Euodius, Gregory of Nyssen, (380), Damascene, (725), Germanus, Bishop of Con-

(1.) In Matth. 1.

(2.) On the Creed, p. 175, Art. 3.

stantinople, Andreas Cretensis, (675), George, bishop of Nicomedia, and others.[1]

The Protevangelion was not condemned by the decree of Pope Gelasius.

Jones was mistaken in supposing that Epiphanius and Austin were the first writers who had recognized the Protevangelion.[2] Origen mentioned it as "the Book of James;" Tertullian was acquainted with it, and still earlier, Justin Martyr.

The fact that Christ was born in a cave, is frequently alluded to in the writings of the fathers. Thus Gregory Nyssen (380) says:

"We are indeed cheered by the gospel, when we revert to the speech at Bethlehem, and when we contemplate the divine mysteries in the cave." "Speelaio musteeria."—[Greg. Nys. Op. vol. 3, p. 348. (See also, the chapter of this work entitled, "Justin Martyr.")

(1.) See Baronius, (1588), Apparat. ad Annal., no. 48.
(2.) Jeremiah Jones, New Method, etc., vol. 2, p. 144.

CHAPTER XI.

THE PROTEVANGELION,
AND THE GOSPELS OF LUKE AND MATTHEW.

THE PROTEVANGELION ONE OF THE MANUSCRIPTS USED IN THE COMPILATIONS OF LUKE AND MATTHEW—THE PROTEVANGELION AND THE FIRST TWO CHAPTERS OF LUKE AND MATTHEW COMPARED.—WHICH WAS FIRST WRITTEN?

Dr. Frederick Schleiermacher, who is styled, in the Imperial Dictionary of Biography, "the most influential theologian of Protestant Germany that has appeared during the present century," in an able essay, has shown, that the Gospel of Luke consists, almost entirely, of a compilation of manuscripts, older than the time of the compiler.

Speaking of the first and second chapters, he says :

"It is impossible, at the outset, to avoid observing the great difference of style between the introductory passage, (ch. 1, vv. 1 to 4), and this section (balance of chs. 1 and 2); since from very tolerable and well constructed Greek, which even makes some attempts at elegance, we suddenly drop into the harshest Hebraistic phraseology; so that one is loth to attribute both to the same hand."—[Critical Essay on Luke, p. 21, Ed. London, 1825.

Again:

"If we compare the end of the first chapter with the beginning of the second, we can scarcely remain in doubt, that the section from verse 5 to the end of the chapter, (ch. 1), was originally an independent whole. In the first place, the 80th verse is an evident form of conclusion. . . . . .

"To this it may be added, that if it were the same narrator who is proceeding in the second chapter, many things ought to be differently stated."—[Ib. p. 22.

"Thus then we begin by detaching the first chapter as an originally independent composition. If we consider it in this light somewhat more closely we cannot resist the impression, that it was originally a a poetical work rather than a proper historical narrative. The latter supposition in its strictest sense, at all events, no one will adopt; or contend that the angel Gabriel announced the advent of the Messiah, in figures so purely Jewish, and in expressions taken mostly from the Old Testament; or that the alternate song between Elizabeth and Mary actually took place in the manner described; or that Zachariah, at the instant of recovering his speech, made use of it to utter the hymn, without being disturbed by the joy and surprise of the company, by which the narrator himself allows his description to be interrupted.

"At all events, then, we should be obliged to suppose that the author made additions of his own, and enriched the historical narrative by the lyrical effusions of his own genius. But even in the historical part, there is much that will not admit of being understood as literal narrative. In the first place, the whole chronology depends on the circumstance which the author was desirous of introducing, that the child in Elizabeth's womb leaped for joy at Mary's approach. Mary is, on this account, made to defer her visit till after the fifth month; and in order to leave no chasm in the whole, the angel, for the same reason, is made to come to her no sooner. Immediately after the annunciation, she sets out, and stays three months with her cousin;—a circumstance also very improbable, on account of her own approaching nuptials—in order that upon her return, the birth of Jesus might be immediately subjoined.

"Similar to this is the circumstance, that Zacharias is punished with dumbness for his unbelief, and thus contrasted with Mary, who breaks forth, under divine inspiration, into songs of praise; and yet that, although his unbelief must long before have ceased, he does not recover his speech till the instant when, by confirming the name, he solemnly recognizes the angel's declaration of his son's calling.

"If to this we add the whole grouping, the angel coming to Zacharias, and announcing the last prophet of the old covenant in the temple, the same coming afterward to Mary, and announcing the advent of the Messiah in the despised Nazareth, the meeting of Mary and

Elizabeth, the winding up of the whole by the restoration of Zacharias to speech, and his hymn, which form the conclusion, there naturally presents itself to us a pleasing little composition, completely in the style and manner of several Jewish poems, *still extant among our apocryphal writings;* written in all probability, originally in Aramaic, by a Christian of the more liberal Judaizing school, and of the general style of which, a faithful image is conveyed in the early severe school of Christian painting."—[Essay on Luke, by Schleiermacher, pp. 24 to 26.

The Protevangelion, which is one of the extant apocryphal writings alluded to, is in the Greek language, but is filled with Hebraisms, showing it to have been written by a Hellenic Jew; and justifying the supposition of our author, that it was originally in the Aramaic tongue.

The following comparison of the two gospels will, it is believed, sustain the inference of Schleiermacher, that the apocryphal gospel, so called, was first written :

(We have consulted the original Greek text, from the Orthodoxographa of Grynæus, p. 71, etc.)

The Protevangelion
Compared with Luke and Matthew.

PROTEVANGELION, ch. 11.	LUKE, ch. 1.
	26. And in the sixth month the angel Gabriel was sent from God, unto a city of Galilee, named Nazareth.
	27. To a virgin espoused to a man whose name was Joseph, of the house of David; and the virgin's name (was) Mary.
And she (Mary) took a pitcher, and went out to fill it with water. And behold, a voice, saying; Hail, full of grace; the Lord is with thee; blessed art thou among women.	28. And the angel came in unto her, and said, Hail (thou that art) highly favored, the Lord is with thee: blessed (art) thou among women.
And she looked around, to the right and to the left, to see whence this voice came. And trembling, she went into her house, and put	29. And when she saw (him,) she was troubled at his saying, and

PROTEVANGELION, ch. 11.

down the pitcher, and taking the purple, she sat down in her seat, to work it. And behold the angel of the Lord (one version reads, "a young man of ineffable beauty,") stood by her, and said: Fear not, Mary; for thou hast found favor with God.

When she heard this, she reasoned with herself, What sort of salutation is this to me? And the angel said unto her, The Lord is with thee, and thou shalt conceive. And shall I conceive, said she, by the living God, and bring forth as other women do?

The angel replied, Not so,Mary, for the Holy Ghost shall come upon thee, and the power of the Highest shall overshadow thee; therefore also the holy thing which shall be born of thee shall be called the Son of the living God.

And thou shalt call his name Jesus, for he shall save his people from their sins.

And behold thy cousin Elisabeth, she has also conceived a son in her old age. And this is the sixth month with her who was called barren.

For nothing shall be impossible with God.

And Mary said,behold the handmaid of the Lord; be it unto me according to thy word.

CHAPTER 12.

And she wrought the purple, and took it to the high priest. And the high priest blessed her, saying: Mary, the Lord hath magnified thy name, and thou shalt be blessed in all generations of the earth.

LUKE, ch. 1.

cast in her mind what manner of salutation this should be.

30. And the angel said unto her, Fear not, Mary; for thou hast found favor with God.

31. And behold, thou shalt conceive in thy womb, and bring forth a son, and shalt call his name JESUS.

32. He shall be great, and shall be called the Son of the Highest; and the Lord God shall give unto him the throne of his father David.

33. And he shall reign over the house of Jacob forever; and of his kingdom there shall be no end.

34. Then said Mary unto the angel, how shall this be, seeing I know not a man?

35. And the angel answered and said unto her, The Holy Ghost shall come upon thee, and the power of the Highest shall overshadow thee; therefore also, that holy thing which shall be born of thee, shall be called the Son of God.

36. And behold, thy cousin Elisabeth, she hath also conceived a son in her old age; and this is the sixth month with her who was called barren:

37. For with God nothing shall be impossible.

38. And Mary said, Behold the handmaid of the Lord; be it unto me according to thy word. And the angel departed from her.

39. And Mary arose in those days, and went into the hill-country with haste, into a city of Juda,

40. And entered into the house of Zacharias, and saluted Elisabeth.

PROTEVANGELION, ch. 12.

Then Mary, filled with joy, went away to her cousin Elisabeth, and knocked at the door.

When Elisabeth heard, she ran, and opened to her, and blessed her.

And said: Whence is this to me, that the mother of my Lord should come to me?

For lo; as soon as the voice of thy salutation came to my ears, that which is within me leaped and blessed thee.

But Mary, being ignorant of those mysterious things, which the archangel Gabriel had spoken to her, lifted up her eyes to heaven, and said: Lord, what am I, that all the generations of the earth should call me blessed?

But as day by day she grew big, being afraid, she went to her home, and hid herself from the children of Israel.

She was fourteen years old when these mysteries happened.

LUKE, ch. 1.

41. And it came to pass, that when Elisabeth heard the salutation of Mary, the babe leaped in her womb; and Elisabeth was filled with the Holy Ghost.

42. And she spake out with a loud voice, and said: Blessed (art) thou among women, and blessed (is) the fruit of thy womb.

43. And whence (is) this to me, that the mother of my Lord should come to me?

44. For lo, as soon as the voice of thy salutation sounded in mine ears, the babe leaped in my womb for joy.

45. And blessed (is) she that believed; for there shall be a performance of those things which were told her from the Lord.

46. And Mary said, My soul doth magnify the Lord, (etc. See the song of Mary, Luke, ch. 1, vv. 46 to 55.)

56. And Mary abode with her about three months, and returned to her own house.

No one can doubt that one of the foregoing narratives was used in the composition of the other.

If, as Schleiermacher supposes, the author of Luke has inserted an entire manuscript, running from verses 5 to 80, then the author of that manuscript drew from the Protevangelion, or the author of the Protevangelion drew from the manuscript, either before or after it was placed in the gospel of Luke.

Grynæus, the author of the Orthodoxographa, believed that the Protevangelion was first written.[1]

(1.) He says, "Multa habet quae narrationibus quatuor evangelistarum pulchre consentiunt, plura autem quae ab illis velut parerga sunt prætermissa."

"It contains many things which perfectly agree with the accounts of the four evangelists, but more which are omitted by (from) them as needless."

If the foregoing parallel passages be carefully examined, in connection with the abstract in the previous chapter, it will be seen that the internal evidence favors the earlier composition of the passages from the Protevangelion. Those are in the midst of a much longer story, forming a natural and consistent part of it; while the account in Luke is a disjointed and unconnected narrative.

The variations in Luke are evidently for a purpose.

For instance, in the 27th verse, it is stated that Joseph was of the house of David; and in the 32d verse, that Jesus should be given the throne of his father David; for neither of which is there any parallel in the Protevangelion. The earlier fathers, who followed this gospel, thought it sufficient to trace the descent of Mary from David. But the author of Luke desired to show that Joseph was descended from David; hence the change, which appears to have been made in support of his genealogy.

In pursuance of the same object, in the 4th verse of the 2d chapter, he represents that Joseph went up from Galilee to Bethlehem, to be taxed, "because he was of the house and lineage of David." The 17th chapter of the Protevangelion represents Joseph as going to Bethlehem to be taxed, but says nothing of his being of the house and lineage of David. If the Protevangelion had been last written, there is no reason why that circumstance, if true, should have been omitted; and especially if that was the reason why Joseph went to Bethlehem to be taxed. On the contrary, the author of the Protevangelion would have inserted the reference to David, as calculated to magnify the importance of Jesus, by showing his royal descent, on the male side of his ancestry.

Then the song of praise with which Mary breaks forth, has a theological look, being composed, almost entirely, from passages in the Old Testament. This, also, is not in the Protevangelion. If, indeed, it was spoken by Mary herself, it may be looked upon as strong evidence of the truth of the statement, that Mary was brought up in the temple ; since in no other way would she have been so conversant with the Jewish scriptures.

Passing on to the second chapter of Luke, Dr. Schleiermacher, commenting on verses 1 to 20, and suggesting that it appears like a separate narrative, says :

"We can recognize neither the same author, nor the prevalence of a poetical character, since this would necessarily have occasioned the introduction of more lyrical passages. Here, therefore, we must refer the main fact, at least, to an historical tradition. But upon this, if we seek grounds for an exact conclusion, there arises in the first place the question, from what source the narrative may be drawn. For two may be conceived, Joseph and Mary on the one side, the shepherds on the other."

After considering the circumstances, he inclines to the opinion, that the narrative came originally from the shepherds. He thinks the shepherds related what occurred, and the affair became known in the neighborhood of Bethlehem. He concludes as follows :

"We must therefore suppose, that this story was only drawn forth from the dust of oblivion, by the recollection of individuals, after the fame of Jesus was already established, and therefore probably did not obtain further publicity until after his death."—[Essay on Luke, pp. 32 to 35.

The following parallel may enable us to determine which of these gospels contains the earlier record of this story :

THE BIRTH OF JESUS.

PROTEVANGELION, ch. 17.

And it came to pass that there went forth a decree from the Emperor Augustus, that all the Jews should be taxed, (apographesthai), who were of Bethlehem of Judea.

And Joseph said, I will take care that my children shall be taxed; but what shall I do with this young woman? To have her taxed as my wife I am ashamed; But if as my daughter, all Israel knows she is not my daughter. The day itself of the Lord shall bring to pass what it will.

And he saddled the ass, and placed her upon it. Joseph and Simeon followed, and arrived within three miles (of Bethlehem.)

CHAPTER 18.

And he found there a cave, and led her into it, and leaving her and his sons in the cave, he went forth to seek a Hebrew midwife in the country of Bethlehem.

(On his way Joseph sees the prodigies mentioned in last chapter.)

(Ch. 19.—He meets a midwife coming down from the mountains. They return together, and find Jesus born, in the cave.)

In subsequent chapters, various remarkable events are related, including the visit of the wise men "to Bethlehem," and the order for the slaughter of the children. The

LUKE, ch. 2.

And it came to pass in those days, that there went out a decree from Cæsar Augustus, that all the world should be taxed.

2. (And this taxing was first made when Cyrenius was Governor of Syria.)

3. And all went to be taxed, every one into his own city.

4. And Joseph also went up from Galilee, out of the city of Nazareth, into Judea, unto the city of David, which is called Bethlehem; (because he was of the house and lineage of David,)

5. To be taxed with Mary, his espoused wife, being great with child.

6. So it was, that while they were there, the days were accomplished that she should be delivered.

7. And she brought forth her first-born son,

PROTEVANGELION, ch. 18.	LUKE, ch. 2.
story proceeds as follows:)	
But Mary hearing that the children were to be killed, being under much fear, took the child, and wrapped him up in swaddling-cloths, and laid him in an ox-manger, because there was no room for them in the inn.—[ch. 22.	and wrapped him in swaddling-clothes, and laid him in a manger; because there was no room for them in the inn.

The account of the vision of the shepherds, etc., does not appear in the Protevangelion; a circumstance which cannot well be accounted for, if Luke was first written. The author of the Protevangelion enlarges upon many unimportant circumstances, and is not in want of space. It is difficult to see why, if his work was last written, he should omit so interesting a portion of the story, as that concerning the shepherds; one too, which would have added so much to the importance of the transaction.

In a subsequent chapter, it will be seen that this account has a parallel in the Gospel of the Infancy. This gospel states also that Jesus was circumcised in the cave.

So with the presentation in the temple: 22d to 40th of 2d chapter of Luke, which, Schleiermacher thinks, was a separate narrative, from another manuscript. This, though not in the Protevangelion, is in the Gospel of the Infancy. The same may be said of the balance of the chapter, verses 41 to 52.

Of this portion of the narrative, Schleiermacher says:

"That the last piece of this division, too, Jesus' first visit to the temple, did not originally belong to the same context with what goes before, is rendered evident by a variety of marks. Verse 40, which some most strangely consider as the beginning of this last piece, against all analogy with 1st. 80, and 2d. 52, is a mere form of conclusion."—[Essay, p. 41.

This learned writer sums up his view of the composition of the first two chapters of Luke, as follows:

"Thus, then, by an apparently gradual annexation of several detached narratives, committed to writing independently of each other, to a piece which was originally composed, not as an historical narrative, but as a poem, did the first division of this gospel, according to these indications, take its rise."-[Essay, p. 44.

The internal evidence going to show that this gospel was written before Luke, is supported by the historical fact, that Justin Martyr (A. D. 150 to 160), who furnishes no evidence of having seen the Gospel of Luke, was acquainted with the Protevangelion history, and received it as true. He refers to Christ being born in a cave, and to various other incidents of the narrative, not found in the canonical gospels.

Let us now pass on to the Gospel of Matthew:

JOSEPH AND THE ANGEL.

PROTEVANGELION, ch. 13.

And when her sixth month was come, Joseph, returning from his building houses, and entering into his house, found the virgin grown big with child.

CHAPTER 14.

Then Joseph was exceedingly afraid, and went away from her, considering what he should do with her: and he thus reasoned with himself:

MATTHEW, ch. 1.

v. 18. Now the birth of Jesus Christ was on this wise: When as his mother Mary was espoused to Joseph, before they came together, she was found with child of the Holy Ghost.

19. Then Joseph her husband, being a just (man,) and not will-

PROTEVANGELION, ch. 14.

If I conceal her crime, I shall be found guilty, by the law of the Lord; and if I discover her to the children of Israel, I fear lest, she being with child by an angel, I shall be found to betray the life of an innocent person. What, therefore shall I do? I will privily put her away.

And night came upon him, and behold, an angel of the Lord appeared to him in a dream, saying: Be not afraid to take the young woman, for that which is within her is of the Holy Ghost.

And she shall bring forth a son, and thou shalt call his name Jesus, for he shall save his people from their sins.

MATTHEW, ch. 1.

ing to make her a public example, was minded to put her away privily.

20. But while he thought on these things, behold, the angel of the Lord appeared unto him in a dream, saying, Joseph, thou son of David, fear not to take unto thee Mary thy wife; for that which is conceived in her is of the Holy Ghost.

21. And she shall bring forth a son, and thou shalt call his name JESUS, for he shall save his people from their sins.

22. Now all this was done that it might be fulfilled which was spoken of the Lord by the prophet saying:

23. Behold a virgin shall be with child, and shall bring forth a son, and they shall call his name Emmanuel, which being interpreted is, God with us.

Then Joseph arose from his sleep, and glorified the God of Israel, who had shown him such grace, and he kept the maiden.

24. Then Joseph, being raised from sleep, did as the angel of the Lord had bidden him, and took unto him his wife.

Here, again, the later and more theological character of the composition, is apparent in Matthew.

Not only does the angel address Joseph as the son of David, which form of address is not in the Protevangelion, but verses 22 and 23 are injected into the Protevangelion history, for the purpose of making the account fit in with a certain prophecy of the Old Testament. These verses are, however, no improvement upon the Protevangelion. When that prophecy is examined, it is found not to relate to Christ at all.

The passage is in the 7th chapter of Isaiah.

In the days of Ahaz, King of Judah, the kings of Syria and Israel went up to Jerusalem, and made war against it. Then the Lord sent Isaiah forth with instructions to meet Ahaz, and to bid him to be quiet, and fear not. He was instructed to assure Ahaz, that within three-score and five years, Ephraim should be broken. The Lord then bid Ahaz ask for a sign. But Ahaz replied, he would not ask, neither would he tempt the Lord. Then the Lord (through Isaiah) said :

"Therefore the Lord himself shall give you a sign; Behold, a virgin shall conceive, and bear a son, and shall call his name Immanuel. Butter and honey shall he eat, that he may know to refuse the evil, and choose the good. For before the child shall know to refuse the evil, and choose the good, the land that thou abhorrest shall be forsaken of both her kings."—[Isaiah, 7. 14. 16.

The 8th chapter proceeds as follows :

"Moreover, the Lord said unto me, Take thee a great roll, and write in it with a man's pen concerning Maher-shalal-hash-baz. And I took unto me faithful witnesses to record, Uriah the priest, and Zechariah the son of Jeberechiah. And I went unto the prophetess, and she conceived, and bare a son. Then said the Lord to me, Call his name Maher-shalal-hash-baz. (In making speed to the spoil, he hasteneth the prey.) For before the child shall have knowledge to cry, My father, and my mother, the riches of Damascus and the spoil of Samaria shall be taken away before the king of Assyria."-[Isa. 8. 1-4.

It is only necessary to read the passage, in connection with the context, to see that it had no reference to Christ whatever. The language does not profess to be prophetic, beyond sixty-five years. Otherwise, it is historical, throughout, and the history needs no interpretation.

VISIT OF THE MAGI — SLAUGHTER OF THE CHILDREN.

PROTEVANGELION, ch. 21.

Then Joseph was preparing to go away. For there was a great commotion in Bethlehem, by the coming of wise men from the east,

MATTHEW, ch. 2.

Now when Jesus was born in Bethlehem of Judea, in the days of Herod the king, behold there came wise men from the east to Jerusalem,

saying: Where is he that is born King of the Jews? For we have seen his star in the east, and are come to worship him.

When Herod heard this, he was exceedingly troubled; and having sent messengers to the wise men and the priests, he inquired of them in the prætorium, saying to them, Where is it written among you, of Christ the king, that he should be born?

Then they say unto him, In Bethlehem of Judea; for thus it is written; And thou Bethlehem, in the land of Juda, art not the least among the princes of Juda; for out of thee shall come a governor, who shall rule my people Israel.

And having sent away the chief priests, he inquired of the wise men in the prætorium, and said unto them: What sign was it ye saw concerning the king that is born? They answered,

2. Saying: Where is he that is born King of the Jews? For we have seen his star in the east, and are come to worship him.

3. When Herod the king had heard (these things), he was troubled, and all Jerusalem with him.

4. And when he had gathered all the chief priests and scribes of the people together, he demanded of them where Christ should be born.

5. And they said unto him, In Bethlehem of Judea; for thus it is written by the prophet:

6. And thou Bethlehem in the land of Juda, art not the least among the princes of Juda; for out of thee shall come a governor, who shall rule my people Israel.

7. Then Herod, when he had privily called the wise men, inquired of them diligently what time the star appeared.

We saw an extraordinary large star, shining among the stars of heaven, and it so outshined all the other stars, that they became not visible; and we know that a great king has come in Israel, and therefore have come to worship him.

Then said Herod to them, Go and make diligent inquiry, and if ye find him bring me word again, that I may come and worship him also.

8. And he sent them to Bethlehem, and said, Go and search diligently for the young child, and when ye have found him, bring me word again, that I may come and worship him also.

PROTEVANGELION, ch. 21.	MATTHEW, ch. 2.
So the wise men went forth, and behold the star which they saw in the east went before them, till it came and stood over the cave where the young child was, with Mary his mother.	9. When they had heard the king, they departed; and lo, the star which they saw in the east, went before them, till it came and stood over where the young child was.
	10. When they saw the star, they rejoiced with exceeding great joy.
	11. And when they were come into the house, they saw the young child, with Mary his mother, and fell down and worshiped him; and when they had opened their treasures, they presented unto him gifts; gold, and frankincense, and myrrh.
Then they brought forth out of their treasures, and offered unto him gold, and frankincense, and myrrh.	
And being warned in a dream by an angel, that they should not return to Herod, through Judea, they departed into their own country, another way.	12. And being warned of God in a dream, that they should not return to Herod, they departed into their own country another way.
	(The warning of Joseph, and the flight to Egypt, not in the Protevangelion. They are however, in the Gospel of the Infancy.)
CHAPTER 22.	16. Then Herod, when he saw he was mocked by the wise men, was exceeding wroth, and sent forth and slew all the children that were in Bethlehem, and in all the coasts thereof, from two years old and under, according to the time which he had diligently inquired of the wise men.
Then Herod, when he perceived that he was mocked by the wise men, being very angry, sent murderers, commanding them to slay all the children, from two years old and under.	
	17. Then was fulfilled that which was spoken by Jeremy the prophet, saying:
	18. In Rama there was a voice heard, lamentation and weeping, and great mourning; Rachel weeping for her children, and would not be comforted, because they are not.

Here is another prophecy, not alluded to in the Protevangelion.

In this case as in the other, it is only necessary to read the prophecy in its connection with the context, in order to determine whether its application here is legitimate.

In the 30th and 31st chapters of Jeremiah, the prophet predicts the return of the children of Israel from their captivity. The revelation was, it appears, communicated to him in a dream ; for in the 26th verse of the 31st chapter, he says, ''Upon this I awaked, and beheld ; and my sleep was sweet unto me.''

The 30th chapter commences thus :

"The word that came to Jeremiah, from the Lord, saying:
Verse 3. "For lo, the days are come, saith the Lord,that I will bring again the captivity of my people Israel and Judah, saith the Lord; and I will cause them to return to the land that I gave to their fathers, and they shall possess it."

v. 5. "For thus saith the Lord: We have heard a voice of trembling, of fear, and not of peace."

v. 10. ......"And Jacob shall return, and shall be in rest, and be quiet, and none shall make him afraid."

v. 18. "Thus saith the Lord, Behold, I will bring again the captivity of Jacob's tents," etc.

v. 20. "Their children also shall be as aforetime," etc.

CH. 31, v. 8. "Behold I will bring them from the north country," etc.

v. 9. "They shall come with weeping," etc.

Then, soon after, with nothing intervening, to change the subject matter, comes the following :

v. 15. "Thus saith the Lord, A voice was heard in Ramah, lamentation, and bitter weeping: Rachel weeping for her children, refused to be comforted for her children, because they were not."

v. 16. "Thus saith the Lord; Refrain thy voice from weeping, and thine eyes from tears; for thy work shall be rewarded, saith the Lord; and they shall come again from the land of the enemy.

v. 17. "And there is hope in thine end, saith the Lord, that thy children shall come again, to their own border."

It needs no argument or construction to show that the children of Israel are the children referred to in this chapter, and that it had no more reference to the infant children of Bethlehem to be slain by Herod, than it had to the children of Chicago.

It is only by applying a principle known to theologians as "accommodation," that any such application of the language can be made. But by the method of accommodation, any conceivable proposition can be proved from any chapter of the bible.

The reference to the prophecy of Micah, "And thou, Bethlehem," etc., is only in some copies of the Protevangelion. It is not in the Ante-Nicene version, and was probably an interpolation.

From the subsequent verses of the 5th chapter of Micah, it appears that the prophecy related to a ruler of Israel who should be able to cope successfully with the king of Assyria.

If the prophecy related to Christ, then it was necessary that he should be born in the village of Bethlehem. But all the copies of the Protevangelion represent that he was born in a cave three miles from Bethlehem. So it is related in the Gospel of the Infancy, that Jesus was born in a cave before his parents reached Bethlehem, though the distance is not stated. But Bethlehem being comparatively a small village, the prophecy would not thus be fulfilled. "For out of thee shall come," etc. Hence the probability that the reference to the prophecy in some copies of the Protevangelion, is an interpolation. Hence also the necessity, that in Matthew, where the verses relating to the prophecy stand on the same footing with the rest, Jesus should be born in the very village of Bethlehem.

If Matthew was first written, and was known to the authors of the other gospels, it is strange that they should have Jesus born outside of Bethlehem, at the risk of disconnecting the event from the prophecy. The authors of those gospels were disposed, neither to deny the Messiahship of Jesus, nor to deprive him of the benefit of any of the Jewish prophecies.

For the reasons given, and because in the Protevangelion all the circumstances are simply and naturally related in their connection, as portions of a longer story, we conclude the Protevangelion was first written.

CHAPTER XII.

THE GOSPEL OF THE INFANCY.

Different Versions—Synopsis of Contents—Testimonies and Citations of the Fathers.

The complete Gospel of the Infancy of the Savior, first appeared in the Arabic language. It was translated into Latin, and was published by Mr. Sike, Professor of Oriental languages at Cambridge, England. It was published at Utrecht, in 1697.

Besides this, there is a fragment of what is thought to be a more ancient gospel, ascribed to the Apostle Thomas, and known as Thomas' Gospel of the Infancy.

It is published in the Ante-Nicene collection, in three forms: two being translations from the Greek, and one from the Latin. It is manifest that these, as well as the publication of Mr. Sike, are but different versions of the one Gospel of the Infancy.

The following is a synopsis of the complete gospel, as published by Mr. Sike:

CHAPTER 1.—"The following accounts we have found in the book of Joseph, the high priest, who lived in the time of Christ; and some say that he is Caiaphas. He has said that Jesus spoke, and indeed, that when he was lying in his cradle, he said to his mother Mary, I am Jesus, the Son of God, the Logos whom thou hast brought forth, as the angel Gabriel announced to thee; and my Father hath sent me for the salvation of the world."

CHS. 2 & 3.—The decree for the taxing; the journey of Joseph and Mary; stopping at the cave; Joseph going after a midwife, and the birth of Jesus in the cave; the general tenor of the story being the same as in the Protevangelion, but the account being in a condensed form, and differing in some details.

CHS. 4, 5 & 6.—The story of the shepherds, the circumcision in the cave, etc. Jesus brought to Jerusalem. Simeon, and Hannah.—[See next chapter of this work].

CH. 7.—The wise men came from the east, "according to the prophecy of Zoradascht," [Zoroaster], and brought offerings, gold, etc. Lady Mary gave them one of the swaddling-cloths of Jesus, "which they received from her, as a most noble present." They followed the star back to their own country.

CH. 8.—On their return to their own country, having made a fire and worshiped it, they cast in the swaddling-cloth, which remained unharmed by the fire.

CH. 9.—Herod inquired concerning the wise men; whereupon Joseph, being warned by an angel, fled into Egypt.

CHS. 10 to 22.—[Here follows a series of most astounding miracles, performed by Jesus, while a baby, in Egypt:

Idols fall down at his approach—people possessed of devils, are cured by touching his swaddling-cloths; in one case, the devils coming out of the mouth of one who had put a swaddling-cloth on his head. A bride who had become dumb, recovers her speech, by taking the infant Jesus in her arms—a girl whose body was white with leprosy, is cured by "being sprinkled with water in which the Lord Jesus had been washed." Another is freed from Satan, who flees away in the form of a young man. A young man who had been changed into a mule, is re-transformed into his proper shape, by the boy Jesus having been placed on the mule's back, etc. etc.]

CH. 23.—In a desert country they met two robbers, named Titus and Dumachus. Titus having interested himself for the safety of the mother and child, St. Mary prophesied that the Lord God would receive him on his right hand, and grant him the pardon of his sins. Jesus also said to his mother, "When thirty years are expired, O mother, the Jews will crucify me at Jerusalem, and these two thieves shall be with me, at the same time, upon the cross, Titus on my right hand, and Dumachus on my left, and from that time, Titus shall go before me into paradise."

CH. 24.—In Matarea, the Lord Jesus caused a well to spring forth, in which St. Mary washed his coat.

CH. 25.—Thence they proceeded to Memphis, and saw Pharaoh. They abode three years; "And the Lord Jesus did very many miracles in Egypt,which are neither to be found in the Gospel of the Infancy, nor in the Gospel of Perfection."

[Mr. Ellicott, in his Essay on the Apocryphal Gospels, which will be noticed hereafter, very ingeniously supposes the writer of the Infancy, by the Gospel of Perfection, here to mean the four canonical gospels; though it is well understood, that one of the lost gospels of the second century was called "The Gospel of Perfection." See that title].

CH. 26.—At the end of three years, they returned out of Egypt, and when they came near Judea, Joseph was afraid of Archelaus. At the same time, he was warned by an angel to go to Nazareth.

The writer then makes this pertinent remark:

"It is strange, indeed, that He who is the Lord of all countries, should be carried backward and forward, through so many countries."

CHS. 27 to 34.—Here follows another series of miracles, similar to those performed in Egypt.

St. Mary had healed a sick boy, by giving his mother one of the swaddling-cloths of the boy Jesus, in exchange for a handsome carpet. Another woman, who was envious, threw Caleb [the boy who had been healed] into a hot oven. When his mother returned, she saw Caleb lying in the middle of the oven, laughing. When the woman told her story, St. Mary replied, "Be quiet, for I am concerned, lest thou shouldst make this matter known." After this, the other woman threw Caleb into a well, but he sat upon the surface of the water, uninjured. The woman who had thrown him in, fell in herself and perished.

A boy whose eyes were closed in death, revived at the smell of the garments of the Lord Jesus.

A girl who was afflicted by Satan sucking her blood, put upon her head, as Satan approached her, one of the swaddling-cloths of Jesus. Thereupon there issued forth from the cloth, flames and burning coals, which fell upon the dragon. Then the dragon cried out, "What have I to do with thee, Jesus, thou son of Mary? Whither shall I flee from thee?" He then left the girl.

CH. 35.—A boy named Judas was possessed by Satan. Whenever Satan seized him, he wished to bite any one present. The mother of the miserable boy took him to St. Mary. In the mean time, James and Jose had taken away the infant Lord Jesus, to play, and were sitting down together. Judas came and sat down, at the right hand of Jesus, and tried to bite him. Because he could not do it, he struck Jesus in the right side, so that he cried out; and at the same moment, Satan went out of the boy, and ran away like a mad dog. This boy was Judas Iscariot.

CH. 36.—When the Lord Jesus was seven years old, he, with other boys of about the same age, was making clay into the shape of asses, oxen, birds, etc. Jesus commanded his to move and walk, which they did. He also made figures of sparrows, and caused them to fly. The fathers of the other children told them that Jesus was a sorcerer.

CHS. 37 to 39.—Other miracles. Jesus, playing with other boys, threw the clothes of a dyer into a furnace. When taken out, they were all dyed, with the desired colors. Jesus accompanied his father Joseph in his carpenter work, and whenever Joseph wanted any thing made longer or shorter, Jesus would stretch his hand toward it, and it became of the proper length. Joseph had spent two years making a throne for the king of Jerusalem. It was short on each side, two spans. Joseph was so afraid of the king's anger, that he went to bed without his supper. In the morning, Jesus took hold on one side, and Joseph on the other, and pulled, and the throne came to the right dimensions.

CH. 40.—Jesus turned some boys into kids; saying to them, "Come hither, O ye kids, to your shepherd." The boys came forth like kids, and leaped about. He then turned the kids back into boys.

CH. 41.—Jesus gathered the boys together, and ranked them as though he had been a king. They spread garments upon the ground for him to sit upon, and crowned him with flowers.

CH. 42.—In the mean time, a boy was brought along upon a couch. Having put his hand into a partridge's nest, to take out the eggs, he had been stung by a poisonous serpent. When the boy came to the place where the Lord Jesus was sitting, like a king, and the other boys standing round him like his ministers, Jesus inquired on what account they carried the boy? When they told him, he returned with them to the nest, and there caused the serpent to suck all the poison out again.

CH. 43. James the son of Joseph was bitten by a viper. Jesus blew upon it, and cured it instantly.

CH. 44.—The Lord Jesus was playing with other boys upon a house-top. One of them fell off and was killed. Jesus being accused of throwing him off, he stood over the dead boy, and said in a loud voice, "Zeinunus, Zeinunus, who threw thee down from the house-top?" Then the dead boy answered, "Thou didst not throw me down, but (such a one) did."

CH. 45.—Jesus, being sent by his mother to the well for water, broke the pitcher. He thereupon gathered the water into his mantle, and brought it to his mother.

CH. 46.—Jesus was with some other boys by a river, drawing water out of the river by little channels, and making fish pools. Jesus made twelve sparrows, and caused them to fly. The son of Hanani, a Jew, came by, and asked if they thus made figures on the Sabbath? And he broke down their fish pools. Coming to the fish pool of Jesus to destroy it, the water vanished away; and the Lord Jesus said to him, "In like manner as this water has vanished, so shall thy life vanish." And presently the boy died.

CH. 47.—"Another time, when the Lord Jesus was coming home, in the evening, with Joseph, he met a boy, who ran so hard against him, that he threw him down; to whom the Lord Jesus said, 'As thou hast thrown me down, so shalt thou fall, nor ever rise!' And that moment, the boy fell down and died."

CHS. 48 and 49.—Jesus was sent to school to Zaccheus. The master told him to say Aleph, which he did. Then, to say Beth. "Then the Lord Jesus said to him, 'Tell me first the meaning of the letter Aleph, and then I will pronounce Beth.'" Jesus explained the meaning of Aleph and Beth, and all the alphabet. He was taken to a more learned master. When the same scene was repeated, the master raised his hand to whip him, but his hand presently withered, and he died.

CH. 50.—Jesus with the doctors in the temple. [See next chapter of this work.]

CH. 51.—Jesus explains to an astronomer, "the number of the spheres and heavenly bodies, as also their triangular, square and sextile aspect; their progressive and retrograde motion; their size, and several prognostications."

CH. 52.—He explains to a philosopher, physics and natural philoso-phy. "The things which were above and below the power of nature; the powers of the body; the numbers of its members, and bones, veins, arteries and nerves; how the soul operated on the body," etc. [The particulars of these explanations are not given.]

CH. 53.—His parents find him among the doctors, in the temple.

CH. 54.—Jesus conceals his miracles and secret works, and devotes himself to the study of the law, till thirty years old.   His acknowledgment by the Father, at the Jordan.

CH. 55.—CONCLUSION.—"The end of the whole Gospel of the Infancy, by the assistance of the Supreme God, according to what we found in the original."

TESTIMONIES AND CITATIONS BY THE FATHERS.

1.   Justin Martyr was acquainted with this gospel, A. D. 150 to 160.   [See Justin Martyr.]

All the arguments, therefore, against its antiquity, drawn from internal evidence, if directed against the gospel as a whole, fall to the ground. Those arguments are based upon modes of expression which were thought not to prevail until the third or fourth century, or even later ; such as "The Lord Christ," "The Lady St. Mary;" etc., also upon the veneration and devotion paid to Mary, and the efficacy ascribed to relics and emblems.   Whatever force there may be in these objections, they can only apply to some portions of the gospel, and to some of its phraseology, which may have been introduced by a copyist or a translator.

2.   It is referred to by Irenæus, (A. D. 190), in an unmistakable manner.

He claims it was a forgery of the Marcosians, of the second century, and relates, with much particularity, the scene between Jesus and the schoolmaster.[1]

3.   It is alluded to by Origen, (A. D. 230), as the Gospel of Thomas.[2]   Also by Epiphanius,

(1.) Adv. Hær. I. 20.
(2.) In Luc. I. I.

(385),[1] by Eusebius, (325),[2] by Cyril, (375),[3] and by Athanasius; (373.)

It is possible that some of the miracles in Egypt may have been added by a later hand, to a changed version of the Gospel of Thomas. Epiphanius, however, refers to the miracles performed by Jesus in his childhood, and does not discredit them. He says:

"Christ wrought his first miracle in Cana of Galilee, the third day after he began to preach; for Christ is not said to have been at the marriage before his temptation. Nor did he work any miracles, or preach any sermons before that time, except some things which some say he did at play, when a child. And indeed it was fit some things should be done by him in his childhood, that there might not be any foundation for the assertion of those heretics, who say that Christ did not come upon him till he was baptized, in Jordan, in the form of a dove."-[Hær. 51, 20.

Both Eusebius and Athanasius relate, that when Joseph and Mary arrived in Egypt, they took up their abode in Hermopolis, a city of Thebais, in which was a superb temple of Serapis. When Joseph and Mary entered the temple, not only the great idol, but all the lesser gods fell down before them.[4]

It is agreed by Origen, Jerome and many others, that the Gospel of the Infancy, or the Gospel of Thomas, was one of "the many," referred to in Luke.

Jones, who has made an elaborate attack upon

(1.) Hær. 51. 20.
(2.) Ecc. Hist. 3. 25.
(3.) Hier. Catech. 4, p. 38.
(4.) Euseb. Demonst. Evang. lib. 6, c. 20; Athan. de Incarn. Verbi, p. 89.

the Gospel of the Infancy, pronouncing its miracles absurd and ridiculous, concedes, nevertheless, that the original of this gospel was written early in the second century.[1]

In the Ecclesiastical History of Sozomen, one of the Greek fathers, who wrote A. D. 439, will be found the following reference to some of the incidents connected with the residence of Christ in Egypt.

"At Ermopolis in Thebais, is a tree called Persea, of which the branches, the leaves, and the least portion of the bark, are said to heal disease, when touched by the sick. It is related by the Egyptians, that when Joseph fled with Christ and Mary, the Holy Mother, from the wrath of Herod, they went to Ermopolis; and, as they were entering the city, this tree bent down, and worshiped Christ. I relate precisely what I have heard, from many sources, concerning this tree. I think that this was the sign of the presence of God in the city; or perhaps, as seems most probable, it may have arisen from the fear of the demon, who had been worshiped in this large and beautiful tree, by the people of the country; for at the presence of Christ, the idols of Egypt were shaken, even as Isaiah the prophet had foretold. On the expulsion of the demon, the tree was permitted to remain as a monument to what had occurred, and was endued with the property of healing those who believed. The inhabitants of Egypt and of Palestine, [referring to another event which he had related, also], testify to the truth of these events which took place among themselves."— [Sozomen's Ecc. Hist. bk. 5, ch. 21.

Such is the testimony, and such are the conclusions, of one of the more moderate of the ancient ecclesiastical historians. There were many miracles ascribed to Jesus, which were fully accredited by the fathers, for several centuries. Those not contained in the canonical gospels, became, after a while, first doubted, then discredited ; the miracles related in those gospels only, being considered finally worthy of belief.

(1.) Jones on the New Testament, vol. 2, p. 259.

CHAPTER XIII.

THE GOSPEL OF THE INFANCY,
COMPARED WITH LUKE AND MATTHEW.

———

THE GOSPEL OF THE INFANCY ONE OF THE MANUSCRIPTS
USED IN THE COMPILATIONS OF LUKE AND MATTHEW—THE
FIRST TWO CHAPTERS OF THOSE GOSPELS AND THE GOSPEL
OF THE INFANCY COMPARED.

In regard to the taxing, etc., the parallel passage
in the Protevangelion has already been given. The
following is the parallel with the Infancy:

THE TAXING, AND THE BIRTH OF CHRIST.

GOSPEL OF THE INFANCY, ch. 2.

In the three hundred and ninth year of the era of Alexander, Augustus published a decree, that all persons should go to be taxed, into their own country.

Joseph therefore arose, and with

Mary his spouse, he went to Jerusalem, and then came to Bethlehem, that he and his family might be taxed, in the city of his fathers.

["When they came by the cave," they stopped, and there Jesus was born.]

GOSPEL OF LUKE, ch. 2.

And it came to pass in those days, that there went out a decree from Cæsar Augustus, that all the world should be taxed.

2. (And this taxing was first made when Cyrenius was Governor of Syria.)

3. And all went to be taxed, every one into his own city.

4. And Joseph also went up from Galilee, out of the city of Nazareth, into Judea, unto the city of David, which is called Bethlehem, (because he was of the house and lineage of David,)

5. To be taxed, with Mary, his espoused wife, being great with child.

(Christ was then born in Bethlehem.)

This reference to "the cave," as something well understood, indicates that the writer of the Infancy was familiar with the Protevangelion.

VISION TO THE SHEPHERDS.

INFANCY, ch. 4.

After this, when the shepherds came, and had made a fire, and they were rejoicing exceedingly, the heavenly host appeared to them, praising and adoring the Supreme God. As the shepherds were engaged in the same employment, the cave at that time seemed like a glorious temple, because both the tongues of angels and men united to adore and magnify God, on account of the birth of the Lord Christ.

LUKE, ch. 2.

8. And there were in the same country shepherds abiding in the field, keeping watch over their flock at night.

9. And lo, the angel of the Lord came upon them, and the glory of the Lord shone round about them; and they were sore afraid.

10. And the angel said unto them, Fear not; for behold I bring you good tidings of great joy, which shall be to all people.

11. For unto you is born this day, in the City of David, a Savior, who is Christ the Lord.

12. And this (shall be) a sign unto you; ye shall find the babe wrapped in swaddling-clothes, lying in a manger.

13. And suddenly there was with the angel a multitude of the heavenly host, praising God, and saying:

14. Glory to God in the highest, and on earth, peace, good will toward men.

15. And it came to pass as the angels were gone away from them into heaven, the shepherds said to one another, Let us now go even unto Bethlehem, and see this thing which is come to pass, which the Lord hath made known to us.

16. And they came with haste, and found Mary and Joseph, and the babe lying in a manger.

The account in the Gospel of the Infancy, though sufficiently marvelous, has much the more natural surroundings.

Mary, on her way to Bethlehem, not being able to continue the journey, stops at a cave, used by shepherds for herding cattle. Here Jesus is born. In the mean time, the shepherds, returning to the cave, build a fire, and as they come to understand the nature of the transaction, they unite in praises to God, in which they are joined by the heavenly host of angels.

In Luke, Jesus is born in Bethlehem, and the shepherds, who are in the field, are informed by an angel of the birth of a Savior, and that he is lying in a manger; but they are left to find the place the best way they can. Then the heavenly host, instead of appearing where Jesus was, is made to appear to the shepherds in the field.

It is manifest that the story has been taken from its natural setting, in order that Jesus might be born at Bethlehem, in fulfillment of the prophecy of Micah.

THE CIRCUMCISION.

INFANCY, ch. 5.	LUKE, ch. 2.
And when the time of circumcision was come, viz. the eighth day, on which the law commanded that a boy should be circumcised, they circumcised him in the cave, etc.	21. And when eight days were accomplished for the circumcising of the child, his name was called JESUS, who was so named by the angel before he was conceived in the womb.

PRESENTATION IN THE TEMPLE.

Here, again, it may be well to note the remarks of Shleiermacher. He says:

"What we read from 22 to 40 in chapter 2, respecting the presentation of the child in the temple, which was combined with the purification of his mother, seems also to have been originally related and committed to writing, without connection with the preceding passage; for at the end, mention is made of the return to Nazareth, just as though the parents had come from that place to Jerusalem, without notice being taken, by a single word, of their residence up to that time in Bethlehem, which would nevertheless, have been so easy and natural.   This narrative, therefore, knows nothing of that residence. Only I would not on that account understand the surprise of Mary at the language of Simeon, as implying that she herself did not know yet who her son was."—[Essay on Luke, p. 39.

While the narrative of the vision to the shepherds, as contained in Luke, had a basis in the Gospel of the Infancy, there has been a wide departure from the story as there given, and much new matter introduced, showing that the whole account had been rewritten.

In the following, however, it will not be difficult to perceive, that we have but different versions of the same narrative:

INFANCY, chs. 5 and 6.	LUKE, ch. 2.
Ten days having intervened, they brought him to Jerusalem; and on the fortieth day of his birth, they presented him in the temple before the Lord, making offerings for him, according to what is prescribed in the law of Moses, to wit: Every male who openeth the womb, shall be called the holy of God.	22. And when the days of her purification, according to the law of Moses, were accomplished, they brought him to Jerusalem, to present (him) to the Lord;
	23. (As it is written in the law of the Lord, Every male that openeth the womb shall be called holy to the Lord;)
	24. And to offer a sacrifice according to that which is said in the law of the Lord, a pair of turtle-doves, or two young pigeons.
Then old Simeon saw him shining as a pillar of light, when the Lady Virgin Mary, his mother, was carrying him in her arms, and rejoicing exceedingly over him. And angels, praising him, stood around him in a circle, like life-guards standing by a king.	25. And behold there was a man in Jerusalem, whose name (was) Simeon; and the same man (was) just and devout, waiting for the consolation of Israel; and the Holy Ghost was upon him.
	26. And it was revealed unto him by the Holy Ghost, that he should not see death before he had seen the Lord's Christ.
	27. And he came by the Spirit into the temple; and when the

INFANCY, ch. 6.	LUKE, ch. 2.

	parents brought in the child Jesus, to do for him after the custom of the law,
Then Simeon, going up before Lady Mary, and stretching out his hands before her, said to the Lord Christ, Now, O my Lord, let thy servant depart in peace, according to thy word.	28. Then took he him up in his arms, and blessed God, and said:
	29. Lord, now lettest thou thy servant depart in peace, according to thy word.
For mine eyes have seen thy mercy,	30. For mine eyes have seen thy salvation
	31. Which thou hast prepared before the face of all people;
Which thou hast prepared for the salvation of all peoples;	32. A light to lighten the Gentiles, and the glory of thy people Israel.
A light to all nations, and a glory to thy people Israel.	
	33. And Joseph and his mother marveled at those things which were spoken of him.
	34. And Simeon blessed them, and said unto Mary his mother, Behold, this (child) is set, etc.
	35. Yea, a sword shall pierce, etc.
Hannah, a prophetess, was also present, and drawing near, she gave	36. And there was one Anna, a prophetess, the daughter of Phanuel, of the tribe of Aser; she was of great age, and had lived with a husband seven years from her virginity.
	37. And she (was) a widow of about fourscore and four years, who departed not from the temple, but served (God) with fastings and prayers, night and day.
thanks to God, and celebrated the happiness of Lady Mary.	38. And she, coming in that instant, gave thanks likewise unto the Lord, and spake of him to all them that looked for redemption in Jerusalem.

JESUS DISPUTING WITH THE DOCTORS.

INFANCY, ch. 50.	LUKE, ch. 2.
	41. Now his parents went to Jerusalem every year, at the feast of the passover.
And when he was twelve years old, they took him to Jerusalem, to the feast.	42. And when he was twelve years old, they went up to Jerusalem, after the custom of the feast.

INFANCY, ch. 50.

And when the feast was finished, they indeed returned, but

the Lord Jesus remained behind, in the temple, among the doctors and elders, and learned men of the sons of Israel; to whom he put various questions in the sciences, and gave them answers in his turn.

[The balance of chapter 50 and the whole of chapters 51 and 52 are taken up with an account of this discussion. It is stated that Jesus explained the books of the law and the mysteries of the prophets; also the sciences of astronomy, philosophy, etc. But the particular explanations are not given.]

CHAPTER 53.

While they were speaking to each other these and other things, the Lady St. Mary came, after having been going about for three days, with Joseph, seeking for him. She therefore, seeing him sitting among the doctors, asking them questions, and answering in his turn, said to him, My son, why hast thou thus dealt with us? Behold, I and thy father have sought thee, with much trouble.

He replied, Wherefore did ye seek me? Did ye not know that I ought to be employed in my father's house? But they understood not the word which he spake unto them.

Then the doctors asked Mary whether he was her son. And when she signified that he was,

LUKE, ch. 2.

43. And when they had fulfilled the days, as they returned, the child Jesus tarried behind in Jerusalem; and Joseph and his mother knew not (of it.)

44. But they, supposing him to have been in the company, went a day's journey; and they sought him among (their) kinsfolk and acquaintance.

45. And when they found him not, they turned back again to Jerusalem, seeking him.

46. And it came to pass, that after three days, they found him in the temple, sitting in the midst of the doctors, both hearing them, and asking them questions.

47. And all who heard him were astonished at his understanding and answers.

48. And when they saw him, they were amazed; and his mother said unto him, Son, why hast thou thus dealt with us? Behold, thy father and I have sought thee, sorrowing.

49. And he said unto them, How is it that ye sought me? Wist ye not, that I must be about my Father's business?

50. And they understood not the saying which he spake unto them.

51. And he went down with

INFANCY, ch. 53.	LUKE, ch. 2.
they said, O happy Mary, who hast brought forth such a son.	
Then he returned with them to Nazareth, and obeyed them in all things; and his mother kept all these sayings in her heart.	them, and came to Nazareth, and was subject unto them; but his mother kept all these sayings in her heart.
And the Lord Jesus grew in stature and wisdom and in favor with God and man.	52. And Jesus increased in wisdom and stature, and in favor with God and man.

The foregoing accounts are closely parallel, with no particular inference as to which was first written.

The next chapter of the Infancy is as follows:

Ch. 54.—"But from this time he began to conceal his miracles and secret works, and gave himself to the study of the law, till he arrived to the end of his thirtieth year; at which time the Father publicly owned him at Jordan, sending down this voice from heaven: This is my beloved Son, in whom I am well pleased; the Holy Ghost being also present, in the form of a dove."

Passing on to the Gospel of Matthew, the parallel commences with the 7th chapter of the Infancy, and the 2d chapter of Matthew, as follows:

VISIT OF THE MAGI.

INFANCY, ch. 7.	MATTHEW, ch. 2.
And it came to pass, when the Lord Jesus was born at Bethlehem, a city of Judea, in the time of Herod the King, behold, wise men came from the east to Jerusalem, as Zoradascht [in the Ante-Nicene copy, Zeraduscht] had predicted; and there were with	Now when Jesus was born in Bethlehem of Judea, in the days of Herod the King, behold, there came wise men from the east to Jerusalem,
	2. Saying: Where is he that is born King of the Jews? For we have seen his star in the east, and are come to worship him.
	[Verses 3 to 10 have a parallel in the Protevangelion, which has been given.]
	11. And when they were come into the house, they saw the

INFANCY, ch. 7.

them gifts, gold, and frankin-cense, and myrrh. And they adored him, and presented to him their gifts.

Then the Lady Mary took one of those swaddling-cloths (in which the infant was wrapped), and gave it to them instead of a blessing; which they received from her as a most noble present. And in the same hour there ap-peared unto them an angel in the form of that star, which had be-fore been their guide in their journey; and they went away, following the guidance of its light, till they returned into their own country.

[On their return, having made a fire and worshiped it, they cast in the swaddling-cloth, which re-mained unharmed by the fire.]

MATTHEW, ch. 2.

young child with Mary his moth-er, and fell down and worshiped him. And when they had open-ed their treasures, they presented unto him gifts; gold, and frankin-cense and myrrh.

12. And being warned of God in a dream, that they should not

return to Herod they departed into their own country, another way.

It will be noticed, that according to the Infancy Gospel, the visit of the magi was made in accord-ance with the prophecy of Zoradascht (Zoroaster).

The reference to the prophecy of Zoroaster can-not well be explained, except on the hypothesis that the Gospel of the Infancy was first written.

THE FLIGHT TO EGYPT.

INFANCY, ch. 9.

But Herod, perceiving that the wise men did delay, and not re-turn to him, called together the priests and the wise men, and said, Tell me in what place the Christ is to be born. And when they replied, In Bethlehem, a city of Judea, he began to contrive in his mind, the death of the Lord Jesus Christ.

Then appeared an angel of the Lord to Joseph in his sleep, and said, Arise, take the boy and his

MATTHEW, ch. 2.

13. And when they were de-parted, behold the angel of the Lord appeareth to Joseph in a dream, saying: Arise and take the young child and his mother, and flee into Egypt; and be there until I bring thee word; for Her-od will seek the young child, to destroy him.

INFANCY, ch. 9.	MATTHEW, ch. 2.
mother and go into Egypt, at the crowing of the cock. So he arose and went.	14. When he arose, he took the young child and his mother, by night, and departed into Egypt. [Here follows the passage of Hosea, ch. 11, v. 1, referring to the calling of Israel out of Egypt, which is applied, as a prophecy, to this transaction.]

In reply to the inquiry of Herod, as to the place where the Christ was to be born, the priests and wise men said, "In Bethlehem." Yet, according to the Infancy Gospel, he was born on the road, before his parents reached Bethlehem. (According to the Protevangelion, three miles distant). The author of Luke, perceiving this inconsistency, has Christ born in the village of Bethlehem. But in so doing, as has been seen, he is obliged to break up the consecutive incidents, and, in several respects, to reconstruct the narrative.

The slaughter of the children is mentioned in the Protevangelion, but not in the Infancy, in this connection.

In the twelfth chapter, there is a reference to it, as also to the prophecy of Micah, thrown in, in the midst of the miracles wrought in Egypt. It is doubtless an interpolation.

Josephus, though he enlarges upon the cruelties of Herod, says nothing of the slaughter of the children.

The account can scarcely be considered historical. It must be looked upon as legendary, and probably first appeared in the Protevangelion.

THE RETURN FROM EGYPT.

INFANCY, ch. 26.	MATTHEW, ch. 2.
	19. But when Herod was dead, behold, an angel of the Lord appeareth in a dream, to Joseph in Egypt,
	20. Saying: Arise, and take the young child and his mother, and go into the land of Israel; for they are dead who sought the young child's life.
At the end of three years, he returned out of Egypt; and when he came near to Judea, Joseph was afraid to enter; for, hearing that Herod was dead, and that Archelaus his son reigned in his stead, he was afraid; and when he went to Judea, an angel of God appeared to him and said; O	21. And he arose, and took the young child and his mother, and came into the land of Israel.
	22. But when he heard that Archelaus did reign in Judea, in the room of his father Herod, he was afraid to go thither. Notwithstanding, being warned of God in a dream, he turned aside into the parts of Galilee.
Joseph, go into the city of Nazareth, and there abide.	23. And he came and dwelt in a city called Nazareth.
It is indeed wonderful, that the Lord of all countries should thus be carried about, through so many regions.	

In the foregoing comparisons, the reader must have noticed, that where, in the account of the birth and childhood of Jesus, as given in Luke and Matthew, there was no parallel in one of the apocryphal gospels, the history was almost invariably supplemented in the other. This will appear more plainly by the following arrangement, where the portions of each which contain parallel passages are indicated:

LUKE.

THE ANNOUNCEMENT, AND THE VISIT TO ELISABETH.

Protevangelion, chs. 11 and 12.   Luke, ch. 1, vv. 26 to 56.

THE TAXING, AND THE BIRTH OF JESUS.

Protevangelion, chs. 17 and 18. }
Also, Infancy, chs. 2 and 3.   }   Luke, ch. 2, vv. 1 to 7.

VISION TO THE SHEPHERDS.

Infancy, ch. 4.   Luke, chapter 2, vv. 8 to 16.

CIRCUMCISION OF JESUS.

Infancy, ch. 5.   Luke, ch. 2, v. 21.

PRESENTATION IN THE TEMPLE.

Infancy, chs. 5 and 6.   Luke, ch.2 , vv. 22 to 38.

JESUS DISPUTING WITH THE DOCTORS.

Infancy, chs. 50 to 53.   Luke, ch. 2, vv. 41 to 52.

MATTHEW.

JOSEPH AND THE ANGEL.

Protevangelion, chs. 13 and 14.   Matthew, ch. 1, vv. 18 to 24.

VISIT OF THE MAGI, AND SLAUGHTER OF THE CHILDREN.

Protevangelion, chs. 21 and 22. }
Also visit of the Magi, Infancy, ch. 7. } Matthew, ch. 2, vv. 1 to 18.

FLIGHT TO EGYPT.

Infancy, ch. 7.   Matthew, ch. 2, vv. 13 to 15.

RETURN FROM EGYPT.

Infancy, ch. 26.   Matthew, ch. 2, vv. 19 to 23.

In considering the question of priority, it must be borne in mind, that these are, so far as is known, the only histories of the birth and childhood of Jesus to be found in the ancient gospels.

There was no such history in the Gospel of the Hebrews, nor in the Gospel of Marcion; nor have we any evidence that there was any such in the gospels still older—those of the first century — nor in any of the lost gospels of the second century.

On the hypothesis that the Protevangelion and the Infancy were first written, it might be interest-

ing to inquire, according to what rule or law the
selections were made by the authors of Luke and
Matthew.   Upon this point we will venture to
make a suggestion.

The Protevangelion and the Infancy were rude
gospels.   They were very inartificially constructed,
and both of them contained accounts which were
inconsistent and irreconcilable.   They were inconsistent, not only with each other, but each with
itself.

Looking at them together, we find, in endeavoring to trace the history of Jesus, that according to
one account, he was taken from Bethlehem to
Jerusalem, and publicly presented in the temple;
thence to Nazareth, where he remained till his dispute with the doctors.   The other account represented his parents fleeing with him, soon after his
birth, from Bethlehem to Egypt, under a warning
from an angel not to return by Jerusalem.   These
conflicting accounts, founded on different traditions, ran through the two gospels, indiscriminately.

Each of the compilers of Luke and Matthew,
wishing to give, as a sort of preface to his gospel,
a history of the birth and childhood of Christ, not
too long, but one which would appear consistent in
itself, selected, we may suppose, such portions of
the other two gospels, as, in his judgment, would
form such a history; the one adopting the theory
of the presentation in the temple, and the other,
the flight to Egypt. This would result in giving us

precisely what we have ; two diverse, inconsistent, and utterly irreconcilable histories of the birth and childhood of Jesus.

"If we compare," says Schliermacher, "without any prepossession, this (Luke, chs. 1 and 2), and the corresponding portion in Matthew, we have two parallel successions of narratives; parallel in the stricter sense of the word, inasmuch as they have no single point, that is, in this case, no entire fact, in common. They are not at all supplemental to each other, but on the contrary, the corresponding members of the two successions, almost entirely exclude each other. Hence, then, if in any one point, the narrative of the one evangelist is correct, that of the other, so far as it relates to the same epoch, cannot be so."—[Essay on Luke, pp. 44, 45.

Again: "All attempts to reconcile these two contradictory statements, seem only elaborate efforts of art, to which one should not needlessly resort; or indeed, should rather give no explanation at all."—[Ibid. p. 48.

Conceding them to be irreconcilable, he undertakes, by an ingenious process, to pick out the truth, a little here from Luke, and a little there from Matthew.

He thinks the accounts rest upon "a totally different tradition, one from the other."—[p. 48.

In the Protevangelion and in the Infancy, the traditions are grouped together. In Luke and Matthew, they are separated.

In the next chapter, we shall endeavor to trace the origin and history of these traditions, and in so doing, some further light may be thrown upon the question of priority as between the two apocryphal and the two canonical gospels.

CHAPTER XIV.

ORIGIN AND HISTORY
OF THE GOSPELS OF THE INFANCY.

We are now to search for the origin of the legendary accounts of the conception, birth and childhood of Jesus.

For the purpose of this investigation, the Protevangelion and the Gospel of the Infancy may be considered together, as Gospels of the Infancy.

While in the subsequent history of the childhood of Christ, there are incidents which may be traced to other countries, there are certain leading features in the first part of the narrative, which stamp it as of Persian derivation. These are, the visit of the magi, guided by a star, and the fact that the visit was made in accordance with the prophecy of Zeraduscht, or Zoroaster.

This prophecy will be found in the life of Zoroaster, in Du Perron's translation of the Zend-Avesta.

Faber thinks the materials from which the Zend-

Avesta was composed, were taken from heathen, rather than from Jewish sources, giving many reasons, based upon the peculiar construction of the legends of the Zend-Avesta. One of these peculiarities consists in the association of a star with the deluge; a circumstance not to be found in the Mosaic account of the flood.

Taschter, the second man bull, of the creation, to whom was committed the charge of bringing on the deluge, was said to be a star, and his light is spoken of, as shining on high, during thirty days and thirty nights, while the waters of the deluge were increasing.

The star may be found in the mythology of other nations. Astarte consecrated, at Tyre, a star, which she found falling from the sky. Electra, the mother of Dardanus, was one of the seven stars of the Pleiades, and was saved from a deluge, both in Arcadia and Samothrace.

The star is older, even than Zoroaster, and according to Faber, older than Hebrew tradition.

There were two Zoroasters. The first, spoken of by Greek writers, flourished, according to these authors, several thousand years before Christ. Pliny speaks of him as thousands of years before Moses; and from that writer and Aristotle, it may be concluded that he lived some six thousand years before Christ. Hermodorus, Hermippus, and Plutarch concur in dating him five thousand years before the siege of Troy.

The other Zoroaster flourished, according to **Dr.**

Prideaux, in the time of Darius Hystaspes.[1] Sir William Jones agrees in assigning him to that period.

It was the opinion of the learned Mr. Faber, that there were two Zeraduschts, or Zoroasters, and that the primeval Zoroaster was none other than Menu, or Mahabad, or Buddha. He traces many analogies and resemblances between the ancient religions and mythologies of the Persians and the Hindus, and thinks the Zend-Avesta a modern compilation, founded upon religious books compiled by the second Zeraduscht; and those again, based upon more ancient legends, which were substantially identical with the older mythology of India.

He ably antagonizes the theory of Dr. Prideaux, that the accounts of the Zend-Avesta concerning the deluge and the antediluvial age, were taken from the Mosaic history.[2]

Malcolm, in his history of Persia, states that Zoroaster first introduced the worship of fire.

In the Recognitions may be found an interesting tradition upon this subject.

Peter states that Zoroaster, being frequently intent upon the stars, and wishing to be considered a god among them, began to draw forth sparks from the stars, that he might astonish, as with a miracle, rude and ignorant men.   That he attempted those

---

(1.) Prideaux's Connect. pt. 1, b. 4, p. 219.

(2.) Origin of Pagan Idolatry, by George Stanley Faber, B. D., Rector of Long-Newton, London, 1816, vol. 2, pp. 58 to 73.

things again and again, until he was set on fire,
"and consumed by the demon himself, whom he
accosted with too great importunity." That the
men of his day, after this, extolled him all the
more ; raised a monument to his honor, and adored
him as a friend of God, and one who had been
removed to heaven in a chariot of lightning. They
then worshiped him as a living star; which, says
the author of the Recognitions, is the meaning of
the name ; from "zoe," life, and "aster," star.

The star, which had previously been an object of
worship, now became associated with Zoroaster.

But what about the prophecy, upon which was
founded the legend of the magi?

In the life of Zoroaster, as given by Du Perron,
in his translation of the Zend-Avesta, is an account
öf the three prophetic sons of Zoroaster, who were
to appear, according to the Pehlvian and Parsian
books of the Persians, at successive periods of time.
They were to be the result of immaculate conceptions, caused by the washing of virgins in the water
in which the wife of Zoroaster had bathed.

"The first is named Oschederbami. He will appear in the last mil-
lenium of the world. He will stop the sun for ten days and ten
nights, and the second part of the human race will embrace the law,
of which he will bring the 22nd portion.

"The second posthumous son of Zoroaster, is Oschedermah. He
will appear 400 years after Oschederbami. He will stop the sun
twenty days and twenty nights, and he will bring the 23rd part of the
law, and the third part of the world will be converted."

This is somewhat different from the prophecy as
given by Hyde, in his work on the religion of the
ancient Persians. But the Oschedermah and the

Oschederbami of Du Perron, are doubtless the same as the Oshanderbega and the Osiderbega of Hyde.[1]

Then follows, in Du Perron, this remarkable prophecy:[2]

"The third is named Sosiosch. He will be born at the end of the ages. He will bring the 24th portion of the law; he will stay the sun thirty days and thirty nights, and the whole earth will embrace the law of Zoroaster. *After him will be the resurrection.* Behold what the books of the Parsees apprise us of the family of the legislator." —[Vie de Zoroastre, in the French translation of the Zend-Avesta, by Du Perron, Paris, 1771, vol. 1, pt. 2, p. 45.

From Abulpharagius, we learn that the prophecy was connected with the appearance of a star, and the visit of magi.

Zoroaster declared, says this writer, that in the latter days, a pure virgin would conceive, and that as soon as the child should be born, a star would appear, blazing even at noonday, with undiminished luster.

"You, my sons," exclaimed the seer, "will perceive its rising before any other nation. As soon, therefore, as you shall behold the star, follow it, whithersoever it shall lead you; and adore that mysterious child, offering your gifts to him, with profound humility. He is the Almighty Word, which created the heavens."—[Abulpharagius, according to Hyde, de Rel. Vet. Pers. c. 3.

Here, from a writer vouched for by Faber as high authority, we have, not only the immaculate conception, the star and the magi of Matthew, but

(1.) See his work, de Rel. Vet. Pers. c. 31.

(2.) The following is the text of Du Perron:

"Le troiseme est nomme Sosiosch. Il naitra a la fin des siecles, apportera le 24 Nosk de la Loi, arretera le Soleil trente jours, et trente nuits; et toute la terre embrassera la Loi de Zoroastre. Apres lui se sera la resurrection. Voila ce que les Livres des Parses nous apprennent de la famille de ce Legislateur."

also the Logos of John. The Rev. Mr. Faber considers thoroughly the question, whether this remarkable prediction was before or after the birth of Christ; and concludes it was a long time before. One reason why he rejects the idea of its being a subsequent forgery, is, that in the old Irish history, there was a Zeraduscht, associated with a similar prophecy, which was first delivered by a Daru or Druid of Bokhara.[1]

The same prophecy was, in the East, ascribed by Abulpharagius to a Zeraduscht who was actually a Daru or Druid of Bokhara. This coincidence is so singular, that Faber thinks it can only be accounted for on the hypothesis of an ancient emigration from Persia to Ireland, by the north-west passage, which carried the legend with it.

Thus, in the prophecy of Zoroaster, we have the origin of the legend of the star and the magi, which appeared early in the second century, in the Infancy gospels, and thence became incorporated into the prefatory chapters of Luke and Matthew. To which may be added, that there was a Christian sect called Prodiceans, whose leader, Prodicus, [about A. D. 120], boasted that they had the secret books of Zoroaster.[2]

Having traced to their source the legends connected with the conception and birth of Jesus, and having found them associated with the central figure of Persian mythology, let us now go farther

---

(1.) As authority, see Vallancey's Vindication of the Ancient History of Ireland, Collect. de Reb. Hibern. vol. 4, p. 202.

(2.) Clement of Alexandria, Stromata, bk. 1, ch. 15.

south, and see what light may be thrown upon subsequent history, as given in the gospels of the Infancy; portions of which, also, are to be found in Luke and Matthew; not forgetting, as we proceed, the intimate connection which existed between the ancient religions of Persia and India.

CHRISHNA.

In the History of Hindostan, by Rev. Thomas Maurice, vol. 2, will be found a complete history of Chrishna, the eighth incarnation of the Hindu God Vishnu; translated by Mr. Maurice from the Bhagavat Purana, one of the sacred books of India.

Chrishna, according to Colonel Tod, was born 1156 years before Christ.[1]

There are many other traditions, that might be collected from different writers, and thrown together, which would show a still closer resemblance between the narratives. But without going into these, except Baldæus, taking the translation of Mr. Maurice from the sacred Hindu scriptures, we have the following parallel between Chrishna and Christ:

CHRISHNA AND CHRIST.

BHAGAVAT PURANA.	GOSPELS OF THE INFANCY.
CHRISHNA	CHRIST
Was believed to be God incarnate, by a miraculous conception.	Was believed to be God incarnate, by a miraculous conception.
Was born in a dungeon.	Was born in a cave.

(1.) Annals and Antiquities of Rajust'han, vol. 1, p. 37.

CHRISHNA	CHRIST
At the time of his birth, the walls of his chamber were illuminated.	The cave was filled with a great light, and seemed like a glorious temple.
At the time of his birth, a chorus of devatas, or angels, saluted the newborn infant.	At the time of his birth, a chorus of angels saluted the newborn infant.
Of royal descent.	Of royal descent.
As soon as born, had the power of speech. (According to Baldæus, Chrishna, immediately when born, conversed with his mother, soothing and comforting her.)	As soon as born, spoke to his mother, informing her of his divine character, his origin and destiny.
Cradled among shepherds.	Cradled among shepherds.
Cansa, the ruler of the country, fears the loss of his kingdom, and seeks the life of the infant.	Herod, the ruler of the country, fears the loss of his kingdom, and seeks the life of the infant.
The child is carried away by night, and concealed in a remote region.	The child is carried away by night, and concealed in a remote region.
Cansa is wroth, and issues an order for the slaughter of all the young children throughout his kingdom.	Herod is wroth, and issues an order for the slaughter of all the children of Bethlehem, from two years old and under.
Has a combat with, and subdues a huge serpent, in his infancy.	Has several combats with serpents; overcomes them, and drives them out of persons possessed.
The serpent vomits streams of fire from his mouth and nostrils.	In one case, there issued forth, from one of his swaddling-cloths, flames and burning coals, and fell on the head of the serpent.
Performs many miracles in his infancy and boyhood.	Performs many miracles in his infancy and boyhood.
While a boy, raises the dead to life.	While a boy, raises the dead to life.
While a boy, strikes dead, persons who have offended him.	While a boy, strikes dead, persons who have offended him.
Was preceded by his elder brother, Ram, who was his associate in the work of purification, and was hurried away as soon as born, to escape the decree of Cansa.	Was preceded by John the Baptist, who was sent into the wilderness, to escape the decree of Herod.
Lived at Mathurea.	On his visit to Egypt, in his childhood, stopped at a place called Maturea. This name it afterward retained.
One of his first miracles was curing a leper.	Among the first miracles, was the curing of lepers.

CHRISHNA	CHRIST
While a boy, is chosen by the other boys as their king.—[Baldæus.	While a boy, is chosen by the other boys as their king.
Learns all the sciences in one day and night.	While a boy, teaches the doctors and philosophers in the temple, the whole circle of the sciences.

This remarkable parallel, which leaves no room for doubt, that one of the narratives was drawn upon in the construction of the other, raises at once the question, which was first written? A question of the utmost importance; since if the Bhagavat Purana preceded the gospels of the Infancy, it could hardly be contended, at the same time, that it was subsequent to Luke and Matthew.

It is considered by evangelical writers, that the Infancy gospels were composed early in the second century, and the same writers do not now claim that the canonical gospels appeared much sooner. If, therefore, the Hindu production was long anterior to that time, the only question remaining would be, whether the parallelisms between the life of Chrishna, and that of Christ as recorded in Luke and Matthew, were taken directly from the Bhagavat Purana, or through the medium of the Infancy gospels.

The Rev. Mr. Maurice, who fully appreciated the importance of the question, and saw that in discussing it the gospels must all be considered together, would have his readers believe, that the Bhagavat Purana was interpolated, from "both the genuine and the spurious gospels." [1]

(1.) Vol. 2, p. 322.

In advocating this theory, however, he found himself embarrassed by the fact, that in various places in this and others of his works, he had contended for the great antiquity of the Hindu books, and had repeatedly hinted at the absurdity of supposing that the Brahmins would ever "descend so far from the conscious superiority of mental distinction" to which they laid claim, as to receive instruction, either in regard to the rites of religion, or the principles of science, from aliens.

But while he did not entertain for a moment, the idea, that the Indian philosophers had taken any thing from Greece or Arabia, from a mythology much akin to their own ; and while he believed many of the Indian legends to be older than the oldest of Greece, he found no difficulty in supposing that eastern magi would travel a year or more, in search of a king of the Jews ; would fall down and worship him, and on their return, would incorporate accounts concerning him, into their own sacred scriptures.

He overlooked the fact, that the prophecy of Zoroaster, in which the magi had been instructed, had no reference to a Jewish king, or to the Jewish people.

What are the facts, upon which an intelligent opinion upon the subject, is to be based? The original Gospel of the Infancy was attributed to the apostle and evangelist, Thomas. In this connection, we cannot ignore the ancient tradition of the church, that Thomas was a missionary to Parthia,

and to India. According to that tradition, and the
testimony of the fathers, when the distribution was
made by the apostles, of the several regions of the
Gentile world, in which they were respectively to
preach the gospel, the vast district of Parthia, and
the more eastern empires of Asia, were allotted to
Thomas.   He visited the various countries then
constituting the Parthian empire; that is, Media,
Persia, Carmania, Hyrcania and Bactria.   The
capital of Bactria was Balkh, the ancient residence
of the magi.   Here, according to eastern tradition,
he had an interview with the sages, and the tradition does not fail to say he converted them.[1]

From Parthia, St. Thomas is said to have visited
India.   It is not claimed that he converted the
Brahmins, but it is thought the Brahmins may
have profited by his visit, to interpolate their sacred
books, from his instructions.

But how did it happen, that after this visit of
Thomas, there appeared among the Christians of
Palestine, and countries west of it, a Gospel of
Thomas, full of stories so closely resembling the
legends of the Bhagavat Purana? If the interpolations were made by the Brahmins, how was it,
that this gospel appeared after the interpolations,
and not before?

In confirmation of the visit of Thomas to India,
it is related by Maffei, that at Cranganor, on the
Malabar coast, St. Thomas instituted an order of

(1.) See a work entitled "Opus Imperfectum in Matthæum," hom. 2. This "Imperfect Commentary on Matthew" was written about A. D, 560.

Christians, still known by his name, and which boasts to retain the records of their institution, and a grant of land to St. Thomas, their pastor, from the reigning king of India. [1]

The records and grant were engraved on tablets of brass, which had been lost for centuries, but were dug up, during the vice-royalty of Don Alfonso Sousa, one of the early governors of Portuguese India.

Thomas is said to have been murdered at Meliapoor; from which circumstance it was afterward called St. Thome.

The conclusion must be, that while for some of the salient points of the Gospels of the Infancy, the authors were indebted to Zoroaster, and the legends of Persia, the outline of the story was largely filled up from the history of Chrishna, as sent back to Palestine, by the Apostle Thomas, from the land of the Brahmins.

As to the slaughtered infants, there was discovered, in a cavern at Elephanta, in India, a sculptured representation, of great antiquity, of a huge and ferocious figure, bearing a drawn sword, and surrounded by slaughtered infants, while mothers were weeping for their slain. [2]

ANTIQUITY OF THE BHAGAVAT PURANA.

The Puranas are eighteen in number. The fifth, which was translated by Maurice, is the Bhagavata.

(1.) History of India, l. 2, p. 85.
(2.) See Forbes' Oriental Memoirs.

The legends concerning Chrishna appear in substantially the same form in several of the others.

Those who may wish to examine further as to the
antiquity of these books, will find the whole subject thoroughly and ably discussed, in a correspondence between Col. Vans Kennedy, and Prof. Horace
H. Wilson, author of a translation of the Vishnu
Purana.

The correspondence is in the form of five letters
from Col. Kennedy, the reply of Prof. Wilson, and
rejoinder of Kennedy.   It was published originally
in the London Asiatic Journal, for 1840 and 1841,
and was republished in the Appendix to the 5th
volume of the work of Prof. Wilson. [1]

This writer inclines to the opinion, that the
Puranas, in their present form, are modern compilations; and gives some countenance to the theory
though he does not fully endorse it, that the Bhagavata was written by one Bopadeva, as late as the
twelfth century.

This position is opposed, with great ability, by
Col. Kennedy, who reminds the learned author of
the "Vishnu Purana," that he had himself, in his
Preface to that work, stated, that there is "abundant positive and circumstantial evidence of the
prevalence of the doctrines which they [the Puran-
as] teach, the currency of the legends which they
narrate, and the integrity of the institutions which

(1.) The Vishnu Purana: A System of Mythology and Tradition, translated from
the original Sanscrit, by Horace Hayman Wilson, F. R. S., etc., London, 1864.

they describe, at least three centuries before the Christian era." [1]

This concession, Col. Kennedy thinks, leaves it comparatively unimportant when the Puranas assumed the exact form they now have. The word "Purana" itself signifies "old," thus indicating the character of the contents. He maintains, however, that they are now essentially the same that they were two thousand years ago.

"It is unquestionable," says Col. Kennedy, "that certain works called Puranas, have been immemorially considered by the Hindus as sacred books. They inculcated the doctrines of the Hindu religion."

And proceeding to consider the theory which had been advanced as to the authorship of the Bhagavata Purana, he says :

"If the Bhagavata was written by Bopadeva, at Doulutabad, in the twelfth century, was the original Bhagavata then in existence or not? If it was, what reason, consistent with probability, can be assigned, for supposing that the Brahmins of all India would have suppressed one of their sacred books, to which they ascribed a divine origin, and received, as entitled to the same reverence, the acknowledged composition of an obscure grammarian? The supposition is evidently absurd."—[Appendix to vol. 5, of Vish. Pur. by Wilson, p. 278.

He concludes, "that the present Puranas are, in fact, in all essential respects, the same works which were current, under that name, in India, in the century prior to the Christian era."

(1.) Vishnu Purana, etc., by H. H. Wilson, Pref. p. 99.

CHAPTER XV.

THE ACTS OF PILATE.

It has been supposed that Pilate made a report to Tiberius Cæsar, of the crucifixion of Christ, and of the circumstances attending it.

Frequent references to such a report were made by early Christian writers, who called it "The Acts of Pilate." That Justin Martyr [A. D. 150] made frequent allusions to a book or writing of some sort, entitled "The Acts of Pilate," will be seen in a subsequent chapter. [See Justin Martyr.]

Some writers have thought that he alluded to the original report, supposed to have been made to Cæsar. It will be seen, however, that he must have alluded to a gospel then in circulation, entitled "The Acts of Pilate, or Gospel of Nicodemus;" since his citations not only were in that gospel, but were such as would not have been in any report made by Pontius Pilate himself. It is possible that he was not able to distinguish between them, or did not care to do so. He was not a critical writer.

The fact that one of the early gospels was confounded by the Christians themselves, with the report of Pilate, renders the existence of such a report somewhat problematical; although it would have been in accordance with the mode of procedure in such cases that a report should have been made.

Tertullian, some sixty years later than Justin, refers to it several times; but not in a manner sufficiently definite, to determine whether or not he distinguishes it from the gospel. He says:

"Tiberius, accordingly, in whose days the Christian name made its entry into the world, having himself received intelligence from Palestine, of events which had clearly shown the truth of Christ's divinity, brought the matter before the senate, with his own decision in favor of Christ. The senate, because it had not given approval itself, rejected his proposal. Cæsar held to his opinion, threatening wrath against all accusers of the Christians."—[Apology, ch. 5, Ante Nicene, vol. 11, p. 63.

Speaking of the darkness at the time of the crucifixion, he says:

"You yourselves have the account of the world portent, still in your archives."—[Apol. ch. 21; Ant. Nic. vol. 11, p. 94.

The account of the darkness at the crucifixion, was in the Gospel of the Acts of Pilate. Whether Tertullian, like Justin Martyr, alluded to this, assuming that it was the same as the Romans had in their archives, or whether he referred to another document, it is impossible to determine. Again, he says:

"All these things Pilate did to Christ; and now in fact a Christian in his own conviction, he sent word of him to the reigning Cæsar, who was at the time, Tiberius."—[Ibid. ch. 21, p. 95.

It would be very important to ascertain whether there was any report of Pilate. That there was such a report, was the general opinion of the fathers; Eusebius, Jerome and others. Also of Grotius, Bishop Pearson, Spanheim, Fabricius, and modern writers generally. But these opinions are all founded upon the testimony of Justin Martyr and Tertullian. The writings of these fathers throw no light upon the subject; every thing referred to by them being contained in the gospel. The report, if any existed, could not have contained much in common with the gospel. For instance, would Pilate, in describing the crucifixion, have quoted from the Jewish scriptures, and said, "Upon his vesture they cast lots?"

Leclerc, Jones and others conclude, with good reason, that if there was such a report, neither Justin nor Tertullian had ever seen it, nor any subsequent Christian writer.

An attempt has lately been made to reproduce the original Report of Pilate. This will be considered in another chapter.

THE ACTS OF PILATE—ABSTRACT OF CONTENTS.

CHAPTER 1.—Annas and Caiaphas, and eight others, who are named, went to Pilate, accusing Jesus of many crimes; declaring they were satisfied that he was the son of Joseph the carpenter, and that he declared himself the Son of God, and a king. Also that he attempted a dissolution of the sabbath, and of the laws of their fathers.

Pilate inquired what Jesus had done?

The Jews replied, that he worked cures on the sabbath, contrary to their law; that he cured the lame and the deaf, those afflicted with the palsy, the blind, the lepers, and demoniacs, by wicked methods.

Pilate sent a messenger after Christ. When the messenger met him, he worshiped him, and spread his cloak for Jesus to walk upon.

The Jews complained of this act of the messenger. When Pilate asked him why he had done it, he replied, "When thou sentest me from Jerusalem to Alexander, I saw Jesus sitting in a mean figure, upon a she-ass, and the children of the Hebrews cried out, 'Hosanna;' holding boughs in their hands; others spread their garments in the way, and said, 'Save us, thou who art in heaven; blessed is he who cometh in the name of the Lord.'" The messenger was again sent, and did as before. "And as Jesus was going in by the ensigns who carried the standards, the tops of them bowed down, and worshiped Jesus." This was repeated, in the presence of Pilate.

Ch. 2.—Pilate's wife sent to him, saying: "Have nothing to do with that just man; for I have suffered much concerning him in a vision, this night."

Pilate, then calling Jesus, said, "Hast thou heard what they testify against thee, and makest no answer?" Jesus replied, "If they had not the power of speaking, they would not have spoken; but because every one has the command of his own tongue, to speak both good and bad, let them see to it."

The elders of the Jews charged him with being born through fornication; also that on account of his birth, the infants were slain in Bethlehem, and his father and mother fled into Egypt, because they could not trust the people. Others of the Jews spoke more favorably, among whom a number are named, including James and Judas. (These are the only names that correspond with those of the twelve apostles.) Then Pilate ordered all to go out, except the twelve, and Jesus to withdraw. He then asked the twelve why the Jews wished to kill Jesus. They replied that they were angry because he wrought cures on the sabbath.

Ch. 3.—Scenes between Jesus and Pilate. (See next chapter of this work.) The closing conversation is as follows:

"Pilate saith to him, 'What is truth?' Jesus said, 'Truth is from heaven.' Pilate said, 'Truth, therefore, is not on earth?' Jesus replied, 'Believe that truth is on earth, among those who, when they have the power of judgment, are governed by truth, and form their judgment aright.'"

Ch. 4.—Scenes between Pilate and the Jews. Pilate finding no fault in Jesus—the report of the Jews as to what Jesus had said about the temple—Pilate declaring himself innocent of the blood of Jesus, etc.

"Then the governor again commanded the Jews to depart out of the hall; and calling Jesus, said to him, 'What am I to do with thee?' Jesus answered him, 'According as it is written.' Pilate said to him,

'How is it written?' Jesus answered, 'Moses and the prophets made known beforehand, concerning my suffering and resurrection.'"

The Jews, hearing this, were enraged, and said to Pilate, "Why will you longer listen to his blasphemy?" Pilate said to them, "If these words seem to you blasphemous, take him, bring him before your synagogue, and try him according to your law." The Jews said to Pilate, "It is contained in our law, that if one man has sinned against another, he is worthy of nine and thirty stripes; but when he has blasphemed in this manner, against the Lord, he is to be stoned."

Pilate replied, "If this speech is blasphemy, then judge him according to your law." The Jews said, "Our law commands us not to put any one to death. [The preceding sentence in some copies only.] We desire that he may be crucified, because he is worthy of death at the cross." Pilate said to them, "It is not proper to crucify him. Let him be whipped and sent away."

"The governor, looking upon the people, and upon the Jews standing around, saw many of the Jews in tears; and said to the foremost of the Jewish priests, 'Not all of the multitude wish him to die.' The Jewish elders said to Pilate, 'We and the whole multitude came hither for this purpose, that he should die.' Pilate said to them, 'Wherefore should he die?' They replied, 'Because he declares himself the Son of God, and a king.'"

CH. 5.—But Nicodemus, a certain Jew, stood before the governor, and said: "I entreat thee, O merciful Judge, that thou wouldst deign to hear me a few words." Pilate said to him, "Speak on."

Nicodemus said, "I have spoken to the elders of the Jews, and the scribes, the priests and the Levites, and to the whole multitude of the Jews in the synagogue, and have asked them what they would do with this man? He is a man who has done many useful and glorious signs and wonders, such as no man on earth has done, or can do. Dismiss him, and do him no harm. If he is from God, his wonderful works will stand. But if from men, they will come to naught. Thus Moses," etc. [Alluding to the miracles wrought in Egypt, by Jannes, Jambres, etc.]

The Jews became angry at Nicodemus for interfering. Colloquy between them and Nicodemus.

CH. 6.—"Another certain one of the Jews, rising up, asked the governor, that he would hear him a word. The governor said, 'Whatever thou hast to say, say.'" [Here follows an account of the miracle at the sheep-pool. See next chapter.]

And another certain Jew, coming forth, said: "I was blind," etc. [See next chapter.]

"And another Jew, starting forth, said: '1 was a leper,'" etc. [See next chapter.]

"And another Jew came forth and said: 'I was crooked and he made me straight by his word.'"

CH. 7.—And a certain woman named Veronica, etc. [See next chapter.]

Then follows, from another Jew, the account of the turning of water into wine; from another, the casting out of a devil at Capernaum.

"Then the following things were also said by a Pharisee:

"'I saw that a great company came to Jesus, from Galilee and Judea, and the sea coast, and many countries about Jordan; and many infirm persons came to him, and he healed them all. And I heard the unclean spirits crying out and saying, 'Thou art the Son of God.' And Jesus strictly charged them that they should not make him known. "

CH. 8.—"After this, another person, whose name was Centurio, said," etc. (See next chapter.)

"And many others, also, from the Jews, both men and women, cried out, saying:

"'He is truly the Son of God, who cures all diseases, only by his word; and to whom all the demons are subjected.' Some from among them said, 'This power is only from God.'

"Others said to Pilate, that he restored Lazarus from the dead, after he had been four days in the tomb."

"The governor, hearing these things, trembling, said to the multitude of the Jews, 'What will it profit you, to shed innocent blood?'"

Chapters 9, 10 and 11 give an account of the sentence of Jesus, and of the circumstances attending his crucifixion. (See next chapter.)

CH. 12.—The Jews, having heard that Joseph had begged and buried the body of Jesus, sought for Joseph and others, his companions and accomplices. They concealed themselves, all but Nicodemus. He showed himself boldly, and disputed with the Jews. Joseph also afterward appeared, and expostulated with them. The elders of the Jews were enraged, "and seizing Joseph, they put him into a chamber, where was no window. They fastened the door, and put a seal upon the lock." They also placed a guard about it.

CH. 13.—When he was ordered brought forth, they found the same seal on the lock of the chamber, but could not find Joseph. While they were all wondering at this, one of the soldiers who had guarded the sepulcher, entered, and reported that while they were guarding the sepulcher, etc. (See next chapter.)

"Then the Jews called together all the soldiers who kept the sepulcher of Jesus, and said to them, 'Who were those to whom the angel spoke? Why did ye not seize them?' The soldiers answering, said, 'We know not who the women were; besides, we became as dead persons, through fear of the angel; and how could we seize the women?'"

The Jews do not believe the soldiers, and an altercation ensues between them. The soldiers say, "Do ye produce Joseph, whom ye put under guard in your chamber, and we will produce Jesus, whom we guarded in the sepulcher." The Jews gathered a large sum of money, and gave it to the soldiers, etc. (See next ch.)

Ch. 14.—Three persons came from Galilee to Jerusalem, and reported that they had seen Jesus in Galilee, talking with his eleven disciples, etc. (See next ch.) The chief priests gave these persons a large sum of money, and had them take oath not to declare what they had seen, and sent them back to their own country. The Jews were now in great consternation.

"But Annas and Caiaphas comforted them, saying: 'Why should we believe the soldiers?'" etc. (See next ch.)

Ch. 15.—On the advice of Nicodemus, men were sent into the mountains, to search for Jesus. They could not find him, but found Joseph. They induced him to return. He related his marvelous escape. Jesus had appeared to him in the room, and having liberated him, had shown him the tomb in which he had been laid, etc.

Ch. 16.—The Jews were astonished. They said, they knew the father and mother of Jesus. A certain Levite said, he knew his relations, etc.

Ch. 17.—Joseph related to the Jews, that the two sons of Simeon had risen from the dead, and were at Arimathea. He suggested visiting them, for the purpose of ascertaining some of the mysteries of their resurrection. Five persons visited their graves, and found them open. They found them in the village, and brought them to Jerusalem, to the synagogue. They took the book of the law of the Lord, and swore them by the God Adonai, and the God of Israel, to tell them how they were raised from the dead, and what they had seen.

Charinus and Lenthius, the two sons of Simeon, called for paper, and wrote down the mysteries which they had experienced.

GOSPEL OF NICODEMUS. PART 2. THE DESCENT
INTO HELL [HADES].—This part of the gospel consists of the story thus written down, which is,
briefly, as follows :

When they were in the depths of hell, suddenly
there was a golden light, as of the sun. Adam then
rejoiced ; also Isaiah the prophet, etc. Then their
father Simeon came, and quoted what he said when
he took Jesus in his arms ; the saints in hell then
rejoiced ; then came John the Baptist, like a little
hermit. Seth appeared, and repeated a long speech
of Michael. Then Satan, the prince and captain of
death, announced to the prince of hell that Jesus
was coming. The prince of hell and Satan made
long speeches. While they were discoursing, there
was heard a voice as of thunder : "Lift up your
gates, O ye princes, and the King of Glory shall
come in."

The prince of hell prepared to resist, but the sound
was repeated, and the mighty Lord appeared in the
form of a man, lighting up the darkness. The King
of Glory tramples upon death, seizes the prince of
hell, and takes father Adam and the saints with
him to glory. In exchange for the loss of Adam
and his righteous sons, he gives Satan over to
Beelzebub, the prince of hell, to be subject to his
dominion forever.

CH. 27.—"These are the divine and sacred mysteries, which we saw and heard." Thus say Charinus and Lenthius.

They, having written all this down, gave one
copy to the Jewish priests, and one copy to Nicodemus and Joseph ; "and immediately they were
exchanged into exceeding white forms, and were
seen no more."

"But immediately, all these things, which were related by the Jews in their synagogue, concerning Jesus, were directly told to the governor, by Joseph and Nicodemus, and Pilate wrote down all the transactions, and placed them all in the public records of the prætorium."

CH. 28.—Pilate went to the temple, and calling together the rulers, and the scribes, and the doctors of the law, he stated that he had heard they had a large book in the temple, and he desired it to be brought. When the great book, carried by four ministers of the temple, and adorned with gold and precious stones, was brought, Pilate adjured them to tell him, if they had found anything in the scriptures about Jesus coming for the salvation of the human race; and at what time of the world he should have come. Annas and Caiaphas being sworn, declared that they had found, in the first of the seventy books, where Michael the archangel gave to the third son of Adam an account concerning the appearance of Christ after 5500 years.

Here follows, in the copy of the gospel which we have adhered to, taken from the Orthodoxographa, vol. 1, tom. 2, p. 643, a list of chronological periods, footing up 4964 years. But in the Latin form of the gospel, published in the sixteenth volume of the Ante-Nicene collection, is a list of dates, which, after a slight correction, foots up 5500 years.

The copy from the Orthodoxographa closes by stating that these Acts were found, in the 19th year of Tiberius Cæsar, by the Emperor, Theodosius the Great, in Jerusalem, in the prætorium of Pontius Pilate, among the public records. That it was in the 17th year of Herod the Tetrarch, and in the 102d Olympiad. That the history was written in Hebrew, by Nicodemus. In the preface to the Latin form it is stated that the Acts were translated by Æneas, from the Hebrew in the 17th consulship of Theodosius, and the 5th consulship of Valentinian. That they had been written by Nicodemus, in Hebrew, in the 19th year of Tiberius. That Pilate laid up a statement of the Acts of Christ in the public records of the prætorium, and wrote a letter to Claudius, stating that Jesus had been crucified, and referring to the miracles which he had wrought. Also, that he rose again the third day, while the soldiers were keeping guard.

CHAPTER XVI.

ACTS OF PILATE
AND THE CANONICAL GOSPELS COMPARED.

Before instituting a comparison of these gospels, it will be necessary to consider more carefully, a custom which prevailed extensively in the first ages of the church, and especially in the first two centuries.

The prevailing religious excitement and enthusiasm, the trusting credulity and love of the marvelous, which were characteristic of the early Christians, led them to accept, unhesitatingly, what came to them, sanctioned by the authority of their bishops and teachers.

When the better educated among them were called upon to translate or to transcribe the religious writings of the day, they saw at a glance, what liberties had been taken with previous materials, and how readily the changes had been accepted. Accordingly, not with any improper motives, but for the purpose of edification, and of increasing somewhat, the volume, not then very large, of current Christian literature, they made additions, more or less extensive, to the writings which they were copying or translating. This process, which may be termed literary accretion, prevailed so extensively and universally, in those times, that it was the rule, rather than the exception; and must be constantly kept in view, in all investigations and discussions of Christian doctrine, as well as in the exegesis of the Christian scriptures.

This practice is well understood by ecclesiastical writers, as well as the disposition and habits of thought to which it is to be referred. "The ancient transcribers of the gospels," says Michaelis, "were always more inclined to insert new passages, than to erase what already existed." [1]

Many passages in the New Testament are thus to be accounted for; notably may be mentioned the last twelve verses of the Gospel according to Mark; which are generally considered a later addition to the narrative. [2]

One of the most remarkable illustrations of the process of interpolation and accretion, is in the Ignatian Epistles. It is now established that the only genuine writings of Ignatius extant, are the Cureton Epistles. These consist of about twelve octavo pages. They were written A. D. 115.

Twenty-five years later, these three epistles had

(1.)   Volume 3, p. 169.

(2.)   It is stated in the religious Encyclopedia of McClintock and Strong, that one of the Greek manuscripts of the New Testament, the one called "Codex Bezæ," or the Cambridge manuscript, "is chiefly remarkable for its bold and extensive interpolations; amounting to some 600 in the Acts alone."—[Article "Cambridge MS."

increased from 12 pages to 20, while four new ones had appeared, making in all, 40 pages. Some time afterward, the 40 pages, which constituted the seven epistles, were found swollen to 60, while eight new epistles had appeared, adding 40 pages more, making 100 pages of the Epistles of Ignatius! These all passed as genuine, for hundreds of years. Here was a natural growth, from twelve pages to 100. They were all for edification. They all breathed the same spirit with the original epistles; some new doctrines had crept in, but no harm had been intended, and no great violence had been done to anything but the truth of history.

While 88 pages had been added to the Ignatian Epistles, how many had been taken away? One half page, and that supposed to be by mistake, from the loss of the last half sheet of the MS.

Of the 150,000 various readings which Griesbach found in the manuscripts of the New Testament, probably 149,500 were additions and interpolations.

Prof. Abbot gives us a list of over 60 passages in the New Testament, the genuineness of which the Bible Revision Committee considered "more or less questionable." They include Mark, ch. 16, vv. 9 to 20, and John 8. 1 to 11; and if published together, would constitute of themselves a gospel of no mean dimensions. What part of the same space would be occupied by the portions which they found to have been erased? Probably not one-hundredth.

In comparing the Gospels of the Infancy with

Luke and Matthew, it was seen that the changes were to be accounted for by other considerations.

Now, however, when we come to the miracles of Christ, which are given in the Acts of Pilate on the one hand, and in the canonical gospels on the other, the principle is allowed full play, and can be applied, as internal evidence, tending to show which were first written.

The fact that in the Acts, the narratives are related to Pilate by Jews, testifying in behalf of their master, is no reason why the accounts should be shortened, but rather the contrary. The witnesses would be anxious to have Pilate impressed with the details of the wonderful occurrences. If the writer of the Acts of Pilate had before him the gospels containing these narratives, we may be assured he would have put into the mouths of the witnesses, every circumstance of an impressive character contained in those accounts, and would probably have added others. Let us see if that was the case.

SOME OF THE MIRACLES OF JESUS.
TURNING WATER INTO WINE.

This miracle is related in only one of the four gospels; the Gospel according to John.

The comparison can be made between the Acts of Pilate and the Gospel of John, with no disturbing forces from the other gospels, to be accounted for:

ACTS OF PILATE, ch. 7.	GOSPEL OF JOHN, ch. 2.
And after other things, a cer-	And the third day, there was a marriage in Cana of Galilee; and the mother of Jesus was there;

ACTS OF PILATE, ch. 7.	GOSPEL OF JOHN, ch. 2.
tain Jew said: I saw Jesus invited to a wedding with his disciples, and there was a want of wine; in Cana of Galilee. And when the wine was all drunk, he commanded the ser-	2. And both Jesus was called, and his disciples, to the marriage. 3. And when they wanted wine, the mother of Jesus saith unto him, They have no wine. 4. Jesus saith unto her, Woman, what have I to do with thee? Mine hour is not yet come. 5. His mother saith unto the servants, Whatsoever he saith unto you, do (it.)
vants, that they should fill six pots that were there, with water;	6. And there were set there, six water-pots of stone, after the manner of the purifying of the Jews, containing two or three firkins apiece. 7. Jesus saith unto them, Fill the water-pots with water. And
and they filled them up to the brim. And he blessed them and turned the water into wine.	they filled them up to the brim. 8. And he saith unto them, Draw out now and bear unto the governor of the feast. And they bare (it.)
And all the people drank, being surprised at this miracle.	9. When the ruler of the feast had tasted the water that was made wine, and knew not whence it was, (but the servants who drew the water knew), the governor of the feast called the bridegroom, 10. And saith unto him, Every man at the beginning doth set forth good wine; and when men have well drunk, then that which is worse; (but) thou hast kept the good wine until now. 11. This beginning of miracles did Jesus, in Cana of Galilee, and manifested forth his glory; and his disciples believed on him.

Which of these accounts was first written?

The process of accretion, which has been alluded to, has two modes of development. The one, by clothing the same facts in a more copious dress, the other, by the interpolation of additional facts. Both these processes are here to be observed.

Not only are the facts constituting the miracle, which, in the Acts of Pilate, are narrated in a plain, concise and impressive manner, enveloped in much additional and useless verbiage, in John, but also, two additional circumstances are inserted ; the size of the water-pots, and the fact that the newly made wine was better than the other. If the author of the Acts had been acquainted with the Gospel of John, is it probable that he would have omitted these circumstances?

The next miracle, also, is related only by John :

HEALING OF THE NOBLEMAN'S SON.

ACTS OF PILATE, ch. 8.

Then a certain nobleman said, I had a son at Capernaum, who lay at the point of death.

And when I heard that Jesus was come into Galilee, I went and besought him, that he would come down to my house, and heal my son;

For he was about to die.

He said to me, Go thy way; thy son liveth. And my son was cured, from that hour.

JOHN, 4. 46 to 53.

46. And there was a certain nobleman whose son was sick at Capernaum.

47. And when he heard that Jesus was come out of Judea into Galilee, he went unto him and besought him that he would come down, and heal his son; for he was at the point of death.

48. Then said Jesus unto him, Except ye see signs and wonders, ye will not believe.

49. The nobleman saith unto him, Sir, come down, ere my child die.

50. Jesus saith unto him, Go thy way; thy son liveth. And the man believed the word that Jesus had spoken unto him, and he went his way.

51. And as he was now going down, his servants met him, and told (him), saying, Thy son liveth.

52. Then inquired he of them the hour when he began to amend. And they said unto him, Yesterday, at the seventh hour, the fever left him.

53. So the father knew that (it was) at the same hour in the which Jesus said unto him, Thy son liveth: and himself believed, and his whole house.

The difference in the narrative consists, almost entirely, in the greater diffuseness of style and copiousness of detail, in John, with no new facts of any importance introduced. This difference indicates a later narrative in John. That the short paragraph in the Acts should, under the hand of the author of John, grow into the nine verses, would be in perfect accordance with the law of accretion, then prevailing.

The next miracle is related in Luke and Mark, but not in John or Matthew. The comparison will be made with the shorter narrative, in Luke.

CASTING OUT THE UNCLEAN DEVIL AT CAPERNAUM.

ACTS OF PILATE, ch. 7.

And another Jew stood forth in the midst of them, and said:

I saw Jesus in Capernaum,

teaching in the synagogue; and there was in the synagogue a certain man who had a devil.

And he cried out, saying: Let me alone; what have we to do with thee, Jesus of Nazareth? Art thou come to destroy us? I know that thou art the Holy One of God.

And Jesus rebuked him, and said to him, Hold thy peace, unclean spirit, and come out of the man. And presently he came out of him, and did not at all hurt him.

LUKE, 4. 31 to 35.

31. And on the sabbath days he taught them.

32. And they were astonished at his doctrine; for his word was with power.

33. And in the synagogue, there was a man who had a spirit of an unclean devil; and he cried out with a loud voice,

34. Saying: Let (us) alone; what have we to do with thee, (thou) Jesus of Nazareth? Art thou come to destroy us? I know thee, who thou art: the Holy One of God.

35. And Jesus rebuked him, saying: Hold thy peace, and come out of him. And when the devil had thrown him in the midst, he came out of him, and hurt him not.

In the foregoing account, there is amplification in Luke. Not satisfied that the man should be possessed of a devil, the writer makes it "a spirit of an unclean devil;" and he has the devil, before leaving the man, "throw him in the midst." In Mark, where the narrative is longer, and the amplification still greater, the devil, when required to come out, is made to cry out with a loud voice.

HEALING OF THE LEPER.

The miracle is related in Luke, Mark and Matthew. The account in Matthew is almost exactly the same as that in Luke. Mark shows some evidence of additional accretion. The comparison will be continued with Luke:

ACTS OF PILATE, ch. 6.	LUKE, 5. 12, 13.
Another Jew, also coming forth, said: I was a leper, and he cured me	12. And it came to pass, when he was in a certain city, behold, a man full of leprosy; who, seeing Jesus, fell on (his) face, and besought him, saying, Lord, if thou wilt, thou canst make me clean.
by his word only; saying, I will, be thou clean. And immediately I was cleansed from my leprosy.	13. And he put forth (his) hand and touched him, saying: I will: be thou clean. And immediately the leprosy departed from him.

HEALING OF THE INFIRM MAN AT BETHESDA.

This miracle, again, is only related in John:

ACTS OF PILATE, ch. 6.	JOHN, 5. 1 to 16.
Then another certain one of the Jews, rising up, desired of the governor, that he would hear him a word. The governor said, What thou wishest to say, say. He said, I lay for thirty-eight years, by the sheep-pool at Jerusalem, suffering under a great infirmity. I was expecting a cure to come from the coming of an angel, who disturbed the water at a certain time. Whoever, after the troubling of the water, first descended into it, was made whole of every infirmity.	After this, there was a feast of the Jews; and Jesus went up to Jerusalem. 2. Now there is at Jerusalem, by the sheep (market), a pool, which is called in the Hebrew tongue, Bethesda; having five porches. 3. In these, lay a great multitude of impotent folk, of blind, halt, withered, waiting for the moving of the water. 4. For an angel went down at a certain season into the pool, and troubled the water; whosoever then first, after the troubling of the water, stepped in, was made

ACTS OF PILATE, ch. 6.	JOHN, 5. 1 to 16.
	whole of whatsoever disease he had.
Jesus, finding me languishing there, said to me,	5. And a certain man was there who had an infirmity, thirty and eight years.
	6. When Jesus saw him lie, and knew that he had been now a long time so, he saith unto him, Wilt thou be made whole?
Wilt thou be made whole? And I answered, Sir, I have no man, when the water is troubled, to put me into the pool.	7. The impotent man answered him, Sir, I have no man, when the water is troubled, to put me into the pool; but while I am coming, another steppeth down before me.
And he said unto me, Rise, take up thy bed, and walk. And I was made whole, and immediately took up my bed, and walked.	8. Jesus saith unto him, Rise, take up thy bed, and walk. 9. And immediately the man was made whole, and took up his bed, and walked.
[Here follows a colloquy concerning the sabbath, of the same general tenor as that in John, but much shorter.]	[Then follows a colloquy concerning the sabbath, verses 10 to 16; varying in detail from that in the other gospel, and considerably longer.]

HEALING OF THE SERVANT OF CENTURIO, OR THE SERVANT OF THE CENTURION.

The comparison will be made with Luke; the account in that gospel being more nearly parallel. In Matthew, the narrative is somewhat shorter, but still it is twice as long as in the Acts of Pilate.

ACTS OF PILATE, ch. 8.	LUKE, ch. 7.
After this a certain person whose name was Centurio, said: I saw Jesus at Capernaum, and I entreated him, saying:	Now, when, (etc.), he entered into Capernaum. 2. And a centurion's servant, who was dear unto him, was sick, and ready to die. 3. And when he heard of Jesus, he sent unto him the elders of the Jews, beseeching him that he would come and heal his servant.
Lord, my servant lieth at home, a paralytic. And Jesus said to me, I will come and cure him. But I said,	4. And when they came to Jesus they besought him instantly; saying that he was worthy, for whom he should do this.

ACTS OF PILATE, ch. 8.	LUKE, ch. 7.
	5. For he loveth our nation, and he hath built us a synagogue.
	6. Then Jesus went with them. And when he was not far from the house, the centurion sent friends unto him, saying unto him, Lord, trouble not thyself, for
Lord, I am not worthy, that thou shouldst come under my	I am not worthy that thou shouldst enter under my roof.
roof; But only speak the word, and my servant shall be healed.	7. Wherefore neither thought I myself worthy to come unto thee: but say in a word, and my servant shall be healed.
	8. For I also am a man set under authority, having under me soldiers; and I say unto one, Go, and he goeth; and to another, Come, and he cometh; and to my servant, Do this, and he doeth (it.)
	9. When Jesus heard these things, he marveled at him, and turned him about, and said unto the people that followed him, I say unto you, I have not
And Jesus said unto me, Go thy way; and as thou hast believed, so be it done unto thee.	found so great faith, no, not in Israel.
And the servant was healed, from that same hour.	10. And they that were sent, returning to the house, found the servant whole, that had been sick.

Here the account in Luke is nearly three times as long as that in the other gospel.

It is manifest, also, that one of the historians made a mistake in the person upon whose servant the miracle was performed; a mistake arising from the use of the word Centurio, or centurion.

In which gospel was the mistake probably made?

If the Acts of Pilate was written last, and the author had at first mistaken the word centurion for the name of the person, he would, as he proceeded with the narrative, discover his mistake, by noticing the character of the person, and his military position, as a commander of men. On the other hand, if Luke was last written, it would be very natural for the author to suppose, inasmuch as Centurio was an unusual name, that centurion was intended. And having once made the change, either by mistake or otherwise, he would naturally, in the usual process of interpolation, make additions to the narrative, illustrative of the peculiar position occupied by the person upon whom the miracle was wrought, and of the willingness of Jesus to cure Gentiles as well as Jews.

THE HEALING OF VERONICA.

ACTS OF PILATE, ch. 7.	LUKE, 8. 43 to 48. (Shortest form.)
And a certain woman, Veronica by name, said: I was flowing with blood for twelve years; and I touched the fringe of his garment, and immediately the flowing of my blood stopped. (Note. The name of the woman is not given in the first Greek form of the Acts of Pilate, as published in the Ante-Nicene Christian Library, vol. 16, pp. 125 to 148.)	43. And a woman having an issue of blood twelve years, who had spent all her living upon physicians, neither could be healed by any, 44. Came behind him, and touched the border of his garment: and immediately her issue of blood stanched. (Then follow four verses, giving a conversation concerning the matter, between Jesus, the people and the woman.)

According to Eusebius, this woman erected a statue to the honor of Christ, on account of the miracle.[1]

The historian says, the woman lived at Cæsarea Philippi; that her house was to be seen in his time, and several monuments of the miracle. That near her house was a brazen statue of the woman, fixed on a pedestal of stone, in the posture of a suppliant,

(1,) Ecclesiastical History, 7. 18.

on bended knees, with outstretched hands. Opposite to it, made of the same metal, was the statue of a man, in a standing posture, with a cloak over his shoulders and stretching forth his hand to the woman. At the foot of this statue, at the very base of the column, grew a certain unknown herb, which, growing up to the hem of the garment, was a present remedy, so said Eusebius, for all sorts of distempers. This statue was said to be like Christ. "It continued," says Eusebius, "to my time, and I went to that city, and saw it myself."

Sozomen, the historian, [A D. 439], mentions the same story, and says that Julian the apostate took down the statue, and placed his own in the room of it. He adds, that a fire from heaven smote the statue erected by Julian, and took off the head and neck, and fixed it in the earth ; where it continued to his day, looking black, as if it had been burnt by lightning.[1]

The statue is also mentioned by the historian Cassiodorus, [A. D. 550], by Theophylact, Epiphanius and Nicephorus. Also by Asterius, a writer of the fourth century, who says it was removed by the Emperor Maximus.[2]

Luebke, who was unacquainted with this tradition, or did not give credit to it, speaks of the first statue of Christ, as having been erected by Alexander Severus.[3]

(1.) Sozomen's Ecc. Hist. 5. 21.

(2.) See Photius, Bib. Cod. 272, p. 1507.

(3.) History of Art, vol. 1, 3d Ed. p. 306.

It is said, also, that the second picture of Christ ever taken, (the first being the one sent by him to Abgarus, King of Edessa), was stamped or impressed upon the handkerchief of Veronica. That when Jesus was led to his crucifixion, Veronica, who followed him, put a handkerchief to his face, on which Christ impressed his picture. This is attested by Methodius, Bishop of Tyre, [A. D. 300], Constantius Porphyrogenitus, and others.[1]

CURING BLIND BARTIMEUS.

ACTS OF PILATE, ch. 6.

And a certain other Jew, rising up, said: I was blind; could hear sounds, but could see no one.

And as Jesus was going along, I heard the multitude passing by, and I asked what was there? They told me that Jesus was passing by. Then I cried out, saying: Jesus, Son of David, have mercy on me.

And he, standing still, commanded me to be brought to him,

and said to me, What wilt thou? I said, Lord, that I may receive my sight.

LUKE, 18. 35 to 43.

35. And it came to pass, that as he was come nigh unto Jericho, a certain blind man sat by the way-side, begging:

36. And hearing the multitude pass by, he asked what it meant.

37. And they told him that Jesus of Nazareth passed by.

38. And he cried, saying: Jesus, thou Son of David, have mercy on me.

39. And they who went before, rebuked him, that he should hold his peace; but he cried so much the more, (Thou) Son of David, have mercy on me.

40. And Jesus stood, and commanded him to be brought unto him; and when he was come near, he asked him,

41. Saying: What wilt thou that I shall do unto thee? And he said, Lord, that I may receive my sight.

(1.) See Durant, de Retib. Cath. Eccles. l. 1, c. 5:

"Altera Christi imago sudario Veronicæ impressa fuit: cum enim Christus ad crucifigedum duceretur, Veronica, quæ Christum sequebatur, faciei sudarium, admovit, in quo Christi effigiem, expressam retulit. Hujus rei, auctores sunt Methodius," etc.

Durant also refers to the image of Christ erected by the woman cured of the flowing of blood.

ACTS OF PILATE, ch. 6.	LUKE, 18. 35 to 43.
And he said to me, Receive thy sight.	42. And Jesus said unto him, Receive thy sight; thy faith hath saved thee.
And immediately I saw, and followed him, rejoicing and giving thanks.	43. And immediately he received his sight, and followed him, glorifying God; and all the people, when they saw (it), gave praise unto God.

The author of Matthew has two blind men; and as Schleiermacher observes, has a habit of duplicating, in such cases.

THE RAISING OF LAZARUS.

ACTS OF PILATE, ch. 8.	GOSPEL OF JOHN.
But others said to Pilate, that he raised Lazarus from the dead, after he had been four days in his grave.	The reader is familiar with the long account of this miracle, contained in the 11th chapter of John, consisting of 44 verses.

The foregoing are all of the gospel miracles which are related in the Acts of Pilate. The result of the comparison may be stated thus:

In every instance, the account in the Acts of Pilate is shorter than the shortest narrative in the canonical gospels.

In view of the practice of interpolation, which prevailed so extensively in the second century, it is for the reader to judge which was last written.

THE CRUCIFIXION OF JESUS.

The account of the crucifixion, as given in the Acts of Pilate, is undoubtedly the nearest historical of any religious writings of the second century. As everything connected with this event is of absorbing interest, the subject cannot be approached with indifference.

Bishop Ellicott, in an able Essay on the Apocryphal Gospels, published in the Cambridge Essays for 1856, admits that this account was used by the earlier fathers.

To show the value of this testimony, we will quote from his prefatory remarks the contemptuous language which he employs, when speaking of the apocryphal gospels as a class:

"Their real demerits, their mendacities, their absurdities, their coarsenesses, the barbarities of their style, and the inconsequence of their narratives, have never been excused or condoned. It would be hard to find any competent writer, in any age of the church, who has been beguiled into saying anything civil or commendatory."

And yet the writer who could not refrain from expressing himself thus strongly toward these unfortunate, bantling gospels, when he comes to consider the Acts of Pilate, feels compelled to speak in a more respectful manner. In commencing, he says:

"We pass onward to a very important document, apparently of a very early date, the first part of the Gospel of Nicodemus, or, as it is commonly called, the Acta Pilati.

"The question of real interest is this.

"Whether the present Acta Pilati are substantially the same with the very ancient document, referred to with such respect by Justin Martyr, Tertullian, and other early and reputable writers. It need scarcely be said that these ancient acts are not the real, judiciary acts of Pilate. The Acta noticed by Tertullian, was probably an account of our Savior's condemnation, written by some early Jewish-Christian, and derived from eye-witnesses, or from important oral traditions, which, in so short a time, and on such an event, could not have become seriously erroneous."

After stating that it would be liable to changes and interpolations, and that there is reason to think the apocryphal Acts of Pilate was one of the interpolated manuscripts, he says:

"When, however, it is remembered that the quotations made by Tertullian and others from the ancient Acta, are all found in the present Acta, it seems fair to conclude, especially from the nature and length of the composition, that these changes or interpolations have not been very serious, and that we have, in this first part of this Gospel of Nicodemus, substantially, the very ancient and important Acta Pilati, of the second century."

Again: "If we strip off the obviously fabulous, it does seem that the writer has related some portions of the trial in a manner so very probable and plausible, that we may well pause before we sweep away the whole as a mere party fiction. There is something very natural in the way in which the Jews heap up indiscriminate accusation; there is an eager ferocity on their part, met by a steady and almost indignant scorn on the part of the governor, that seems, at any rate, very happily depicted. The desire of the Jews, not only that Christ should die, but that he should be crucified, that he should die the death of a malefactor,—is brought out very distinctly.

"There are minor incidents,— the weeping populace — the appearance of witnesses in favor of the accused (though here there is evidently much interpolated) — the steady defense of Nicodemus — the persecution of the pious Joseph—the cloth wound round the crucified Savior—the crown of thorns still retained on the brow — the account given by the centurion to Pilate, and the distress of that unjust man and his wife,— which all tend to make us regard these interpolated, but still very ancient records, with a greater interest than we can feel for any other member of the apocryphal family."

After so respectable a testimony for this gospel, from one who cannot be accused of any prejudice in its favor, we proceed to contrast its narrative of the crucifixion and resurrection of Jesus, with the parallel accounts in the canonical gospels :

THE PROPOSAL TO RELEASE A PRISONER.

This account is given in all four of the canonical gospels. The narrative is, however, so divergent, that it can scarcely be considered parallel, except in Mark and Matthew. Of these, the comparison will be made with the shorter form :

ACTS OF PILATE, ch. 9.	MATTHEW, 27. 15 to 23.
Pilate, again calling the multitude, said to them, Since there is a custom among you, on the day of passover, that I should release to you one that is bound; I have a noted murderer, called Barabbas, also Jesus who is called Christ; in whom I find no cause of death.	15. Now at (that) feast, the governor was wont to release unto the people a prisoner, whom they would. 16. And they had then a notable prisoner, called Barabbas. 17. Therefore, when they were gathered together, Pilate said unto them, Whom will ye that I release unto you? Barabbas, or Jesus who is called Christ? 18. For he knew that for envy they had delivered him. 19. [Omitted. Parallel in another part of the Acts of Pilate.] 20. But the chief priests and elders persuaded the multitude, that they should ask Barabbas, and destroy Jesus.
Which, therefore, of these two do you wish to have released? They all cried out, saying, Release unto us Barabbas. Pilate saith unto them, What then shall I do with Jesus who is called Christ? They all say unto him, Let him be crucified.	21. The governor answered and said unto them, Whether of the twain will ye that I release unto you? Thay said, Barabbas. 22. Pilate saith unto them, What shall I do then with Jesus who is called Christ? (They) all say unto him, Let him be crucified. 23. And the governor said, Why, what evil hath he done? But they cried out the more, saying: Let him be crucified.

The foregoing accounts are closely parallel. But the canonical gospel exhibits considerable accretion. There is some amplification of language, and the introduction of the dream of the wife of Pilate.

PILATE WASHING HIS HANDS OF THE BLOOD OF JESUS.

ACTS OF PILATE, ch. 9.	MATTHEW, ch. 27.
Then Pilate, taking water, washed his hands before the people, saying: I am innocent of the blood of this just person; see ye to it. The Jews answered, saying: His blood be upon us, and upon our children.	24. When Pilate saw that he could prevail nothing, but (that) rather a tumult was made, he took water, and washed (his) hands before the multitude, saying: I am innocent of the blood of this just person; see ye (to it). 25. Then answered all the people, and said, His blood (be) on us, and on our children.

Not in either of the other gospels.

In the Acts of Pilate, Jesus is now sentenced, as follows :

"Then Pilate commanded Jesus to be brought before him, and spake to him the following words:

"'Thy own nation hath charged thee, as making thyself a king. Wherefore, I, Herod, sentence thee to be whipped, according to the laws of former governors; and that thou be first bound, then hanged upon a cross, in that place where thou art now a prisoner; and also two criminals with thee; whose names are Demas and Gestas.'"

JESUS TAKEN TO EXECUTION.

As the account is less connected in the canonical gospels, we shall be obliged here, in order to preserve the parallel, to put several passages together :

ACTS OF PILATE, ch. 10.	MATTHEW, ch. 27.
Then Jesus went out of the hall, and the two thieves with him. And when they were come to the place which is called Golgotha, they stripped him of his raiment, and girt him about with	26. And . . . he delivered him to be crucified. 33. When they were come unto a place called Golgotha, that is to say, a place of a skull, 28. They stripped him, and put on him a scarlet robe, 29. And when they had platted
a linen cloth, and put a crown of thorns upon his head, and put a reed in his hand.	a crown of thorns, they put (it) upon his head, and a reed in his right hand.

PRAYING FOR HIS ENEMIES.

ACTS OF PILATE, ch. 10.	LUKE, 23. 34.
But Jesus said, My Father, forgive them; for they know not what they do.	Then said Jesus, Father, forgive them; for they know not what they do.

HIS GARMENTS ARE DIVIDED.

ACTS OF PILATE, ch. 10.	MARK, 15. 24.
And they divided his garments, and upon his vesture they cast lots.	And when they had crucified him, they parted his garments, casting lots upon them, what every man should take.

MATTHEW, 27. 35.

And parted his garments, casting lots; that it might be fulfilled which was spoken by the prophet: They parted my garments among them, and upon my vesture did they cast lots.

LUKE, 23. 34.

And they parted his raiment, and cast lots.

The law of accretion is well illustrated here, by comparing the short statements in Luke and the Acts of Pilate, on the one hand, with Mark and Matthew on the other. Luke being a compilation, this portion of it is probably from a manuscript older, even, than the Acts of Pilate.

In John, the account is extended, with the additional statement, that the garments were divided into four parts, to every soldier a part, and that lots were cast for the coat, which was without seam.

MOCKED BY THE CHIEF PRIESTS AND SOLDIERS.

ACTS OF PILATE, ch. 10.

The people in the mean time stood by, and the chief priests and elders of the Jews mocked him, saying:

He saved others, let him now save himself if he can; if he be the Son of God, let him now come down from the cross.

The soldiers also mocked him, and taking vinegar and gall, offered it to him to drink, and said to him: If thou art King of the Jews, deliver thyself.

MARK, 15. 29 to 32, 36.

29. And they that passed by railed on him, wagging their heads, and saying: Ah, thou that destroyest the temple, and buildest (it) in three days,

30. Save thyself, and come down from the cross.

31. Likewise, also, the chief priests, mocking, said among themselves, with the scribes, He saved others, himself he cannot save.

32. Let Christ, the King of Israel, descend now from the cross, that we may see and believe.

36. And one ran and filled a sponge full of vinegar, and put (it) on a reed, and gave him to drink.

JESUS PIERCED IN THE SIDE.

ACTS OF PILATE, ch. 10.	JOHN, 19. 34.
Longinus, a soldier, taking a spear, pierced his side; and directly, there came forth blood and water.	But one of the soldiers with a spear pierced his side, and forthwith there came out blood and water.

THE TITLE UPON THE CROSS.

ACTS OF PILATE, ch. 10.	JOHN, 19. 19, 20.
And Pilate wrote a title upon the cross, in Hebrew, Latin and Greek letters, to wit: "THIS IS THE KING OF THE JEWS."	19. And Pilate wrote a title and put (it) on the cross. And the writing was, "JESUS OF NAZARETH, THE KING OF THE JEWS." 20. This title then read many of the Jews: for the place where Jesus was crucified, was nigh to the city: and it was written in Hebrew, (and) Greek, (and) Latin.

In the synoptic gospels, it is not stated who wrote the title. In Luke, it is "This is the King of the Jews." In Mark, "The King of the Jews." In Matthew, "This is Jesus, the King of the Jews." In Luke, it is stated to have been in Greek, Latin and Hebrew.

THE THIEVES ON THE CROSS.

ACTS OF PILATE, ch. 10.	LUKE, 23. 39 to 43.
But one of the two thieves who were crucified with Jesus, whose name was Gestas, said to Jesus, If thou art the Christ, deliver thyself and us. But the thief who was crucified on the right hand, whose name was Demas, answering, rebuked him, and said: Dost not thou, who art condemned to this punishment, fear God? We, indeed, justly and rightly, according to what we have done, receive our reward. But this Jesus, what evil hath he done?	39. And one of the malefactors who were hanged, railed on him, saying: If thou be Christ, save thyself and us. 40. But the other answering rebuked him, saying: Dost thou not fear God, seeing thou art in the same condemnation? 41. And we indeed justly; for we receive the due reward of our deeds: but this man hath done nothing amiss.

ACTS OF PILATE, ch. 10.	LUKE, 23. 39 to 43.
After this. groaning, he said to Jesus, Lord, remember me when thou comest into thy kingdom.	42. And he said unto Jesus, Lord, remember me when thou comest into thy kingdom.
Jesus, answering, said unto him, Verily I say unto thee, to-day shalt thou be with me in paradise.	43. And Jesus said unto him, Verily I say unto thee, to-day shalt thou be with me in paradise.

The account in the compilation of Luke, is the shortest, and indicates a manuscript of greater antiquity than the Acts of Pilate. The accretion is in the latter gospel, which gives as additional circumstances, the names of the thieves, the crucifixion of Demas on the right hand and Gestas on the left hand of Jesus, and the groaning of Demas, before making his dying request.

In Mark and Matthew, both of the thieves revile Jesus.

Attention might here be called to the fact, that while there are older manuscripts concerning the crucifixion, etc., which found their way into the Gospel of Luke, the case is different with the miracles. The shortest, and, as there is reason to believe, the earliest accounts of these, are in the Acts of Pilate.

THE DARKNESS AT THE CRUCIFIXION.

ACTS OF PILATE, ch. 11.	LUKE, 23. 44, 45.
And it was about the sixth hour; and there was darkness over the whole earth until the ninth hour. And while the sun was eclipsed, etc.	44. And it was about the sixth hour, and there was a darkness over all the earth, until the ninth hour. 45. And the sun was darkened, etc.

In Mark and Matthew, it is stated, "There was darkness over all the land, until the ninth hour."

RENDING OF THE VAIL OF THE TEMPLE.

ACTS OF PILATE, ch. 11.	MATTHEW, 27. 51.
Behold, the vail of the temple was rent from the top to the bottom; and the rocks also were rent.	And behold, the vail of the temple was rent in twain from the top to the bottom; and the earth did quake, and the rocks rent.

In Matthew, there is the work of a later hand, which interpolated the earthquake. In Luke and Mark, there is only the rending of the vail.

RISING OF THE SAINTS.

ACTS OF PILATE, ch. 11.	MATTHEW, 27. 52, 53.
And the graves opened, and many bodies of saints who slept, arose.	52. And the graves were opened; and many bodies of the saints who slept, arose,
	53. And came out of the graves after his resurrection, and went into the holy city, and appeared unto many.

No such account in any of the other gospels. The interpolation by the author of Matthew, of the Acts of Pilate or of some common manuscript, is manifest. The whole of the 53d verse is accretion; and by a strange anachronism, though the author of Matthew has the graves opened by the earthquake, at the time of the crucifixion, and manifestly intends to represent their inhabitants as coming forth in consequence of that event, they do not arise until several days afterward.

Michaelis, Farrar, Dean Milman and others attribute this scene to the excited imaginations of some of the disciples.

THE DYING WORDS, AND DEATH OF JESUS.

ACTS OF PILATE, ch. 11.	MARK, 15. 34.
And about the ninth hour, Jesus cried out with a loud voice, Heli, Heli, lama, zabathani? Which interpreted, is, My God, my God, why hast thou forsaken me?	And at the ninth hour, Jesus cried with a loud voice, saying: Eloi, Eloi, lama sabachthani? Which is, being interpreted, My God, my God, why hast thou forsaken me?
	LUKE, 23. 46.
And after these things, Jesus said, Father, into thy hands I commend my spirit. And having said this, he gave up the ghost.	And when Jesus had cried with a loud voice, he said, Father, into thy hands I commend my spirit; and having said thus, he gave up the ghost.

SCENES AT THE CROSS AFTERWARD.

ACTS OF PILATE, ch. 11.	LUKE, 23. 47, 48.
The centurion, when he saw that Jesus, crying out, thus gave up the ghost, glorified God, and said: Of a truth, this was a just man.	47. Now when the centurion saw what was done, he glorified God, saying: Certainly this was a righteous man.
And all the people who stood by, were accordingly troubled at the sight, and reflecting upon what had passed, smote upon their breasts, and returned to the city of Jerusalem.	48. And all the people that came together to that sight, beholding the things which were done, smote their breasts, and returned.

In one of the canonical gospels, the centurion is made to say, "Truly this was the Son of God;" and in another, "Truly this man was the Son of God."

THE WOMEN AT THE CRUCIFIXION.

ACTS OF PILATE, ch. 11.	LUKE, 23, 49.
But all his acquaintances stood at a distance, as also the women who had followed him from Galilee; beholding these things.	And all his acquaintance, and the women who followed him from Galilee, stood afar off, beholding these things.

JOSEPH OF ARIMATHEA.

ACTS OF PILATE, ch. 11.	JOHN, 19. 38.
And, behold, a certain man of Arimathea, named Joseph, who	And after this, Joseph of Arimathea, being a disciple of Jesus,

ACTS OF PILATE, ch. 11.

also was a disciple of Jesus, but secretly for fear of the Jews, came to the governor, and entreated the governor, that he would permit him to take the body of Jesus from the cross. And the governor permitted it.

JOHN, 19. 38.

(but secretly for fear of the Jews) besought Pilate, that he might take away the body of Jesus; and Pilate gave (him) leave.
[Longer accounts in Luke and Mark.]

THE BURIAL OF JESUS.

ACTS OF PILATE, ch. 11.

And Nicodemus came, bringing

with him a mixture of myrrh and aloes, about a hundred pound weight.

And with tears, they took down Jesus from the cross, and bound him in linen clothes, with spices, according to the custom of burying among the Jews, and placed him in a new tomb, which Joseph had built and caused to be cut out of a rock; in which no man

had yet been placed; and they

rolled a great stone to the door of the sepulcher.

JOHN, 19. 39 to 41.

39. And there came also Nicodemus, (who, at the first, came to Jesus by night), and brought a mixture of myrrh and aloes, about a hundred pounds (weight.)

40. Then took they the body of Jesus, and wound it in linen clothes, with the spices, as the manner of the Jews is to bury.

41. Now, in the place where he was crucified, there was a garden;

and in the garden a new sepulcher wherein was never man yet laid.

42. There laid they Jesus, therefore, because of the Jews' preparation (day); for the sepulcher was nigh at hand.

MATTHEW, 27. 60.

And he rolled a great stone to the door of the sepulcher, and departed.

THE RESURRECTION OF JESUS.

ACTS OF PILATE, ch. 13.

And while they (the priests and rulers of the Jews assembled) were all wondering (at the miraculous escape of Joseph), behold, one of the soldiers who were guarding the sepulcher (of Jesus), spake in the synagogue, and said:

While we were guarding the sepulcher of Jesus, there was an earthquake; and we saw an angel of God, who rolled away the stone from the sepulcher, and sat upon it; and his countenance was like

MATTHEW, 28. 1 to 7.

In the end of the sabbath, as it began to dawn, toward the first (day) of the week, came Mary Magdalene, and the other Mary, to see the sepulcher.

2. And behold, there was a great earthquake; for the angel of the Lord descended from heaven, and came and rolled back the stone from the door, and sat upon it.

3. His countenance was like

ACTS OF PILATE, ch. 13.	MATTHEW, 28.
lightning, and his garment like snow; and we became through fear, as dead persons.	lightning, and his raiment white as snow.
And we heard the angel saying to the women at the sepulcher of Jesus, Fear not; I know that ye seek the crucified Jesus. He has risen, as he foretold. Come and behold the place where he was laid;	4. And for fear of him, the keepers did shake, and became as dead (men.)
	5. And the angel answered and said unto the women, Fear not ye; for I know that ye seek Jesus, who was crucified.
	6. He is not here; for he is risen, as he said. Come, see the place where the Lord lay.
and go quickly, and say to his disciples, He has risen from the dead, and will go before you into Galilee. There ye shall see him, as he told you.	7. And go quickly, and tell his disciples, that he is risen from the dead; and behold, he goeth before you into Galilee. There shall ye see him; lo, I have told you.

BRIBING THE SOLDIERS.

ACTS OF PILATE, ch. 13.	MATTHEW, 28. 11 to 15.
The Jews, hearing this, were afraid; and said among themselves, If by any means these things become public, everybody will believe in Jesus.	11. Now when they were going, behold, some of the watch came into the city, and showed unto the chief priests all the things that were done.
Then gathering a large sum of money, they gave it to the soldiers, saying: Tell the people, that while ye were sleeping, the disciples of Jesus came by night, and stole the body of Jesus. And if this should come to the ears of Pilate the governor, we will satisfy him, and secure you.	12. And when they were assembled with the elders, and had taken counsel, they gave large money unto the soldiers,
	13. Saying: Say ye, His disciples came by night and stole him (away,) while we slept.
	14. And if this come to the governor's ears, we will persuade him, and secure you.
The soldiers, accordingly, receiving the money, said as they were instructed by the Jews. And their report was spread abroad, among all the people.	15. So they took the money, and did as they were taught. And this saying is commonly reported among the Jews until this day.

The account in Matthew, which is most nearly parallel with the Acts of Pilate, differs from it in one very important feature. In the Acts of Pilate, the resurrection is only stated upon the report of the soldiers. In Matthew, it is related as a distinct narrative, on the authority of the historian himself; while the report of the soldiers is brought in afterward, as confirmatory testimony. But in the bribing of the soldiers, for the purpose of keeping the resurrection a secret, the narratives again run together.

The closing sentence in the Acts of Pilate, is,

"And their report was spread abroad, among all the people."

In Matthew it reads, "And this saying is common among the Jews, until this day."

The language of Matthew appears to be that of the later document.

THE ASCENSION OF JESUS.
ACTS OF PILATE, AND APPENDIX TO MARK.

It is generally agreed, that the last twelve verses of the Gospel of Mark, are an interpolation; a sort of appendix to the gospel, added by some transcriber.

There is the following parallel between the Acts of Pilate and a portion of this appendix:

ACTS OF PILATE, ch. 14.	MARK, ch. 16.
But a certain priest named Phineas, Ada, a schoolmaster, and a Levite named Ageus, they three came from Galilee to Jerusalem, and told the chief priests and all who were in the synagogues, saying: We have seen Jesus, whom you crucified, talking with his eleven disciples, and sitting in the midst of them on Mount Olivet, and saying to them:	14. Afterward, he appeared unto the eleven, as they sat at meat, and upbraided them with their unbelief, and hardness of heart, because they believed not them who had seen him after he was risen.

ACTS OF PILATE, ch. 14.

Go ye into all the world; preach to all nations; baptizing them in

the name of the Father, and the Son, and the Holy Spirit; and he who shall believe and be baptized, will be saved.

And when he had said these things to his disciples, we saw him ascending into heaven.

MARK, ch. 16.

15. And he said unto them, Go ye into all the world, and preach the gospel to every creature.

16. He that believeth and is baptized, shall be saved; but he that believeth not, shall be damned.

17. And these signs shall follow them that believe: In my name shall they cast out devils; they shall speak with new tongues.

18. They shall take up serpents; and if they drink any deadly thing, it shall not hurt them; they shall lay hands on the sick, and they shall recover.

19. So then, after the Lord had spoken unto them, he was received up into heaven, and sat on the right hand of God.

This parallel would indicate that the Acts of Pilate was antecedent to the gospel, since if it were subsequent, this portion of the Acts could not be accounted for; it not being in the original of Gospel of Mark.

In the Acts of Pilate, the narrative is continued in the following manner:

The chief priests, being alarmed at the news of the resurrection of Jesus, and his appearance to the Galileans, gave them money, and sent them back.

The Jews then assembled for consultation, and Annas and Caiaphas comforted them, saying:

"Why should we believe the soldiers who guarded the sepulcher of Jesus, telling us that an angel rolled away the stone from the door of the sepulcher? Perhaps his own disciples told them this, and gave them money, that they should declare these things; and that they, the disciples, might bear away the body of Jesus. Besides, consider this: That there is no credit to be given to the foreigners, because they also took a large sum from us, and have declared to all, according to the instructions we gave them. They have to maintain faith either to us, or to the disciples of Jesus."

The foregoing are all the parallels between the Acts of Pilate and the canonical gospels.

It is impossible not to perceive, that the narrative in the Acts of Pilate is more natural and consistent, and better sustained throughout.

In LUKE, there is a preliminary trial before Herod; who has Jesus arrayed in a gorgeous robe, and sent back to Pilate. Then, after the trial, he is taken to execution, addressing the women by the way. After the mocking and deriding, the dividing of the raiment, etc., and the inscription on the cross, the historian gives the prayer of Jesus for his enemies. Then the scene between the two thieves on the cross, and between one of them and Jesus. It is stated that the sun was darkened at the cruci- fixion. After describing the other scenes in a man- ner somewhat similar to the other synoptics, the author of this gospel states that on the first day of the week, early in the morning, the women who came with him from Galilee, came to the sepulcher, bringing spices, etc., for the purpose of embalming the body of Jesus. They found the stone rolled away, and the sepulcher empty. They then saw two men, clothed in shining garments, who told them Jesus had risen, and reminded them of his words, that he should rise the third day. Then Peter went, and saw the grave empty. Jesus after- ward appeared to the two disciples, on their way to Emmaus, and to the eleven apostles, at Jerusalem. Then, leading them to Bethany, he blessed them, and ascended into heaven.

In MARK, Jesus is delivered to Pilate, directly, by the chief priests, who, after holding a consultation with the elders and scribes, and with the council, had apprehended and bound Jesus; nothing being said about the examination before Herod. Then follows the trial or examination, before Pilate—the clamor of the Jews—the show of resistance and final yielding by Pilate—scenes on the way to the crucifixion, and at the cross, differing from Luke, in various details, with which the reader is familiar. Then, after the death and burial of Jesus, when the sabbath was past, three women, whose names are mentioned, went with spices, to anoint him. They found the stone rolled away, and entering into the sepulcher, they saw a young man, sitting, clothed in a long white garment. He told them Jesus had gone into Galilee. Jesus then appeared, first to Mary Magdalene, after that to the two disciples. Then to the eleven, as they sat at meat. Then follows the remainder of the spurious appendix.

In MATTHEW, the author relates nearly all the incidents given in Luke and Mark, concerning the crucifixion, and several of his own besides. He has two earthquakes, and many other incidents, unknown to the other synoptics. After the death and burial, the two Marys came to the sepulcher; there they saw one who is now represented as the angel who had rolled away the stone from the sepulcher. He stated, also, that Jesus had gone into Galilee. Jesus appeared to the women, as they were returning.   He then appeared to the eleven, on a mountain in Galilee.

The narrative in JOHN differs still, in many particulars, from all three of the synoptics; not only omitting many incidents, but adding important additional matter, not always consistent with the other accounts.   Among such might be mentioned much that Jesus said to Pilate, sayings of Jesus on the cross, etc., the piercing of his side; the scene with Thomas after the resurrection; the appearance of Jesus, after that event, to the fishermen on the Sea of Tiberias, and the miraculous draft of fishes, which are manifestly confounded with scenes in Christ's ministry.

If we turn to the narrative of all these events, as found in the Acts of Pilate, while there is sufficient that is marvelous, there will be found, nevertheless, a degree of unity and consistency, which is wanting in the other gospels.

In the first place, there is the trial before Pilate; and in the language of Bishop Ellicott, the Jews "heaping up indiscriminate accusation;" "an eager ferocity on their part, met" at first "by a steady and almost indignant scorn on the part of the governor." At the same time, "the weeping populace; the appearance of witnesses in favor of the accused." These witnesses testify to many miracles Jesus had wrought, hoping thereby to save his life.

All this having failed, Pilate, overborne by the Jews, passes sentence on Jesus; something quite natural in a judicial proceeding, but which is entirely omitted in the other gospels, except that in Luke it is stated, that Pilate gave sentence that it should be as the Jews required.

Then Jesus is taken to execution. The scenes at the cross are stated briefly, and in natural order.

Coming to the resurrection, we find it related on the report of the soldiers. The appearance of Jesus was to the Galileans and to Joseph of Arimathea.

When considered in reference to the length of the accounts, it will be found that the narratives in the Acts of Pilate are generally, though not invariably, shorter than those in the canonical gospels.

Upon the whole, we may reasonably conclude, that the older gospels—those of the first century—contained fragmentary accounts of the crucifixion ; that these were first put together, in a connected form, in the Acts of Pilate, to which there was added, for the first time, the material resurrection. This event, at first stated at second hand, as coming from the soldiers, was afterward incorporated into the canonical gospels, as a part of the principal narrative.

CHAPTER XVII.

OTHER EXTANT GOSPELS.

HISTORY OF JOSEPH THE CARPENTER—NARRATIVE OF JO-
SEPH OF ARIMATHEA—PSEUDO MATTHEW — THE SUPPOSED
GOSPEL OF THE NATIVITY OF MARY—LETTER OF PONTIUS
PILATE—REPORT OF PILATE—THE GIVING UP OF PONTIUS
PILATE—AVENGING OF THE SAVIOR—THE NEWLY DISCOVERED
ACTS OF PILATE.

The remaining extant gospels must be considered
very briefly; since none of them have fully established their claims to the great antiquity accorded
to those which have been examined. As a part of
the literature connected with the early history of the
Christian religion, they cannot be passed unno-
ticed.

HISTORY OF JOSEPH THE CARPENTER.—Tischendorf thinks this
gospel was written in the fourth century. There is no reason for
placing it earlier. The early fathers knew nothing of it.

It purports to be a discourse of Jesus Christ himself to his disciples, on the mount of Olives, in which he relates to them the history
of his father, Joseph.

He speaks of the former marriage of Joseph, and the death of his
first wife; his marriage to the virgin Mary. Says she brought up
James, one of the sons of Joseph's former wife; whence she was called
the mother of James. Refers to the birth at Bethlehem, the flight to
Egypt and return. Joseph lived to be 111 years old. A large part of

the gospel is occupied in a minute and affecting account of the scenes attending the death of Joseph.

The last part of the narrative is as follows:

"Having thus spoken, I embraced the body of my father Joseph, and wept over it; and they opened the door of the tomb, and placed his body in it, near the body of his father Jacob. And at the time when he fell asleep, he had fulfilled a hundred and eleven years. Never did a tooth in his mouth hurt him, nor was his eyesight rendered less sharp, nor his body bent, nor his strength impaired: but he worked at his trade of a carpenter, to the very last day of his life; and that was the six-and-twentieth of the month of Ahib."

This having been related to the apostles, they rose up and prostrated themselves, making an address to Jesus, to which he replied, referring to the prophecies, and to the return into the world of Enoch and Elias, etc.

NARRATIVE OF JOSEPH OF ARIMATHEA.— The full title of the gospel is,

"*The Narrative of Joseph of Arimathea, that begged the Lord's Body; in which also he brings in the Cases of the Two Robbers.*"

It is not known when it was written. It was popular in the middle ages.

It is based upon the Gospel of Nicodemus, or the Acts of Pilate. The narrative in the Acts is closely followed. But Judas charges Jesus with stealing the law from the temple, and betrays him. Judas was son of the brother of Caiaphas the priest. Trial of Jesus, and crucifixion with the thieves.

In the incidents taken from the Acts of Pilate, there is the customary accretion. For instance, the thief says to Jesus:

"Before, then, O Lord, my spirit departs, order my sins to be washed away, and remember me, the sinner, in thy kingdom, when upon the great, most lofty throne, thou shalt judge the twelve tribes of Israel."

This sentence is sufficient evidence, that the composition of the book was subsequent to the second century. The law of accretion is also aptly illustrated in the address of the other thief on the cross:

"If thou art the Christ, come down from the cross, that I may believe thee. But now I see thee perishing along with me, not like a man, but like a wild beast."

The gospel contains original matter, also, of a wonderful and startling character.

PSEUDO MATTHEW.—A mere compilation of portions of the Gospel

of the Infancy, with such accretions as may be expected after two
hundred years.

There is reason to believe that it did not appear much before the
time of Jerome. Some have thought it to have been the publication
of Seleucas, alluded to in the correspondence between Jerome and the
bishops. Others have thought it to have been the translation which
Jerome made at the request of the bishops. But that, as will be seen,
was another document.

THE SUPPOSED GOSPEL OF THE NATIVITY OF
MARY.—In all the collections of apocryphal gospels,
will be found a Gospel of the Birth of Mary. It is
sometimes spoken of as among the most ancient.

We are satisfied that there was anciently no such
gospel; that its supposed existence is based upon a
misapprehension. The facts are these:

In the works of Jerome is found a correspondence
between him and two bishops, named Chromatius
and Heliodorus. The bishops, addressing their
beloved brother and presbyter, Jerome, state that
they had found in some apocryphal books, "an
account of the birth of the Virgin Queen Mary, as
also the birth and infancy of our Lord and Savior
Jesus Christ;" in which they had observed many
things contrary to their faith. They say they had
heard that he (Jerome) had found a volume in
Hebrew, written in St. Matthew the Evangelist's
own hand, "in which was described the infant state
of the Virgin Mary and our Savior." They therefore entreat him to translate it out of Hebrew into
Latin; that they may know what the famous things
concerning Christ were and to refute the heretics,
who had mixed other things "with the genuine history of the Savior's nativity."

Jerome replies, saying it was a difficult task which they had imposed on him,

"Because the holy apostle and evangelist Matthew did not himself wish to have it written for the public; [nec voluit in aperto conscribi.] For if it was not to have been a secret, he would certainly have annexed it to his own gospel which he published.

"But he composed this little book in Hebrew letters, [sed fecit hunc libellum Hebraicis literis obsignatum,] which he so published, in order that this book might be in the hands of religious men, written in his own hand, in Hebrew characters; [ex manu ipsius scriptus Hebraicis literis.] They have transmitted it from preceding to subsequent times. They have taken care, however, never to have it translated by any one, and have given different accounts of its contents; textus ejus aliter atque aliter narraverunt.

"But the truth is, that the book was published by a certain Manichæan disciple, Seleucas by name, who also composed a false history of the Acts of the Apostles."

He speaks of the publication as injurious, and not to be listened to by the church. He then accedes to their request.

In another epistle, he says he will translate it "as well as he can remember;" [in quantum recordari possum ;] and notifies them, that not only will the translation be not literal, but that he will feel at liberty to wander considerably from the original. He says he will translate, following the meaning rather than the words, saying only "what has been written, or what may be supposed consistently, to have been written;" [et non alia dicam, quam quae aut scripta sunt ibi, aut consequenter scribi potuerunt ;] "sometimes walking in the same path with the author, though not in the same steps ; and though sometimes turning a little one side, returning the same way again," (nunc eadam semita non iisdem vestgiis incedens, nunc quibusdam diverticulis, et eandem viam recurrens).

It will be noticed that nowhere in the correspondence is either the gospel which the bishops had seen,
or the one which Jerome claimed to have seen in
Matthew's handwriting, spoken of as a Gospel of
the Birth or Nativity of Mary only, but in connection with the Infancy of the Savior.

Jerome proceeded to make his translation, but the
publisher of his works, for some reason, omitted
the last part, and published only that relating to
the birth and infancy of Mary. This was placed
after the correspondence, and the whole was entitled "De Nativitate Mariæ;" indicating that all
that followed, was concerning the nativity of Mary.
The translation was only what Jerome remembered
of the Gospels of the Infancy; he having probably
seen a version purer than that published by Seleucas.

The translation, under the very wide latitude
which the pious father had given himself, doubtless
differed from any version of those gospels which
had previously been seen. Hence it was thought
to be a new gospel; an impression which was
strengthened by the title placed by Jerome's publisher before the correspondence; "De Nativitate
Mariæ."

This view of the matter is confirmed by the historical evidence. The first writers who refer to this
gospel, are Epiphanius and Gregory Nyssen, both
of whom were contemporary with Jerome. Neither
of these writers speak of it as "the Gospel of the
Birth of Mary," but as "De Nativitate Mariæ."[1]

(1.) See Epiphanius, Hæres. 26. Gnost. No. 12, and Hæres. 79. Collyr. No. 5.
Also Gregory Nyssen, Hom. de Nativ. S. Mari. Vir. tom. 3. Opp. p. 346.

LETTER OF PONTIUS PILATE.—This letter may be seen in translation from Latin and Greek manuscripts, the date of which is uncertain. The Greek text is given in "The Acts of Peter and Paul."

There is a discussion between the Emperor Nero, Peter, and Simon Magus. Peter appeals to the writings of Pontius Pilate, sent to Claudius. Nero orders them to be brought and read, which was done. The letter stated,

That the fathers of the Jews had promised, that God would send Jesus from heaven, who should be their king, and he should come to earth by means of a virgin. That he came into Judea, and was enlightening the blind, cleansing lepers, healing paralytics, expelling demons from men, raising the dead, subduing the winds, walking upon the waves of the sea, and doing many other wonders. That the Jews seized him and delivered him up to Pilate, who, after scourging him, gave him up to their will. That they crucified him, but Jesus rose on the third day, while the soldiers of Pilate were guarding him. That the Jews bribed the soldiers. That the soldiers could not keep silence, and had testified that they had seen Jesus after he was risen.

Another and probably older form of this letter is in one version of the Acts of Pilate. It is not materially different.

REPORT OF PILATE.—There are two forms of this in the Greek. It is similar to the foregoing. It enlarges upon the miracles, and is written in a more fervid style.

It is possible that some ancient form of the letter or Report, was the original from which the Acts of Pilate, or the first part of the Gospel of Nicodemus, was constructed. In their present form the letter and Report are manifestly of a later date.

THE GIVING UP OF PONTIUS PILATE.—Cæsar, filled with rage at what had happened, sent soldiers, and ordered them to bring Pilate a prisoner. When brought to Rome, he was arraigned for what he had done.

While Cæsar was addressing Pilate, when he named the name of Christ, all the multitude of Gods fell down in a body. Pilate making his defense, and throwing the blame on the Jews, Cæsar sent, and had "all the nation of the Jews" seized. He ordered Pilate to be beheaded. Pilate prayed to the Lord, and received assurances that he should be blessed, because under him the prophecies had been fulfilled.

When he was beheaded, an angel of the Lord received his head. His wife Procla, seeing this, filled with joy, immediately gave up the ghost, and was buried with her husband.

THE DEATH OF PILATE.—A variation of the foregoing.

Tiberius Cæsar, emperor, had a disease, and sent for Jesus to come and cure him. The messenger, on arriving in Palestine, found that Christ had been crucified. But on his journey, he met Veronica, who lent him the cloth on which was impressed an image of the Savior, which, she said, would cure Cæsar.

"Cæsar therefore ordered the way to be strewn with silk cloths, and the picture to be presented to him. As soon as he had looked upon it, he regained his former health."

Pilate was brought to Rome, where the emperor was furious against him. But Pilate appearing before him in the seamless tunic which Jesus had worn, all the anger of Tiberius at once disappeared.

Having been condemned to die a disgraceful death, Pilate killed himself with his own knife. His body was bound to a great mass, and sunk in the River Tiber.

"But malignant and filthy spirits, in his malignant and filthy body, all rejoicing together, kept moving themselves in the waters, and in a terrible manner, brought lightnings and tempests, thunders and hail-storms, in the air, so that all men were kept in horrible fear." Wherefore the Romans, driving him out of the Tiber, carried him to Vienna, and sunk him in the River Rhone. "But there evil spirits were present, working the same things in the same place. Those men, therefore, not enduring such a visitation of demons, removed from themselves that vessel of malediction, and sent him to be buried in the territory of Losania. And they, seeing that they were troubled by the aforesaid visitations, removed him from themselves, and sunk him in a certain pit, surrounded by mountains; where, to this day, according to the account of some, certain diabolical machinations are said to bubble up."

THE AVENGING OF THE SAVIOR.—There are, in this document, two distinct legends: one of Veronica, the other, that of Nathan's embassy.

In the days of Tiberius Cæsar, Titus, a prince under Tiberius, in Equitania, was afflicted with a cancer in his face. And Tiberius was ill, and full of ulcers and fevers, having nine kinds of leprosy. Nathan was sent from Judea, to carry a treaty to Rome. He tells about Christ, his miracles, his crucifixion and his resurrection. Titus addresses Tiberius strongly in condemnation of the Jews who had slain Jesus. Whereupon the wound fell from the face of Titus, "and his flesh and his face were restored to health. And all the sick who were in the same place, were made whole, in that hour." He then sent for

Vespasian, who brought five thousand armed men. With them they went and made war on the Jews for killing Jesus.

Jerusalem was taken with great slaughter. A search was made, and Veronica was found, who had the portrait of Jesus.   When the emperor saw the portrait, he was immediately cured.   And all the blind, the lepers, and those affected in divers ways, were healed.

Nathan then came forward, and baptized Tiberius, who ascended his throne, and publicly returned thanks to God.

THE NEWLY DISCOVERED ACTS OF PILATE. — A learned German, while traveling in Missouri, some years ago, became the guest of a clergyman by the name of W. D. Mahan, at Boonville.   In conversation, he mentioned to this clergyman, that he had seen, in the Vatican Library, at Rome, the original Acts of Pilate.

After the German had left, Mr. Mahan, deeming the matter of great importance, wrote to him, in Europe, and at considerable expense, had the manuscript copied. He then published it, with the correspondence.

Afterward, the same document was published, under an arrangement with the proprietor, by Rev. George Sluter, A. M., of the Presbyterian Synod of Missouri.

The publication is preceded by a statement of the discovery and procuring of the document; an introduction, giving the references to the Acts of Pilate by Justin Martyr and Tertullian, and the subsequent comments of Eusebius.   The volume contains, also, remarks and critical notes.

Without doubt, these clergymen are acting in good faith, and think they have obtained the orig-

inal Acts of Pilate. There is none the less doubt
that they are mistaken. One sentence alone is sufficient to show that the document published by
them is of comparatively modern date ; if indeed
the whole affair is not an imposition upon them,
by some astute adventurers.

When Pilate requested Jesus to be more circum-
spect in his language, while discoursing to the Jews,
he is represented in this document, as replying to
Pilate, as follows :

"Say to the torrent, Stop in the midst of the mountain home, because it will uproot the trees of the valley."—[Page 55, Sluter's Ed.

This, with considerable more of the same sort, is
sufficient, without taking time with other reasons,
to brand the document, not only as a forgery, but
as a modern, and a vulgar one. Any person of
but a small degree of literary skill, would have
come nearer to the simple and impressive style of
Jesus. "Brief and concise utterances," says Justin Martyr, "fell from him, for he was no sophist,
but his word was the power of God."

CHAPTER XVIII.

WRITERS OF THE THIRD PERIOD.

MENANDER—SATURNINUS—BASILIDES—PRODICUS—ARISTI-
DES—QUADRATUS—BARNABAS—AGRIPPA CASTOR — ARISTION
—JOHN THE PRESBYTER. — ANONYMOUS WRITINGS. — PRO-
VERBS OF XYSTAS—PREACHING AND DOCTRINE OF PETER—
TESTIMONY OF THE TWELVE PATRIARCHS—SIBYLLINE ORACLES
—PREACHING OF PAUL—SYRIAC DOCUMENTS.

Most of the Christian writers of the second century who immediately succeeded the apostolic fathers, advocated doctrines which were afterward considered heretical.

"Heresy," says Dr. Lardner, "in Greek, *hairesis*, signifies election,
or choice; and is used for any opinion which a man chooseth as best,
or more probable."—[Works, vol. 4, p. 505.

Menander, Saturninus and Basilides, are generally classed together, by the orthodox fathers, and
their heresies considered in the order here named.

MENANDER,—A. D. 120,

Is said to have been the fellow countryman and
disciple of Simon Magus.[1]   This is denied, however, by some.   He is said to have aspired to the
honor of being a Messiah, and one of the Æons,

(1.) Westcott Canon, p. 252.

sent from the pleroma, or celestial regions, to suc-
cor souls oppressed by the demons of earth.   He
had a form of baptism in his own name.   His influence continued for several centuries.   He was
written against by Justin Martyr, by Irenæus, Eusebius, and several others.   Justin speaks of him
as follows:

"And a man, Menander, also a Samaritan, of the town of Cappare-
tæa, a disciple of Simon, and inspired by devils, we know to have deceived many, while he was in Antioch, by his magical art.   He persuaded those who adhered to him, that they should never die.   And
even now, there are some living, who hold this opinion of his."
—[Apology, 1. 25.

SATURNINUS,—A. D. 125.

Saturninus, like Menander, held that there was
one Father, unknown to all, who made angels,
archangels, principalities and powers.   He said the
world and all things therein were made by a company of seven angels.   The Savior, he taught to be
unbegotten and incorporeal; and that he was a
man in appearance only.   "He says that marriage
and generation are of Satan." [1]

BASILIDES,—A. D. 125,

Was a Gnostic of Alexandria.   Is said to have
written a commentary, in 24 books, on "The Gospel."   This was refuted by Agrippa Castor.

Fragments of his writings are given by Hippolytus, who wrote in the third century.   They have
caused much discussion in reference to the gospel
upon which he commented; whether it was in writing, and whether his own or another's.

(1.) Irenæus, adv. Hær. lib. 1, c. 24.

He made use of "The traditions of Matthias ;" or, as Miller supposes, the traditions of Matthew. These "claimed to be grounded on private intercourse with the Savior.'' [1] They were, possibly, the much talked of Oracles of Matthew.

The fact that Basilides made use of such a collection, is significant, and may go far to explain the source of many of the sayings of Christ, so often quoted by the fathers before Irenæus, and which have been supposed to be evidence of the existence of the canonical gospels.

Some have claimed Basilides as a witness to the four gospels, more particularly to Luke. The arguments upon which the claim is based, are vague and unsatisfactory. Perhaps it will be sufficient, upon this question, to take the judgment of Dr. Davidson. He says :

"As to Basilides, his supposed quotations from the New Testament, in Hippolytus, are too precarious to be trusted."—[Canon, p. 86. See also his Introduction to the N. T., vol 2, p. 388.

Any apparent use of Luke may be explained by the fact, that Basilides had access to the same manuscripts from which the Gospels of Marcion and Luke were compiled.

DOCTRINES.—"Basilides," says Irenæus, "that he may appear to have discovered something more sublime and plausible, gives an immense development to his doctrines. He sets forth that Nous was first born of the unborn Father; that from him again was born Logos, from Logos Phronesis, from Phronesis Sophia and Dynamis; and from Dynamis and Sophia, the powers and principalities, and angels, whom he calls the *first;* and that by them the first heaven was made. Then other powers, being formed by emanation from these, created another heaven, similar to the first," etc.

(1.) Westcott, Canon, p. 264.

The chief of the angels who occupy the lowest heaven, is the God of the Jews, and he and his angels created the world.

That Jesus himself was not crucified, but Simon of Cyrene, who bore the cross, and assumed the form of Jesus. Salvation belongs to the soul alone, for the body is by nature subject to corruption.—[Irenæus adv. Hæres. bk. 1, ch. 24. Ante Nic. vol. 5, p. 90.

Eusebius makes the doubtful statement, that like Pythagoras, Basilides enjoined upon his followers, a silence of five years.[1] A gospel is attributed to him. But this is thought to be the same as the commentaries.

PRODICUS.—A. D. 120.

But little is known of this writer, except that he was leader of a sect called Prodiceans; and that they were accused, by Clement of Alexandria, of licentious practices.

"They say," says Clement, "they are by nature the children of the supreme deity; but they dishonor their high birth and freedom; for they live as they choose, and they choose to live in pleasure. They scorn to be controlled, as being lords of the sabbath, and the King's children."—[Clem. Alex. Str. 3. 4.

They also held that prayer was needless.[2]

They did not separate themselves from the Christian churches.

The followers of Prodicus boasted of having the secret books of Zoroaster.[3]

Baring-Gould thinks they may have used the Gospel of Philip.[4]

(1.) Ecclesiastical History, 4. 7; attributing it to Agrippa Castor.
(2.) Stromata, 7. 7.
(3.) Strom. 1. 15.
(4.) Lost and Hostile Gospels, p. 293.

ARISTIDES AND QUADRATUS.—A. D. 126.

They delivered to the Emperor Hadrian, Apologies for the Christian Religion. That of Quadratus is said to have procured the Rescript of the emperor to Minucius, in favor of the Christians.

Eusebius says that this was in circulation among the brethren, and that he had a copy of it. He gives an extract, in which there is reference to the miracles of Christ.[1] If we could rely upon the correctness of the statement, this might be recorded as the earliest historical reference to the miracles of Jesus.

The same historian, speaking of Quadratus and others, "who held the first rank in the apostolic succession," makes a statement, by which he manifestly intends to leave the impression, that the canonical gospels were in circulation at that time. He says:

"Afterwards, leaving their country, they performed the office of evangelists to those who had not yet heard the faith, whilst with a noble ambition to proclaim Christ, they also delivered to them the books of the holy gospels."—[Ecc. Hist. 3. 37.

Westcott, after speaking of the apologies of Quadratus and Aristides, says: "Nothing, it will be seen, can be drawn directly from these scanty notices, in support of the Canon."[2]

BARNABAS.—About A. D. 130.

The Epistle of Barnabas is often classed among the writings of the apostolic fathers. There is much

(1.) Ecc. Hist. 4. 3.
(2.) Canon, p. 76.

difference of opinion as to its date, but those writers who place it after A. D. 120, comprise a large majority.

The ancient fathers of the church held it in high esteem, and attributed it to Barnabas, the companion of Paul. Such was the opinion of Clement of Alexandria.[1] Origen called it a "catholic epistle," and ranked it among the sacred scriptures.[2]

In the introduction to the epistle, in the Anti-Nicene Collection, it is stated, the ancients unanimously attribute it to Barnabas the Levite, of apostolic times.

"Certainly," says the editor, "no other name is even hinted at in Christian antiquity, as that of the writer."[3] The editor is equally explicit in asserting, that scarcely any scholars now ascribe it to the illustrious friend and companion of St. Paul. What a commentary upon the credit to be given to the opinions of the fathers, upon such questions!

THE GOSPELS.—Some writers have supposed they saw in this epistle, evidence of the use of the canonical gospels. It is not, however, much relied upon. The reader will remember the verdict of Dr. Less, upon this subject.

Dr. Davidson says he has apparently a citation from Matthew, but it is uncertain.[4]

Dr. Westcott, speaking of this class of evidence, says :

(1.) Strom. 2. 6; 2, 7, etc.
(2.) Contra Celsum, 1. 63, Comm. in Rom. 1. 24.
(3.)Ante. Nic. vol. 1, p. 99, et seq.
(4.) Canon, p. 94.

"References in the sub-apostolic age, to the discourses or actions of our Lord, as we find them recorded in the gospels, show, so far as they go, that what the gospels relate was then held to be true; but it does not necessarily follow that they were already in use, and were the actual source of the passages in question."—[Canon, p. 49.

THE MIRACLES.—In the 5th chapter of the Epistle of Barnabas, is the first reference to the miracles of Christ; if we except those in the apocryphal gospels, which appeared about the same time. Speaking of Jesus, he says:

"Morever, teaching Israel, and doing such great miracles and signs, [*Peras ge toi dedaskon ton Israel, kai peelikauta terata kai seemeia toion*], he preached the truth to him, and greatly loved him."

AGRIPPA CASTOR.—A. D. 130.

According to Eusebius, Agrippa Castor wrote books against Basilides.[1] Eusebius says he was one of the most distinguished writers of that day.[2]

These, with many other writings of the kind, are lost or destroyed. It was a natural source of information, and would have disclosed, almost certainly, the nature of the gospels or other writings used by Basilides.

It is somewhat remarkable, that all the writings of the second century which would have furnished the most direct evidence as to the gospels then in use, have perished.

ARISTION.—About A. D. 130.

It might be inferred from a passage in Eusebius, that Aristion had preserved written traditions of

[1] Ecclesiastical History, 4. 7.
[2] See also Jerome, Catal. Script. c. 20.

the time of Christ. Speaking of Papias, he says :

"He moreover hands down, in his own writing, other narratives given him by the previously mentioned Aristion, of the Lord's sayings, and the traditions of the presbyter John."—[Ecc. Hist. 3. 29.

A fair inference would be that these "narratives" were in writing ; as they are distinguished from the "traditions" of the presbyter.

JOHN THE PRESBYTER,—About A. D. 130,

Is supposed by some, to have written the Revelation.   This was the opinion of Eusebius.[1]

He is also, not without reason, believed to have been the author of the epistles of John.   It will be noticed that in the 2d and 3d of these epistles, the writer styles himself "the elder," or presbyter.

The theory that he wrote the Gospel of John, has less plausibility ; since there is no sufficient evidence of its existence, until about half a century later.

ANONYMOUS WRITINGS.

There are also some anonymous writings, belonging to the third period, which will be briefly considered.

THE PROVERBS OF XYSTAS.

Written, about A. D. 119. The genuineness of the book is doubted by Westcott and others. Ewald places it among the most valuable relics of early Christian literature.—[Gott. Gel. Anz. 1859, p. 261; and Gesch. 7. 321.

Westcott says it contains no definite references to the New Testament.—[Hist. Canon, p. 174.

(1.) Ecc. Hist. 3. 39.

THE PREACHING, AND DOCTRINE OF PETER.

These books were well known in the second century.

The Preaching of Peter was condemned by Eusebius, in the same language used in reference to the Gospel of Peter. He pronounced it a forgery, and stated that none of the ancients, nor any ecclesiastical writers had taken testimonies from it.—[Ecc. H. 3. 3.

On the contrary, it is referred to by Heracleon, A. D. 190, according to Origen, (Tom. 1, in Joan, p. 211), and repeatedly by Clement of Alexandria. — [Stromata, 1. 29; 2. 15; 6. 5; 6. 6, and 6. 15.]   Also by Lactantius; all before Eusebius.   Clement took numerous testimonies from it, and endorsed it in the most emphatic manner; declaring that Christ said to his disciples, what he is reported to have said, in the Preaching of Peter.—[Strom. 6. 6.

It was also referred to in the epistle of Peter to James, published by Cotelerius.—[See Ante-Nic. Ch. Lib. vol. 17, p. 1.

The book was subsequently cited by Theodotus, Byzantius, and Gregory Nazianzen, of the ancients, and among the moderns has been very favorably spoken of by Dr. Grabe, Mr. Toland, Mr. Whiston, Dr. Mill, and others.

The Doctrine of Peter was a small book, in use in the 2d century, of which little is now known. It was referred to and condemned by Origen. From him we learn that it contained the same passage which Jerome says was in the Gospel of the Hebrews, in which Christ says to those who were with Peter, "Lay hold, handle me, and see that I am not an incorporeal spirit."—[Origen, de Princip. Præf. sec. 8.

TESTAMENTS OF THE TWELVE PATRIARCHS.

Supposed to have been written, about A. D. 125.   The character of the book is indicated by the title.   Each of the sons of Jacob gives his dying testimony on some important subject.—"The Testament of Reuben concerning Thoughts;" "The Testament of Simeon concerning envy;" etc.

Dr. Lardner thought he discovered in it some slight evidence of the use of some of the canonical gospels. Nothing better illustrates the dearth of evidence, than the necessity of searching for it in a document of this kind.

THE SIBYLLINE ORACLES

Belong properly to an earlier age, but are supposed to have been interpolated about this time, in order to furnish additional evidence for the Christian religion.   They were extensively quoted, from Justin

Martyr down; though the quotations of Justin have reference, for the most part, to the utterances of the ancient sibyl.

THE PREACHING OF PAUL.

This, as well as the Preaching of Peter, was referred to by Lactantius and others, and was generally known in the second century. It contained references to the Sibylline writings. Also to the fire in Jordan, at the time of the baptism of Jesus.—[See Anonymous Treatise on Re-Baptism, Ante-Nicene, vol. 13, p. 426.

It has been favorably referred to by Cardinal Baronius, Dr. Grabe, and others. Sixtus Senensis believed it to have been written by Paul. —[Bib. Sanc. lib. 2, p. 113.

SYRIAC DOCUMENTS.

The late Dr. Cureton found among the Syriac manuscripts of the British Museum, several documents purporting to have been written in the first and second centuries.—[See 20th volume of Ante-Nicene Collection.

They are full of mistakes and anachronisms, and cannot be considered of much value.—[Consult "Revelations of Anti-Christ;" Boston and N. Y. 1879; an able work, but written in an objectionable style.

FORTY YEARS OF CHRISTIAN WRITERS.

CHAPTER XIX.

FIRST HALF OF FOURTH PERIOD.—A. D. 130 TO 150.]

CARPOCRATES—EPIPHANES—CERDO—HERMAS—CERINTHUS
—ISIDORUS—VALENTINUS—PAPIAS—EPISTLE TO DIOGNETUS
—THE CLEMENTINES.

CARPOCRATES.—About A. D. 135.

Irenæus, in his first book against Heresies, writes
as follows:

"Carpocrates, again, and his followers, maintain that the world and
the things which are therein, were created by angels greatly inferior
to the unbegotten Father. They also hold that Jesus was the son of
Joseph, and was just like other men, with the exception that he differed from them in this respect, that inasmuch as his soul was stead-
fast and pure, he perfectly remembered those things which he had
witnessed within the sphere of the unbegotten God. On this account,
a power descended upon him from the Father, that by means of it, he
might escape from the creators of the world."

After enlarging upon this idea, and stating that
they believe the human soul, which is like that of
Christ, can rise above the creators of the world, he
says:

"This idea has raised them to such a pitch of pride, that some of them declare themselves similar to Jesus; while others, still more mighty, maintain that they are superior to his disciples, such as Peter and Paul, and the rest of the apostles, whom they consider to be in no respect inferior to Jesus."

He then charges them with practicing magical arts and incantations; of using philters and love potions; of having recourse to familiar spirits, dream-sending demons, "and other abominations;" and of leading a licentious life.[1]

Dr. Lardner thinks the charge of licentiousness a slander.[2]

Clement of Alexandria speaks of Carpocrates and Epiphanes as both advocating a community of wives. Clement argues against it in the second chapter of the third book of the Stromata.[3]

EPIPHANES,—About A. D. 140,

Was the son of Carpocrates, and was, like his father, a Gnostic. He believed in an infinite, eternal principle. It is ignorance and passion, which, in disturbing the equality and community of goods, have introduced evil into the world. The idea of property forms no part of the divine plan. All unequal laws should be abolished, and equality should be re-established. He is reported to have advocated the community of wives, as well as of the fruits of the earth.

He died at the early age of seventeen years.

A temple was consecrated to him in Cappadocia,

(1.) Adv. Hær. 1. 25.   Ante-Nic. vol. 5, p. 93.

(2.) Lard. Works, vol. 4, p. 562.

(3.) Ante-Nic. vol. 12, p. 86.

and according to Clement of Alexandria, he was honored as a god.[1]

CERDO OR CERDON.—About A. D. 140.

Cerdon, also, was a Gnostic. Irenæus says he came to Rome from Syria, in the time of Hyginus. His views were adopted and amplified by Marcion. Like Marcion, he is accused of mutilating the Gospel of Luke; and with as little reason. [See "Marcion."]

HERMAS.—A. D. 145.

Hermas, like Barnabas, is often classed with the apostolic fathers. He is, however, placed after 120, by a large majority of writers, and most of them date his works near the middle of the second century.

The authorship of the Pastor or Shepherd of Hermas, as stated in the Muratorian Fragment, is generally accepted. "The Pastor, moreover," says the Fragment, "did Hermas write, very recently, in our times, in the city of Rome, while his brother, Bishop Pius, sat in the chair, in the church of Rome."

According to the "Handbuch der Kirchengeschichte," a work extensively used as a text book among Catholics, Pius was Bishop from A. D. 142 to 157.

This, which may now be considered the settled verdict of scholars as to the authorship of the Pastor,

(1.) Stromata, bk. 3, ch. 2.

by no means accords with the opinions of the fathers.

With them, Hermas, the author of the Shepherd, was the Hermas of apostolic times. Origen distinctly ascribes the Shepherd to the Hermas mentoned in the Epistle to the Romans.[1] This is favored by Eusebius,[2] and by Jerome.[3]

The early writers considered it an inspired book.

Irenæus quotes it as scripture.[4] Clemens Alexandrinus thought it divinely inspired.[5] It was read in the churches as scripture.

Here we have the same phenomenon as in the case of the Epistle of Barnabas. A work universally attributed to a co-worker and companion of Paul, which modern scholars of all shades of religious opinion concur in deciding was never written by him, nor even in that century. In view of such facts, it is impossible not to perceive that the books finally admitted into the canon, were selected with reference to their contents, rather than to any question of authenticity, or of proof of apostolic origin.

The Shepherd of Hermas was one of the most popular books among the Christians of the second century.

About the year 494, it was condemned in the de-

(1.) Comment. in Rom. 16. 14; lib. 10, 31. Origen there states that he thinks it divinely inspired.

(2.) Ecce. Hist. 3. 3.   (3.) De Viris Illust. c. 10.

(4.) Adv. Hær. 4. 20. 2.

(5.) Strom. 1. 29.

cree of Pope Gelasius ; from which time it began to decline in public favor.

As late as the 15th century, a translation of the Shepherd of Hermas was found in a MS. of the Latin bible.

The Pastor or Shepherd consists of three books. The first is entitled Visions, the second, Commandments, the third, Similitudes. There is in it all, nothing attractive to the modern mind. It is not easy to understand how, in any age, its wild vagaries and crude piety could have been found interesting, and even been considered inspired. A partial explanation may be found in its supposed semi-apostolic origin.

ITS EVIDENCE FOR THE GOSPELS.—Dr. Westcott says it contains no definite quotation from either the old or New Testament.[1]

"From the Shepherd of Hermas," says Dr. Less, "no inference whatever can be drawn."

CERINTHUS AND HIS GOSPEL.—About A. D. 145.

The history as well as the writings of Cerinthus are strangely blended with those of John the presbyter, and even with John the apostle.

By the ancient writers on heresies, he is generally placed after Carpocrates.

A sect called the Alogi, attributed to him (so says Epiphanius), the gospel, as well as the other writings of John.

(1.) Canon, p. 181.

Cerinthus had both a gospel and a revelation.

Toland states that the Gospel of John was attributed to Cerinthus.[1]

Cerinthus is believed to have been a Jew by birth. He was educated at Alexandria, and taught philosophy there.[2]

Irenæus says :

"He represents Jesus as not having been born of a virgin, but as being the son of Joseph and Mary according to the ordinary course of human generation; while he, nevertheless, was more righteous, prudent and wise than other men." "Moreover, after his baptism, Christ descended upon him in the form of a dove, from the Supreme Ruler, and that he proclaimed the unknown Father, and performed miracles."—[Adv. Hær. 1. 26.

The same writer says, John's Gospel was written to confute the errors spread abroad by Cerinthus.[3]

This may be accepted, as throwing some light on the time when the Gospel of John was written. Jerome also asserts that John wrote against Cerinthus.[4]

ISIDORUS.—A. D. 150.

Isidorus was the son of Basilides. He wrote works of an exegetical and ethical character. Fragments are preserved by Clement of Alexandria and Epiphanius. There are other fragments by Hippolytus. Isidorus maintained the doctrine of his father.

"No references to the gospels," says Westcott.[5]

(1.) Amyntor, London, 1699, p. 64.
(2.) Mosheim, vol. 1, pp. 93 to 95.
(3.) Adv. Hær. 3. 11.
(4.) See Michaelis, vol. 3, p. 278.
(5.) Canon, p. 267.

VALENTINUS, AND THE GOSPEL OF TRUTH.—A. D. 150.

Valentinus was one of the most famous Gnostics in the early history of the church. According to Tischendorf, he came from Egypt to Rome, about A. D. 140. He was by birth an Egyptian, and possibly of Jewish descent. Lardner says he was a man of letters.[1]

The Valentinians did not admit that Christ had a human body. Such a body, they said, must have sprung, not from spirit, or from God, but from the will of man.[2]

The Gospel of Truth is generally attributed to Valentinus; though Westcott says it was composed by his followers.

There was a tradition among the Valentinians, that Jesus remained among his disciples eighteen months after his resurrection.[3]

THE CANONICAL GOSPELS.—An effort has been made to make Valentinus a witness for the canonical gospels.

Davidson says it is doubtful whether Valentinus' alleged citations from the New Testament can be relied upon.[4]

PAPIAS.—A. D. 125.

Papias, who had long been considered an immediate successor to the apostles, is now generally relegated to the second century.

(1.) Vol. 4, p. 526.
(2.) Tertullian, de Carne Christi, c. 15.
(3.) Irenæus adv. Hær. I. 3. 2.
(4.) Canon, p. 87.

Papias was bishop of Hierapolis, in Phrygia. He was a millenarian. The doctrine that the end of the world was near at hand, was extensively believed and may be considered as orthodox in the second century.

FRAGMENTS FROM PAPIAS.— Œcumenius represents him as saying that Judas came to his death in this manner:

"His body having swollen to such an extent, that he could not pass where a chariot could pass easily, he was crushed by the chariot, so that his bowels gushed out."

The writer of this could hardly have seen the Gospel of Matthew. Irenæus, in the 33d chapter of the 5th book against heresies, cites from Papias, sayings of Christ unlike anything in the New Testament:

"The elders who saw John, the disciple of the Lord, related that they had heard from him, how the Lord used to teach, in regard to these times, and say:

"'The days will come, in which vines shall grow, each having ten thousand branches, and in each branch ten thousand twigs, and in each twig ten thousand shoots, and in each one of the shoots ten thousand clusters, and on every one of the clusters ten thousand grapes, and every grape, when pressed, will give five and twenty metrets of wine.'" etc.

Also that 1,000,000,000 pounds of clear, pure, fine flour would be produced from one grain of wheat; and that animals should become peaceful and harmonious, and perfectly subject to man.

Irenæus adds, that these things were borne witness to by Papias, the hearer of John, and companion of Polycarp.

The famous testimony of Eusebius, concerning

Papias, which, in some form, will be found in every work on the canon of the New Testament, is is as follows:

That Papias wrote five books, called an Exposition of the Oracles of the Lord, citing Irenæus.

That Papias affirmed that he received the sayings of the apostles from those who accompanied them, and that he heard in person Aristion, and the presbyter John; and gives their trāditions.

That there was a narrative received by Papias from the daughters of Philip, of the raising of a man from the dead, and how Justus, surnamed Barsabas, swallowed a deadly poison, and received no harm.

That Papias had set down, as coming to him from unwritten tradition, "some strange parables and instructions of the Savior, and some other things, of a more fabulous nature."

Eusebius then adds, "as a matter of primary importance, a tradition regarding Mark, who wrote the gospel."

That the presbyter said that Mark, having become the interpreter of Peter, wrote down accurately, whatsoever he remembered. It was not, however, in exact order that he related the sayings or deeds of Christ. For he neither heard the Lord, nor accompanied him. But afterward, he accompanied Peter, who accommodated his instructions to the necessities (of his hearers), but with no intention of giving a regular narrative of the Lord's sayings. Wherefore Mark made no mistake in thus writing some things as he remembered them. For of one thing he took especial care, not to omit anything he had heard, and not to put anything fictitious in the statements.

That "Matthew put together the oracles (of the Lord) in the Hebrew language, and each one interpreted them as best he could."

That Papias gives a story of a woman who was accused of many sins before the Lord, which was to be found in the Gospel of the Hebrews.

Also that Papias considered, "That the information which he could derive from books, was not so profitable as that which was preserved in a living tradition.—[Eusebius, Ecc. Hist. bk. 3, ch. 39.

Such is this far-famed testimony. That portion relating to the Gospels of Mark and Matthew, may be stated as follows:

Eusebius says, that Papias said, that John the presbyter told, in what manner certain writings of Mark and Matthew had been constructed.

The value to be attached to any statements of Eusebius, will be considered hereafter.

One important circumstance will be noted, in the evidence, as it stands :

Notwithstanding this explanation of the apostolic origin of the books, it appears that Papias considered them, as evidence, inferior to oral tradition. That, too, a hundred years after the time, when, as is claimed, they were written.

Again, it is contended by able critics, that the language here attributed to Papias, concerning the book written by Mark, cannot be applied to the gospel which bears his name.[1] They insist that it must be referred to the Preaching of Peter, or some other document more ancient than the Gospel of Mark. So also of the logia, oracles or sayings of Christ, by Matthew, which were not the same as the Gospel of Matthew.

EPISTLE TO DIOGNETUS.—About A. D. 140.

This is an apology, or argument, in favor of the Christian system, and in defense of the Christians of that day. It is well written. It has been variously attributed to Quadratus, to Aristides, Justin Martyr, and others. Bunsen thought part of it was written by Marcion.[2] Westcott thinks he

---

(1.) Credner, Davidson, Guericke, Griesbach, Neander, and many others.
(2.) Analecta Ante-Nic. I. 103.

sees indications of John's Gospel in this document, but says there are no direct references.[1] This epistle is only to be found in a single manuscript of a late date, and hence has been suspected of being a forgery.

The Clementines.—A. D. 150.

The Recognitions, the Homilies, Epitome, etc. These are Ebionite productions. The writer appears to have had the same gospels which were used by Justin.

Tischendorf thinks the Gospel of the Hebrews was used by Justin Martyr, by the author of the Clementines, and by Tatian and Hegesippus.[2]

(1.) Canon, p. 81.
(2.) Origin of the Four Gospels, p. 78.

CHAPTER XX.

MARCION.—A. D. 145.

Marcion, the great heresiarch, was born at Sinope, in the second century. He came to Rome about the year 142.

Tertullian says, the fiercest and most barbarous nations lived upon the Euxine Sea—that nothing had the glow of life there—that all things were torpid and stiff with cold — that nevertheless, nothing in Pontus was so barbarous and sad, as that Marcion was born there.

Dr. Lardner, on the authority of Jerome and Augustine, credits Marcion with being a man of letters.[1] He preached and disseminated his doctrines, for twenty years; and with such success, that in the time of Epiphanius, his followers were in every nation under heaven.

The story that before he came to Rome, he had seduced a young woman, Dr. Lardner thinks an invention of Epiphanius.[2] It probably originated

(1.) Lardner's works, vol. 4, p. 526.
(2.) Ibid. vol. 4, p. 591.

in the fact, which we learn from Jerome, that Marcion had sent before him to Rome, a woman, to prepare the minds of the people for his doctrines.[1]

Marcion is said to have rejected the Old Testament entirely; not considering it of any authority after the coming of Christ. He wrote a work entitled "Antithesis," in which he contrasted the old system with the new—the God of the one, with the God of the other—the law with the gospel. He represented Christianity as a new system, abrogating the old, and as entirely disconnected from it. The Creator of the world described in the Old Testament, [The Demi-ourgos], was different from the God of the new dispensation, and inferior to him. From the superior God, Jesus had come, endued with divine power, commencing with the beginning of his ministry.

He maintained the doctrine of the impurity of matter and could not therefore believe in the immaculate conception. According to Tertullian,[2] he even denied the corporeal reality of the flesh of Christ. But this statement may be received with some allowance.

Marcion denied the resurrection of the body, and believed in the doctrine of necessity.

He was a follower of Paul, and accused the other apostles of having perverted the gospel doctrines.

Tertullian ingeniously endeavors to treat this accusation as aimed at the four gospels; and argues

(1.) Jerome, adv. Ctesiph. t. 4, p. 477.
(2.) Adv. Marcion, 3. 8.   See also de Pr. c. 33, 34.

thence that they must have been in existence before Marcion. His argument, however, destroys itself; since the apostles denounced, were Peter, James and John; only one of whom has credit for writing either of the four gospels, while to the other two were attributed two of the apocryphal gospels. Marcion probably referred to the corruption of "the gospel," and not to any written books.

Marcion taught and permitted the baptizing by women. It may be inferred, also, from Epiphanius, that he did not treat with much respect those who refused them this privilege.[1]

MARCION'S NEW TESTAMENT.

The first New Testament that ever appeared, was compiled and published by Marcion. It was in the Greek language. It consisted of "The Gospel," and "The Apostolicon." No Acts—no Revelation, and but one gospel. The Apostolicon comprised ten of Paul's Epistles, as follows: Galatians, 1st and 2d Corinthians, Romans, except the 15th and 16th chapters, 1st and 2d Thessalonians, Ephesians, Colossians, Philemon and Philippians; arranged in the order as here named.[2]

This canon of the New Testament was prepared and published soon after his arrival at Rome; probably about A. D. 145. Baring-Gould thinks he brought the gospel with him from Sinope.[3]

(1.) Adv. Hær. 42. 4.

(2.) Also part of the Epistle to the Laodiceans.

(3.) Lost and Host. Gospels, p. 241.

Tertullian accuses Marcion of giving no name or title to his gospel. It was called simply "the Gospel;" and sometimes, "the Gospel of the Lord." Marcion claimed for it the authority of Paul himself. It closely resembles the Gospel of Luke, but is much shorter.

Ever since the time of Tertullian, it has been, by many, charged against Marcion, that he corrupted the Gospel of Luke. This charge, it will be seen as we proceed, cannot be sustained.

Nearly all we have concerning the Gospel of Marcion, comes through Tertullian and Epiphanius, both of whom were violently opposed to him, and neither of whom was particularly scrupulous in the means employed against an adversary. Hence it has become difficult to reproduce the gospel. Several German critics have attempted to reconstruct it, and it is published in the Codex Apocryphus of Thilo, from the works of Hahn.

In Marcion's Gospel, there was nothing corresponding to the first three chapters of Luke.

The first chapter of Marcion was similar to the fourth of Luke, but had many variations from it; and it is here that the critics have had the most difficulty.

After passing the first chapter of Marcion and fourth of Luke, the progress is somewhat easier. Tertullian furnishes but little aid; but Epiphanius, writing in the same language with Marcion, gives a list of 78 passages, in which, as he claims, Marcion corrupted the text of Luke. As he mentions the most trivial deviations, giving the exact words in every instance, we think it may be taken as the correct text of Marcion.

This opinion is confirmed by the fact, that in his scholia, he recapitulates every reading in almost precisely the same words; the deviations being few and unimportant.

Tertullian, in his work against Marcion, has a running commentary on Luke, with a constant invective against Marcion, and an occasional allusion to his gospel.   From this some little further assistance may be obtained.   Too much reliance has been placed upon it by some critics, as it is quite uncertain, in many cases, whether Tertullian is referring to the Gospel of Marcion, or to the text of Luke, as it prevailed in his day.   By comparing all that is said by these two writers, the text of Marcion may be pretty nearly discovered.

We have not been able to procure a copy of this important gospel, as it appears in Thilo, or elsewhere.

From the works of Tertullian and Epiphanius, we have, however, attempted to reproduce it; occasionally invoking the aid of some of the German critics.

THE GOSPEL.   [According to Marcion.]

CHAPTER 1.—(Mostly in the 4th chapter of Luke.)

In the fifteenth year of the reign of Tiberius Cæsar, (Part of Luke 3. 1), Jesus came down to Capernaum, a city of Galilee, and taught them on the sabbath days. (Luke 4. 31.)

Verse 2. And they were exceedingly astonished at his doctrine, for his word was with power.   (For parallel with verses 2 to 9 inclusive, see Luke, ch. 4. vv. 32 to 39.)

3.   And in the synagogue there was a man who had a spirit of an unclean devil, and who cried out with a loud voice,

4.   Saying: Let us alone, what have we to do with thee, Jesus? (omitting the words "of Nazareth.")   Art thou come to destroy us? I know thee who thou art, the holy one of God.

5.   And Jesus rebuked him, saying: Hold thy peace, and come out of him.   And when the devil had thrown him in the midst, he came out of him, and hurt him not.

6.   And they were all amazed, and spake among themselves, saying: What a word is this?   For with authority and power he commandeth the unclean spirits, and they come out.

7.   And the fame of him went out into every place, in the country round about.   (This verse is omitted by Volkmar, but retained by Hahn, Hilgenfeld and others.   See Sup. Rel. vol. 2, p. 128. Note. Baring-Gould, who reproduces this chapter, follows Volkmar.   The two following verses are omitted by Ritschl and Bauer, but retained by others.)

8.   And he arose out of the synagogue, and entered into Simon's house.   And Simon's wife's mother was taken with a great fever; and they besought him for her.

9.   And he stood over her and rebuked the fever; and it left her; and immediately she arose and ministered unto them.   (Following this, Volkmar has the last part of Luke 4. 14 and 15; but he is not supported by other critics.)

10.   And he came to Nazareth, and, as his custom was, he went into the synagogue on the sabbath day, and began to preach to them. (See Luke 4. 16.)

11.   And he sat down, and the eyes of all who were in the synagogue, were fastened on him.   (Luke 4. 20.)

12.   And he began to speak to them.   And all bare him witness, and wondered at the gracious words which proceeded out of his mouth. (Luke 4. 21, 22.)

13.   And he said unto them, Ye surely will say unto me this proverb: Physician, heal thyself; whatsoever ye have done in Capernaum, do also here.   (Luke 4. 23.)   (The next verse, 24th of Luke, was not in Marcion.   Neither were verses 25 and 26, according to Hahn, Ritschl and DeWette.   We accordingly omit them, though they were retained by Volkmar and Hilgenfeld.   Verse 27 is also

omitted by most critics.   Baring-Gould, who follows Volkmar, retains these three verses.)

14. And all they in the synagogue, when they heard these things, were filled with wrath. (Luke 4. 28.)

15. And rose up, and thrust him out of the city, and led him to the brow of the hill whereon their city was built, that they might cast him down headlong. (Luke 4. 29.)

16. But he, passing through the midst of them, went his way. (Volkmar says "to Capernaum.") (See Luke 4. 30.)

17. Now when the sun was setting, all they that had any sick with divers diseases, brought them unto him; and he laid his hands on every one of them, and healed them. (Luke 4. 40.)

18. And devils also came out of many, crying out and saying, Thou art Christ, the Son of God. And he, rebuking them, suffered them not to speak: for they knew that he was Christ.   (For parallel to verses 18 to 21, inclusive, see Luke 4. 41 to 44.)

19. And when it was day, he departed, and went into a desert place. And the people sought him, and came unto him, and staid him, that he should not depart from them.

20. And he said unto them, I must preach the kingdom of God to other cities also; for therefore am I sent.

21. And he preached in the synagogues of Galilee.

CHAPTER II.   (See Luke, ch. 5.)

Verses 1 to 13, same as in the Gospel of Luke.

14. And he charged him to tell no man, But go and show thyself to the priest, and offer for thy cleansing, according as Moses commanded, for a testimony unto you.

Verses 15 to 39 inclusive, same as in Luke.

CHAPTER III.   (Luke, ch. 6.)

Verses 1 to 16, same as in Luke.

17. And he came down among them, (*en autois*), and stood in the plain, and there was the company of his disciples, and a great multitude of people, out of all Judea and Jerusalem, and from the sea coast of Tyre and Sidon, who came to hear him, and to be healed of their diseases.

18. Same as in Luke.

19. And the whole multitude sought to touch him.

20, 21 and 22, Same as in Luke.

23. Rejoice ye in that day, and leap for joy; for behold your reward

is great in heaven; for in the like manner did your fathers unto the prophets.

24 to 49 inclusive, same as in Luke.

CHAPTER IV. (Luke, ch. 7.)

Verses 1 to 28, same as in Luke, except some unimportant verbal differences.

(Verses 29 to 35 inclusive, of Luke, not in Marcion.)

29. (36 of Luke.) And going into the house of a Pharisee, he ate with him.

30. (37 and 38 of Luke.) But a sinful woman, standing near, before his feet, washed his feet with her tears, and anointed them, and kissed them.

31 to 35 inclusive, same as 39 to 43 of Luke.

36. (44, 45 and 46 of Luke.) And he turned to the woman, and said unto Simon, See'st thou this woman? I entered into thy house, thou gavest me no water for my feet. She has washed my feet with her tears, and has anointed them, and kissed them.

37 to 40 inclusive, same as 47 to 50 of Luke.

CHAPTER V. (Luke, ch. 8.)

Verses 1 to 18 inclusive, same as in Luke. (Verse 19 of Luke not in Marcion.)

19, 20 and 21 inclusive, same as 20, 21 and 22 of Luke. But Volkmar has, in verse 20 of Marcion, (21 of Luke), "Who is my mother? and who are my brethren? My mother and my brethren are," etc.

22. (23 and 24 of Luke.) He was sleeping with the sailors. And he arose, and rebuked the wind, and the sea.

23 to 40 inclusive, same as 25 to 42 of Luke.

41. (43, 44 and 45 of Luke.) And a woman, touching him, was healed of an issue of blood; and the Lord said, Who has touched me?

42 to 52 inclusive, same as 46 to 56 of Luke.

CHAPTER VI. [Luke, ch. 9.]

Verses 1 to 15 inclusive, same as in Luke.

16. Same as in Luke, except, "he asked blessing upon them." [*Ep autois.*]

17 to 21 inclusive, same as in Luke.

22. Saying, the Son of Man must suffer many things, and be put to death, and after three days rise again.

23 to 29 inclusive, same as in Luke.

30. (30 and 31 of Luke.) And behold two men talked with him; Elias and Moses, in glory.

31 to 33 inclusive, same as 32 to 34 of Luke.

34. (35 of Luke.) From the cloud a voice saying: This is my beloved Son.

35 to 38 inclusive, same as 36 to 39 of Luke.

39. (40 of Luke.) And I besought thy disciples, and they were not able to cast him out. (*ouk eedunestheesan ekballein auto.*)

40. (41 of Luke.) And he said to them, O faithless generation, how long shall I suffer you?

41 to 61 inclusive, same as in 42 to 62 of Luke.

CHAPTER VII. (Luke, ch. 10.)

Verses 1 to 20 inclusive, same as in Luke.

21. In that hour, he rejoiced in the spirit, and said: I thank thee, Lord of heaven, that those things which were hidden from the wise and prudent, thou hast revealed unto babes. Even so, Father, for it seemed good in thy sight.

22. All things are delivered to me of my Father, and no man hath known the Father save the Son, nor the Son save the Father, and he to whom the Son hath revealed.

23 and 24, same as in Luke.

25. And behold, a certain lawyer stood up, and tempted him, saying: Master, doing what shall I obtain life? (*aionion* omitted.)

26. He said unto him, What is written in the law?

27 and 28, same as in Luke, except that instead of *orthos apekrithees*, Marcion had *orthos eipes*.

29 to 42 inclusive, same as in Luke.

CHAPTER VIII. (Luke ch. 11.)

Verse 1, same as in Luke.

2. And he said unto them, When ye pray, say, Father, may thy Holy Spirit come to us. Thy kingdom come. Thy will be done, as in heaven, so on earth.

3 and 4, same as in Luke.

5. And he said: Which of you shall have a friend, and shall go unto him at midnight, asking for three loaves? [*aiton treis artous;*]

(Verses 6, 7 and 8 of Luke, not in Marcion.)

6. [9 of Luke.] Ask, and it shall be given. (Verse 10 of Luke, not in Marcion.)

7. [11 and 12 of Luke.] Who of you, being a father, if his son ask a fish, instead of a fish, will give to him a serpent? Or, instead of an egg, a scorpion?

8. [13 of Luke.] If, therefore, you being evil, know how to give good things unto your children, how much more your Father, who is in heaven?

9 to 23 inclusive, same as 14 to 28 of Luke.

24. [29 of Luke.] And when the people were gathered thick together, he began to say: This is an evil generation; they seek a sign; no sign shall be given them.

[Verses 30, 31 and 32 of Luke, not in Marcion.] 25 to 33 inclusive, same as 33 to 41 of Luke.

34. [42 of Luke.] Wo unto you, Pharisees! For ye tithe mint and rue, and all manner of herbs, and pass over the calling [*kleesin*], and the love of God. These ought ye to have done, and not to leave the other undone.

35 to 40 inclusive, same as 43 to 48 of Luke. [Verses 49, 50 and 51 of Luke, not in Marcion.] 41, 42 and 43, same as 52, 53 and 54 of Luke.

CHAPTER IX. (Luke, ch. 12.)

Verses 1, 2 and 3, same as in Luke.

4. (4 and 5 of Luke.) I say unto you, be not afraid of them who kill the body; fear him who has power, after killing, to cast into hell.

(Verses 6 and 7 of Luke, not in Marcion.)

5. (8 of Luke.) Also I say unto you, whosoever shall confess me before men, him shall the Son of Man also confess before God.

6. (9 of Luke.) But he that denieth me before men, shall be denied before God.

7 to 24 inclusive, same as 10 to 27 of Luke. (Verse 28 of Luke, not in Marcion.)

25, same as 29 of Luke.

26. (30 of Luke.) For all these things do the nations of the

world seek after. And your Father knoweth that ye have need of these things of the flesh.

27. (31 of Luke.) *Pleen* before *zeeteite*, omitted.

28. (32 of Luke.) Instead of *ho pateer humon*, Marcion had *ho pateer;* "the Father."

29 to 33 inclusive, same as 33 to 37 of Luke.

34. (38 of Luke.) And if he shall come in the evening watch, (*hesperieen phulakeen*), and shall find them so, blessed are those servants.

35 to 41 inclusive, same as 39 to 45 of Luke.

42. (46 of Luke.) The Lord of that servant will come, and will cut him in sunder, and will appoint his portion with the unbelievers.

43 to 53 inclusive, same as 47 to 57 of Luke.

54. (58 of Luke.) Instead of *se parado*, Marcion has *paradosei se.*

55, same as 59 of Luke.

CHAPTER X. (Luke, ch. 13.)

(Verses 1 to 10 of Luke, not in Marcion.) Verses 1 to 5 inclusive, same as 11 to 15 of Luke.

6. (16 of Luke.) Ought not this daughter of Abraham, whom Satan hath bound, lo these eighteen years, be loosed from this bond, on the sabbath day?

7 to 17 inclusive, same as 17 to 27 of Luke.

18. (28 of Luke.) There shall be weeping and gnashing of teeth, when ye shall see all the righteous in the kingdom of God, and yourselves cast out, and held back.

(Verses 29 to 35 of Luke, not in Marcion.)

CHAPTER XI. (Luke, ch. 14.)

Verses 1 to 6 inclusive, same as in Luke. (Verses 7 to 11 inclusive of Luke, not in Marcion.)

7 to 30 inclusive, same as 12 to 35 of Luke.

CHAPTER XII. (Luke, ch. 15.)

This chapter consisted of the first 10 verses only, of 15th Luke.

CHAPTER XIII. (Luke, ch. 16.)

Verses 1 to 11 inclusive, same as in Luke.

12. And if ye have not been faithful in that which was another man's, who will give you that which is mine?

13 to 16 inclusive, substantially the same as in Luke.

17. Heaven and earth may pass, but one tittle of my words shall not fail.

18 to 28 inclusive, substantially the same as in Luke.

29. (In place of the last three verses of 16th Luke.) Abraham saith unto him, They have Moses and the prophets, let them hear them. Not after one has risen from the dead, will they listen. (*epei oude tou egeiromenou apo nekron akouousin.*)

CHAPTER XIV. (Luke, ch. 17.)

Verse 1, same as in Luke.

2. (According to Volkmar.) It would be better for him, if he had not been born; or if a millstone were hanged about his neck, and he were cast into the sea, than that he should offend one of these little ones.

3 to 9 inclusive, same as in Luke.

10. So, likewise ye, when ye shall have done all those things which are commanded you.

11, 12, and 13, substantially as in Luke.

14. And he sent them away, saying: Go, show yourselves unto the priests. And it came to pass, that as they went, they were cleansed.

15, 16, and 17, same as in Luke.

18. These are not found returning, to give glory unto God. And there were many lepers, in the days of Eliseus the prophet, and none of these were cleansed, except Naaman the Syrian.

19 to 37, substantially the same as in Luke.

CHAPTER XV. (Luke, ch. 18.)

Verses 1 to 18 inclusive, same as in Luke.

19. Jesus said to him, Do not call me good; one is good: the Father.

20 to 30 inclusive, same as in Luke. (Verses 31 to 34 inclusive, of Luke, not in Marcion.)

31. (In place of 35 to 43 inclusive, in Luke, were this verse and the following:) And it came to pass, as he came near Jericho, a blind man cried out, Jesus, thou son of David, have mercy on me.

32. And when he had healed him, he said, Thy faith hath saved thee.

CHAPTER XVI. (Luke, ch. 19.)

Verses 1 to 8 inclusive, same as in Luke.

9. And Jesus said unto him, This day is salvation come unto this house.

10 to 28 inclusive, same as in Luke.

(Verses 29 to 48 of Luke, not in Marcion.)

CHAPTER XVII. (Luke, ch. 20.)

Verses 1 to 8 inclusive, same as in Luke. (Verses 9 to 18 of Luke, not in Marcion.)

9, (19 of Luke.) And the chief priests and the scribes the same hour sought to lay hands on him, and they feared the people.

10 to 24 inclusive, same as 20 to 34 of Luke.

25. (35 of Luke.) But they who shall be accounted worthy of God, to obtain that world, and the resurrection from the dead, neither marry nor are given in marriage.

26, same as 36 of Luke. (Verses 37 and 38 of Luke, not in Marcion.)

27 to 35 inclusive, same as 39 to 47 of Luke.

CHAPTER XVIII. (Luke, ch. 21.)

Verses 1 to 17 inclusive, same as in Luke. (Verse 18 of Luke, not in Marcion.)

18 and 19, same as 19 and 20 of Luke. (Verses 21 and 22 of Luke, not in Marcion.)

20 to 35 inclusive, same as 23 to 38 of Luke.

(Dr. Lardner thought, the first 18 verses of 21st Luke were not in Marcion. But later authorities include vv. 1 to 17.)

CHAPTER XIX. (Luke, ch. 22.)

Verses 1, 2 and 3, same as in Luke.

4. And he communicated with the captains, how he might betray him unto them.

5, 6 and 7, same as in Luke.

8. And he said to Peter and the rest, Go and prepare, that we may eat of the passover.

(Kai eipe, to Petro kai tois loipois, apelthontes etoimasate, hina phagomen to pascha.)

9 to 13 inclusive, same as in Luke.

14. And he sat down, and the twelve apostles with him.

15. Same as Luke, except *pros autous* in Luke.

(Verses 16, 17 and 18 of Luke, not in Marcion.)

16 to 24 inclusive, same as 19 to 27 of Luke.   (Verses 28, 29 and 30 of Luke, not in Marcion.)

25 to 28 inclusive, same as 31 to 34 of Luke.   (Verses 35 to 38 of Luke, not in Marcion.)

29 to 38 inclusive, substantially the same as 39 to 48 of Luke.

(Verses 49, 50 and 51 of Luke, not in Marcion.)

39 to 49 inclusive, same as 52 to 62 of Luke.

50, substantially the same as 63 of Luke.

51. (64 of Luke.) And striking him, they said: Prophesy: Who is it that smote thee?

52 to 58 inclusive, same as 65 to 71 of Luke.

CHAPTER XX.   (Luke, ch. 23.)

Verse 1, same as in Luke.

2. And they began to accuse him, saying: We found this fellow perverting the nation, and destroying the law and the prophets; forbidding to give tribute to Cæsar, and turning away the women and children.

3 to 32 inclusive, same as in Luke.

33. And coming to the place called the place of Calvary, (place of a skull, *kraniou topos,*) they crucified him and divided his garments; and the sun was darkened.

34 to 42 inclusive, same as in Luke, excepting from Luke the portions contained in verse 33 of Marcion.

(Verse 43 of Luke, not in Marcion.)   43, same as 44 of Luke.

44. (45 of Luke.) And the vail of the temple was rent in the midst.

45. (46 of Luke.) And crying out with a loud voice, he expired.

46, 47 and 48, same as 47, 48 and 49 of Luke.

49. (50 to 53 of Luke.)   And behold, a man named Joseph taking down the body, wrapped it up, and placed it in a hewn tomb.

50 and 51, same as 54 and 55 of Luke.

52. (56 of Luke.) And returning, they rested the sabbath day, according to the commandment.

CHAPTER XXI. (Luke ch. 24.)

Verses 1 to 4 inclusive, same as in Luke.

5. And as they were afraid, and bowed down their faces to the earth, those in white clothing said to them, Why seek ye the living among the dead?

6. He has risen; remember what he said while yet living, (*eti on.*)

7. That it was necessary for the Son of Man to suffer, and be delivered up.

8 to 24, same as in Luke.

25. Then he said to them, O fools, and slow to believe all that he said unto you!

26, same as in Luke. [Verse 27 of Luke not in Marcion.]

27 to 30 inclusive, same as 28 to 31 of Luke.

31. (32 of Luke.) And they said one to another, Did not our hearts burn within us, while he talked with us by the way?

32 to 36 inclusive, same as 33 to 37 of Luke.

37. (38 and 39 of Luke.) And he said unto them, Why are ye troubled? Behold my hands and my feet; a spirit hath not bones, as ye see me have.

38 to 41 inclusive, same as 40 to 43 of Luke.

42. (44 of Luke.) These are the words which I spake unto you while I was yet with you.

(Verse 45 of Luke, not in Marcion.)

43. (46 of Luke.) That thus it behooved Christ to suffer, and to rise from the dead, the third day.

44 to 48 inclusive, same as 47 to 51 of Luke.

(Verses 52 and 53 of Luke, not in Marcion.)

From the foregoing synopsis the reader can write out the Gospel of Marcion, and will have the text of that gospel, very nearly as it stood in the fourth century. The English reader may pass over, as unimportant, the Greek readings not translated, and may adopt the corresponding text of Luke.

MARCION AND LUKE.

The question of priority, as between these gospels, is one of the most interesting connected with the history of early Christian literature.

From the commencement of the third, down to the beginning of the present century, it has been fashionable to accuse Marcion of corrupting the Gospel of Luke; the emphatic and oft-repeated assertions of Tertullian and Epiphanius to that effect, having been deemed sufficient authority.

Bishop Marsh was one of the first to do Marcion justice. He said there was no proof that Marcion used Luke's Gospel at all.[1]

Since then, many of the most intelligent German critics have come to the same conclusion.

Baring-Gould also says : ''Marcion was too conscientious and earnest a man, wilfully to corrupt a gospel.''[2]

This author thinks that the Church of Sinope, where Marcion formerly resided, had been furnished by Paul with a collection of the records of the life and teaching of Christ; that Marcion thus obtained his gospel, and brought it to Rome.[3]

Again: "Marcion's Gospel contained a different arrangement of the narrative, from the canonical Luke, and was without many passages which it is not possible to believe he wilfully excluded."—[Ibid. p. 242.

(1.) Notes to Michaelis, vol. 3, pt. 2, p. 160.
(2.) Lost and Hostile Gospels, p. 241
(3.) Ibid.

He afterward speaks of differences of arrangement, which are unaccountable on the theory that Marcion corrupted Luke, and says that Marcion's Gospel was without several passages which apparently favor his views.[1]

Canon Westcott is equally explicit in acquitting Marcion from the accusation made against him by the early fathers of the church.

He says: "Tertullian and Epiphanius agree in affirming that Marcion altered the text of the books which he received, to suit his own views; and they quote many various readings in support of the assertion. Those which they cite from the epistles, are certainly insufficient to prove the point; and on the contrary, they go to show that Marcion preserved without alteration, the text which he found in his manuscript. Of the seven readings noticed by Epiphanius, [in the epistles], only two are unsupported by other authority: and it is altogether unlikely that Marcion changed other passages, when, as Epiphanius himself shows, he left untouched those which are most directly opposed to his system."—[History of the Canon, p. 284.

It is one of the most hopeful signs of the times, that men, even in religious matters, can vindicate the character of an adversary, after it has been aspersed for fifteen hundred years.

Some writers still persist in repeating the old slander. But the more candid and intelligent opinion of Westcott and Baring-Gould, is supported by Semler, Griesbach, Loeffler, Schmidt, Schleiermacher, Hahn, and many others.

These writers, perceiving how little reliance is to be placed upon the statements of the fathers, in matters of critical exegesis, or of authorship, or upon their assertions concerning the heretics, have

(1.) Ibid, p. 243; referring to Luke 11. 51; 13. 30, 34, and 20. 9 to 16.

examined carefully the text of Marcion, and finding the statements of Tertullian and Epiphanius unsupported by internal evidence, have rejected them altogether.

WHICH WAS FIRST WRITTEN?—Let us now see if we cannot ascertain with reasonable certainty which was first written ; the Gospel of Luke or the Gospel of Marcion.

The question of priority, in this case, is closely connected with that of brevity.

The first three chapters of Luke were entirely wanting in Marcion, except the opening clause in the third chapter, which was the commencement of the Gospel of Marcion : "In the fifteenth year of the reign of Tiberius Cæsar." The balance of the first chapter of Marcion is contained with some variations in the fourth of Luke. About half that chapter is wanting entirely, in Marcion.

After passing this, the different chapters of the two gospels correspond, the 2d of Marcion with 5th of Luke, 3d of Marcion with 6th of Luke, and so on.

The Gospel of Luke is the most copious throughout. The number of verses in Luke in excess of those in Marcion, is as follows : In chapter 7, seven verses : in ch. 8, one ; in ch. 11, ten ; in ch. 12, three ; in ch. 13, seventeen ; in ch. 14, five ; in ch. 15, twenty-two ; in ch. 18, four ; in ch. 19, twenty ; in ch. 20, twelve ; in ch. 21, three ; in ch. 22, thirteen ; in ch. 23, one, and in ch. 24, four : total 122 verses. To this add the excess of 23 verses in the 4th chapter of Luke, and we have altogether 145 verses, or more than three average chapters. Add the first three chapters of Luke, which are entirely wanting in Marcion, and the result is, more than six chapters, or more than one-fourth of the entire Gospel of Luke, wanting in Marcion.

But this is not all. In a number of places, the verses of Marcion are shorter. Then, again, two or more verses of Luke are contained, in substance, in one of Marcion, and in one place, nine verses of Luke in two of Marcion.

THE LAW OF ACCRETION.

LUKE AND MARCION COMPARED.

Leaving out of view, for the present, the whole-sale accumulation of matter, aggregating 315 verses, the law of accretion will be well illustrated by those cases where one or more verses in Marcion are found swollen into several in Luke, or where a single passage has additions. They are as follows:

I.

MARCION, ch. 1, v. 4.	LUKE, ch. 4, v. 34.
Saying, Let us alone; what have we to do with thee, Jesus?	Saying, Let (us) alone; what have we to do with thee, Jesus of Nazareth?

The difference is important. According to Matthew, the parents of Jesus, when they returned from Egypt, being warned of God in a dream, turned aside, (they were going to Bethlehem or Jerusalem,) into the parts of Galilee, that a certain prophecy might be fulfilled. The language does not imply that Nazareth was their residence.

The theory of the author of Luke was, that Nazareth was their residence. Accordingly, in this passage, which, though followed in Mark, has no parallel in Matthew, Jesus is addressed as "of Nazareth," a phrase not in Marcion.

II.

A corresponding variation will be found in

MARCION, 1. 10.	LUKE, 4. 16.
And he came to Nazareth, and as his custom was, etc.	And he came to Nazareth, where he had been brought up; and as his custom was, etc.

These are probably interpolations, made for the purpose of establishing Nazareth as the birth-place of Jesus.

III.

MARCION, 3. 19.	LUKE, 6. 19.
And the whole multitude sought to touch him.	And the whole multitude sought to touch him; for there went virtue out of him, and healed (them) all.

There is no reason why Marcion, who had not rejected the miracles of Christ, should omit the closing sentence. It is more probable that it was added in Luke, to give expression to a very natural inference on the part of the writer, as to the object of the multitude in pressing forward toward Jesus, and seeking to touch him.

There is no parallel in the other gospels.

IV.

MARCION, 4. 29	LUKE, 7. 36.
And going into the house of a Pharisee, he ate with him.	And one of the Pharisees desired him that he would eat with him. And he went into the Pharisee's house, and sat down to meat.

V.

JESUS AND THE SINFUL WOMAN.

MARCION, 4, 30.	LUKE, 7. 37 and 38.
But a sinful woman, standing near, before his feet, washed them with tears, and anointed them, and kissed them.	37. And behold, a woman in the city, who was a sinner, when she knew that (Jesus) sat at meat in the Pharisee's house, brought an alabaster box of ointment,
	38. And stood at his feet, behind (him,) weeping, and began to wash his feet with tears, and did wipe (them) with the hairs of her head, and kissed his feet, and anointed (them) with the ointment.

This touching incident, simply and beautifully told in the sixteen Greek words of Marcion, is spun out, by the author of Luke, into more than three times the number, with no improvement in the story. The washing of the feet of Jesus, which in Marcion is left as a figurative expression, denoting the great grief of the woman, is stated in Luke as an actual fact. While weeping, "she began to wash his feet with tears." Then, having washed them, she must needs "wipe them with the hairs of her head."

There can be but little doubt, that Marcion was first written, and that the author of Luke drew upon his imagination in filling up the text.

Again, there is a similar variation, in the following reference to the same transaction :

VI.

MARCION, 4. 36.	LUKE, 7. 44 to 46.
And he turned to the woman, and said unto Simon, Seest thou this woman? I entered into thy house; thou gavest me no water for my feet. She has washed my feet with her tears, and has anointed them, and kissed them.	44. And he turned to the woman, and said unto Simon, Seest thou this woman? I entered into thine house; thou gavest me no water for my feet. But she hath washed my feet with tears, and wiped (them) with the hairs of her head. 45. Thou gavest me no kiss; but this woman, since the time I came in, hath not ceased to kiss my feet. 46. My head with oil thou didst not anoint; but this woman hath anointed my feet with ointment.

The use here, by Jesus himself, of the figurative expression, "she hath washed my feet with tears," misled the author of Luke into conceiving, and hence expressing, a literal and complete washing of feet, followed by wiping them in the manner described.

This account is not in the other canonical gospels. It is simply a question between Marcion and Luke.

VII.

JESUS REBUKING THE STORM.

MARCION, 5. 22.	LUKE, 8. 23, 24.
He was sleeping with the sail-	23. But as they sailed, he fell asleep: and there came down a storm of wind on the lake; and they were filled (with water), and were in jeopardy.
	24. And they came to him, and awoke him, saying: Master, Master, we perish! Then he arose,
ors, and he arose, and rebuked the wind, and the sea.	and rebuked the wind, and the raging of the water: and they ceased, and there was a calm.

The language of Marcion, as given by Epiphanius, is highly elliptical.   It was probably preceded by some sentence having reference to the storm. The text of the synoptics is more copious; especially Mark, in which a pillow is provided for the head of Jesus.

VIII.

HEALING OF THE WOMAN.

MARCION, 5. 41.

And a woman, touching him,

was healed of an issue of the blood. And the Lord said, who has touched me?

LUKE, 8. 43 to 45.

43. And a woman, having an issue of blood twelve years, who had spent all her living upon physicians, neither could be healed by any,

44. Came behind (him), and touched the border of his garment; and immediately her issue of blood stanched.

45. And Jesus said, Who touched me? When all denied, Peter and they who were with him, said, Master, the multitude throng thee and press [thee], and sayest thou, Who touched me?

If these accounts come from a common manuscript, it had passed through many hands, before reaching the author of Luke.

IX, X.

MARCION, 6. 22.

Saying: The Son of Man must suffer many things, and be put to death, and after three days, rise again.

LUKE, 9. 22.

Saying: The Son of Man must suffer many things, and be rejected by the elders, and chief priests and scribes, and be slain, and be raised the third day.

MARCION, 6. 30.

And behold two men talked

with him; Elias and Moses in glory.

LUKE, 9. 30, 31.

30. And behold, there talked with him two men, who were Moses and Elias;

31. Who appeared in glory, and spake of his decease, which he should accomplish at Jerusalem.

XI, XII, XIII, XIV.

MARCION, 6. 34.	LUKE, 9. 35.
From the cloud a voice, saying: This is my beloved son.	And there came a voice out of the cloud, saying: This is my beloved son. Hear him.

MARCION, 6. 40.	LUKE, 9. 41.
And he said to them, O, faithless generation; how long shall I suffer you?	And Jesus answering said: O faithless and perverse generation! How long shall I be with you, and suffer you?

MARCION, 7. 21.	LUKE, 10. 21.
In that hour, he rejoiced in the spirit, and said: I thank thee, Lord of heaven, that, etc. (balance of the verse substantially as in Luke.)	In that hour, Jesus rejoiced in spirit, and said, I thank thee, O Father, Lord of heaven and earth, that, etc.

MARCION, 7. 25.	LUKE, 10. 25.
Master, doing what shall I obtain life?	Master, what shall I do to inherit eternal life?

The word *aionion*, (eternal,) was inserted by the author of Luke, to make more clear the meaning of Marcion.

The argument of Tertullian, (adv. Mar. 4. 25), that Marcion struck out *aionion*, so that the question might be confined to this life, is weak and untenable.

XV, XVI, XVII.

MARCION, 7. 26.	LUKE, 10. 26.
And he said unto him, What is written in the law?	He said unto him, What is written in the law? How readest thou?

MARCION, 8. 5.	LUKE, 11. 5.
And shall go unto him at midnight, asking for three loaves?	And shall go unto him at midnight, and say unto him, Friend, lend me three loaves.

MARCION, 8. 6.	LUKE, 11. 9.
Ask and it shall be given. (*Aiteite, kai dotheesetai.*)	Ask, and it shall be given you. (*Aiteite, kai dotheesetai humin.*)

XVIII, XIX, XX.

MARCION, 8. 7, 8.

Who of you, being a father, if his son ask a fish, instead of a fish, will give to him a serpent? Or instead of an egg, a scorpion?

If ye, then, being evil, know how to give good gifts unto your children, how much more your Father who is in heaven?

LUKE, 11. 11 to 13.

11. If a son shall ask bread of any of you that is a father, will he give him a stone? Or if (he ask) a fish, will he for a fish, give him a serpent?

12. Or if he shall ask an egg, will he offer him a scorpion?

13. If ye then, being evil, know how to give good gifts unto your children, how much more shall (your) heavenly Father give the Holy Spirit to them that ask him?

MARCION, 8. 24.

This is an evil generation; they seek a sign; no sign shall be given it.

LUKE, 11. 29.

This is an evil generation; they seek a sign, and there shall no sign be given it but the sign of Jonas the prophet.

MARCION, 9. 4.

I say unto you, be not afraid of

them that kill the body; fear him who has power after killing, to cast into hell. [*eis geennan.*]

LUKE, 12. 4, 5.

4. But I say unto you, my friends, be not afraid of them that kill the body, and after that, have no more that they can do.

5. But I will forewarn you whom ye shall fear; fear him who, after he hath killed, hath power to cast into hell. [*eis teen geennan.*] Yea, I say unto you, fear him.

The last passage illustrates, throughout, the prevailing practice of verbal accumulation. The language of Jesus, "I say unto you," becomes, when it reaches the author of Luke, "I say unto you, my friends;" "Be not afraid of them that kill the body," becomes, "Be not afraid of them that kill the body, and after that, have no more that they can do;" etc.

XXI, XXII, XXIII, XXIV, XXV, XXVI.

MARCION, 9. 5.	LUKE, 12. 8.
Him shall also the Son of Man confess before God.	Him shall the Son of Man also confess before the angels of God. [Similar difference in the next verse.]

MARCION, 9. 34.	LUKE, 12. 38.
And if he shall come in the evening watch, and shall find them so, blessed are those servants.	And if he shall come in the second watch, or come in the third watch, and find (them) so, blessed are those servants.

MARCION, 9. 42.	LUKE, 12. 46.
And the Lord of that servant will come, and will cut him in sunder, and will appoint his portion with the unbelievers.	The Lord of that servant will come in a day when he looketh not for (him), and at an hour when he is not aware, and will cut him in sunder, and will appoint him his portion with the unbelievers.

MARCION, 13. 29.	LUKE, 16. 29 to 31.
Abraham saith unto him, They have Moses and the prophets, let them hear them. Not after one has risen from the dead, will they listen.	29. Abraham saith unto him, They have Moses and the prophets; let them hear them. 30. And he said, Nay, father Abraham; but if one went unto them from the dead, they will repent. 31. And he said unto him, if they hear not Moses and the prophets, neither will they be persuaded, though one rose from the dead.

MARCION, 14. 10.	LUKE, 17. 10.
So likewise ye, when ye shall have done all those things which are commanded you.	So likewise ye, when ye shall have done all those things which are commanded you, say, We are unprofitable servants: we have done that which was our duty to do.

MARCION, 15. 31, 32.	LUKE, 18. 35 to 43.
31. And it came to pass, as he came near to Jericho, a blind	35. And it came to pass, that as he was come nigh unto Jericho, a

certain blind man sat by the way-side, begging:

36. And hearing the multitude pass by, he asked what it meant.

37. And they told him, that Jesus of Nazareth passeth by.

man cried out, Jesus, thou Son of David, have mercy on me.

32. And when he had healed him, he said, thy faith hath saved thee.

38. And he cried, saying: Jesus (thou) Son of David, have mercy on me!

39. And they who went before, rebuked him, that he should hold his peace; but he cried so much the more, (Thou) Son of David, have mercy on me!

40. And Jesus stood, and com-manded him to be brought unto him; and when he was come near, he asked him,

41. Saying: What wilt thou that I shall do unto thee? And he said, Lord, that I may receive my sight.

42. And Jesus said unto him, Receive thy sight. Thy faith hath saved thee.

43. And immediately he re-ceived his sight, and followed him, etc.

XXVII, XXVIII, XXIX, XXX.

MARCION, 18. 9.

And Jesus said unto him, This day is salvation come to this house.

LUKE, 19. 9.

And Jesus said unto him, This day is salvation come to this house, forasmuch as he also is a son of Abraham.

MARCION, 19. 4.

And he communicated with the captains, how he might betray him unto them.

LUKE, 22. 4.

And he went his way, and com-muned with the chief priests and captains, how he might betray him unto them.

MARCION, 19. 14.

And he sat down, and the twelve apostles with him.

LUKE, 22. 14.

And when the hour was come, he sat down, and the twelve apos-tles with him.

MARCION, 19. 51.

And striking him, they said Prophesy; who is it that smote thee?

LUKE, 22. 64.

And when they had blindfolded him, they struck him on the face; and asked him, saying: Prophesy, who is it that smote thee?

The account in Marcion, besides being shorter, is the more natural. Being struck from behind, or by a stranger, Jesus was called upon to tell who struck him. It was an impulsive action.

But the author of Luke has the Jews deliberately blindfold Jesus, before striking him.

XXXI.

MARCION, 20. 45.	LUKE, 23. 46.
And crying out with a loud voice, he expired.	And when Jesus had cried with a loud voice, he said, Father, into thy hands I commend my spirit; and having said thus, he gave up the ghost.

These dying words of Jesus are not in either of the other three canonical gospels. They may have been taken by the author of Luke from the Acts of Pilate, or from a later version of the manuscript used by Marcion.

XXXII.

MARCION, 20. 49.	LUKE, 23. 50 to 53.
And behold, a man named Joseph, taking down the body, wrapped it up, and placed it in a hewn tomb.	50. And behold, (there was) a man named Joseph, a counselor; (and he was) a good man, and a just;
	51. (The same had not consented to the counsel and deed of them;) he was of Arimathea, a city of the Jews; who also himself waited for the kingdom of God.
	52. This man went unto Pilate, and begged the body of Jesus.
	53. And he took it down, and wrapped it in linen, and laid it in a sepulcher, that was hewn in stone, wherein never man before was laid.

XXXIII, XXXIV, XXXV, XXXVI.

MARCION, 20. 52.	LUKE, 23. 56.
And returning, they rested the sabbath day, according to the commandment.	And they returned, and prepared spices and ointments; and rested the sabbath day, according to the commandment.

MARCION, 21. 6.	LUKE, 24. 6.
He has risen; remember what he said, while yet living.	He is not here, but is risen; remember how he spake unto you, when he was yet in Galilee.

MARCION, 21. 7.	LUKE, 24. 7.
That it was necessary that the Son of Man should suffer, and be delivered up.	Saying: The Son of Man must be delivered into the hands of sinful men, and be crucified, and the third day rise again.

MARCION, 21. 37.	LUKE, 24. 38 and 39.
And he said unto them, why are ye troubled? Behold my hands and my feet, a spirit hath not bones, as ye see me have.	38. And he said unto them, Why are ye troubled? and why do thoughts arise in your hearts? 39. Behold my hands and my feet, that it is I, myself; handle me and see; for a spirit hath not flesh and bones, as ye see me have.

THE OTHER SIDE.

We will now give the cases where the text of Marcion is the more copious:

I.

MARCION, 5. 20.	LUKE, 8. 21.

According to Volkmar, (though not in the schedule or scholion of Epiphanius), in this verse, after the words, "And he answered and said unto them," is the question, "Who are my mother and my brethren?" Balance of the verse, same as in Luke.

Volkmar may have taken some of his variations from the "Dialogues," etc., attributed to Origen, to which he appears to have given too much attention.

II, III, IV, V, VI.

MARCION, 9. 26.	LUKE, 12. 30.
And your Father knoweth that ye have need of these things of the flesh; (*ton sarkikon.*)	And your Father knoweth that ye have need of these things.

MARCION, 14. 2.	LUKE, 17. 2.
(On the authority of Volkmar.) It would be better for him if he had not been born; or if a millstone were hanged about his neck, etc. (This may have been the reading of Luke at that time. See Tertullian adv. Marcion, 4. 35.)	It were better for him, that a millstone were hanged about his neck, etc.

MARCION, 17. 25.	LUKE, 20. 35.
But they who shall be accounted worthy of God, to obtain that world, etc.	But they who shall be accounted worthy to obtain that world, etc.

MARCION, 20. 2.	LUKE, 23. 2.
And they began to accuse him, saying: We found this fellow perverting the nation, and destroying the law and the prophets, and forbidding to give tribute to Cæsar, and turning away the women and children.	And they began to accuse him saying: We found this (fellow) perverting the nation, and forbidding to give tribute to Cæsar, saying that he himself is Christ, a king.

MARCION, 21. 5.	LUKE, 24. 5.
And as they were afraid, and bowed down their faces to the earth, those in white clothing said to them, etc.	And as they were afraid, and bowed down (their) faces to the earth, they said unto them, etc.

Here are six cases in Marcion, against thirty-six in Luke; or 35 new words in Marcion, to 660 in Luke. If to these we add 315 verses of Luke which are not in Marcion in any form, we have a ratio of 1 to 230.

The strength of the argument, then, based upon the principle of accretion, would be 230 to 1, that the Gospel of Marcion was first written.

But there is other evidence of priority. The Gospel of Marcion is more simple and natural, not only in the mode of expression, but in the order of arrangement.

In the fourth chapter of Luke, Jesus is represented as being tempted in the wilderness, immediately after his baptism; thence he returned into Galilee, and came to Nazareth; [Luke, 4. 16]; where his public ministry commenced. But though commencing, at Nazareth, he is made to refer [v. 23], to works which he had done at Capernaum; a place to which he goes, afterward; [v. 31.]

In Marcion, on the contrary, his public ministry commenced at Capernaum; [Marcion, 1. 1]; whence, [v. 10], he came to Nazareth, and preached; and here, in the natural order, [v. 13], he refers to the works done at Capernaum.

This accords with the Gospel of Matthew, which represents that Jesus did not commence preaching until after he had taken up his residence in Capernaum. [Matt. 4. 13 to 17.] Mark follows Luke. Matthew and Marcion were probably from a common manuscript.

In the Gospel of John, Jesus is represented as performing his first miracle in Cana of Galilee, after which he went down to Capernaum. [John 2. 11, 12.] This, therefore, is confirmatory of Marcion.

It is probable that in Luke, the manuscripts were

put together out of their natural order, and that this disorder was followed in Mark. It was the opinion of Griesbach that the author of Mark had before him the whole of the present Gospel of Luke. Schleiermacher thinks he had some of the manuscripts which comprise the Gospel of Luke.[1]

At the same time, the fact that nearly every word of Marcion is in Luke, besides much additional matter, is strongly suggestive of the theory, that the author of Luke had before him, besides other material, the Gospel of Marcion entire. On the supposition that Marcion was last written, it is difficult to conceive why he should have excluded so large a part of the Gospel of Luke, especially as it is now conceded that it was not done for dogmatic purposes. On the other hand, if Luke was written last, the accumulations were in accordance with the spirit of the age, and the practice of the times. Besides, it was necessary to have a gospel different from that of Marcion, who was a heretic. There is no satisfactory evidence that Marcion had seen either of the canonical gospels, or had even heard of them.

The first two chapters of Luke were wanting in the gospels of the first century. They were also wanting in the Gospel of the Hebrews, or Nazarenes, about A. D. 125, as well as in the Gospel of Marcion, A. D. 145. They first appeared in the Protevangelion, about A. D. 125, and were probably not deemed by Marcion, authentic.

(1.) Schleiermacher on Luke, p. 91.

CHAPTER XXI.

SECOND HALF OF FOURTH PERIOD.

JUSTIN MARTYR.—A. D. 150 to 160.

There has been much diversity of opinion as to the time when Justin Martyr lived, and wrote his far-famed Apologies.

His first Apology was supposed by Page, Neander, Otto, Semisch and others, to have been written A. D. 139. But the reason given for the opinion was, that Verissimus became Cæsar in 139, and it was thought, if the First Apology had been written after that date, he would have been styled Cæsar by Justin. He calls him "the philosopher;" a title in which Justin himself took great pride. He says :

"Do you then, since ye are called pious and philosophers, guardians of justice and lovers of learning, give good heed, and hearken to my address."—[1st Apology, ch. 2.

And again: "This judgment of yours, O Urbicus, does not become the Emperor Pius, nor the philosopher, the son of Cæsar, nor the sacred senate."—[2d Apology, ch. 2.

Here Verissimus is called the philosopher, in the Second Apology, also, which is admitted by all to have been written after 139. The title "philosopher" was at that time esteemed a very honorable one. The embassy or apology of Athenagoras, A. D. 177, was addressed as follows:

"The Embassy of Athenagoras, the Athenian, a philosopher and a Christian, concerning Christians, to the Emperors Marcus Aurelius Antoninus, and Lucius Aurelius Commodus, Armeniaci, Sarmatici, and above all, philosophers."

There are other considerations, which go strongly against so early a date.

Justin was born, A. D. 114, and therefore would be but 25 years of age in 139.

Again: Marcion did not come to Rome, until about 140. The date is generally fixed at 142. But Justin, in the First Apology, speaks of him in terms which imply that he had been a long time disseminating his doctrines.

"And there is Marcion, a man of Pontus," says he, "who is even at this day alive, and teaching his disciples to believe in some other god greater than the Creator."—[1st Apology, ch. 26.

Still further: Justin himself says impliedly, that he was writing 150 years after Christ:

"But lest some should, without reason," says he, "and for the perversion of what we teach, maintain that we say that Christ was born one hundred and fifty years ago, under Cyrenius, and subsequently, in the time of Pontius Pilate, taught what we say he taught," etc. —[1st Apology, ch. 46.

Those who contend for an early date, claim that Justin is here speaking in round numbers merely. But if, when writing in 139, he wished to speak in round numbers, would he not have said 140? Some writers, seeing that for this reason the date should be nearer 150 than 140, have placed it at 146 to 148.   Burton has 148.[1]

We think it consists better with the age of Justin, and with what he says of Marcion, as well as with a true construction of this passage, to take the 150 years as the true time, certainly the minimum time after the birth of Christ, when the First Apology was written.   This is the opinion of Tillemont, Fleury, Ceillier, Dr. Grabe and others, and is sanctioned by the authority of Norton.   Dr. Davidson speaks of Justin as flourishing about 150, though he is inclined to date the Apology two or three years earlier.

We have thought it necessary to review the evidence on this question, because of its importance, and because, though the evidence of a later date than 139, appears almost overwhelming, we find, in the very valuable encyclopedia of McClintock and Strong, it is still stated, that the First Apology was written A. D. 139.[2]

WHAT GOSPELS WERE USED BY JUSTIN?

This is a question of the highest importance. We have now come to the middle of the second century, and to one of the ablest and most celebrated of the fathers; one whose works are famous for the zeal and piety which they display.

(1.) Ecc. Hist. Vol. 2, p. 111.

(2.) Article, "Marcion." The article is accredited to Prof. Worman, of Drew Theological Seminary.

Canon Westcott, through some seventy-five pages, labors with great earnestness, and with much ability, to show that Justin Martyr was acquainted with the canonical gospels.

At the very threshold of the subject, we are met by the fact, that nowhere in all the writings of Justin, does he once so much as mention any of these gospels. Nor does he mention either of their supposed authors, except John. Once his name occurs; not, however, as the author of a gospel, but in such a connection as raises a very strong presumption, that Justin knew of no gospel of John the Apostle.

"And further," says he, "there was a certain man with us, whose name was John, one of the apostles of Christ, who prophesied, by a revelation that was made to him, that those who believed in our Christ, would dwell a thousand years in Jerusalem; and that thereafter, the general, and, in short, the eternal resurrection and judgment of all men, would likewise take place."—[Dialogue with Trypho, ch. 81.

This language is quite inconsistent with the theory that John was the author of a gospel then well known and generally received, and which was a part of the "Memoirs of the Apostles," used and referred to by Justin.

The failure of Justin Martyr to refer to either of the supposed authors of the four gospels, as a writer of such a book, becomes still more significant, when it is considered how often he refers to the Old Testament writers by name, (nearly 200 times in all), and that besides the "Memoirs of the Apostles," the title of which is somewhat indefinite, he specifically mentions two gospels, one of which, the

Acts of Pilate, is still extant.   The other, the Gospel of Peter, is lost.

The argument of Westcott and others is, that inasmuch as there are found in the canonicals gospels, passages closely resembling those quoted by Justin, and in two or three instances, passages exactly the same, that by the Memoirs of the Apostles, which Justin frequently refers to, he must mean the canonical gospels.

On the contrary, it has been shown, by Hilgenfeld, Credner, Mayerhoff and others, and more lately by the author of "Supernatural Religion," who has reviewed the whole subject with great ability, that the argument based upon the similarity of these passages, is entirely inconclusive; and that except in two or three instances, it becomes necessary, in order to obtain parallels, to put together, not only passages from different portions of the same gospel, but in some cases, passages from different gospels.   Also, that by this process the connection is broken up, while the quotations in Justin have, for the most part, a consecutive order, and, as is shown in the context, had such an order in the gospel from which they were taken.

There are also a number of sayings of Christ, given by Justin as quotations, which are not in the canonical gospels at all.

Again, the references of Justin to the various incidents in the life of Jesus, show a divergence from the canonical gospels, not only in the mode of stating facts, but in the facts themselves.   In some instances, they point to a known source, whence they were taken.

While in Luke and Matthew the genealogy of Jesus is traced through Joseph, Justin traces it through Mary. In the Protevangelion, of the use of which by Justin there is much evidence, Mary is said to be of the lineage of David.[1]

Justin, in relating the announcement to Mary, has the angel say, "Behold, thou shalt conceive of the Holy Ghost, and shalt bear a Son, and he shall be called the Son of the Highest, and thou shalt call his name Jesus, for he shall save his people from their sins."[2]

In the Protevangelion, the angel says to Mary :

"The power of the Most High shall overshadow thee; wherefore also the holy thing which shall be born of thee shall be called the Son of the Highest, [in one version, the 'Son of the living God,'] and thou shalt call his name Jesus; for he shall save his people from their sins." —[Chapter 11.

In Luke, the closing of the salutation is,

"Therefore also, that holy thing which shall be born of thee shall be called the Son of God."—[Luke, 1. 35.

The closing phrase, "for he shall save his people from their sins," which is exactly the same in the Apology and in the Protevangelion, is not in this passage of Luke ; neither is it in the 31st verse, which reads, "And behold, thou shalt conceive in thy womb, and bring forth a son, and shalt call his name Jesus."

(1.) Protevangelion, ch. 10.
(2.) Apology, I. 33.

Again, in one version of the Protevangelion, the angels say to Mary, "Fear not, Mary, for thou hast found favor before the Lord, and thou shalt conceive of his Word."[1]

Justin, after quoting what the angel said to Mary, but without giving his authority, says:

"It is wrong, therefore, to understand the spirit and power of God, as anything else than the Word, who is also the first-born of God, as the aforesaid prophet Moses declared; and it was this which, when it came upon the virgin and overshadowed her, caused her to conceive; not by intercourse, but by power."

Nothing of this in Luke.   Justin then adds:

"And the name Jesus, in the Hebrew language, means Savior in the Greek tongue;" and continuing, he repeats the closing words in the announcement to Mary, thus:

"Wherefore, too, the angel said to the virgin, Thou shalt call his name Jesus, for he shall save his people from their sins."—[Apology, ch. 33.

This deliberate repetition of the sentence, in the same words, indicates, quite conclusively, that he was quoting the words of the Protevangelion, from that gospel, or from some other now lost.

Tischendorf himself thinks this passage was a recollection from the Protevangelion, and that it was "unconsciously added, by Justin, to the account in Luke."[2]

Justin, when speaking of the journey of Joseph and Mary to Bethlehem, says:

"On the occasion of the first census, which was taken in Judea, under Cyrenius, he (Joseph) went up from Nazareth, where he lived.

(1.) Ch. 11, as given by Tischendorf, Evang. Apoc. p. 21.
(2.) Wann wurden, etc. p. 77.

to Bethlehem, to which he belonged, to be enrolled; for his family was of the tribe of Judah, which then inhabited that region."—[Dialogue with Trypho, ch. 78.

The differences between the account of Justin, and that in Luke, are manifest.

In the one, the census was taken in Judea. (In the Protevangelion, all the Jews were to be taxed, who were of Bethlehem, in Judea.) In the other, the census was to extend to all the world, or in other words, to the whole Roman Empire. In the one, (not in this passage, but in 1st Apology, ch. 34), Cyrenius is styled "your first procurator in Judea," and in this passage it is stated, that the going to Bethlehem was on the occasion of the first census which was taken under him. In the other, the census is spoken of as being made when Cyrenius was governor of Syria. In the one, the descent of Joseph is said to be from the tribe of Judah. In the other, it is asserted that he was of the house and lineage of David, and that is given as the reason for going to Bethlehem, it being the city of David.

Justin represents Jesus as having been born in a cave,[1] So do the Protevangelion, and the Gospel of the Infancy. In the 70th and 78th chapters of the Dialogue, Justin quotes from Isaiah 33. 16, to prove that it was necessary, for the fulfillment of prophecy, that Christ should be born in a cave. That the birth of Christ took place in a cave, was believed generally by the fathers. Origen and

(1.) Dialogue, ch. 78.

Eusebius state that the cave was shown in their day.[1]

"Later Fathers," says Westcott, "speak of the cave, without any misgivings that they contradict St. Luke."[2]

Justin, when referring to the magi, nearly every time speaks of their coming from Arabia; making the assertion no less than nine times. This must have been taken from some gospel now lost.

Justin says, speaking of Christ,

"He was deemed a carpenter, (for he was in the habit of working as a carpenter, when among men, making plows and yokes; by which he taught the symbols of righteousness and an active life.)"—[Dial. ch. 88.

In the copy of the Gospel of the Infancy published by Tischendorf,[3] it is said of Jesus,

"Now his father was a carpenter, and made at that time, plows and yokes."

Justin speaks of a fire in the River Jordan, when Jesus was baptized. So did the Gospel of the Hebrews.[4] It is also mentioned in "The Preaching of Paul."[5]

Justin has the Holy Spirit say to Jesus, at his baptism, "This is my beloved Son; to-day have I

(1.) Origen, cont. Cels. 1. 51, and Euseb. Vita Const. 3. 40. See also Socrates, Ecc. Hist. 1. 17; Sozomen, Ecc. Hist. 2. 2; Epiph. Hær. 20. 1; Jerome, Ep. 58, ad Paul. The reference to the cave by Gregory Nyssen, has already been given. (Ch. 10.) Origen refers to the Gospel of the Infancy.

(2.) Canon, p. 92, note; referring to Origen and Epiphanius.

(3.) Ev. Apoc. p. 144.

(4.) See chopter 4 of this work, fragment from Epiphanius.

(5.) Treatise on Re-Baptism, apppended to Cyprian's works.

begotten thee." The same form of expression was in the Gospel of the Hebrews, and was quoted by others of the fathers.

These are some of the indications, and it must be admitted they are plain ones, showing that Justin made extensive use of other gospels.

Some of those used by him, are expressly named. —Not only does he allude to the Gospel or Memoirs of Peter,[1] but he twice cites by name, the Acts of Pilate, or Gospel of Nicodemus.

In the 35th chapter of the First Apology, he says of Christ,

"And after he was crucified, they cast lots upon his vesture, and they that crucified him, parted it among them. And that these things did happen, you can ascertain from the Acts of Pontius Pilate."

Some writers have thought that the reference here is to the official report, said to have been made by Pilate to Tiberius. At the same time it is conceded, that even if such a report was made, Justin had never seen it. These writers do not explain, how he could so confidently refer to a report which he had never seen, or how such a report could contain an account so manifestly founded upon Jewish prophecies.

In the text of the gospel called "The Acts of Pilate," as published in the Orthodoxographa of Grynæus, is the following:

"And divided his garments, and upon his vesture they cast lots."— [Acts of Pilate, ch. 10.

Justin says:

"They cast lots upon his vesture, and they that crucified him, parted it among them;"

And refers to the Acts of Pilate, as authority for the statement. There is but little doubt, that the gospel by that name now extant, was the work referred to by Justin.[1] It will be seen that the phraseology is different from that in the canonical gospels. Davidson also thinks Justin had this gospel.[2]

Again : in the 48th chapter of the First Apology, Justin says :

"And that it was predicted that our Christ should heal all diseases, and raise the dead, hear what was said: There are these words: 'At his coming, the lame shall leap as an hart, and the tongue of the stammerer shall be clear speaking; the blind shall see, and the lepers shall be cleansed; and the dead shall rise and walk about.' And that he did those things, you can learn from the Acts of Pontius Pilate."

A number of these miracles are reported in the Gospel of the Acts of Pilate, including the raising from the dead. It is undoubtedly the authority referred to in this passage of Justin Martyr. If any official report was ever made by Pilate to Tiberius, it would scarcely contain admissions that a person whom he had put to death, had performed such miracles.

If, then, as there is every reason to believe, the Gospel of the Acts of Pilate was the work alluded to, we have, on the supposition that the canonical gospels then existed, the extraordinary spectacle presented, of a writer of the middle of the second

(1.) This is the opinion of Tischendorf. — Evang. Apoc. Proleg. p. 64; — Wann wurden, etc. p. 82.

(2.) Canon, p. 100.

century, one of the most prominent fathers of the church, passing over gospels in general circulation, and which were considered authoritative, and as evidence of the miracles of Jesus, citing an apocryphal and discredited gospel.

Various other considerations might be mentioned, affecting, with more or less force, the question, as to what gospels were used by Justin. But let these suffice.

When it is considered, That no one of the canonical gospels is expressly mentioned, nor either of the supposed writers, except John, and he under such circumstances as negative the presumption that Justin knew of him as the author of a gospel—that Justin refers by name to the writers of the Old Testament Scriptures nearly 200 times—that from a large number of quotations from written accounts of the sayings of Christ, only two or three agree literally with the canonical gospels—that in nearly all cases, parallel passages can only be obtained by patching together different passages, and sometimes from different gospels—that Justin quotes sayings of Christ not in the canonical gospels—that he refers to incidents in the life of Jesus, not found at all in those gospels, but which are in other known gospels—and finally that he cites two or three such by name, and one of them as authority for the miracles of Jesus ; it cannot be denied, that the evidence that the canonical gospels were unknown to Justin Martyr, is very strong, and indeed, well nigh conclusive.

There are two circumstances which should be mentioned, which are sometimes relied upon to break the force of this accumulated evidence.

One is, that Justin quotes from the Old Testament loosely, the difference between his quotations and the passages themselves, being, in several instances, as great as between the quotations which have been referred to, and the corresponding passages in the New Testament. The proportion of exact quotations is, however, much greater in the one case than the other, there being over sixty from the Old Testament, or nearly one-half of the whole number; while in a large number of other instances the variation is very slight.

In the citations, on the other hand, relating to the sayings and doings of Christ, the number of exact quotations will not exceed three, out of nearly a hundred. Those which are the same, consist of the sayings of Christ, which were preserved in other gospels, and by oral tradition. Thus, where the quotations are the most important, and should therefore more exactly correspond, they are found, on the contrary, the more divergent.

The other circumstance is, that Justin does not expressly mention Paul, or his writings. Hence, it is argued, his omission to mention other New Testament writers, should not be looked on with surprise. There is some force in the suggestion. At the same time, it is claimed on the other side, that there were special reasons for this omission. The silence concerning Paul has been referred to the well-known schism between him and Peter. Justin's works have been considered as standing upon the Petrine side, or at least, as anti-Pauline. It is possible that some further explanation of the silence of Justin, may be found in the fact, that the only collection of Paul's epistles then in circulation, had been made by Marcion, a heretic, who was peculiarly obnoxious to Justin.

In regard to the "Memoirs of the Apostles," which are referred to some fifteen or twenty times by Justin, as the source of many of his quotations, those who contend that he meant the Gospel of the Hebrews,[1] in support of their theory, point to the significant fact that the Gospel of the Hebrews was also known as The Gospel of the Twelve Apostles." This, they think, was "The Memoirs of the Apostles," referred to by Justin Martyr.

Justin was of Greek descent, but was born at Flavia Neapolis, a city of Samaria. He studied in the various schools of philosophy, and afterward became an earnest and devoted Christian. He lived for a while at Ephesus, and then settled in Rome. Here he suffered martyrdom, about the year 165.

DOCTRINES.—Dr. Priestly held that Justin was the first who advanced the doctrine of the divinity of Christ.[2]

From the time of Justin Martyr, the doctrine of the Logos, or Word, which had prevailed in various

(1.) Davidson, Ewald, Credner, Tischendorf, De Wette, and many others.
(2.) History of the Corruptions of Christianity, vol. 1, p. 46.

forms from ancient times, and which had been so extensively treated by Philo, became associated with the person of Jesus Christ.

The "Word" of Philo, was "The first begotten Son of God," [1] "the first begotten Word," [2] "the Image of God," "the Divine Word," [3] "his most ancient Word," [4] "the Image of God, by which the whole world was created." But Philo was a Jew, and knew nothing of Christ as the Word.

In the writings of Justin Martyr, this phraseology was applied to Jesus.[5] A similar application of the term was afterward adopted in the Gospel of John.

Paul had applied to Jesus the language of the Psalmist, "Thou art my Son; this day have I begotten thee;" but he had not identified the Son and the Word as the same. The "Word" of Paul was the written word of Scripture.

Philo had said the Word was the first begotten Son; Justin Martyr, applying these terms to Christ, asserted that he was the Word, the first and only begotten Son of God. In the writings of Justin, however, he is still subordinated to the Father. It remained for the author of the Gospel of John to boldly and unqualifiedly announce that "the Word was with God, and the Word was God."

(1.)   De Agricult. sec. 12.
(2.)   De Confus. Ling. sec. 28.
(3.)   De Somniis, 1, sec. 12.
(4.)   Ibid, 1. 39.
(5.)   Dialogue, chs. 87 to 100, 105, and other places.

CHAPTER XXII.

SECOND HALF OF FOURTH PERIOD.—Continued.

Apelles—Peregrinus—Marcellina—Philip — Soter— Montanus—Tatian.

Apelles.—A. D. 160.

Apelles is said to have been excommunicated by Marcion. He afterward had a sect and a gospel of his own. He was a Gnostic. There were various Gnostic sects. One of their cardinal doctrines was that Jesus was a man, begotten by man. Some of them held that he became Christ, the Son of God, at the time of his anointing and baptism.

"When," says Baring-Gould, "Gnosticism fixed on the anointing as the communication to Christ of his divine mission and Messiahship, their mention of it was cut out of the gospels in possession of the church, and consequently the canonical gospels are without it to this day."—[Lost and Hostile Gospels, p. 202.

Others believed that Jesus and Christ were different. That Jesus suffered, but Christ only in appearance. These were called Docetæ. Christ, as distinct from the man Jesus, had a pre-existence.

According to the fathers, Apelles denied the resurrection of the dead. He published a collection of revelations which he had received from a noted courtezan, by the name of Philumene.[1]

Not much reliance is placed upon these assertions. They are considered slanders by Dr. Lardner and other candid historians. Especially are such statements against prominent women, who held heretical opinions, entitled to but little credit.

Neander defends the character of Apelles, and considers his intimacy with Philumene altogether blameless.[2]

THE GOSPEL OF APELLES.

But little is known of this gospel. Jerome, in the preface to his Commentary on Matthew, and Venerable Bede, in his Commentary on Luke, refer to the Gospel of Apelles, as one of those alluded to in Luke: "Forasmuch as many have taken in hand to set forth," etc. (Luke, 1. 1.) According to these writers, then, the Gospel of Luke was written in the latter part of the second century.

PEREGRINUS.—A. D. 150 to 169.

Lucian, author of the Dialogues, A. D. 165, gives a history of Peregrinus. He says he learned a wonderful doctrine of the Christians, by conversing with their priests and scribes, near Palestine.

"And in a short time, he showed they were but children to him; for he was prophet, high priest, ruler of a synagogue; uniting all offices in himself alone. Some books he interpreted and explained; others he wrote. They spoke of him as a god, and took him for a law-giver,

(1.) See Tertullian, de Præs. adv. Hær. c. 30; Epiph. Hær. 44; Austin, de Hær. ad Q. 23 in Ap.

(2. Church History, vol. 2, p. 151.

and honored him with the title of master. They still, therefore, worship that great man who was crucified in Palestine, because he introduced into the world this new religion." [1]

Lucian was contemporary with Peregrinus, having been born A. D. 124,[2] and living until after 180.[3] The same writer says further, that Peregrinus was a person who rambled from place to place, and from one sect of philosophy to another. "Having been guilty of parricide and other crimes, he was obliged for a while to leave his native country and travel abroad." He was afterward imprisoned. While in prison, he was visited by Christians, who administered to his necessities. The Governor of Syria set him at liberty. He then returned to Parium, his native place, and afterward, about the year 169, he ascended a funeral pile, which he had voluntarily prepared, and perished in the flames, in the sight of all Greece.

Peregrinus was also called Proteus. His death is mentioned by some of the fathers.[4]

Athenagoras refers to it thus:

"Of the statues of Alexander and Proteus, (the latter, you are aware, threw himself into the fire near Olympia), that of Proteus is likewise said to utter oracles."—[Plea for the Christians, ch. 26.

There is reason to believe that the picture drawn by Lucian, was, like his portraiture of Alexander Abonotichus, and his casual mention of Apollonius of Tyana, colored by the pen of prejudice.

(1.) De Morte Peregrin. t. 1, p. 565.
(2.) Moyle's Works, vol. 2, p. 363.
(3.) Lardner, vol. 4, p. 149.
(4.) Tertullian, ad Mart. cap. 4, p. 157; Athenagoras, see above.

From other writers there are more favorable accounts :

Ammianus Marcellinus, (3d century), mentions his death, and calls him an illustrious philosopher.[1]

Philostratus (210), refers to his death, and speaks of him as a cynic philosopher.[2]

Aulus Gellius, (2d century), speaks of him as follows :

"I saw, when I was at Athens, a philosopher named Peregrinus, and surnamed afterward Proteus; a man of dignity and fortitude, who resided in a little cottage, without the city. As I used to go to him frequently, I heard from him many useful and excellent remarks, among which this is what I chiefly remember:

"He said, 'A wise man would not be guilty of sin, although gods and men were alike ignorant of it.' For he thought a wise man would avoid sin, not from the fear of punishment or disgrace, but from his sense of duty and love of virtue."—[Noctes Atticæ, bk. 12, ch. 11.

He then represents Peregrinus as quoting these lines of Sophocles :

"Nor vainly think your skill can aught conceal;
Time, that knows all things, shall all truths reveal."

It is as difficult to reconcile this sprightly picture by the author of the Attic Nights, with what is said by Lucian, as it is to reconcile the extant Epistles of Apollonius with the notice which Lucian chose to take of that philosopher.

MARCELLINA.—A. D. 160.

Marcellina was the founder of a sect called Mar-

(1.) Amm. i. 29, cap. i.
(2.) De Vit. Soph. i. 2, n i, sec. 13.

cellians. She was a Gnostic—a disciple of Carpo-crates.

The fathers are almost entirely silent concerning her. If we are left in ignorance of desirable information, her name has at least been handed down free from detraction and calumny.

SOTER.—A. D. 164.

Soter was Bishop of Rome, about A. D. 175. Dr. Lardner puts him down as one of the writers of the second century, whose works are lost, and dates his writings, A. D. 164. He may have flourished as a writer before he was made bishop.

PHILIP.—A. D. 170.

This writer is in the same category with the preceding. He is mentioned with Soter and others, as writers of the second century, whose works are lost.[1]

MONTANUS.—A. D. 170.

Dr. Priestly thinks many of the Montanists were Unitarians.

Epiphanius gives extracts from the writings of Montanus, and shows him to have been a millenarian.

Apollonius, the Christian writer of the third century, became an active opponent of Montanism, and endeavored to counteract the impulse which had been given to it by Tertullian. This great father had left the catholic church, and had gone

(1.) Lardner, vol. 1, p. 436.

over to Montanism, about the end of the second century.

Tischendorf says, the opponents of Montanism rejected the Gospel of John.[1]

Epiphanius mentions the Pepuzians, a sect of Montanists, who permitted women to baptize.[2]

TATIAN.—A. D. 170.

Tatian was by birth an Assyrian. He was converted by Justin Martyr, but afterward became a Gnostic, a follower of Marcion. He joined the Encratites, and has been considered by some as the founder of that sect.

His Oration against the Greeks is still extant. It contains no mention of any of the canonical gospels. Some writers claim there are passages parallel with those gospels. They consist of the sayings of Christ, and the better opinion appears to be, that they were taken from the Gospel of the Hebrews.

THE GOSPEL OR HARMONY OF TATIAN.

There is a Harmony of the Gospels attributed to Tatian. It is sometimes called, "The Gospel of Tatian."

The work is first heard of in Eusebius, who says,

"Tatian, however, their former chief, having put together a certain amalgamation and collection, I know not how, of the Gospels, named this the Diatessaron; which even now is current with some."—[Ecc. Hist. 4. 29.

(1.) Origin of the Four Gospels, p. 123.
(2.) Hæer. 49. 2.

The next reference to the Gospel of Tatian is by Epiphanius. He says :

"It is said that he (Tatian) composed the Gospel by Four, which is called by some the Gospel of the Hebrews."—[Hær. 46. 1.

It does not appear that either of these writers had seen any such gospel. They wrote from hearsay ; and the statement of Epiphanius as to the name of the gospel, is no doubt based upon the passage in Eusebius.

The third writer is Theodoret. He says :

"He (Tatian) also composed the gospel which is called the Diatessaron, excising the genealogies, and all the other parts which declare that the Lord was born of the seed of David, according to the flesh. This was used, not only by his own sect, but also by those who held the apostolic doctrines, who did not perceive the evil of the composition, but made use of the book in simplicity, on account of its conciseness. I found, myself, upwards of two hundred such books held in honor among your churches, and collecting them all together, I had them put aside, and instead, introduced the Gospels of the Four Evangelists."—[Haeret. Fab. 1. 20.

The next century, Victor of Capua, referring to Tatian's Gospel, called it "Diapente ;" "The Gospel by Five."[1]

Such is the evidence concerning the Gospel or Harmony of Tatian. Let us attempt to analyze it :

Epiphanius only states, that it was then said that he (Tatian) composed the Gospel by Four ; and immediately adds that it was called by some the Gospel of the Hebrews. This was about A. D. 385. Half a century later, Theodoret asserts that it was

---

(1.) Fabricius, Cod, N. T. 1, p. 378.

then called the Diatessaron, and states something about its composition.

Independently of Eusebius, then, it only appears that in the fourth and fifth centuries it was called the Diatessaron, and in the sixth, the Diapente.

But Eusebius says that Tatian himself called it the Diatessaron. This is not the first statement of Eusebius tending to give an early date to the canonical gospels, in which he is unsupported by earlier authorities.

The importance of the question renders it necessary to examine into the credibility of this witness, and to endeavor to ascertain whether his unsupported statement may be relied upon. This subject will be treated in the next chapter.

In the mean time, there is a circumstance disclosed, which in itself goes strongly to rebut the presumption that Tatian made use of the four gospels.

It appears from the testimony of Theodoret himself, that he felt under the necessity of suppressing this gospel, though it was held in high respect, and two hundred were in use in the churches which he visited.

The fact that Theodoret felt obliged to suppress it, is inconsistent with the theory that it was a harmony of the four gospels, and throws suspicion upon a statement made manifestly for the purpose of supporting such an inference.

(See Note III.)

CHAPTER XXIII.

VALUE OF THE TESTIMONY OF EUSEBIUS.

THE ESTIMATE OF FRIENDLY WRITERS.

Those who are disposed to take the most favorable view of this historian, hold him in low repute as a chronicler of facts.

"The great fault of Eusebius," says canon Westcott, "is a want of independent judgment. He writes under the influence of the last informant, and consequently his narrative is often confused and inconsistent. This is the case, in some degree, with his statements on the canon."—[Canon, p. 283.] He believes it possible, however, to ascertain his real judgment on the question.

Jones charges him with being too credulous, and thinks he was imposed upon, in the correspondence between Christ and Abgarus, or else that the correspondence had been interpolated into the history of Eusebius.[1] The historian affirms, that he found the letters written in the Syriac language, in the public records of the city of Edessa, and that he himself translated them into Greek. The letters are very generally discredited, as well as the statements of Eusebius concerning them.

(1.) Jones, vol. 2, p. 18.

"No one," says Scaliger, speaking of Eusebius, "has contributed more to Christian history, and no one is guilty of more mistakes."[1]

His Falsehoods and Forgeries.

The statements of this historian are made, not only carelessly and blunderingly, but in many instances, in falsification of the facts of history.

Not only the most unblushing falsehoods, but literary forgeries of the vilest character, darken the pages of his apologetic and historical writings.

His misstatements made for the purpose of bringing into disrepute the Gospel of Peter and other writings of the first century, have already been noticed.

As the greater includes the less, we will not stop to consider the countless other merely false statements to be found in his works, but will proceed at once to some of the forgeries of which he has been convicted.

Forgeries on Josephus.

One of the most notorious of these, is in the account of the death of Herod Agrippa.

In the 12th chapter of Acts, it is stated that Herod, while sitting upon his throne, arrayed in royal apparel, and as the people were shouting and calling him a god, was smitten by the angel of the

---

(1.) Elench. Trihær. c. 29. See also, Father Maimberg's Hist. of Arianism, in French, Tom. 1, 1. 1, p. 32; and Valesius' Life of Eusebius, prefixed to his Ecclesiastical History.

Lord, and was eaten by worms, and gave up the ghost.[1]

Josephus says, ''Agrippa, casting his eyes upward, saw an owl, sitting upon a rope, over his head.''[2]

Eusebius, in order to make Josephus agree with the Acts of the Apostles, struck out of the text of the Jewish historian, a whole Greek phrase, meaning an owl sitting upon a rope or cord, and substituted the word meaning angel; so as to make Josephus state that Herod, looking up, saw an angel over his head.[3]

This forgery has been known for centuries, and is not denied by any. Some endeavor to excuse or palliate it, while others pass it over in silence, or as a matter of small importance.

Again: It was the opinion of the learned Dr. Lardner, that Eusebius was the one who was guilty of the forgery of the passage in Josephus concerning Christ.

In the third volume of his works, Dr. Lardner did not openly charge this forgery upon Eusebius, though he more than hinted that he believed him to be the author of it; saying,

"Probably some learned Christian, who had read the works of Josephus, thinking it strange that this Jewish historian should say nothing of Jesus Christ, wrote this paragraph, in the margin of his copy, and thence it came to be afterward inserted into many copies of Josephus."

(1.) Acts, 12. 21 to 23.

(2.) Antiquities, bk. 19, c. 8, 2.

(3.) Ecc. Hist. bk. 2, ch. 10. Eusebius omitted the words "boubona epi skoiniou tinos," "an owl on a certain rope," and substituted "anggelon," "angel."

"Who was the first author of this interpolation," said he, "cannot
be said. Tanaquil Faber (ap. Havercamp, p. 272), suspected Eusebius.
I do not charge it upon him, but I think it was first made about his
time."—[Works, vol. 3, p. 542.

Afterward, however, in the preface to the fourth
volume, he speaks more plainly, and says:

"Indeed, it is not Josephus, but Eusebius or some other Christian
about this time, who composed this paragraph. Every one must be
inclined to think so, who observes the connection in the Evangelical
Demonstration, where is the first quotation of it. In the third book
of that work, Eusebius has a chapter or section, against those who do
not give credit to the history of our Savior's wonderful works. ('*Pros
tous apenthountas tee tou soteeros heemon peri ton paradoxon prax-
eon dieegeeset.*'—[Dem. Ev. l. 3, c. 7, p. 109.] Where follows an excellent argument, taken from the internal characters of credibility in
the evangelical history, the success of the gospel among the Greeks
and Romans, and barbarians, and the zeal, intrepidity and sufferings
of Christ's apostles and the first Christians. Then he says:

" 'Though the testimony of such men concerning our Savior, must
be esteemed fully sufficient, it cannot be amiss for me to add, over
and above, the testimony of Josephus, a Hebrew; who, in the eigh-
teenth book of the Jewish Antiquities, writing the history of affairs
in the time of Pilate, speaks of our Savior in these words:' where
follows the paragraph which we are considering: where" continues
Dr. Lardner, "our Lord is said to be 'a worker of wonderful works,'
('*Heen gar paradoxon ergon poieetees:*') which way of speaking is so
agreeable to Eusebius, and has such a similitude with his style, that
I am disposed to put down below, some instances from him; which
must be of use to satisfy us, that the style of this paragraph is very
Christian, if it be not the composition of Eusebius himself; as Tanaquil Faber suspected."

(Here follow several quotations from the 'Evangelical Demonstration' in the original Greek, showing the frequent use by Eusebius, of
the phrase, *poieetees ergon paradoxon*, 'worker of wonderful works.')
—[Lardner's Works, vol. 4, p. 6.

Thus it appears that Dr. Lardner, who, in the
third volume, only intimated a strong suspicion
against Eusebius, as the author of this forgery,
now, in the commencement of the fourth volume,
after considering the matter more fully, draws an

indictment, charging him openly with the crime; and calling up the case, introduces the evidence. The words "or some other Christian about this time," contained in the indictment, are to be considered as surplusage; since the evidence and the argument are directed against Eusebius himself.

There are other gross liberties taken by Eusebius with the writings of Josephus.

He transcribes Josephus' account of Theudas, and applies it as confirmatory of Acts, 5. 36; while in fact, it disagrees with the account in Acts so much as to have made commentators great trouble. He quotes the passage from the fifth chapter of the twentieth book of the Antiquities, and asserts that the Theudas there mentioned is the same referred to in the Acts; skillfully suppressing the fact, that the Theudas mentioned by Josephus, led that rebellion in the year 45 or 46, at least 38 years after the time mentioned in the Acts of the Apostles.

Again, in regard to the question of the taxing:

Eusebius, in his Chronicles, p. 76, asserts that Cyrenius "made a census of goods and persons" in the time of Herod. In the Ecclesiastical History, bk. 1, ch. 5, he says that Christ was born "the same year when the first census was taken, and Quirinus was Governor of Syria." He adds, "This census is mentioned by Flavius Josephus, the distinguished historian among the Hebrews." If a census was taken in the time of Herod, it is not mentioned by Josephus, who states distinctly, that after the death of Herod, Archelaus reigned nine years and was banished, and then Cyrenius had the assessment and the taxing.[1]

Dr. Lardner, referring to this disingenuous passage, says he ascribes it, not to ignorance, but "to somewhat a great deal worse."

"It is impossible," says he, "that a man of Eusebius' acuteness, who had the New Testament and Josephus before him, should think a census made after Archelaus' banishment, was the same with that before Herod died; but Eusebius was resolved to have St. Luke's history confirmed by the express testimony of the. Jewish historian, right or wrong."—[Lardner's works, vol. 1, p. 179.

THE FORGERY ON PHLEGON.

Origen, in his work against Celsus, says :

"But of the eclipse, which happened in the time of Tiberius, in whose reign Jesus was crucified, and of the great earthquakes which were at that time, Phlegon writes in the thirteenth, or as I think, the fourteenth book of the Chronicle."—[Cont. Celsum, lib. 2, c. 33.

Phlegon was a heathen historian, who wrote about the middle of the second century, and whose works are lost.

The statement of Origen, which was open to suspicion from the first, was severely handled by contemporary writers, who urged that an eclipse of the sun could not then have taken place, as the crucifixion occurred at the time of the Jewish passover, which was at the full of the moon ; when an eclipse of the sun is impossible.

Whether it was further shown that the passage was misquoted, we know not.   At all events, Origen, afterward, in his Commentary on Matthew,

(1.) Antiquities, bk. 17, ch. 13; also bk. 18, ch. 1.

27. 45, in reply to the objections which had been made, said, that Phlegon did not assert that the eclipse mentioned by him, happened at the time of the full moon, and finally concludes that we must not too positively maintain, against heathen people, that Phlegon spoke of the darkness which happened at the death of Jesus Christ.

Now comes Eusebius ; who, writing a hundred years later, not only repeats the original statement, which had been substantially retracted by Origen, but undertakes to quote the very words of Phlegon. The passage in Eusebius is as follows :

"Jesus Christ, the Son of God, our Lord, according to the prophecies concerning him, came to his passion on the 19th year of the reign of Tiberius; about which time, we find these things related in other, even Gentile memoirs, in these very words: 'The sun was eclipsed; there was an earthquake in Bithynia, and many houses were overturned in Nice.' All which things he relates with what happened at our Savior's passion. So writes and says the author of the Olympiads, in the thirteenth book, in these words: 'In the fourth year of the two hundred and second Olympiad, there was an eclipse of the sun, the greatest of any known before. And it was night at the sixth hour of the day, so that the stars appeared in the heavens. And there was a great earthquake in Bithynia, which overturned many houses in Nice.' So writes this aforementioned author."—[Eusebius' Chronicle, p. 77.

This is one of the most manifest of the forgeries of Eusebius.   If there had been any such passage in Phlegon, stating that there was an eclipse of the sun, at the very hour when Christ was crucified, it would have been found out by Origen, who would have availed himself of it, when hard pressed by his adversaries.

Besides, the passage bears internal evidence of being a fabrication.

Eusebius had already quoted the passage from
Phlegon, giving the very words.   In the first quotation, Phlegon says: "The sun was eclipsed;
there was an earthquake in Bithynia, and many
houses were overturned in Nice."   This is given
as the language of Phlegon.   Afterward, Phlegon
is made to say, "In the fourth year," etc., "there
was an eclipse of the sun, the greatest," etc., "and
it was night, the sixth hour of the day," etc., and
"there was a great earthquake in Bithynia which
overturned many houses in Nice."   All this new
matter prefixed to the quotation, and the quotation
itself different.   What was only "an earthquake,"
(giving the very words, as he said, of Phlegon), becomes, in the second quotation, "a great earthquake," and the statement that "the sun was
eclipsed," becomes swollen into a long sentence,
full of additional circumstances.   Then a heathen
historian, for the purpose of sustaining the Christian religion, narrates an earthquake, and an eclipse
of the sun, taking place at the very hour when
Christ was crucified, although the moon was at the
full !

This was only equaled by making a Jewish historian declare that Jesus "was the Christ."

THE FORGERY ON THALLUS.

Eusebius makes Thallus, another heathen historian, who wrote about 220, testify to the eclipse of
the sun.   The following is the language of our historian :

"There was a dreadful darkness over the whole world, and the

rocks were rent by an earthquake, and many buildings were overturned in Judea, and in other parts of the earth. This darkness
Thallus calls an eclipse of the sun, in the third book of his histories;
but as seems to me very improperly; for the Jews keep the passover
in the fourteenth day of the moon; at which time an eclipse of the
sun is impossible."-[Eusebius, Canon. Chron. Græce, by Scaliger, p. 77.

Since quoting from Phlegon, Eusebius appears
to have become enlightened in regard to the possi-
bility of an eclipse of the sun when the moon is at
its full.   Nevertheless, he persists in perpetrating
these forgeries on the heathen writers.   He has no
compunction in making Thallus, a heathen, in his
anxiety to support the gospel historians, declare
that there was an eclipse of the sun at the crucifixion of Christ.

This forgery Eusebius undertakes to father upon
Africanus, quoting as from that writer the words
which are attributed to Thallus.   As the works of
Africanus are lost, there is no way of determining
the question with complete certainty.   There is no
reasonable doubt, however, that the passage emanated, in the first instance, from the author of the
church history.

Thallus was a Syrian, and wrote in Greek.   He
is cited by Justin Martyr, Tertullian, Minucius
Felix, Lactantius and Theophilus, no one of whom
ever claimed that his works contained any such
passage, nor was the passage known, so far as we
have any evidence, to any other ancient writer.

THE FORGERY ON PORPHYRY.

Eusebius quotes, as evidence of the truth of the
Christian religion, from a pretended work of Por-

phyry, entitled "The Philosophy of Oracles," a work never heard of before the time of Eusebius, and never since, but from those who accept as authority the author of the ecclesiastical history. The majority of scholars are pretty well satisfied that such a work never existed.

Porphyry flourished in the latter part of the third century. He was an active opponent of the Christian religion. He wrote so strongly and powerfully against it, that his writings were, by an edict of Constantine, condemned to the flames. Porphyry is made to speak of Christianity as the "prevailing religion;" which it was not, until some time after Porphyry.

It was probably not until after the destruction of the writings of Porphyry, in accordance with the decree of Constantine, that this bold attempt was made to bring him in as a witness in favor of the very religion which he so powerfully opposed.

The "Philosophy of Oracles" has been branded as spurious by Van Dale,[1] by Fontenelle,[2] and other able writers.

Other portions of the works of the church historian, have been suspected.

Dr. Dodwell, Thirlby, and Dr. Jortin thought the letter of rescript of Antoninus Pius, as given by Eusebius, was a forgery. It is generally suspected that the correspondence between Christ and Abgarus is a literary work of the same character.

(1.) De Orac. Ethnic. p. 14.
(2.) Hist. of Oracles, Diss. I, ch. 4.
[See Note IV.]

Such was the first chronicler of church history whose works have come down to us. Such is the witness, the only witness to any thing which would indicate, with any definiteness, the existence of any of the canonical gospels earlier than about A. D. 170.

"Reject Eusebius," says Prof. Stowe, "and what have we for a history of the Christian churches of the first three centuries, or of the books used as scripture in those churches?"—[History of the Bible, p. 47.

And yet, the truth requires that he should not at all be relied upon, except where he is supported by earlier, or at least contemporary writers, or by strong circumstantial evidence.

CHAPTER XXIV.

A. D. 120 to 170.

Since leaving the apostolic fathers, we have traveled, by the uncertain light of patristic literature, through half a century;—the last half of a period well characterized by Dr. Westcott as the dark age of church history. (A. D. 70 to 170.)

We have met with twenty-six Christian writers, some of them persons of much celebrity, and all of them writers of considerable repute, besides others of less note, and with various anonymous works, including the three most famous so-called apocryphal gospels.

In all this mass of Christian literature, there is not to be found a single mention of any of the canonical gospels. Not one of all these writers, in any work which has been preserved, has mentioned Luke, Mark, John or Matthew, as the author of a gospel.

The Gospel of Marcion, written about A. D. 145, bears internal evidence of having preceded Luke, and in like manner the Protevangelion and the Gospel of the Infancy were manifestly written before Luke and Matthew, and the Acts of Pilate before any of the canonical gospels.

Coming to Justin Martyr, who wrote fully as late as the middle of the second century, there· is no satisfactory evidence that he used or knew of the existence of any such gospels as those which afterward became canonical.

Continuing through the remainder of the period, we meet with several writers, nearly all of whose works are lost. These end with Tatian. There is no sufficient evidence that the so called Diatessaron of this writer was a harmony of the Four Gospels.

The character of Eusebius has been examined, and he has been found to be, as an unsupported witness, entirely unreliable. The facts to which this witness testifies, are not, by any means, of a conclusive character. But they are skillfully thrown together in such a manner as to create the impression, that the canonical gospels were in existence during the time of which he was writing.

In every instance, the assertion is by implication. But the intent to deceive is manifest. The silence, even of Eusebius, as to any evidence earlier than A. D. 126, is significant.

CHAPTER XXV.

THE FOUR CANONICAL GOSPELS.

More than fourteen hundred years ago, Faustus, a Manichæan bishop, a Christian, in his discussion with Augustine, after calling attention to the fact that his opponent himself rejected many portions of the Old Testament, said:

"If there are parts of the Testament of the Father which we are not bound to observe, (for if you attribute the Jewish law to the Father, and it is well known that many things in it shock you, etc.) the testimony of the Son must be equally liable to corruption, and may equally well contain objectionable things; especially as it is allowed not to have been written by the Son himself, *nor by his apostles; but long after, by some unknown men*, who, lest they should be suspected of writing things they knew nothing of, gave to their books the names of the apostles, declaring the contents to be *according* to these originals. In this, I think they do grievous wrong to the disciples of Christ, by quoting their authority for the discordant and contradictory statements in these writings, saying that it was according to them that they wrote the gospels, which are so full of errors and discrepancies, both in facts and opinions, that they can be harmonized neither with themselves, nor with one another. This is nothing else than to slander good men, and to bring the charge of dissension on the brotherhood of the disciples. In reading the gospels, the clear intention of our heart perceives the errors, and to avoid all injustice, we accept whatever is useful in the way of building up our faith, and promoting the glory of the Lord Christ, and of the Almighty God, the Father, while we reject the rest, as unbecoming the majesty of

God and Christ, and inconsistent with our belief."—[Works of Augustine.—On the Manichean Heresy, bk. 32, 1. 2.

Again, in a subsequent passage, continuing his argument, he says:

"I do not suppose you will even consent or listen to such things, as that a father-in-law should lie with his daughter-in-law, as Judah did; or a father with his daughters, as Lot; or with harlots, like Hosea; or that a husband should sell his wife for a night, to her lover, like Abraham; or that a man should marry two sisters, like Jacob; or that the rulers of the people, and the men you consider most inspired, should keep their mistresses by hundreds and thousands; or according to the provision made in Deuteromony about wives, that the wife of one brother, if he die without children, should marry the surviving brother, and that he should raise up seed for her instead of his brother, and if the man refuses to do this, the fair plaintiff should bring her case before the elders, that the brother may be called, and admonished to perform this religious duty, and that if he persists in his refusal, he must not go unpunished, but the woman must loose his shoe from his right foot, and strike him in the face, and send him away, spat upon and accursed, to perpetuate the reproach in his family.

"These, and such as these, are the examples and precepts of the Old Testament. If they are good, why do you not practice them? If they are bad, why do you not condemn the Old Testament, in which they are found? But if you think that these are spurious interpolations, that is precisely what we think of the New Testament. You have no right to claim from us an acknowledgment for the New Testament which you do not make for the Old."—[Ibid. bk. 32, 4.

Again, he says:

"So, then, with the help of the Paraclete, we may take the same liberties with the New Testament, as Jesus enables you to take with the Old, unless you suppose that the Testament of the Son is of greater value than that of the Father, if it is really the Father; so that while many parts of the one are to be condemned, the other must be exempted from all disapproval. That too, *when we know, as I said before, that it was not written by Christ or his apostles.*"—[Ibid.

To this charge, thus repeated, Augustine, after treating other points at length, replies as follows:

"We can now answer the question, how we know that these books were written by the apostles. In a word, we know this in the same way that you know that the books whose authority you are so deluded as to prefer, were written by Manichæus. For suppose some one should raise a question on this point, and should contend, in arguing with you, that the books which you attribute to Manichæus, are not of his authorship. Your only reply would be, to ridicule the absurdity of thus gratuitously calling in question a matter confirmed by successive testimonies, of such wide extent. As, then, it is certain that these books are the production of Manichæus, and as it is ridiculous in one born so many years after, to start objections of his own, and to raise a discussion on the point; with equal confidence may we pronounce it absurd, or rather, pitiable, in Manichæus or his followers, to bring such objections against writings originally well authenticated, and carefully handed down from the times of the apostles to our own day, through a constant succession of custodiers."—[Ibid.

FAUSTUS IN REPLY.—"It is not without reason that we bring a critical judgment to the study of the scriptures, where there are such discrepancies and contradictions. By thus examining every thing, and comparing one passage with another, we determine which contains Christ's actual words, and what may or may not be genuine. For your predecessors have made many interpolations in the words of our Lord, which thus appear under his name while they disagree with his doctrine. *Besides, as we have proved again and again,* the writings are not the production of Christ or of his apostles, but a compilation of rumors and beliefs, *made long after their departure,* by some obscure semi-Jews, not in harmony even with one another, and published by them under the name of the apostles, or of those considered the followers of the apostles, so as to give the appearance of apostolic authority to all these blunders and falsehoods."—[Ibid. bk. 33.

Augustine, in response, repeats the argument already given, and illustrates it by reference to certain books which had appeared under the name of Hippocrates, and had been rejected by physicians, because when compared with the genuine writings of Hippocrates, they were seen to be inferior. As to the genuine writings of that author, he says:

"There is a succession of testimonies of books from the time of Hippocrates to the present day, which makes it unreasonable now or hereafter to have any doubt on the subject. How do we know the authorship of the works of Plato, Aristotle, Cicero, Varro, and other similar writers, but by the unbroken chain of evidence?"—[Ibid.

He afterward speaks of "the ability of the church of the apostles—a community of brethren as numerous as they were faithful, to transmit their writings unaltered to posterity, as the original seats of the apostles have been occupied by a continuous succession of bishops to the present day."

This closed the argument.

Such was the state of the controversy early in the fifth century ; a controversy within the church itself.

On the one side, Faustus had stated, first, that it was "allowed" that the New Testament was not written by Christ or his apostles, but long after, by some unknown men. Then, that they "knew" it was not written by Christ or his apostles, and finally that they "had proven it, again and again."

To this, Augustine, not expressly denying the assertions of Faustus, or challenging him to the proof, replies with the argument founded on tradition. This he illustrates by a comparison with books ascribed to Hippocrates, Aristotle and other writers.

As to the proof that may have been offered by Faustus on former occasions, we are entirely ignorant. But that such proof of some kind had been adduced, may be safely inferred, since the statement was not expressly denied by Augustine.

The argument of Augustine was the same as has been relied upon since his day.

The bold challenge of Faustus would seem to have required something more at the hands of his adversary ; at least, an enumeration or mention of some of those by whom the tradition had been preserved and handed down.

The argument of Augustine was not good, because the statement upon which it rested was not true. It was not true that the books had been "confirmed by successive testimonies from the times of the apostles ; that they were originally well authenticated and carefully handed down," etc., unless, indeed, we are to suppose, that every successive link in this chain of evidence has been lost, and that of all the writings of the Christian fathers to the latter part of the second century, only those which made no mention of the books were preserved, while those which mentioned them were in every instance lost. Such a supposition, if not actually preposterous, is in the highest degree incredible ; and we are forced to the conclusion, that such a chain of evidence existed only in the imagination of Augustine.

The tradition cannot be traced further back than Irenæus, A. D. 190. No one of the four gospels was mentioned earlier, except the Gospel of John, A. D. 180, by Theophilus of Antioch.

He does not say it was written by the apostle, but "by an inspired man."

For nearly a hundred and fifty years after the events related in the canonical gospels, there is no evidence of any such tradition as was necessary to sustain the argument of Augustine. The controversy cannot, therefore, be looked upon as having been settled in his discussion with Faustus ; and as no new light has since been thrown upon the question, it is still an open one.

As such, we propose to consider it. It is the duty of the historian to do what he can toward settling truthfully, important facts ; and surely no fact can be of more importance in religious history, than the time when the four gospels were written.

The external evidence has been considered as our history progressed. It was necessarily of a negative character, but has pointed strongly toward the non-existence of the books, previous to the year 170. We are now to examine the internal evidence. This naturally comes last, and is not ordinarily to be resorted to, except when the historical evidence fails to bring a satisfactory conclusion. "History " says Westcott, "must deliver its full testimony, before internal criticism can find its proper use."

That the external evidence is unsatisfactory, and justifies the resort to internal evidence, is distinctly asserted by Rev. Dr. Davidson, who says :

"The evidence in favor of the authors traditionally assigned to the gospels, and some of the epistles, is still uncertain. A wide gap intervenes between eye witnesses of the apostles or apostolic men that wrote the sacred books, and the earliest fathers who assert their authorship. The additional bridge between them is a precarious one. As the chasm cannot be filled by adequate external evidence, we are thrown back on the internal character of the works themselves."— [Davidson on the Canon, p. 126.

Before proceeding to the internal evidence, there

are certain considerations which are necessary to a complete view of the subject.

1. No one of the four gospels is mentioned in any other part of the New Testament.

2. No work of art of any kind has ever been discovered, no painting, or engraving, no sculpture, or other relic of antiquity, which may be looked upon as furnishing additional evidence of the existence of those gospels, and which was executed earlier than the latter part of the second century. Even the exploration of the Christian catacombs failed to bring to light any evidence of that character.

3. The four gospels were written in Greek, and there was no translation of them into other languages, earlier than the third century.

It has been supposed by some, that Matthew was a translation from a Hebrew gospel. But the tendency of modern thought and criticism is strongly toward the conclusion, that Matthew, as well as the others, was an original Greek production.

The oldest known translations are the Peshito, in the Syriac, and in the Latin, an old translation, the original of the Vulgate.

Efforts have been made to show that there were Latin translations in the second century. They have resulted in nothing tangible, and may be looked upon as mere speculations.

In Germany, Semler made an elaborate attempt to prove that Tertullian had a Latin translation, which had been used before his time ; but the effort cannot be pronounced successful. The view taken by the author of the article in the Encyclopedia of McClintock and Strong, is doubtless the correct one : that Tertullian did not make use of a translation, but translated for himself. The article was written originally for Kitto, by Dr. Alexander, and is entitled "ANTE-HIERONYMIAN VERSIONS." The writer says :

"The early and extensive diffusion of Christianity among the Latin-speaking people, renders it probable that means would be used to supply the Christians who used that language with versions of the scriptures in their own tongue, especially those resident in countries where the Greek language was less generally known. That from an early period such means were used, cannot be doubted; but the information which has reached us is so scanty, that we are not in circumstances to arrive at certainty on many points of interest connected with the subject. It is even matter of debate, whether there were several translations, or one translation, variously corrupted or emended.

"The first writer by whom reference is supposed to be made to a Latin version, is Tertullian; in the words, 'sciamus plane non sic esse in Græce authentico, quomodo in usum exiit per duarum syllabarum aut callidam, aut simplicem eversionem,' etc.—[De Monogamia, c. 11.] 'We may certainly know, that in the Greek original, it does not stand in the form in which, (through the either crafty or simple alteration of two syllables), it has gone out into common use,' etc.—[Ante-Nicene, 'in the form which (through, etc.) has gone out,' etc.]

"It is possible Tertullian has in view here, a version in use among the African Christians: but it is by no means certain that such is his meaning, for he may refer merely to the manner in which the passage in question had come to be usually cited, but without intending to intimate that it was so written in any formal version. The probability that such is really his meaning, is greatly heightened when we compare his language with similar expressions in other parts of his writings. Thus, speaking of the Logos, he says:

"'Hanc Græci *logon* dicunt, quo vacabulo etiam *Sermonem* appellamus. Ideoque in usu est nostrorum per simplicitatem interpretationis, Sermonem, dicere, in primordio apud deum esse,' etc.—[Adv.

Prax. c. 5.] 'This the Greeeks call 'Logos' by which term we also designate Word (or Discourse); and therefore it is now usual, owing to the simple interpretation of our people, to say that the Word was in the beginning with God,' etc.

"Where he seems to have in view, simply, the colloquial usage of the Christian compatriots."

From this it appears, there is no sufficient evidence of a Latin translation of the gospels, up to the time of Tertullian, at the opening of the third century.

The fact that Tertullian did not use a Latin translation, is made more manifest by a passage in the 9th chapter of the second book against Marcion. Speaking of the nature of the soul, he says :

"We must, at the outset, hold fast the meaning of the Greek scripture, which has *afflatus*, not spirit. (*pnoeen*, not *pneuma*.) Some interpreters of the Greek, without reflecting on the difference of the words, and careless about their exact meaning, put spirit for efflatus;" etc.

Here Tertullian would very naturally have referred to the translation, had there been one in use, and would have commented upon the meaning given to the Greek words by the translator. On the contrary, he speaks of the meaning attached to the words by different "interpreters of the Greek." Tertullian was a Greek scholar, and, doubtless, did his own translating.

In the passage referred to by Tertullian, the word is SPIRACULUM in the Vulgate, not EFFLATUS. If a Latin translation was then in use, it is not probable the Vulgate would afterward have differed from it, in the use of this word.

Again, in his citations from Marcion, Tertullian quoted in Latin, as he did from the four gospels. There is still less reason to suppose that he had before him a translation of the Greek of Marcion. The reasonable conclusion is, therefore, that he gave his own rendering to the text of all these gospels.

Tertullian aside, there is absolutely no evidence of any Latin translation of the gospels earlier than the third century.

There is, in fact, nothing very definite until the fourth century. But as the language of Augustine, Jerome and Hilary would seem to imply the existence of at least one translation before their time, it may be assumed that there was a Latin translation in the third century.

THE VULGATE.—This may be said to date properly from the revision of Jerome, A. D. 383. It is not certain whether it extended beyond the gospels, though he was requested by Damasus to revise the New Testament, and his work is sometimes spoken of as a revision of the whole.

If any revision of the balance was made, it was less carefully and thoroughly done; so that the Vulgate was a composite work, consisting of a complete translation of the gospels, and some corrections and emendations of the then current Latin version of the balance of the New Testament.

THE PESHITO.—Efforts have been made, also, to date the Syriac version in the second, or even in the first century; but with no better success. The whole subject was carefully examined by Bishop

Marsh, who came to the conclusion that we had no reliable evidence concerning the Peshito, earlier than Ephraem, who lived in the fourth century. How much earlier than that the version existed, was a matter of speculation.[1]

Dr. Davidson goes somewhat farther, but stops at the third century.   He says :

"In Syria, a version of the New Testament for the use of the church, was made early in the third century." This was the Peshito.—[Canon, p. 114.

The Latin and Syriac were the languages spoken by the great body of Christians who did not understand the Hebraistic Greek, in which the scriptures were written.   There being, then, no translations into these languages before the third century, why, if the gospels were written in the times of the apostles, were all the churches where those languages prevailed, deprived of the use of the books for more than a hundred and fifty years?

4.)   No manuscripts of the gospels are in existence, dating farther back than the fourth century. Of that century or the next, there are three or four ; and some twenty or thirty, more than a thousand years old.

Not only are there no older manuscripts now in existence, but there is no evidence, so far as we are aware, that older copies have existed, at any time, for hundreds of years past.   They are said to have been destroyed in the persecution of Diocletian, about A. D. 303 ; but how could every hidden

(1.)   Notes to Michaelis, vol. 2, p. 554.

manuscript be thus reached and destroyed?

5.   No autograph manuscript of any of the gospels has ever been known, so far as there is any authentic record ; nor has any credible witness ever claimed to have seen such a manuscript.   Jerome did claim that the gospel concerning the birth of Mary, and the infancy of the Savior, which he translated for the bishops, was in the handwriting of Matthew.   But we are not aware that he or any one else ever claimed to have seen a manuscript of a gospel, in the handwriting of either Luke, Mark, Matthew or John.   If the autograph manuscripts had ever existed, they would have been preserved among the most sacred relics of the church.

If they once existed, and were destroyed, where is the record of their existence, and when and where were they destroyed, by whom and under what circumstances?   Who made the first copies and when, and what evidence have we that they were correctly transcribed?

6.   During the first two centuries, tradition was esteemed of more value, and better evidence of the gospel history, than any written book or manuscript.

Of this the reader has had repeated evidence in these pages.   Papias, writing early in the second century, considered that the information which he could derive from books, was not so profitable as that which was preserved in a living tradition.

The great outlines of the life of Christ, says Irenæus, were received by barbarous nations, without written documents, by "ancient tradition."[1]

The extent to which tradition was relied upon, is well illustrated by the letter of Ptolemæus to Flora about A. D. 190. He says he will explain to her the particulars of that doctrine which he had just been mentioning, "by the help of tradition received from the apostles, and handed down to us." He adds, "All must be tried by, and made to square with, the doctrine of the Savior himself, which was to be the rule."[2]

This extensive use of tradition, and the preferring it to any written books, is inconsistent with the general use of gospels which were deemed authoritative and inspired records.

7. The dialect in which the New Testament books were written, a sort of Hebraistic Greek, has been considered evidence of their antiquity. But this dialect prevailed for three centuries after Christ, and was in full use during the second century. The same or similar Hebraisms abound in the apocryphal gospels of that age.

8. The canonical gospels were selected by the bishops from a large number then in circulation. This is asserted by Origen, who says:

"And that not four gospels, but very many were written, *out of which those we have were chosen, and delivered to the churches,* we may perceive," etc.—[In Proem. Lucæ, Hom. 1, t. 2, p. 210.

(1.) Adv. Hær. 3. 4. 2.
(2,) In App. ad Iren. Grabe, Spi. Pat. vol. 2, p. 77.

CHAPTER XXVI.

THE GOSPELS AS A GROUP.

Considered together, as a history, the gospels are fragmentary and incoherent, and far from harmonious.

In the first place, there is a radical difference between the Gospel of John on the one side, and the three synoptics on the other.

In the synoptics, Jesus speaks in parables and proverbs. Short, pithy sayings are ever on his lips. In John, he indulges in theological discourses. In the Synoptics, his ministry lasted one year. Scene, Galilee, except the last few days of his life. In John his ministry lasted some three years, and the time was spent mostly in Jerusalem, and other parts of Judea.

There are a few places where the four gospels run parallel. There are parallel passages, more or less similar, concerning the feeding of the multitude on five loaves and two fishes—Jesus riding into Jerusalem—the reference to his betrayal, when in conversation with his disciples—the prediction of his denial to Peter—the smiting by Peter of the servant of the high priest—the denial of Christ by Peter—the question of Pilate to Jesus, asking him if he was the king of the Jews—the scene concerning the release of Barabbas—the crucifixion of Jesus, with some few of the circumstances attending it—the parting of his garments—the crucifixion of the thieves—the title on the cross—the begging of the body of Jesus, his burial, and the visit to the sepulcher. In these, however, there is considerable diversity, and even contrariety of statement.

Then, again, John is parallel with Mark and Matthew, in the account of Jesus walking on the sea; and of the woman who poured ointment upon him.

John is also parallel with Mark, in the appearance of Jesus to Mary Magdalene, after the resurrection, though the account is much amplified in John, and is parallel with Luke, in the report of Pilate to the Jews, that he found no fault in Jesus, and with the visit of Peter to the sepulcher; with, as in the case of Mary, much amplification.

With the exception of these, and perhaps two or three other passages, everything in John is different from the other gospels, or very differently related.

Any consideration of the gospels as a group, must therefore be confined to the other three.

The Synoptic Gospels.

No question connected with gospel history, has attracted more attention, or elicited more discussion, than that of the origin and formation of the synoptic gospels, Luke, Mark, and Matthew. Volumes have been written upon it, but with very unsatisfactory results. That they are not merely copied, one from the other, with changes, is the almost unanimous verdict of biblical scholars. At the same time the resemblance, not in incident merely, but in language also, is so close, as to indicate some common source, which was drawn upon in their construction. As to the nature of this source, some have supposed an original gospel, others, several original fragmentary gospels; others again, have believed them written mainly from oral traditions.

Eichhorn thought but one document was used by the three evangelists; that additions had been made to different copies of it; that some of the evangelists had some of those copies; others, others; that everything found in common in the three synoptics, was in the common document.

In one respect, the theory of Eichhorn deserves especial attention; recognizing as it does, the natural result of accretion. He considered those portions which were common to Matthew and Mark, and not in Luke, additions made in the copies of a common document, which were used by Matthew and Mark; and in like manner, that those portions found in common in Mark and Luke, and not in

Matthew, were additions made in the copies used by Mark and Luke.[1]

Bishop Marsh made a thorough examination of the subject, and his views may be condensed as follows :

1. The three evangelists used copies of a common Hebrew document.

2. Matthew used this with some additions, in writing his original gospel, which Marsh supposes to have been in Hebrew.

3. Mark and Luke translated the common document into Greek, and used, besides, another Greek translation of it.

4. Afterward, Matthew was translated into Greek, by some one who made use of Mark and Luke.

5. In addition to the common document, there was another, containing only precepts, parables and discourses of Christ, which was used only by Matthew and Luke, who had different copies. [2]

This theory, though quite complicated, comes nearer, probably, than any other, to explaining all the facts, on the hypothesis that Matthew is a mere translation.

That hypothesis is, however, pretty nearly abandoned.

Schleiermacher, not looking upon the theory of Marsh as satisfactory, discarded the hypothesis of a common, original gospel, and undertook to show that Luke, which he considered the principal, and the most reliable gospel, consisted merely of a collection of a large number of manuscripts, compiled and arranged by some one, who wrote nothing more than was necessary to adapt the phraseology to a

(1.) Michaelis, by Marsh, vol. 3, pt. 2, p. 192.
(2.) Notes to Michaelis, vol. 3, pt. 2.

continuous narrative. This theory deserves the most careful attention. It may prove to be the key to the whole subject; especially if it shall become established, as we believe it will be, that Luke was the first of these gospels, and was written after Marcion.

Ewald supposes an original gospel, containing the record of the baptism, the temptation, and the passion.

This was the substructure used by Paul, and composed, perhaps, by the evangelist Philip. It was in Greek. Then followed the Hebrew Oracles, by Matthew, which, with some narratives, contained nearly all the discourses of Christ. Then came Mark, and after that Matthew and Luke.[1]

In all these theories, too little attention appears to have been given to the evidence indicating a late date to these gospels; too little account taken of their close relation to the apocryphal gospels; and the law of accretion, in its application to the question, has not been sufficiently considered.

Other things being equal, the shortest document is the oldest. Not until this fact is recognized, can the complicated questions connected with the synoptic gospels, ever be solved.

The character of the synoptics is well delineated by Mr. Sunderland, as follows:

"At least three of the four gospels can have had no real authors, as we usually understand that word. They are the work of editors; they are compilations; (they are 'mosaics';) the material which enters

(1.) Jahrbuecher, 1848, 1849.

in to make them up being real utterances of Jesus, real events of his life, together with more or less of legendary elements and deviations from historic facts, occasioned by the lapse of years and the necessary imperfections of the human memory."—[What is the Bible, etc., p. 65.

THE LAW OF ACCRETION,

APPLIED TO THE CANONICAL GOSPELS.

The result of a careful comparison of the four gospels, noting all the parallels which consist, not of short passages merely, but of continuous narratives, may be stated as follows :

1. LUKE COMPARED WITH MATTHEW.

In 92 parallels, Luke is the shorter in 44, and the longer in 32.   The others about equal.

2. LUKE COMPARED WITH MARK.

In 95 parallels, Luke is the shorter in 57, and the longer in 21.   The others equal.

3. LUKE COMPARED WITH JOHN.

In 19 parallels, Luke is the shorter in 13, the longer in 4.

The preponderance of shorter passages in Luke,

As compared with Matthew, is as 11 to 8.

As compared with Mark, as 19 to 7.

As compared with John, more than 3 to 1.

Of all the parallels, 206 in number, Luke is the shorter in 114, the longer in 57. Proportion, 2 to 1.

This points to Luke as the older gospel, unless some other reason can be assigned for its greater brevity.

4. MATTHEW COMPARED WITH MARK.

In 105 parallels, Matthew is the shorter in 44 and the longer in 35.

5. MATTHEW COMPARED WITH JOHN.

In 22 parallels, Matthew is the shorter in 13, and the longer in 7.

6. MARK COMPARED WITH JOHN.

In 23 parallels, Mark is the shorter in 12, and the longer in 10.

According to the law of accumulation, or accretion, the order of date of these gospels would be, Luke, Matthew, Mark, John.

We think for reasons that will be given in a subsequent chapter, that the Gospel of Matthew constitutes an exception to the rule, and the true order is, Luke, Mark, John, Matthew.

This order for the synoptics, agrees with the conclusions of the Rev. Mr. Sanday, as to the relative correctness of the three gospels.

"The very same investigation," says he, "which shows that our present St. Mark was not an original (gospel), tells with increased force against St. Matthew. When a document exists dealing with the same subject matter as two other documents, and those two other documents agree together, and differ from it, on as many as 944 separate points, there can be little doubt, that in a great majority of those points, it has deviated from the original, and that it is, therefore, secondary in character. It is both secondary, and secondary on a lower stage than St. Mark; it has preserved the features of the original with a less amount of accuracy.

"The points of the triple synopsis, on which Matthew fails to receive verification, are in all, 944; those on which Mark fails to receive verification, 334; or in other words, the inaccuracies of Matthew are to those of Mark, nearly as three to one."—[Gospels in the Second Century, p. 152.

The inaccuracies of Matthew as compared with Luke, he estimates at five to one.

The time when the four gospels were written, cannot be definitely determined, but may be approximately stated, thus :

Luke, A. D. 170, Mark, 175, John, 178, Matthew, 180.

The theory of a common document for the synoptic gospels, so ably advocated by Eichhorn, cannot

360 FIFTH PERIOD—A. D. 170 TO A. D. 185.

be considered as overthrown. The fragmentary character of Luke has, it is true, been quite conclusively shown by Schleiermacher. But suppose the common document was of a like fragmentary character, and was itself a compilation. Suppose one copy of this came to the hands of Marcion, and was afterward used by the author of Luke, each of whom made additions from other manuscripts. Suppose other copies of the same document, in later stages of accretion, came afterward to the hands of the other gospel historians, successively, and were used by them, with additions of their own, or from other manuscripts. This would account for the complicated phenomena which are presented by the gospels, and which have proved so perplexing to commentators.

Eichhorn did not believe, from a comparison of the four gospels with each other and with older documents, that they came into use before the end of the second century.

Thus his theory, based upon internal criticism, harmonizes with the historical evidence; a fact which entitles it to greater consideration.

CHAPTER XXVII.

THE FOUR CANONICAL GOSPELS.—Continued.

HISTORY OF JESUS, AS GIVEN IN THE GOSPELS.

The genealogy, birth and childhood of Jesus, are narrated in two only of the canonical gospels, Luke and Matthew.

1. THE GENEALOGY OF JESUS.

If immaculately conceived, Christ had no human genealogy, except upon the mother's side ; a fact which was recognized in some of the earlier gospels, and by the earlier fathers, who deemed it sufficient that Mary was of the race of David. [1]

But the compilers of Luke and Matthew, not satisfied that the genealogy of Jesus should be traced through a woman, undertook, strangely enough, to show that Joseph was descended from David. That this was an afterthought, is sufficiently manifest from the result of the undertaking. Both historians give a long line of ancestry ;

(1.) Protevangelion, ch. 10; Justin Martyr, Dialogue with Trypho, chs. 23, 43, 45, 100; Clement of Alex. Strom. I. 21.

but Matthew has Christ descended from Solomon, son of David, while, according to Luke, he descended from Nathan, brother of Solomon.

From that point on, the chain would necessarily be different. Where the names given are alike, if not all fictitious, and thrown in merely to fill up, they were, of course, different persons having the same name; and the genealogy ends as might be expected; the chroniclers assigning to Joseph different fathers.

Many attempts have been made to explain this palpable contradiction, but there is no substantial agreement concerning it, among commentators. The theory that Luke intended the genealogy of Mary, though flatly opposed to the grammatical construction of the Greek, finds probably, at the present time, the most supporters.

Perhaps the reader will be satisfied with the following explanation of Augustine:

"St. Matthew descends through Solomon, by whose mother David sinned; St. Luke ascends through Nathan, another son of the same David, through whom he was purged from his sin. For we read that Nathan was sent to reprove him, and that he might, through repentance, be healed. Both evangelists meet together in David, the one in descending, the other in ascending."—[Sermon 51.

Again: "Now in the generations which Matthew enumerates, the predominant number is forty. For it is the custom of the holy scriptures, not to reckon what is over and above certain round numbers."—[Ibid.

2. THE BIRTH AND INFANCY OF JESUS.

Here, again, the only canonical historians are the authors of Luke and Matthew, and they agree no better in this, than in the genealogy of Joseph.

According to Luke, Jesus having been born in Bethlehem, his parents remained there until the forty days expired for the purification of Mary, when they brought him to Jerusalem, where he was publicly presented in the temple. Joseph and Mary then returned to Nazareth, which, according to the historian, had been their former residence. It has been seen in a former chapter, that the author of Luke made several changes in Marcion's Gospel, to accommodate it to his theory that the parents of Jesus had formerly resided in Nazareth.[1]

The author of Matthew, on the other hand, did not recognize Nazareth as having been the former residence of Joseph and Mary. Instead of returning to that place from Bethlehem, through Jerusalem, they are warned to flee into Egypt, since Herod would seek to destroy the child. And when, after the death of Herod, they returned from Egypt, being warned in a dream, they "turned aside" into the parts of Galilee.

In Luke, nothing is said of the magi, the slaughter of the infants, or the flight to Egypt. In Matthew, nothing is said of the announcement to Mary, the appearance to the shepherds, or the presentation in the temple.

The public presentation of Jesus at that time, in the temple, at Jerusalem, is utterly inconsistent with the seeking of his life by Herod, and the warning to his parents at Bethlehem.

(1.) This theory was supported by the Gospel of the Infancy.

"All attempts," says Schleiermacher, "to reconcile these two contradictory statements, seem only elaborate efforts of art."—[Essay on
Luke, p. 48.

But this is not all. There is a difference between
Luke and Matthew, of about eleven years, in the
time of the birth of Christ.

According to Matthew, Jesus was born during
the reign of Herod, and some time, say two years,
before his death. Herod was succeeded by Archelaus, who reigned nine years, and was then banished. The country of Archelaus was then added
to the province of Syria, and Cyrenius was sent out
as governor, with instructions to take an account
of the people's effects, for the purposes of taxation.[1]

This, which was more than nine years after the
death of Herod, was, according to Luke, the time
when Jesus was born.—[Luke, 2. 1 to 7.]

Numberless attempts have been made to solve
the difficulty. Dr. Lardner has handled the subject at great length, and with much skill and ingenuity.[2]

It may be safely said, however, that the difficulty has never been removed. In the language of
Schleiermacher, the "most indispensable conditions" to a solution of these chronological difficulties, "are wanting." For which reason, he asserts
that in the attempt to solve them, "no one has yet
met with the slightest degree of success."[3]

(1.) Josephus, Antiq. bk. 17, ch. 13; bk. 18, ch. 1.
(2.) Lardner's Works, vol. 1, pp. 136 to 179.
(3.) Essay on Luke, p. 38.

Perhaps the most plausible theory is that of Zumpt, who supposes Cyrenius was twice Governor of Syria.[1]

The argument of Zumpt, though ingenious, is far from satisfactory. It is rather a speculation as to what might possibly have been. The two governorships are inconsistent with the language of Josephus, who speaks of Cyrenius as one who had been consul, and who had passed through various magistracies before becoming consul. His governorship is then spoken of, in such a way as indicates it to be a new magistracy.

Besides, even if Cyrenius had before been Governor of Syria, the difficulty would not be removed, except by supposing an assessment and taxing, under his first administration. But the taxing referred to by Josephus, was a new thing. It was manifestly the first attempt of the kind, as it resulted in a revolt, of a very serious character.

In regard to the place of residence of the parents of Jesus, and the journey to Bethlehem, some light may be thrown upon the subject by Jerome's translation, from memory, of one of the gospels of the Infancy, a translation which has usually been known as the Gospel of the Birth of Mary.[2]

It is there stated, (ch. 1.), that the family of Mary's father was of Nazareth, and the family of her mother of Bethlehem. According to the Gos-

(1.) See Smith's Bible Dictionary, Article "Cyrenius."
(2,) See ch. 17, of this work.

pel of the Infancy, also, Joseph and Mary were residing at Nazareth.

It would be very natural that as the time of her
delivery drew near, Mary should desire to be with
her mother, who, probably, was not able to visit
her.   This furnishes a much more plausible reason
for the journey to Bethlehem, than that of the en-
rollment for taxation, as given in Luke; since the
personal presence of Mary, for that purpose, would
not, under such circumstances, have been required.

3.   THE CHILDHOOD OF JESUS.

Here Luke is the only historian, and relates but
a single incident: the dispute of Jesus with the
doctors in the temple, when he was but twelve
years of age.   This narrative, which Schleiermacher supposes to have been contained in a separate manuscript, was no doubt the same which,
with accumulations, constituted the 50th chapter
of the Gospel of the Infancy.

With this exception, the whole life of Jesus, except one year or perhaps three years at its close, is
buried in oblivion.

In the Gospel of the Infancy there are further
accounts of the childhood of Jesus.   But as some
of them are not to his credit, while all are of an
extravagant nature, they are prudently omitted
from the canonical history.

4.   THE MINISTRY OF JESUS.

The plain inference from the synoptic gospels is,

that the ministry of Christ lasted but one year. Every thing related appears to have taken place in or near Galilee, and within the year. He goes up to Jerusalem to but one passover.

But according to John, the ministry must have lasted much longer, as he goes up to three or four passovers, at least. A large part of the time was passed in Judea and Jerusalem.

To add to the confusion, Irenæus, the first writer who mentions the four gospels, asserts that the ministry of Jesus lasted about twenty years, and that he was more than fifty years old when he was crucified. He discusses the question at considerable length. The following is his statement, with the argument by which he supports it :

IRENÆUS AGAINST HERESIES, BOOK II, CHAPTER XXII.

CHRIST DID NOT SUFFER IN THE TWELFTH MONTH AFTER HIS BAPTISM; BUT WAS MORE THAN FIFTY YEARS OLD WHEN HE DIED.

"I have shown that the number thirty fails them (the heretics) in every respect; too few æons, as they represent them, being at one time found within the Pleroma, and then again too many.

"There are not, therefore, thirty æons, nor did the Savior come to be baptized when he was thirty years old for this reason, that he might show forth the thirty silent æons of their system; otherwise they must first of all separate and eject (the Savior) himself from the Pleroma of all.

"Moreover, they affirm that he suffered in the twelfth month, so that he continued to preach for one year after his baptism. They endeavor to establish this point out of the prophet; (for it is written, 'To proclaim the acceptable year of the Lord, and the day of retribution;') being truly blind, inasmuch as they affirm they have found out the mysteries of Bythus; yet not understanding that which is called by Isaiah, the acceptable year of the Lord, nor the day of retribution. For the prophet neither speaks concerning a day which includes a space of twelve hours, nor of a year the length of which is twelve months.

"For even they themselves acknowledge, that the prophets have very often expressed themselves in parables and allegories, and not according to the mere sound of the words."

2. [In this section, Irenæus comments further upon the meaning of the phrases, 'acceptable year of the Lord,' and 'day of retribution.' He claims that the day of retribution has not come, and therefore the acceptable year of the Lord has not passed, and hence it must be more than a year of twelve months.]

3. [The argument in this section is based upon the Gospel of John, Irenæus claiming, that according to the record of "John, the disciple of the Lord," Christ went up to Jerusalem to three passovers. Besides the three mentioned by Irenæus, there would appear to be another; four in all, as follows: (1), John, 2. 23; (2), John, 5. 1; (3), John, 6. 4; (4), John, 13. 1. The first, second and fourth are mentioned by Irenæus. He closes the section thus:]

"Their explanation, therefore, both of the year and the twelfth month, has been proved false, and they ought to reject, either their explanation, or the gospel; otherwise, how is it possible, that the Lord preached for one year only?

"4. Being thirty years when he came to be baptized, and then possessing the full age of a master, (or teacher,) he came to Jerusalem, so that he might be properly acknowledged by all as a master. For he did not seem one thing while he was another, as those affirm who describe him as being man only in appearance; but what he was, that he also appeared to be. Being a master, therefore, he also possessed the age of a master, not despising or evading any condition of humanity, nor setting aside in himself that law which he had appointed for the human race, but sanctifying every age, by that period corresponding to it, which belonged to himself. For he came to save all through means of himself—all I say, who through him are born again to God—infants and children, and boys, and youths, and old men.

"He therefore passed through every age; becoming an infant for infants, thus sanctifying infants; a child for children, thus sanctifying those who are of this age, being at the same time made to them an example of piety, righteousness and submission; a youth for youths, becoming an example to youths, and thus sanctifying them for the Lord.

"So likewise, he was an old man for old men, that he might be a perfect master for all; not merely as respects the setting forth of the truth, but also as regards age; sanctifying at the same time, the aged also, and becoming an example to them likewise. Then, at last, he came on to death itself, that he might be 'the first born from the dead, that in all things he might have the pre-eminence;' the Prince of Life, existing before all, and going before all.

"5. They, however, that they may establish their false opinion regarding that which is written, 'To proclaim the acceptable year of the Lord,' maintain that he preached for one year only, and then suffered in the twelfth month. They are forgetful to their own disadvantage, destroying his work, and robbing him of that age which is both more necessary and more honorable than any other; that more advanced age, I mean, during which also, as a teacher, he excelled all others. For how could he have had disciples if he did not teach? And how could he have taught, unless he had reached the age of a master? For when he came to be baptized, he had not yet completed his thirtieth year, but was beginning to be about thirty years of age. (For thus Luke, who has mentioned his years, has expressed it: 'Now Jesus was, as it were, beginning to be thirty years old,' when he came to receive baptism.) And, (according to these men), he preached only one year, reckoning from his baptism; and on completing his thirtieth year, he suffered, being, in fact, still a young man, who had by no means attained to advanced age.

"Now, that the first stage of early life embraces thirty years, and that this extends onward to the fortieth year, every one will admit; but from the fortieth and fiftieth year a man begins to decline toward old age; which our Lord possessed, while he still fulfilled the office of a teacher, even as the gospel and all the elders testify; those who were conversant in Asia with John, the disciple of the Lord, that John conveyed to them that information. And he (John) remained among them, up to to the times of Trajan. Some of them, moreover, saw not only John, but the other apostles also, and heard the same account from them, and bear testimony to the statement.

"Whom, then, should we believe? Such men as these, or Ptolemæus, who never saw the apostles, and who never, even in his dreams, attained to the slightest trace of an apostle?

"6. But besides this, those very Jews who then disputed with the Lord Jesus Christ, have most clearly indicated the same thing. For when the Lord said to them, 'Your father Abraham rejoiced to see my day, and he saw it, and was glad;' they answered him, 'Thou art not yet fifty years old; and hast thou seen Abraham?' Now, such language is fittingly applied to one who has already passed the age of forty, without having yet reached his fiftieth year, yet is not far from this latter period. But to one who is only thirty years old, it would unquestionably be said, 'Thou art not yet forty years old.' For those who wished to convict him of falsehood, would certainly not extend the number of his years far beyond the age which they saw he had attained. But they mentioned a period near his real age, whether they had truly ascertained this out of the entry in the public register, or simply made a conjecture from what they observed, that he was above forty years old, and that he certainly was not one of only thirty years of age.

"It is altogether unreasonable to suppose that they were mistaken by twenty years, when they wished to prove him younger than the times of Abraham. For what they saw, that they also expressed; and he whom they beheld, was not a mere phantom, but an actual being of flesh and blood. He did not then want much of being fifty years old; and in accordance with that fact, they said to him, 'Thou art not yet fifty years old, and hast thou seen Abraham?'

"He did not, therefore, preach for only one year, nor did he suffer in the twelfth month of the year. For the period included between the thirtieth and fiftieth year, can never be regarded as one year, unless, indeed, among their æons there be so long years assigned to those who sit in their ranks, with Bythus, in the Pleroma. Of which beings, Homer, the poet, too, has spoken; doubtless being inspired by the mother of their error:

> " 'The gods sat round, while Jove presided o'er,
> And converse held upon the golden floor.' "

This extraordinary passage from Irenæus, we have given almost entire. It is a very important chapter in the history of the times ; one which has hitherto been kept in the background. It is time an attempt was made to estimate its historical value.

As to the reasoning of Irenæus, much of it is of an *a priori* character, and as applied to such a subject, entitled to but little consideration. But the argument founded upon the passage, John, 8. 56, 57, is a good one. If Jesus was then but about thirty years of age, the Jews might have said, ''Thou art not yet forty years old ;'' but they would scarcely have said, for any purpose, ''Thou art not yet fifty years old." Much less, when their object was to remind him of the few years which he had spent upon the earth, would they have added eighteen or twenty years, in specifying the limit which he had not reached.

Our author was fully aware of the force of the argument, and accordingly he elaborates it with the confidence of one conscious of writing from a strong position. His conclusion cannot well be avoided. We may, therefore, put down the author of the Gospel according to John, as the second witness of the second century, to the fact, that Jesus was nearly fifty years old at his crucifixion.

Besides these two, there is also, unless Irenæus tells an absolute falsehood, the testimony of all the elders in Asia, who were conversant with John, and some of them with the other apostles also. It must be remembered that Irenæus had been a companion of Polycarp and of others who had seen John, and that he was speaking of what had come to his personal knowledge from the elders in Asia. If, then, Irenæus tells the truth, the evidence in favor of the fact, is almost overwhelming. If, on the other hand, he would deliberately falsify in a matter of this importance, what is his testimony worth, as to the origin of the four gospels?

Against this evidence, we have only the silence of the gospels. But if the silence of the synoptics is consistent with a ministry of three or four years, why is not the further silence of all the gospels, consistent with a ministry of twenty years?

How would such a theory affect the received chronology concerning Christ? The date of the crucifixion at not later than A. D. 36, or when Christ was by the received chronology, forty years old, is settled by the fact, that in that year, Pontius Pilate was removed from his government. That the death of Jesus occurred while Pilate was procurator is attested, not only by five extant gospels, but by the historian Tacitus, who, in speaking of the Christians, says :

"They had their denomination from Christus, who, in the reign of Tiberius, was put to death as a criminal, by the procurator, Pontius Pilate.—[Annals, lib. 15, ch. 44.] (Tiberius reigned till A. D. 37.—See Note V.)

If, then, it be accepted as a historical fact that Christ was about fifty years old at his crucifixion, the date of his birth would have to be set back at least ten years.

It having already been found necessary to date his birth four years before the time first settled upon for the commencement of the Christian era, there can be no objection to extending the four to fourteen, if the facts require it.

It is well known that the date of the Christian era was fixed, in the year 525, by the Roman Abbot, Dionysius Exiguus. It was based upon the account of the birth of Christ as given in Matthew, which is a legend of but little historic value. It is now agreed that Dionysius was mistaken in his date, by at least four years. It is agreed that Jesus was born at least four years before the commencement

of the Christian era, and it may have been fourteen
or even twenty.

5. THE CRUCIFIXION OF JESUS.

In a former chapter, we have given the reasons
for believing that the extant gospel, called the Acts
of Pilate, contains the most reliable historical
account of the crucifixion.

The accounts in the canonical gospels are by no
means consistent or harmonious. The four historians agree that Jesus was apprehended and brought
before the high priest, and taken thence before
Pilate, where he was examined. Luke has him
then sent by Pilate to Herod, who mocked him,
arrayed him in a gorgeous robe, and sent him back
to Pilate; an episode of some importance in the
trial, not mentioned in the other gospels. Passing
over some minor discrepancies, such as that Barabbas was a murderer in Mark and Luke, while in
John he was only known as a robber, and the difference in the color of the robe placed upon Jesus,
we come to the statement of John, that Jesus bore
his own cross, (which was customary in such cases),
to the place of crucifixion. The synoptics, on the
other hand, unite in saying that the cross was borne
by Simon the Cyrenian. This discrepancy, on the
face of it a somewhat serious one, is explained in
one of the apocryphal gospels, which states that
Jesus himself bore the cross a portion of the way,
and Simon the remainder.

Proceeding with the narrative, we find that in
Luke only is related an address of Jesus to the wo-

men, on the way to his execution. When arrived there, he is given to drink, according to Mark, wine mingled with myrrh; according to Matthew, he was given vinegar, mingled with gall, in fulfillment of a prophecy; Luke has the vinegar without the gall.

Mark says, Jesus was crucified at the third hour. (Ch. 15, v. 25.) According to John, (19. 14,) it was about the sixth hour, when he was brought forth to the Jews by Pilate, after which he had to be led to execution. According to Matthew and Mark, there was darkness all over the land, from the sixth to the ninth hour; to which Luke adds, that the sun was darkened. The dying words of Jesus do not agree; Matthew and Mark giving the same as those in the Acts of Pilate, while the words in Luke are different, and those in John different from all the others.

Jesus was upon the cross from three to six hours. Even the latter period was much less than usual. Persons crucified generally lingered at least twelve hours, and sometimes two or three days. The remarkably short time that he remained upon the cross, before being taken down by his disciples, has led some writers to adopt the theory of suspended animation, to account for the supposed resurrection of his body.

The inscription on the cross is given in four different ways, and Luke and John state that it was written in Greek, Latin and Hebrew. According to Mark, it consisted of four Greek words; according to Luke, it consisted of six; acccording to Matthew, seven; according to John, seven also; but with a very important difference in two of the words.

In Mark and Matthew, both of the thieves on the cross are represented as reviling Jesus, while, according to Luke, which follows the Acts of Pilate, but one of them did so; he being rebuked by the other.

The synoptics state that the vail of the temple was rent; to which Matthew adds an earthquake, the rending of the rocks, the opening of the graves, and the coming forth of the dead, though this last is deferred until after the resurrection. The graves are opened at the crucifixion, and remain open two days, the inhabitants waiting till Jesus should first arise, in order that certain prophecies might be fulfilled.

In the Gospel of John, it is stated that in fulfillment of certain prophecies, the side of Jesus was pierced with a spear, and the soldiers refused to break his legs, according to the custom in such cases, though it is to be inferred that they had been commanded to do so.

These narratives throughout bear the impress of having been constructed with reference to the fulfillment of divers Jewish prophecies. It is not probable that the details of the crucifixion had been preserved in any authentic record, made contemporaneously with the event. If such record existed, it was disregarded in the prevailing anxiety to sustain the Messianic character of Jesus, in accordance with the prophecies. The Acts of Pilate, which, in its account of the crucifixion, was probably the most authentic of any existing record, was followed, in the canonical gospels, in some particulars; in others, it was entirely disregarded.

THE RESURRECTION OF JESUS.

The resurrection of the crucified body of Christ, is a doctrine which cannot be traced back beyond the second century.

Paul, who believed in visions, thought he had seen Jesus, and enumerates various other occasions when Christ had been seen by his disciples. First, he was seen by Cephas, then by the twelve, then by more than five hundred brethren at once, then by James, then by all the apostles, and last of all by Paul himself.

It is a fair inference, that these were all apparitions. Paul had seen, or thought he had seen, the spirit, or spiritual body of Jesus, and he heard that the others mentioned had seen the same. That such was the nature of his own vision of Christ, is evident, not only from his explanation of the nature of the resurrection, but from the fact that the appearance to him was after the time when, according to the canonical gospels, Jesus had ascended to heaven. If, then, Jesus appeared on earth, in the same body in which he was crucified, it was not to Paul.

The appearance to the others, to which Paul alludes, was no doubt, of the same character as that to himself. The disciples believed they had seen the spirit or spiritual body of Jesus.

But the Christians of the second century demanded a doctrine concerning the resurrection, of a more material and tangible character.

Accordingly, in the canonical gospels, the very body in which Jesus was crucified, and which was buried by Joseph of Arimathea, is raised from the dead, appears to the disciples, is not only seen but felt, and Jesus himself, in the flesh, as he was before he was crucified, calls for meat, to satisfy his disciples that he was not a spirit; that his body was not spiritual, but material and human like theirs.

As might have been expected, the accounts framed for the purpose of establishing this doctrine, are far from being harmonious or consistent.

In Matthew, two women first come to the sepulcher; in Mark, three; in Luke, a larger number; in John, one. As to the time of day, in Matthew, it had begun to dawn; in John, it was early, while it was yet dark; in Mark, it was at sunrise.

According to Matthew, after the women had arrived at the sepulcher, there was another earthquake, and an angel descended from heaven, rolled back the stone, and then addressed the women. According to the other historians, the women, upon arriving at the sepulcher, found the stone rolled away.

According to Mark, entering into the sepulcher, they saw a young man, clothed in a long white garment. According to Luke, there were two men, in shining garments. According to John, there being but one woman, when she saw the stone rolled away, she ran and told Peter, who, with another, came to the sepulcher. The other disciple, outrunning Peter, came and looked in. Then Peter came, and going in, saw the linen clothes, and the napkin only. The other disciple went in, and saw the same. They returned home, after which, Mary, who remained, saw two angels. Turning round, she saw Jesus, whom she did not know, even after he had spoken to her, she supposing him to be the gardener.

Paul had known no rolling away of the stone from the door of the sepulcher. The spiritual body in which he believed would require no such assistance. But the Petrine and material element in the church prevailed; the spiritual resurrection was set aside, and Christ was made to rise in the very body in which he had been crucified and buried.

CHAPTER XXVIII.

The Gospel according to Luke.

There is good reason to believe that Luke was the first of the canonical gospels. This is rendered probable, partly by internal evidence, (it is compiled from the oldest manuscripts), and partly by the necessity that would exist, of having the first gospel one which would counteract the influence of Marcion. This could best be done through a gospel which, while differing from his, would not vary from it so much as to be repulsive to his followers.

Besides, Marcion, who was a man of learning, had, with much care, compiled the most ancient gospel manuscripts which he could obtain, and the church authorities were under the necessity of using, to a considerable extent, the same materials.

According to Schleiermacher, Luke consists of a compilation of at least 33 different manuscripts; as follows:

MANUSCRIPTS IN LUKE.

1. Introduction.
2. Chapter I.
3. Ch. II, vv. 1 to 20 inclusive.
4. "   "   v. 21.
5. "   "   22 to 40.
6. "   "   41 to 52.
7. " III, v. 1, to ch. IV, v. 15.
8. " IV, vv. 16 to 30.
9. "   "   " 31 to 44.
10. " V, "   1 to 11.
11. "   "   " 12 to 16.
12. "   "   " 17 to 26.
13. "   "   " 27 to 39.
14. " VI, "   1 to 11.
15. "   " v. 12, to ch. VII, v. 10.
16. " VII, vv. 11 to 50.
17. "VIII," 1 to 21.
18. "   "   " 22 to 56.
19. " IX, "   1 to 45.

20. Ch. IX, vv. 46 to 50.
21. "   "   v. 51 to ch. X, v. 24.
22. " X, vv. 25 to 37.
23. "   "   " 38 to 42.
24. " XI, "   1 to 13.
25. "   "   14, to ch. XIII, v. 9.
26. " XIII, vv. 10 to 22.
27. "   "   23, to ch. XIV, v. 24.
28. " XIV, vv. 25 to 35.
29. " XV, 1, to ch. XVII, 19.
30. " XVII, 20, to XIX, 48,
    Consisting of three others;
    XVII 20 to XVIII 14, XVIII
    15 to XIX 28, and XIX 29 to
    XIX 48.
31. Chapters XX and XXI.
32. Ch. XXII v. 1, to XXIII 49.
33. " XXIII v. 50, to the end
    of the gospel.

No 32, consisting, also, of two or more, blended.

Some of these divisions may be too artificial, and may have been established to maintain some supposed unity of purpose in the gospel historian ; but the analysis itself appears to be founded in fact, and is, in the main, pursued in a scientific manner.

If, now, the same process be applied to the Gospel of Marcion, it will be found to consist of a compilation of 26 manuscripts.

An analysis of the two gospels develops the fact that every manuscript after the first eight of Luke, appears in both gospels.

This circumstance favors the theory, that one of these gospels was used in the construction of the other. Which was probably the model?

Not only is Marcion much the shorter, but its narratives are simpler and more natural than those of Luke.

The subject may be illustrated by reference to some of the more important and extensive differences between the two gospels.

The first three chapters of Luke were not in Marcion. The first part of the fourth chapter of Luke which appears in Marcion, is that commencing at verse 16. "And he came to Nazareth." This, in Marcion, comes in its regular order, after the ministry at Capernaum ; while in Luke, Jesus here refers to his doings at Capernaum, though his visit there is not stated until afterward.

We find the whole of the fourth chapter of Luke in Marcion, substantially, except the first 15 verses. But these 15 verses, together with the preceding chapter, none of which was in Marcion, constitute altogether, according to Schleiermacher, a single manuscript. The German critic was writing without any reference to Marcion. This coincidence may therefore be considered confirmatory, at the same time, of the theory of Schleiermacher, and of the priority of Marcion.

In closing the fourth chapter, the author of Luke having arranged sufficient preliminary matter, we may suppose that he now took up the Gospel of Marcion, which he found to be a compilation of manuscripts carefully collected, and made it from this point onward, the basis of the Gospel according to Luke.

382 FIFTH PERIOD—A. D. 170 TO A. D. 185.

Let us see how, upon this supposition, he proceeded with his work.

The style is much the same in the additional matter, as in that which is common to both gospels. Changes and additions are found here and there, some having been made for dogmatic reasons; others apparently for no other purpose than to compose a new gospel.

The first addition of much importance, is Luke, ch. 7, vv. 29 to 35. This contains a saying of Christ, in which is a reference to John the Baptist. V. 34; "The Son of Man is come, eating and drinking," etc. This Hahn supposed was omitted by Marcion, because the representation of Jesus eating and drinking, etc., was opposed to Marcion's view of the spiritual and ethereal nature of Christ's person.[1] But in the very next verse of Marcion's Gospel, Jesus is represented as going into a Pharisee's house, and sitting down to meat. Whatever reason existed for adding these verses in Luke, we can see no reason for omitting them in Marcion.

2. The next place where there is a difference of several verses entire, is Luke, 11, vv. 6, 7 and 8. This is a mere amplification of v. 5, which, in a condensed form, is in Marcion.

3. Luke, 11. 30, 31 and 32.—These verses relate to Jonas, whose name had been inserted in the 29th verse. In Marcion the reading is, "This is an evil generation; they seek a sign, no sign shall be given it." In Luke, "no sign shall be given it, but the sign of Jonas the prophet." The following three verses explain in what manner the preaching of Jonas might be regarded as a sign. It is a continuation of the idea, and the whole passage must stand or fall together.

4. Luke, 11. 49, 50, 51.—This consists of a quotation from an apocryphal book, called "The Wisdom of God." The quotation is of a suspicious character. It contains the statement concerning Zacharias, who perished between the altar and the temple; a statement which, as repeated in Matthew, (23. 35), with the addition of the words "Son of Barachias," has caused commentators so much trouble.[2]

(1.) Das Evangel. Mar. p. 147.
(2.) See Chapter on The Gospel according to Matthew.

Marcion has no allusion to Zacharias, and contains, no doubt, the more ancient form of this passage. Much of the trouble comes from interpolations.

The interpolation in Luke, led to the worse interpolation in Matthew.

5. Luke, 13. 1 to 10, contains the legend concerning Pilate mingling the blood of the Galileans with their sacrifices; also reference to those slain by the falling of the town of Siloam; also the parable of the unfruitful fig-tree. None of it in Marcion.

6. Luke, 13. 29 to 35. This passage is doubtless an interpolation. The portions of it are much disconnected, and the words "Go ye and tell that fox," referring to Herod, can scarcely be accepted as the language of Jesus.

7. One of the most extensive differences is in the parable of the prodigal son, Luke 15. 11 to 32; no part of which is in Marcion. It is essentially Pauline in spirit, as has been well remarked.[3]

There is no reason why so beautiful an illustration of his own views, should have been omitted by Marcion.

8. Luke, 18. 31 to 34.—Jesus predicts to the twelve, his suffering, his death and resurrection. The prediction had already been recorded, (Marcion 6. 22; Luke, 9. 22), and there is no reason why it should be repeated. This entire passage in the 18th chapter, is probably an interpolation.

9. The last twenty verses of the 19th Luke, are entirely wanting in Marcion. The riding upon an ass's colt, is an awkward episode, and was probably inserted to set forth the fulfillment of the prophecy in Zech. 9. 9. Then follows the prediction concerning the destruction of Jerusalem. The other reference, in less explicit language, to the same event, (Luke 13. 34, 35), is also wanting in Marcion. There is no certainty that the prediction was ever uttered by Christ himself. Justin Martyr, who would have found this prophecy so pertinent to enforce his argument, made no allusion to it. The remainder of this passage appears to have been written to illustrate the fulfillment of the prophecy in Jeremiah 7. 11.

10. Luke, 20. 9 to 18. The parable of the vineyard.

This is essentially Pauline in spirit, and has a manifest application to the preaching of the gospel to the Gentiles, after it had been rejected by the Jews. There is no reason why Marcion should have omitted it.

(3.) Hahn, Das Evang. Mar. p. 182; Olshausen, Can. Ev. p. 208.

11. **Luke, 22. 16 to 18.** The paschal supper has been the cause of much controversy in all ages of the church, and was the occasion of the first exercise of a general jurisdiction by the church of Rome. Without entering into the controversy, suffice it to say, if, as there is reason to believe, this passage in 22d Luke is an interpolation upon Marcion, the question becomes much simplified. The supper described in that chapter appears to have been an ordinary meal, having been eaten the evening before the crucifixion; and yet, in verses 16 to 18, it is referred to as the passover.

12. **Luke, 22. 28 to 30.** This is a literal application of certain prophecies to Jesus; an application such as the Jews were constantly making, but such as he himself would scarcely have made, in the form here presented.

13. **Luke, 22. 35 to 38.** Here for the first time, Jesus is made to allude to his coming end. And when his disciples told him there were two swords, he said, "It is enough."

14. **Luke, 22. 49 to 51.**

These are all of the more extended passages in Luke, which are not in Marcion's Gospel. This analysis, equally with the one in a former chapter, affords strong evidence that Marcion was first written.

There are other considerations, indicating a late origin to this gospel.

1. It is expressly stated, in the introduction, that many gospels had been written before this one :

"Forasmuch as many have taken in hand to set forth in order, a declaration of those things which are most surely believed among us, even as they who from the beginning were eye-witnesses and ministers of the word, delivered unto us; it seemed good to me, also," etc., [Translated by the author.]

It is the universal conclusion, that the author of

Luke does not here refer to any of the canonical gospels.[1]

The fact that the other three of those gospels are impliedly excluded by the language used in Luke, raises a strong implication, that they were not then written.   Why would the author refer to many unauthorized gospels, and make no allusion to three which were received as authority?   It is an opinion quite generally entertained, that several gospels are referred to in Luke, which are known to have been written in the second century.

Origen considered that the gospel of the Egyptians and the Gospel of the Twelve Apostles, (of the Hebrews) were among the number.[2]

Jerome extends the list as follows :

"The evangelist Luke declares that there were many who wrote gospels, when he says, 'forasmuch as many,' etc. (c. 1, v. 1), which being published by various authors, gave rise to several heresies. They were such as that according to the Egyptians, and Thomas, and Matthias, and Bartholomew, that of the Twelve Apostles, and Basilides, and Apelles, and others which it would be tedious to enumerate."—[Hieron, Præf. in Comm. in Matth.

The Gospel of Basilides was written about A. D. 125, and that of Apelles, about 160.   Of course, then, according to Jerome, Luke was after 160.

Epiphanius says, in expounding Luke, 1. 1,

(1.)   Origen, Homil. in Luc. 1. 1; Ambrose, Com. on Luke, 1; Augustine, de Cons. Ev. 1. 4, c. 8; Eusebius, Ecc. Hist. 3. 24; Erasmus in Luc. 1. 1; Bellarm. de Mat. Sacr. 1. 1, c. 16; Grotius, in Luc. 1. 1; Father Simon, Crit. Hist. of N. T. par. 1, ch. 3; Jones vol. 1, p. 25; Stowe's Hist. of the Bible, p. 142.

(2.)   Homily in Luc. 1. 1.

"Saying: 'Forasmuch as many have taken in hand,' by which he would intimate that there have been many undertakers of the like work. Among them, I suppose, were Cerinthus, Merinthus, and others." (See also Epi. Hær. 51. 7.)

Cerinthus flourished and wrote about A. D. 145, which Epiphanius thinks was before Luke.

Venerable Bede (A. D. 734) agrees with Jerome, that the Gospels of Basilides and Apelles were among those referred to in Luke.[1]

Erasmus thought the Acts of Pilate, or Gospel of Nicodemus, was among the number.[2]

Jones includes the Gospel of Marcion.[3]

All these writers, in thus dating the Gospel of Luke subsequent to those here named, impliedly renounce the theory of its apostolic origin.

2. The discrepancies betweeen this gospel and that according to Matthew, have already been pointed out. These differences indicate a late origin for one or both of these gospels, and involve in confusion every thing connected with the early history of Christ.

It is impossible, in the present state of the inquiry, to name the author of this gospel.

Westcott thinks it circulated mostly about Alexandria and Antioch,[4] when first published.

(1.) Bede's Works, London, 1844, vol. 10, p. 273.
(2.) Annot. in Luc, 1, 1.
(3.) Jones, vol. 3, Vindication, p. 26.
(4.) Canon, p. 68. Note.

It may have been written at or near Antioch. In that case, the person to whom it was addressed, was probably none other than Theophilus, the writer, who afterward, about A. D. 180, became Bishop of Antioch.

Basnage thinks Luke was the first of the canonical gospels,[1] and there are many reasons for believing he was correct in that opinion.

Michaelis did not consider it inspired ;[2] nor does the author of this, or of either of the canonical gospels, lay any claim to inspiration.

(1.) Ann. 60, num. 31.
(2.) Vol. 1, p. 95.

CHAPTER XXIX.

The Gospel according to Mark.

Mark is the shortest of the four gospels. Its brevity is due partly to the omission of the biography of Christ, which is contained in Luke and Matthew.

It was probably constructed from the Gospel of Peter, as a basis, with many changes, and the incorporation of new material.

If the analysis of Luke be applied to Mark, the following will be the result:

The first seven manuscripts are wanting.

MS. No. 8, Luke, 4. 16 to 30, is omitted in Mark entirely, in place of which is inserted the calling of the apostles; Mark, 1. 16 to 20.

The previous account of the preaching of John, Mark, 1. 1 to 8, is so much different from that in Luke, that it is plain it was not from the same manuscript.

No. 9, Luke, 4. 31 to 44, is closely followed in Mark, (1. 21 to 39.) There is just sufficient expansion of language to justify the presumption that the same manuscript was used; or possibly here, as well as in a few other places, the Gospel of Luke itself.

In point of correctness, it has been already noticed that Sanday places this gospel below Luke. The same view is taken by Schleiermacher. Speaking of the synoptics, he says, that in comparing Luke with Matthew and Mark he sees evidence that the corresponding narratives in the latter gospels, were originally more hastily taken down, or were obscured by passing through many hands.[1]

Pursuing the analysis,

MS. No. 10, Luke, 5. 1 to 11, is not in Mark, though there is a shorter account of a similar transaction.

No. 11, Luke, 5. 12 to 16, is contained in Mark, (1. 40 to 45), but with such an important change at the close, as to draw from Schleiermacher the following remark:

"By this alteration, the history assumes almost an apocryphal character; and if, on the one hand, we acknowledge the instruction we receive by this very circumstance of Mark's narrative, it is no less true, on the other hand, that the comparison is the more unfavorable to him, as his additions frequently tend to this sort of exaggeration."—[Essay on Luke, p. 78.

No. 12, Luke, 5. 17 to 26, all but the first verse, is found substantially the same in Mark, 2. 2 to 12.

No. 13, also, Luke, 5. 27 to 39, is closely followed in Mark, 2. 14 to 22.

So also No. 14, Luke, 6. 1 to 11, in Mark, 2. 23 to 3. 5.

In No. 15, Luke, 6. 12 to 7. 10, we first find a break in a manuscript; hitherto, such as were used being inserted entire, though with alterations.

Mark contains the first and last portion of this, while the middle part, containing portions of the sermon on the mount, is omitted.

The circumstances connected with the choosing of the twelve, Schleiermacher thinks, were misunderstood by Mark. "He had hitherto," he says,

(1.) Essay on Luke, p. 77.

"followed Luke. Not that I would assert, with Griesbach, that he had before him the whole of the present Gospel of Luke, but this collection he most probably had."[1]

After showing that the matter was not properly understood by Mark, he says :

"Under these circumstances, I do not at all see why one should take pains, trying all possible explanations, some of them in the highest degree improbable, to show how Jude, the son of James, and Lebbeus who was named Thaddeus, may be one person."—[p. 93.

No. 16, Luke, 7. 11 to 50, not in Mark.

Schleiermacher is perplexed at not finding the miracle of Nain related by any evangelist but Luke ; especially "considering the scanty number of instances of restoration to life." He thinks the event was recorded by some one who had heard of it at Capernaum, or Jerusalem, and who did not wish to trouble the apostles by applying to them for confirmation of the account.[2]

No. 17, Luke, 8. 1 to 21, is, again, broken up, being found neither entire, nor in the same order, in Mark. The most of it finds a parallel, with much amplification, in Mark, 4. 1 to 25, and 3. 31 to 35.

Commenting upon the contents of this manuscript, Schleiermacher says :

"This addition belongs, undoubtedly, to the number of accumulations and exaggerations which are so very common with Mark, both in the introductions to the several incidents in his gospel, and in the general statements which he occasionally inserts, to fill up a chasm. "
—[Essay; p. 128.

No. 18, Luke, 8. 22 to 56, finds a close parallel in Mark, 4. 36 to 5. 43.

(1.) Essay, p. 91.
(2.) Essay, p. 169.

The manuscript was inserted entire; not, however, without the usual amplification in the different narratives.

No. 19, Luke, 9. 1 to 45. This manuscript, with many variations, and the insertion of much new matter, may be traced as follows: Mark, 6. 7 to 16; same ch. vv. 30 to 44; ch. 8. 27 to 31; same, 34 to 38; ch. 9, vv. 1 to 11; same, 17 to 29, and verses 31 and 32.

No. 20, Luke, 9. 46 to 50. Paralleled in Mark, 9. 33 to 40, to which is subjoined much not in Luke, but parallels to which may be found in Matthew.

MSS. Nos. 21 to 25 inclusive, comprising Luke, 9. 51 to 13. 9, not in Mark, except a few verses, Mark, 3. 22 to 27, parallel with part of No. 25.

Nos. 26 to 29 inclusive, Luke, 13. 10 to 17. 19, not in Mark.

No. 30, Luke, 17. 20 to 19. 48.   First division, 17. 20 to 18. 14, not in Mark. The first part of the second division, Luke, 18. 15 to 43, finds parallel in Mark 10. 13 to 34, and vv. 46 to 52. The balance of the 2d division, Luke, 19. 1 to 28, has no parallel in Mark; while, again, the third division, Luke, 19. 29 to 48, will be found followed more or less closely, in Mark, 11. 1 to 18.

No. 31. Luke, chs. 20 and 21.   Parallel, Mark, 11. 27 to 31, and chs. 12 and 13.

No. 32. Luke, 22. 1 to 23. 49.   Parallels, Mark, 14. 1, 2; same ch. vv. 10 to 17; vv. 22 to 24; v. 26; v. 32; vv. 35 to 38; vv. 43 to 49; vv. 53, 54, and 61 to 72. Also, ch. 15, vv. 1 to 15, 21 to 33, and 37 to 41.

In all this we discover parallels, by no means complete, to only a portion of No. 32. It is impossible to believe that the authors of Luke and Mark here used a common manuscript. The author of Mark, we may suppose, drew somewhat from manuscripts, something from tradition, and much from his imagination.

No. 33. Luke, 23. 50, to the end. Whatever parallel to this there may be in Mark, is in the last part of the gospel.   But Mark here diverges much from the others. The last twelve verses are generally by scholars considered spurious. [1]

(1.) Canon Farrar, in his "Messages of the Books," (London and N. Y., 1887), thus sums up the evidence against the authenticity of the last twelve verses of Mark:

1. There are many remarkable peculiarities of style and expression in the Greek text which are specified, and which do not accord with the balance of the gospel.

2. These verses are wanting in the Sinaitic and Vatican MSS., and are omitted in

As the result of the foregoing analysis, it will be seen, that of the 33 manuscripts in Luke, the first 8 are wanting in Mark, being the same, except No. 8, which were wanting also in Marcion. Of the other 25, 10 are omitted entirely, and 8 are inserted entire, while the others are more or less broken and disjointed ; some of them so much so, as to lose their identity completely.

This result, while it confirms the theory of Schleiermacher, recognizing, as it does, the identity and completeness of most of the manuscripts, at the same time would indicate that the German theologian had, in some instances, carried his division too far ; and had specified, as distinct manuscripts, some portions of Luke, which were founded upon tradition, and composed by the author himself.

The Gospel according to Mark is supposed to have been written at Rome.

It was not quoted by Tertullian, in Africa.

At Rome, where the gospel was probably composed, the stories in Luke, concerning the infancy of Jesus, so manifestly of Eastern original, had not yet obtained much credence. They were accordingly omitted. In this respect, the Gospel of Marcion was, in that portion of Christendom,

many ancient copies of other MSS.

3. Eusebius, Jerome and Gregory of Nyssa say that in their day they were wanting in almost all the Greek copies of the gospels.

4. They must have been unknown to Cyril of Jerusalem, Tertullian and Cyprian, and were not mentioned by Clement of Rome or Clement of Alexandria.

This passage in Mark corresponds with a portion of the 14th chapter of the Acts of Pilate; the usual allowance being made for interpolations, in copying from the Acts.

considered the most reliable, and was looked upon as evidence that the early biography of Jesus was unknown.

The Gospel of Peter is supposed to have contained the substance of the Oracles of Matthew; and as the former was at the basis of Mark, and the latter, of Matthew, that would account for much of the similarity between Mark and Matthew, without assuming that any portion of either was copied directly from the other. Mark has almost a complete parallel in Luke and Matthew taken together. There are but 24 verses which have no parallel in either of the other synoptics.

As to the order in which these gospels were written, much has been said, but the subject is in the utmost confusion and uncertainty.

"That St. Mark wrote later than St. Luke," says Michaelis, "I have no doubt."—[Vol. 3, p. 96. Note.

Baronius, Bellarmine and some others, think this gospel was first written in Latin. This is not improbable, if it was composed at Rome, late in the second century.

That the gospel in its present form was not the work of Mark, the companion of the apostles, is the opinion of Credner,[1] and several other evangelical writers, among whom Mr. Sanday may be included.

(1.) Einleit. Sec. 56.

CHAPTER XXX.

The Gospel according to John.

But little light can be thrown upon the Gospel of John, by any comparison with the manuscripts of Luke.

The first manuscript to which any similarity can be found, is No. 19; the account of the feeding of the multitude, by a miracle. But the differences in the narratives are very great. According to all the synoptics, Jesus had retired to a desert place; in Luke it is stated that it belonged to the city of Bethsaida. According to John, he had gone up into a mountain. According to this historian, it was on the eve of a Jewish passover. This the synoptics say nothing about; nor do they connect Jesus with any passover, except the one at which he suffered. According to Mark and Matthew, who continue the narrative, Jesus sent away the multitudes, and retired into a mountain to pray; according to John, he departed into a mountain, (though he was already in a mountain), to avoid the multitude who wished to take him by force, and make him a king. It will be remembered that this manuscript could not be fully identified in Mark. These were probably different versions of a common tradition.

The essential features of the tradition were, that a multitude consisting of 5000 men, besides the women and children, had been fed by Christ, upon five loaves and two fishes.

The next parallel is No. 30. Of the contents of this long manuscript, there is but the circumstance of Jesus riding on a colt, the foal of an ass, which is briefly noticed, as the fulfillment of a prophecy. This manuscript, also, could not be recognized distinctly in Mark, and there is no reason to believe it was used in John.

No. 32. Luke 22. 1 to 23. 49. Portions of this MS. have partial parallels, in John, 13. 1 to 30; vv. 36 to 38; ch. 18, vv. 1 to 18; 24 to 28; 33 to 40; ch. 19, vv. 15 to 25; 28 to 30.

No. 33. Luke, 23. 50, to the end.

The first part of this manuscript, narrating the begging of the body of Jesus, and his burial, by Joseph of Arimathea, has a closer parallel in John than any of the previous ones; (John, 19. 38 to 42.) The balance of it, however, after the coming of Mary Magdalene to the sepulcher, cannot be recognized.

Thus, it will be seen, that not a single manuscript in Luke can be completely traced in John. In some instances, the writer may have used Luke or Mark.

The inference is, that Luke and John were not composed from common sources.

The same result will follow, upon comparing John with Mark and Matthew.

The Gospel of John stands alone.   It has every mark of being an original gospel, while the synoptics are compilations made, for the most part for the purpose of preserving the early traditions of the disciples, concerning the life and teachings, the sufferings, the death and the resurrection of Jesus.

The Gospel of John is a theological document, written for theological purposes.

The first express testimony to the existence of this gospel, is that of Theophilus, Bishop of Antioch, A. D. 180, who speaks of it thus:

"And hence the holy writings teach us, and all the spirit-bearing (inspired) men, one of whom, John, says, 'In the beginning was the Word, and the Word was with God,'" etc.—[Ad Autolycum, 2. 22.

Here John is not spoken of as an apostle, but as a spirit-bearing, or inspired man.   Such the writer may have considered John the Presbyter, of the second century, who is by many thought to be the author of the gospel.

The internal character of this gospel, is quite inconsistent with the theory of its having been written by the unlettered fisherman, the son of Zebedee.   It is hardly possible that such a person could have become the educated and philosophical theologian, whose pen is to be traced in the Gospel of John.

It is written in purer, and less Hebraistic Greek, than the other gospels, and its style is elegant and graceful.

John the apostle, son of Zebedee, was a Jew. But the author of the Gospel of John, refers to the Jews in the third person. He speaks of the feasts "of the Jews," "the passover of the Jews," "the manner of the purifying of the Jews," etc. The law of Moses is spoken of as "your law," and "their law." Furthermore, the Jews are denounced as the children of the devil.

The fact that in this gospel, the full and absolute divinity of Christ is first distinctly taught, is evidence, also, that it was not written by a Jew. The divinity of Jesus was not a doctrine of the Jewish Christians. It originated with Gentiles, formerly idolaters. To the Jew, it meant polytheism. The early Jewish Christians held Christ to be a man only.

There are also many errors in reference to the geography of the country. The author speaks of Ænon, near to Salim, in Judea; also of Bethany, beyond Jordan, and of "a city of Samaria, called Sychar." If there were any such places, they were strangely unknown to other writers. The learned Dr. Bretschneider points out such mistakes and errors of the geography, chronology, history and statistics of Judea, as no person who had ever resided in that country, or had been by birth a Jew, could possibly have committed.

Even the birthplace of John himself, Bethsaida, or Julias, is assigned to Galilee, when it was situated in another country. This mistake alone, is fatal to the authority of the gospel. This is conceded by Hug,[1] provided it cannot be explained. An attempt has been made to explain it by showing that it was the custom of the people to speak of the Gaulonite country as Galilee. Josephus is cited, as calling Judas, the Galilean, a Gaulonite. Josephus four times refers to Judas as a Galilean.[2] The only place where he is spoken of otherwise,[3] is manifestly a mistake on the part of some transcriber, and arose from the fact, that there were two cities by the name of Gamala, one in Gaulonitis, the other in Galilee. No doubt the passage in Josephus, "a Gaulonite, of a city whose name was Gamala," should read, "a Galilean, of a city whose name was Gamala." It would then correspond with the other passages in Josephus, and with the Acts of the Apostles, [5. 37] ; in all of which he was called Judas of Galilee.

Galilee was a well known district of country, with well defined boundaries ; and it is absurd to suppose that another country, entirely disconnected with it, was called Galilee, without further evidence than this passage of Josephus.

(1.) Introduction to N. T. p. 24.

(2) Antiquities, bk. 18 1. 6; bk. 20, 5. 2; Jewish War, bk. 2, 8. 1, and bk. 2, 17. 8.

(3.) Antiquities, bk. 18, 1. 1.

The conclusion is, that the author of the Gospel of John, was ignorant of the birthplace of John the apostle.

This gospel differs from all three of the synoptics, in relating several events which occurred when John the apostle was not present ; while, strangely enough, other transactions in which, according to the synoptics, the apostle John was present, are not related in the Gospel of John at all ; particularly the transfiguration, which, according to all the synoptics, took place in the presence of Peter, James and John.

That John had neglected to testify, where his testimony would naturally be expected, was noticed, very anciently, by Faustus, the Manichæan, in his controversy with Augustine.   Speaking of the passage, "Think not that I am come," etc. (Matt. 5. 17), he says :

"Who testifies that Jesus said this? Matthew. Where did he say it? On the mountain. Who were present? Peter, Andrew, James and John. Others, but not Matthew himself. He had not as yet chosen Matthew. But one of these four, John, wrote a gospel. Well, then, he relates this somewhere? No, not at all. How is it, then, that John, who was on the mountain, does not testify? And that this was written by Matthew, who became a follower of Jesus some time after he descended from the mountain? It is therefore very doubtful whether Jesus said this; because a proper witness is silent, while an improper witness testifies."—[Augustinus contra Faustum, lib. 17, ch. 1.

The writer of this gospel quotes the Old Testament prophecies, almost as loosely, and with as little regard to their applicability, as the author of Matthew. Psalms, 41. 9, quoted in John 13.

18, did not refer to Christ, nor to Judas. So of John 17. 12.

So strong is the evidence of a late date to this gospel, that its apostolic origin is being abandoned by the ablest evangelical writers. Westcott says, "The earliest account of the origin of the gospel, is already legendary." [1]

Dr. Davidson, author of the article on the canon in the new edition of the Encyclopedia Britannica, says, its Johannine authorship must be abandoned, and its existence prior to A. D. 140, cannot be maintained. [2] Both Irenæus and Jerome assert that John wrote against Cerinthus. Cerinthus flourished about A. D. 145.

Again, there is evidence that in the construction of this gospel, as in that of Matthew, the author had in view the building up of the Roman hierarchy, the foundations of which were then (about A. D. 177—8,) being laid. In the 21st chapter is a detailed account of an appearance of Jesus, after his resurrection, to seven of his disciples, at the Sea of Tiberias, something not heard of in the synoptic gospels, and which bears the impress of an original narrative, suggested by scenes in Christ's ministry. After they had dined, Jesus is made to say to Peter, "Feed my sheep;" an injunction which was afterward repeated.

In Matthew only, is Peter made the rock on

which the Church was to be built, and in John
only, is he enjoined to feed the sheep of Christ.
There is reason to believe that both gospels were
written in the interest of the supremacy of the
Church of Rome.

CHAPTER XXXI.

THE GOSPEL ACCORDING TO MATTHEW.

The Gospel of Matthew presents at once phenomena of the most varied and inexplicable character. While many of its narratives and of its records of the sayings of Christ, from their brevity and simplicity, are recognized as among the oldest traditions, and as having been taken from near the fountain head, the gospel itself bears, in other places, internal evidence of a comparatively late origin.

The persistent statements of Jerome, supported by Epiphanius, that the Gospel of the Hebrews was the Hebrew form of the Gospel of Matthew, statements not at all borne out by the fragments of the Gospel of the Hebrews, which they have given, still further complicate a question, in other respects sufficiently difficult.

Many writers, not willing to discard altogether

the assertions of Jerome and Epiphanius, have
supposed our Matthew to be a translation from a
more correct version of the Hebrew gospel, than
that quoted by those fathers; and that the differences between those quotations and the Greek
Matthew, are to be accounted for, partly by the
difference in the Hebrew versions, and partly by
the freedom of translation. Among these, Bishop
Marsh is one of the most eminent.

Others, giving but little credit to these fathers,
whom in other matters, they have found so unreliable, and resting the case upon internal evidence,
have pronounced the Gospel of Matthew an original Greek production. This view is strongly
maintained by Jones and other modern critics.

THE MANUSCRIPTS OF LUKE COMPARED WITH MATTHEW.

There is a partial parallel, in the third chapter of Matthew, to the
first part of manuscript No. 7; [Luke 3, 1 to 22.] Omitting the genealogies, which are entirely different, the parallel is resumed, and
more closely followed, in the history of the temptation; [Luke, 4. 1 to
13; Matthew, 4. 1 to 11.]

MS. No. 8, Luke, 4. 16 to 30, has no parallel in Matthew.

No. 9, Luke, 4. 31 to 44, which had a complete parallel in Mark, finds
only a partial parallel in Matthew, commencing with verse 38, of
Luke, [Matt. 8. 14], and giving an account of the healing of Simon's
wife's mother, and other sick people.

We early find evidence of that tendency to amplification and exaggeration which is characteristic of
the author of this gospel. Although, in accordance with the accounts in the other synoptics, he
states, in verse 16, that "when the even was come,
they brought unto him many that were possessed

of devils, and he cast out the spirits with his word, and healed all that were sick;" adding, according to his custom, a reference to the fulfillment of prophecy; and though he had also stated, in ch. 4, v. 23, that Jesus went about all Galilee, teaching, etc., and healing all manner of sickness, and all manner of disease, among the people; he there adds, after the narrative has been closed by the other historians, the following:

v. 24. "And his fame went throughout all Syria, and they brought unto him all sick people that were taken with divers diseases and torments, and those who were possessed with devils, and those who were lunatic, and those who had the palsy; and he healed them."

MS. No. 10, Luke, 5. 1 to 11, cannot be traced in Matthew, though there is a shorter account of the calling of the four disciples, corresponding to that in Mark.

No. 11. Luke, 5. 12 to 16. The parallel account in Matthew is shorter than in Luke or Mark. This is one of the places which indicate Matthew as containing the earlier narrative. The account of this miracle, as related in the Acts of Pilate, is shorter than either of these.

No. 12. Luke, 5. 17 to 26. Parallel, Matthew, 9. 1 to 8.

No. 13. Luke, 5. 27 to 39. See Matthew, 9. 9 to 17, which has a close resemblance.

So also No. 14, Luke, 6. 1 to 11; Matthew, 12. 1 to 13.

No. 15. Luke, 6. 12 to 7. 10. The last ten verses of this manuscript, describing the healing of the centurion's servant, are paralleled in Matthew, 8. 5 to 13. The other portion, which commences with the choosing of the twelve, and consists, principally, of sayings of Jesus, can hardly be considered paralleled by the sermon on the mount, which is much more extensive.

No. 16. Luke, 7. 11 to 50, which has no parallel in Mark, has a partial parallel in Matthew. See Luke, 7. 18 to 35, and Matthew, 11. 2 to 19.

No. 17. Luke, 8. 1 to 21. See Matthew, 13. 1 to 25, and 12. 46 to 50, where the parallel is nearly complete.

No. 18. Luke, 8. 22 to 56. Parallel, Matt. 8. 18; vv. 23 to 34; ch. 9, 18 to 25.

19. Luke, 9. 1 to 45. Matt. 10. 1 to 15; 14. 1, 2; vv. 13 to 21; ch. 16 13 to 16, 20; vv. 21 to 28, and ch. 17, 1 to 23. This manuscript, if used at all, is completely broken up.

20. Luke, 9. 46 to 50; Matthew, 18. 1 to 6.

21. Luke, 9. 51 to 10. 24. Partial parallel in Matt. 8. 19 to 22.

MSS. 22, 23 and 24, Luke, 10. 25 to 11. 13. No parallel in Matthew.

No. 25. Luke, 11. 14 to 13. 9. Partial parallel, Matthew 12. 22 to 30 and vv. 38 to 45.

26 to 29. Luke, 13. 10 to 17. 19. No parallel.

No. 30. Luke, 17. 20, to 19. 48. The first division, 17. 20 to 18. 14, has no parallel. First part of second division, 18. 15 to 30, has as parallel, Matt. 19. 13 to 30. Luke, 18. 31 to 43, has Matt. 20. 17 to 19, and 20. 29 to 34. Luke, 19. 29 to 38, has Matthew, 21. 1 to 9, and Luke, 19. 45, 46, has Matt. 21. 12, 13. These partial parallels do not, however, identify the manuscript.

No. 31. Luke, chs. 20 and 21. Partial parallels, Matt. 21. 23 to 27; 33 to 45; ch. 22, vv. 15, 32; vv. 41 to 46; ch. 23, vv. 5 to 7; v. 14; and ch. 24, vv. 1 to 44; following which, are lengthy sayings of Christ, found in Matthew alone.

No. 32. Luke, 22. 1 to 23. 49. Matt. 26. 3 to 5; 14 to 25. The parallel considerably broken. Matt. 27. 1, 2; 11 to 56.

No. 33. Luke, 23. 50, to the end. Some partial parallels, in Matt. 27. 57, to the end.

RECAPITULATION.—Five of the manuscripts are complete in Matthew, though with the customary changes and accumulations. Some dozen of the others have parallels more or less extensive. There is indicated a common use of manuscripts, though not to so great an extent as by the authors of Luke and Mark.

We will now proceed to consider some of the indications of a late date for the construction of the Gospel of Matthew.

1. That Matthew was written for theological purposes, and for the use of the church, after it

had become pretty well established, is shown by
the frequent reference to the prophecies, and the
manifest anxiety to show that the events related,
were in fulfillment of the predictions referred to.
True, the author is quite uniformly unfortunate,
in his selection of prophecies, scarcely one of which
has any reference to the subject matter to which it
is applied.[1] But the object of the writer is nevertheless apparent.

2. The comparatively late composition of this
work may be inferred from the many additions of
incidents of a striking and marvelous character,
not contained in the other gospels. Notably
among these, are the earthquakes at the crucifixion
and the resurrection, both of which were known
to this historian only. Also, the opening of the
graves, and the rising of the saints.

Schleiermacher, in comparing Luke with Mark
and Matthew, sees evidence that the corresponding
narratives in the latter gospels, were originally
more hastily taken down, or were obscured by passing through a great number of hands.[2]

Speaking of the account of casting out the devils,
(Matt. 8. 28 to 33), he says:

"The alteration made here, by introducing two demoniacs, in itself
improbable, as it is not usual for madmen to contract a close friend-
ship and intimacy with each other, might, indeed, admit of a different
explanation, as other instances of a similar duplication are found in
Matthew."—[Essay, p. 137.

(1.) For some instances, see the comparisons between Matthew and the Infancy
gospels.

(2.) Essay on Luke, p. 77.

In regard to the feeding of the multitudes, notwithstanding the statement in Matthew 16, Schleiermacher thinks there was but one feeding, and that Matthew was misled, by having two different accounts of the same transaction.[1]

Speaking of Matt. 16. 13 to 28, he says:

"No one will readily believe, that Christ, in the same breath, as it were, would deliver to Peter the key of the kingdom of heaven, and then call him a Satan, who did not favor the things which be of God."—[Page 153.

He thinks the manner in which Matthew represents the transfiguration, shows that the account had passed through several hands.

"In this narrative," he says, "one perceives the exclusive direction of the reporter's imagination toward the marvelous. On this account, the assertion that the two figures were Moses and Elias, appears far more confident than in Luke, in whose narrative every attentive reader easily sees that it is founded merely on the expression of Peter, in a state between sleeping and waking."—[Page 156.

"In the same way, we may remark, likewise, in the healing of the epileptic in Matthew, a distortion into extravagance."—[Essay, p. 157.

After commenting at length upon the circumstance, he says:

"Matthew, therefore, either has had a less authentic reporter here, or perhaps only obscured the state of the case, by his habit of annexing analogous matter."—[Ibid. p. 159.

In the account in Matthew, corresponding to Luke 9. 46 to 50, Schleiermacher thinks much is annexed which was not spoken on the occasion.[2]

(1.) Essay on Luke, p. 144.

(2.) Essay, p. 162.

He comments on the incoherence in the narratives of Matthew.[1]

Referring to the duplication of the blind men at Jericho, he says, Matthew "had before done something of the same sort, in the case of the demoniac at Gadara." How the mistake happened, he does not undertake to determine.[2]

Speaking of Matt. 21. 1 to 17, he says:

"As to what is said in Matthew, somewhat strangely indeed, of two animals, I can only explain it by the attempt to make the application of the fact to the passage in Zechariah, as close as possible. Any other explanation appears to be lost labor. For if Matthew is to be reconciled with the rest, it must have been properly the *polos* which Christ bespoke for himself; but when the *polos* is able to bear the weight of a man, though it has never been ridden, the she ass no longer runs by its side, but has long left it to itself."—[Essay on Luke, p. 258.

He thinks the rending of the vail poetical. So, also, the opening of the graves, and the rising of the saints from the dead, as related by Matthew.[3]

3. One circumstance indicating a late date for this gospel, is the passage, Matt. 23. 35:

"That upon you may come all the righteous blood shed upon the earth, from the blood of righteous Abel, unto the blood of Zacharias, son of Barachias, whom ye slew, between the temple and the altar."

In Luke, this is quoted from an apocryphal book, called the "Wisdom of God;" and is applied to Zacharias who perished between the altar and the temple." (Luke, 11. 49 to 51.)

The passage was not in Marcion. In Luke,

(1.) Essay on Luke, pp. 190 to 199.
(2.) Ibid. p. 249.
(3.) Ibid. p. 305.

though the place of the death of Zachariah is not described with entire correctness, the reference is in all probability to Zechariah, the son of Jehoida. [See 2d Chron. 24. 20, 21.] But this was ending, a long way back, the list of prophets whose blood had been shed unjustly. The author of Matthew, wishing to bring it down to a later date, adds, "son of Barachias." This changes the personage at once, and brings the scene down to a date subsequent to the time of Christ. Zacharias, son of Barouchos, was massacred by the zealots, inside the temple, shortly before the siege of Jerusalem; about A. D. 69.[1] [See Appendix, Note II.]

It is evident that this portion of the Gospel of Matthew was written, not only after the destruction of Jerusalem, but a long time after. It will be noticed that these words are not here, as in Luke, quoted from the Wisdom of God. They are put into the mouth of Jesus himself, who is made to allude to an event as in the past, which took place more than thirty years after. No one, writing immediately after the destruction of Jerusalem, could have made such a mistake. But a writer living more than a hundred years afterward, might do so. Suppose, a thousand years hence, a history should be under examination, which should represent Andrew Jackson as speaking of something as then past, which had occurred near our own time; say the death of Senator Chandler. Would not that be evidence that the history was written, not only after the death of Chandler, but a long time after?

(1.) Josephus, Jewish War, bk. 4, ch. 5, 4.

4. In Matt. 27. 8, after stating that the chief priests took the silver pieces which Judas had thrown away, and bought with them the potter's field, to bury strangers in, it is added,

"Wherefore, that field was called the field of blood, unto this day."

The phrase, "unto this day," implies a very long time between the transaction and the time of relating it.

So again, Matt. 28. 15. In relating the bribing of the soldiers by the chief priests, there is the following :

"So they took the money, and did as they were taught, and this saying is commonly reported among the Jews, until this day."

5. Evidence of the late construction of Matthew, is to be found in the attempt, in the 16th chapter, to specially connect Peter with the foundation of the Christian church. The narrative of the conversation between Jesus and Peter, as given in Luke and Mark, contains nothing of the kind.

That this was a later interpolation in the gospel history, made in the interest of the Roman Catholic hierarchy, then being established, will become more manifest by comparing the accounts in the synoptic gospels, as follows :

LUKE, ch. 9.	MARK, ch. 8.	MATTHEW, ch. 16.
18. H i s disciples were with him; and he asked them, saying: Whom say the people that I am?	27. And by the way, he asked his disciples, saying unto them: Whom do men say that I am?	13. He asked his disciples, saying: Whom do men say that I, the Son of Man, am?
19. They answering said, John the Bap-	28. And they answered, John the	14. And they said, Some (say) John the Baptist; some, Elias;

LUKE, ch. 9.	MARK, ch. 8.	MATTHEW, ch. 16.
tist; but some (say), Elias; and others (say) that one of the old prophets is risen again. 20. He said unto them, But whom say ye that I am? Peter answering, said, The Christ of God.	Baptist; but some (say), Elias; and others, one of the prophets. 29. And he saith unto them, But whom say ye that I am? And Peter answereth and saith unto him, Thou art the Christ.	and others, Jeremias, or one of the prophets. 15. He saith unto them, But whom say ye that I am? 16. And Simon Peter answered and said, Thou art the Christ, the Son of the living God. 17. And Jesus answered and said unto him, Blessed art thou, Simon Bar-jona; for flesh and blood hath not revealed (it) unto thee, but my Father who is in heaven. 18. And I say also unto thee, that thou art Peter, and upon this rock I will build my church; and the gates of hell shall not prevail against it. 19. And I will give unto thee the keys of the kingdom of heaven; and whatsoever thou shalt bind on earth, shall be bound in heaven; and whatsoever thou shalt loose on earth, shall be loosed in heaven.
21. And he straitly charged them, and commanded (them), to tell no man that thing.	30. And he charged them, that they should tell no man of him.	20. Then charged he his disciples, that they should tell no man, that he was Jesus the Christ.

From the closeness of the parallel it is obvious, that the account was taken from a common manuscript, or from a common tradition.

The saying of Christ to Peter, "Blessed art thou," etc., if it had ever been uttered, was too important

to be omitted by the other historians.   It is a manifest interpolation, made to give gospel sanction to
the hierarchy said to have been established by
Peter.

About this time, A. D. 180 to 190, a violent dispute had arisen, concerning the celebration of
Easter.   The church at Rome was endeavoring to
control the question, and to make it the occasion
for the establishment of a supreme power.   The
Asiatic churches had rebelled against its pretensions.   It was very important to conciliate them.
Let us suppose that at this juncture this gospel had
appeared at Alexandria, whose bishop supported
Rome.   It would at once be adopted in the
churches of Africa, Gaul and Italy, all of which
were favorable to the papal claims.   It would then
be circulated in Asia Minor, among the churches
imbued with Jewish traditions, and among whom
the name of Peter was all powerful, and would
have an immense influence in favor of consolidation.

The epistle of Clement of Rome to James, was,
it is to be presumed, already in circulation.   In
that it was stated that Peter had, at Rome, given
to Clement, in the presence of the congregation,
the keys of the Kingdom, and had used almost the
very words here attributed to Jesus.   Peter had
said of Clement, to the church,

Wherefore, I communicate to him the power of binding and loosing, so that with respect to everything which he shall ordain in the
earth, it shall be decreed in the heavens.   He shall bind what ought
to be bound, and loose what ought to be loosed, as knowing the rule
of the church.

It only needed a gospel, showing that Christ had conferred this power upon Peter, and the chain of title of the Roman pontiff was complete.

WHEN, WHERE AND BY WHOM WRITTEN.—No writer of the first centuries ever assigned a date to the Gospel of Matthew, except Irenæus, whose testimony is generally discarded. He states that it was written for the Jews while Peter and Paul were founding the church at Rome.[1]

"If," says Bishop Marsh, "the arguments in favor of a late date for the composition of St. Matthew's Gospel, be compared with those in favor of an early date, it will be found that the former greatly outweigh the latter."—[Notes to Michaelis, vol. 3, pt. 2, p. 98.

According to the law of accretion, Matthew would stand next to Luke, in point of antiquity.

On the other hand, it has been seen, that several considerations point forcibly to a late date for its composition.

It remains to be considered, whether there is any theory which will explain these seemingly contradictory phenomena. We venture to make a suggestion, which, if not entirely correct, may lead to such inquiries as will result in a correct solution.

About A. D. 180, Pantænus was sent from Alexandria, as a missionary to India. It is said that he there found a Gospel of Matthew, which had been left in India many years before, by Bartholomew, who had preached in that country. There has been much discussion, as to what this Gospel of Matthew, sometimes called the Gospel of Bartholomew, was.

(1.) Irenæus, adv. Hær. 3. 1.

Let us suppose it was a copy of the Oracles of Matthew, to which had been attached some brief narrative of the ministry of Christ. It would be, in that case, one of the oldest copies in existence.

Suppose this copy was brought back to Alexandria, accompanied with some old manuscripts of genealogies; that some zealous Christian in that city, wishing to aid in the consolidation of the church then going on, undertook, from these and other materials, to write a new gospel; that it was published in Alexandria.

Such a work would fulfill all the conditions, and would exhibit the complex character now found in the Gospel of Matthew. The Oracles and accompanying narrative would furnish, in some cases, the most authentic records, and in the shortest and simplest form of any yet published; and this would of itself justify an addition to the gospels then in circulation.

The author would have before him the gospels of the Infancy and the Gospels of Mark and Luke.

That Pantænus was a Jew, we learn from Clement of Alexandria, who speaks of him as a Hebrew of Palestine, whom he found concealed in Egypt, and who "was the true Sicilian bee, gathering the spoil of the flowers of the prophetic and apostolic meadow."—[Stromata, bk. 1, ch. 1.

CHAPTER XXXII.

ACTS OF THE APOSTLES.

The book entitled the "Acts of the Apostles" does not much differ, in its general character, from other writings of the kind which were in circulation among the Christians of the second century. There were Acts of the Apostles supposed to have been written by Leucius; there were The Acts of the Holy Apostles Peter and Paul, The Acts of Peter and Andrew, The Acts of Philip, The Acts of Paul and Thecla, etc.

The same bold appeal to the love of the marvelous—the same disregard of historical facts and geographical and chronological accuracy, which are to be seen in those writings, characterize also, the Acts of the Apostles.

Gaza is spoken of as a deserted place, though at that time it was a flourishing city.

In Acts, 5. 34 to 36, Gamaliel is represented as referring, in a speech, to Theudas, and to acts of his, which were not performed until some forty years after the time referred to, and more than ten years after the time when Gamaliel was delivering his address.   Again, the reference in the 21st chapter, to the Egyptian impostor, does not at all agree with the historical account of the same transaction as given by Josephus.

There is the same loose reference to the prophecies, as in John and Matthew.

This work had but an indifferent standing among the fathers.   As late as at the commencement of the fifth century, Chrysostom said,

"This book is not so much as known to many. They know neither the book, nor by whom it was written."—[Prolegomena to Acts. See also Mill, Prœf. in Act. p. 254.

The text has always been very uncertain.[1]   The Cambridge MS., (Codex Bezæ), has six hundred interpolations.[2]

The author is supposed to have been the same as the compiler of the Gospel of Luke ; a theory based upon the preface to each, and which finds some confirmation in linguistic peculiarities, and similarity of style.

That it was written late in the second century, may be safely assumed.

The following passage is from the writings of Aristides, the sophist, who flourished about A. D. 176.

The similarity in style and incidents to the 27th

(1.) Westcott, Canon, p, 215.
(2.) McClintock & Strong, Article "Cambridge MS."

chapter of Acts, will be at once apparent.

"We were going to Cephalenia, and again we had a high sea, and a contrary wind, and we were tossed up and down, to the great detriment of my health, and beyond what my constitution could bear. Afterward, the like happened in the straits of Achaia, when truly the good mariners would put out from Patræ, at the very time of the equinox, against my will, and very much to my prejudice, under my indispositions. The like things happened again, in the Ægean Sea, through the obstinacy of the master of the ship, and of the mariners; when they would sail, though the winds were contrary; nor would they hearken to me. So we were carried about by the tempest, over that whole sea, for fourteen days and nights, and were oftentimes without food, and at length, with difficulty, got to Miletus."—[Sacrorum Sermon. 2, tom. 1, p. 306.

There is no reason to believe that Aristides had ever seen the Acts, or any other book of the New Testament.

That the Acts of the Apostles, also, was written in the interest of the Roman Catholic hierarchy, must be obvious to any one who will give the matter careful consideration.

In the Acts, a prominence is given to Peter, not to be found elsewhere in the New Testament, if we except the two passages already spoken of. It was Peter who made a speech showing the necessity of selecting another apostle in place of Judas, (the Catholic historians add, that he presided over the election of Matthias)—it was Peter who made the great speech on the day of Pentecost, and who first preached to the Jews—it was he who first announced that the gospel was to go to the Gentiles—it was Peter whom Paul came to Jerusalem to see, and as Bossuet says, to "study"—it was Peter who was a prominent actor at (and, as the Catholic historians have it, presided over) the council of Jerusalem.

Peter is everywhere prominent ; everywhere making speeches, and directing the affairs of the church. He is the "pillar apostle," of both Jews and Gentiles.

Several of these accounts, giving such prominence to Peter, are in direct conflict with the writings of Paul. It was the policy of the author of the Acts, writing in the interest of the Catholic Church, and aiming at unity of doctrine, to ignore the well-known differences that existed all through the early age of the church, between Peter and James, and their Judaistic followers, on the one hand, and Paul and the Gentile Christians on the other. Accordingly, in the Acts, Paul is represented as preaching to the Jews at Samaria and Jerusalem, immediately after his conversion ; although he himself distinctly informs us, in the epistle to the Galatians, that he preached to the Gentiles seventeen years before preaching to the Jews at all. Three years after his conversion, he went up to Jerusalem, but saw only Peter and James. Fourteen years afterward, he went up by revelation, and communicated to the Jews, even then privately at first, the gospel which he had been preaching among the Gentiles. [Galatians, ch. 2.]

In the Acts, not only does Paul preach at once to the Jews, but Peter becomes an apostle to the Gentiles. He is made to say,

"Ye know how that a good while ago, God made choice among us, that the Gentiles, by my mouth, should hear the word of the gospel, and believe."—[Acts, 15. 7.

Thus the distinction so much dwelt upon by Paul,

between himself as the apostle of the Gentiles—of the uncircumcision, and Peter, as the apostle of the Jews—the circumcision, is entirely broken down. Peter preaches to Gentiles and Jews, and Paul to Jews and Gentiles. This is contrary to what is known of the history of the Christian church in the first century, and inconsistent with the declaration of Paul:

"The gospel of the uncircumcision was committed to me, as the gospel of the circumcision was to Peter. For he that wrought effectually in Peter to the apostleship of the circumcision, the same was mighty in me toward the Gentiles."—[Galatians, 2. 7, 8.

Even after the conference at Jerusalem, Paul was obliged to withstand Peter face to face, at Antioch. [Galatians, 2. 11.]

It is plain that the Acts of the Apostles was written in the interest of the Roman Catholic Church, and in support of the tradition that the Church of Rome was founded by the joint labors of Peter and Paul.

This tradition has no foundation except in the writings of one or two fathers of the latter part of the second century; fathers who had in view the same general object as the author of the Acts of the Apostles.

CHAPTER XXXIII.

ORIGIN AND HISTORY OF CHRISTIAN DOCTRINES.

A complete history of Christian doctrines would require volumes. It is obvious, that within the limits of a single chapter, but a meager outline can be given. The completeness of our work requires at least a brief sketch of the doctrines prevailing in the first two centuries.

THE IMMACULATE CONCEPTION.

The first allusion to the immaculate conception of Jesus is in the Epistles of Ignatius; A. D. 115. The belief in the miracles of Jesus, a belief which became common early in the second century, was naturally connected with his deification, and his assignment to a supernatural origin. A being who can disregard and overthrow the laws of nature, must needs be a god, and a god must be begotten by a god. Thus the three doctrines may be said to postulate and prove each other.

The doctrine of the immaculate conception of Jesus, when once announced, rapidly grew into favor, and was firmly established as a doctrine of the church, before the close of the second century.

THE MIRACLES OF JESUS.

The first mention of these was in the Epistle of Barnabas, A. D. 130, and in the Acts of Pilate and other apocryphal gospels, which are supposed to have been written about the same time.

A hundred years of silence by Christian writers, is at least wonderful, if such miracles were then believed. And equally wonderful is the fact, that no Jewish or heathen historian, during that period, has recorded that such events were reported of Jesus, and believed by his followers.

It is not probable that Christ ever claimed or pretended to work miracles. Such pretensions would have detracted from his exalted character, and would have placed him upon a level with Simon Magus, Apollonius, and other miracle workers of that age.

MIRACLES IN THE CHURCH.

Beyond what is contained in the epistles of Paul, it does not appear that any claim was made to the power of working miracles in the church, until about the middle of the second century.

THE MATERIAL RESURRECTION.

The doctrine of the resurrection of the material

body of Christ, must be placed in the same category.

Nothing is heard of it earlier than in the Gospel of the Hebrews, which is generally thought to have been written early in the second century. In the writings of the fathers, the doctrine first appeared in the middle of the second century.

According to the opinion of many in the first century, the soul or spirit of Jesus had gone below, to a place understood as hades, under or beneath the earth, and the resurrection was the calling back of the soul to earth, and its ascension to heaven. To this doctrine Paul may have alluded, when he asked "Who shall descend into the deep? That is, to bring up Christ again from the dead?" [Romans, 10. 7.]

The prevailing view of the resurrection, however, as taught by the earlier fathers, is well explained by Neander, the celebrated church historian. He quotes from Origen, who distinguished "from the mutable phenomenal form, the proper essence lying at the foundation of the body, which remains the same through all the changes of earthly life, and which, moreover, is not destroyed at death. This proper essence, lying at the foundation of the body, would, by the operation of the divine power, be awakened to a nobler form, corresponding to the ennobled character of the soul ; so that as the soul had communicated its own peculiar stamp to the body, it would then communicate the same to the transfigured body." [1]

(1.) Neander's Christian Hist. vol. 2, p. 436.

The spiritualism of the first century was destined to be obscured, after the death of its most illustrious advocates, Paul and Clement. The Christians of the second century required a grosser form of doctrine.

Justin Martyr argued for a resurrection of the flesh.[1]

So Athenagoras, in his Treatise on the Resurrection, maintained that every particle of matter which constitutes the human body, would be brought back to its proper place, and thought it a reflection on the power of God, to object that the same particles of matter enter into the composition of different bodies.

Tertullian thought the dead would be raised with a material body, and afterward, the bodies would be changed. A real fleshly body was to be reproduced, and when Christ should appear, it was to be caught up into the air, and then the material body would be changed into a spiritual body.[2]

Irenæus maintains the identity of the future with the present body.

In the midst of all this materialism, however, Clement of Alexandria and Origen maintained the spiritualistic views of Paul and Clement of Rome.

In the construction of the canonical gospels, the materialistic side prevailed. We there find the resurrection of a material body, which required the

(1.) Works of Justin, Ante-Nicene, vol. 2, p. 345.
(2.) Tertul. adv. Marcion, bk. 5, ch. 20.

stone to be rolled away from before the sepulcher.

DIVINITY OF CHRIST.

Paul, though drawing a broad distinction between God and Jesus Christ through all his epistles, repeatedly designating the latter as a man, "of
the seed of David," at the same time, in other passages, [Philippians, 2. 5, 6 ; 2d Cor. 5. 19, etc.],
used language capable of another construction ; and
from which was drawn a doctrine, which, by successive steps, ended in the complete deification of
Christ, as an essential part of a Triune God.

The Jewish Christians and many of the Gentiles, steadily maintained that Jesus was a man
only, born in the ordinary course of generation.
To which the Gnostics added, that Christ, as an
æon or divine spirit, entered into him at the time
of his baptism ; from which time he was divinely
inspired.

Among the mass of Gentile Christians, however,
the tendency to deify their great teacher and exemplar was early manifested, and rapidly gained in
strength and power.

This tendency can be traced among all the orthodox fathers. Ignatius speaks of him as "Jesus
Christ, our God ;" and similar expressions are to
be found in other early Christian writers.

The testimony of Pliny is, that the Christians
were accustomed to meet before daybreak, and sing
a responsive hymn, ("carmen dicere secum in-

vicem"), to Christ as to God. ("Christo quasi Deo.")[1]

Whether, in so doing, they were not giving countenance to polytheism, the Christians of that day did not stop to inquire. They were too enthusiastic in the new religion to formulate scientific creeds, or to take time to establish consistency of doctrine.

Justin Martyr was the first who undertook to give a definite shape to the doctrine. He maintained that the God of Abraham, Isaac and Jacob, who appeared to Moses in the flaming bush, was the Word, or Christ, who, he says, was also called angel and apostle. While he was God, he was entirely distinct from God the Father, in every respect, except that he was begotten or produced from him, by emanation, as a ray of light proceeds from the sun.[2]

He is very emphatic in maintaining that Christ is really different from the Father.

"This rational power," he says, "is not, like the light of the sun, merely nominally different [from the Father], but really another, numerically." (*Alla kai arithmo heteron ti esti.*)—[Dialogue with Trypho, chs. 128, 129.

This he illustrates by fire kindled from a fire; "which," says he, "we see to be distinct from it." [3]

He repeatedly speaks of Christ as God, but so far from asserting his identity with the Father, either in person or essence, he says:

"They who affirm that the Son is the Father, are proved neither to have become acquainted with the Father, nor to know that the Father of the Universe has a Son."—[1st Apology, ch. 63.

In the same passage, he asserts the divinity of Christ, and says he was the first-begotten Word of God.

Not only does Justin deny the identity of the Son with the Father, but he is equally explicit in excluding the idea of equality between them. Speaking of the Son, he says:

"We esteem him in the second place. (*chora.*)" "For they pro-

(1.) Ep. 10. 97.
(2.) 1st Apology, chs. 13, 63; Dialogue with Trypho, chs, 113, 128, 129, etc.
(3.) Dialogue, ch. 128.

claim," says he, "our madness to consist in this; that we give to a crucified man, a place second to the unchangeable and eternal God, the Creator of all."—[1st Apology, ch. 13.

The tendency to polytheism, which naturally resulted from an attempt to deify Christ, had thus culminated in Justin Martyr. Here were two Gods, the one entirely distinct from, and subordinate to the other. A reaction followed, which resulted in the doctrine of the Trinity. The divinity of Christ could not be abandoned. It had taken too firm a hold upon the hearts of the multitude of his disciples. It must now be reconciled with monotheism. This required that the Son should, in some way, be identified with the Father. The object was accomplished through the growth and development of the doctrine of the Logos. In the writings of Philo, in the first century, the doctrine of the Word, as the only begotten Son of the Father, existing with Him, as the creative power, was fully taught and elaborated. But Philo, a Jew, knew nothing of Jesus Christ, as the Word.

Justin Martyr applied this doctrine to Christ, who then became, to the Christian, the Logos so much dwelt upon by Philo. But Justin did not, as we have seen, identify the Son, or the Word, with the Father. It was for the author of the Gospel of John, a quarter of a century later, boldly to announce, without qualification, that "In the beginning was the Word, and the Word was with God, and the Word was God."

This was the culmination of the doctrine of the Logos, and at the same time, the foundation of the Trinity. The disposition to deify Christ, had been gaining ground for nearly a century, and had finally prevailed, without overthrowing monotheism, which was an essential part of the Christian system.

No wonder that a gospel which thus so distinctly struck, for the first time, the key note of that grand anthem which was already in the hearts of multitudes, waiting only for expression, should at once become popular—should be received as canonical—should take its place among the gospels which had already been selected—that it should be ascribed to an apostle, and should maintain its ground, without any examination as to its authenticity, as an apostolic production.

THE TRINITY.

A solid foundation for the doctrine of the Trinity having thus been laid, the completion of the structure was the work of the next century and a half. The doctrine was scientifically formulated at the Council of Nice, A. D. 325.

From what has been said, it will be seen that it was not a belief of the first two centuries. Those who would trace the doctrine to that age, refer to the formula of baptism, in the name of the Father, Son and Holy Spirit. Those who used this formula, however, did so without any adequate conception of the doctrine of the Trinity, so far as we have any evidence from the writings of the Ante-Nicene fathers. Dr. Shedd, speaking of the formulas employed in the so-called Apostles' Creed, says:

"This is as definite a statement of the doctrine of the Trinity as was made in any public document, previous to those Sabellian and Arian controversies which resulted in the more exhaustive and technical definitions of the Nicene symbols."—[History of Christian Doctrine, by William G. T. Shedd, D. D., Prof. of Bib. Lit. in Union Theological Seminary, N. Y., 1871, vol. 1, p. 262.

Again :

"Those of the primitive fathers who speculated at all upon the Trinity, confined their reflections mostly to the relations of the first and second persons."—[Ibid, vol. 1, p. 268.

Origen speaks of the Trinity, in de Principiis, bk. 4, 1. 30, according to the Latin of Rufinus, which is not very reliable.

NATURE OF THE SOUL.

Tertullian held that both body and soul are propagated.

"The soul of a man," he says, "like the root of a tree, is drawn out, (deducta) into a physical progeny, from Adam, the parent stock." [De Anima, ch. 19.

And again, "Both substances, (body and soul), are conceived, finished, and perfected together."—[De Anima, ch. 27.

In the third century, Origen advocated pre-existence.[1]

IMMORTALITY OF THE SOUL.

The doctrine of the immortality of the soul does not appear to have been generally held at that time.

"The soul is not in itself immortal, O Greeks," says Tatian, "but mortal. If, indeed, it knows not the truth, it dies, and is dissolved with the body, but rises again at last, at the end of the world, with the body, receiving death by punishment in immortality."—[Address to the Greeks, bk. 1, ch. 13.

Similar views were held by Theophilus of Antioch, who says :

"Neither immortal, nor yet mortal did he make him, but capable of both."—[Ad Autolycum, bk. 2, ch. 27.

The nature of the soul, as explained by Tertullian, has been seen to be entirely inconsistent with its immortality.

FREE WILL AND PREDESTINATION.

Justin Martyr argued in favor of the freedom of the will, and against predestination.[2]

The Alexandrian fathers, while they conceded the apostacy, held that the human will has a plenary power of good action, and is able to turn by its own inherent power.[3]

Clement of Alexandria asserts that to believe or disbelieve, is as much at the command of the will,

(1.) De Princip. 4. 1. 16; Ibid. 2. 9, 3. 5; Contra Celsum, 4. 39.
(2.) 1st Apology, 43, 10.
(3.) "autexousion."

as to philosophize or not to philosophize; that the first act in regeneration proceeds from man.

THE ATONEMENT.

Dr. Priestley, in his work on the corruptions of Christianity, claims that the atonement is not taught in the New Testament. The statement, as applied to the doctrine in its theological sense, may be technically correct. But we do not see how it can be denied, that Paul preached, in general terms, a doctrine of atonement.

The earlier fathers generally followed the language of Paul, without attempting any definite statement of the doctrine. They do not appear to connect it with original sin or total depravity.

"For our sins," says Polycarp, "he has even taken death upon himself."—[Epist. to the Philippians.

Basilides maintains that penal suffering, or suffering for the purposes of justice, of necessity implies personal criminality in the sufferer, and therefore cannot be endured by an innocent person like Christ.

According to Marcion, the suffering was not real; it was only apparent.

Clement of Rome speaks of the blood of Christ, shed for our salvation, and of being justified by faith.[1]

"There was," says Dr. Shedd, "no scientific construction of the doctrine of the atonement, in the writings of the apostolic fathers."—[History of Doct. vol. 2, p. 208.

(1.) Epistle to the Corinthians, 7. 32.

Clement of Alexandria and Origen held qualified views in regard to the atonement.

It was a favorite view with Ignatius, that the death of Christ brings the human soul into communion with him.

ORIGINAL SIN.

Wiggers says :

"All or at least the greater part, of the fathers of the Greek Church before Augustine, denied any real, original sin."—[Augustinism and Pelagianism, p. 43, Emerson's Translation.

This doctrine had a gradual growth, and was fully developed by Augustine, A. D. 420.

The maxim of Tertullian was, "Tradux animæ, tradux peccati." "The propagation of the soul is the propagation of sin."

Dr. Shedd says, no controversy arose respecting original sin and regenerating grace, until the fifth century.

Inherited guilt was first distinctly announced by Augustine.

ETERNAL PUNISHMENT,

Was taught by Justin Martyr, and some others of the second century.

"We believe," says Justin, "that those who live wickedly, and do not repent, are punished in everlasting fire." [2]

(1.) History of Doctrines, vol. 2, "Anthropology."

(2.) 1st Apology, ch. 21.

The eternal duration of future punishment was denied by Origen and Clement of Alexandria.

"The good God," says Clement, "corrects for these three causes: First, that he who is corrected may become better than his former self; then, that those who are capable of being saved by examples, may be driven back, being admonished: and thirdly, that he who is injured, may not readily be despised, and be apt to receive injury."— [Stromata, bk. 4, ch. 24.

Origen believed in the final restoration of the whole human race.

THE INTERMEDIATE STATE.

Justin Martyr represents the souls of the righteous as taking up a temporary abode in a happy, and those of the wicked, in a wretched place; and stigmatizes as heretical the doctrine that souls are immediately received into heaven at death.[1]

Tertullian held that martyrs went at once to the abode of the blessed, but that this was a privilege peculiar to them, and not granted to other Christians.[2]

PROVIDENCE.

Neander considers that the doctrine of providence, as now held throughout Christendom, is peculiarly new.[3]

We look in vain for any distinct statement of the doctrine, in the words of the Ante-Nicene fathers.

(1.) Dialogue with Trypho, 5. 80.
(2.) De Anima, 55; De Resur. 43.
(3.) Hist. of Doct. vol. 1, p. 123.

CREATION OUT OF NOTHING.

This was held by some of the fathers. It is distinctly announced in the Shepherd of Hermas; the author of which speaks of God, "who brought all things into being out of nothing."[1]

INSPIRATION.

There was at this time, says Neander, "no coherent and systematic doctrine of inspiration."[2]

The Old Testament was held to be inspired, and inspired men were spoken of, under the new dispensation.

Hagenbach says, that Irenæus first taught the doctrine of inspiration, as connected with New Testament books; and cites Irenæus against Heresies, 3. 16. 2.

MILLENARIANISM.

Barnabas, Hermas and Papias were millenarians. So also were Justin Martyr, Irenæus, and Tertullian.[3]

Justin not only held to the doctrine, but he declared it the belief of all but the Gnostics.[4]

THE SABBATH.

The Jewish Christians insisted upon maintaining the Jewish institutions, particularly, circumcision and the sabbath.

(1.) Commandment, 1.

(2.) Hist. of Doctrines. vol. 1, p. 90.

(3.) Justin Martyr, Dialogue with Trypho; Irenæus, adv. Hær. 5. 25. 36; Tert. adv. Mar. 3. 24.

(4.) Dialogue with Trypho.

Paul protested against it, and urged that the Christians were freed from those observances. He cautioned them against permitting any man to judge them in respect of the sabbath.—[Colossians, 2. 16.]

There is no scriptural evidence of the transfer of the Jewish sabbath to the first day of the week.

On that day, Christians met, to commemorate the resurrection of Christ.

BAPTISM.

Peculiar efficacy was attached to this rite, by the early Christians.

That the form of baptism was by immersion, or at least by a washing of the whole body, must be the conclusion from an impartial examination of the writings of the Ante-Nicene fathers.

The constitution of the church of Alexandria, which is thought to have been established about the year 200, required the applicant for baptism to be divested of clothing, and after the ordinance had been administered, to be anointed with oil. (See ch. 2 of this work.)

Justin Martyr speaks of the laver, and of baptism as a washing.[1]

When the mother of Clement was converted, she was baptized in the sea.[2]

Nothing is heard of infant baptism before Ire-

(1.) 1st Apology, ch. 65. He speaks of the ceremony "in the water."—Ch. 61.
(2.) Recognitions, bk. 7, ch. 38.

næus. He is supposed to refer to it in the chapter
on the ministry of Christ, which is quoted at length,
in another part of this volume.

TRANSUBSTANTIATION.

This doctrine is expressly sanctioned by Justin
Martyr, who says :

"So likewise have we been taught that the food which is blessed by
the prayer of his word, and from which our flesh and blood by trans-
mutation are nourished, is the flesh and blood of that Jesus who was
made flesh."—[1st Apology, ch. 66.

The doctrine is apparently sanctioned, also, in
the Epistle to the Smyrnæans, incorrectly attributed to Ignatius, and in other early writings of the
church.

RELIGIOUS INTOLERANCE.

Tertullian did not admit the right of the heretics
to use the scriptures :

"We oppose to them," he says, "this step above all others, of not admitting them to any discussion of the scriptures. If in these lie their
resources, it ought to be clearly seen to whom belongs possession of
the scriptures, that none may be admitted to the use thereof, who has
no title at all to the privilege."—[Prescription against Heretics, ch.15.

SECRET DOCTRINES AND CEREMONIES.

There were exoteric and esoteric doctrines. The
esoteric were taught only to members of the church.
The instruction in these may have been what is
meant by the initiatory proceedings occasionally
spoken of in the writings of the early Christians.

In the 38th chapter of the 7th book of the Recognitions, a work written in the second or third century, it is stated of the mother of Clement, who had been converted,

"She was then baptized in the sea, and returning to the lodging, was initiated in all the mysteries of religion in their order."—[Ante-Nicene Ch. Lib. vol. 3, p. 358.

The secret character of some of the proceedings among the early Christians, is alluded to by Dr. Doellinger in the following terms:

"The vail of mystery in which the Christians shrouded their assemblies for divine service from the beginning, fostered the suspicion of indulging in a criminal secret worship."—[First Age of the Church, p. 100.

The mysteries of the church must be distinguished from the mere secrecy of their meetings, which was a necessity in times of persecution.

The esoteric and exoteric doctrines are alluded to by Origen, who says:

"To the carnal they taught the gospel in a literal way; preaching Jesus Christ, and him crucified. But to persons farther advanced, and burning with love for divine, celestial wisdom, they communicated the Logos."—[Origen, Pref. to Comm. on John, Opera, vol. 2, p. 255.

Whether there were other secrecies than those of doctrine, is uncertain.

DOCTRINE OF THE MESSIAH.

That Christ was the Messiah whose advent had been predicted by the prophets, was believed by all the fathers, and is a doctrine too well understood to require further comment.

ANTIQUITY OF CHRISTIAN DOCTRINES.

Many of the more prominent doctrines of the Christian religion prevailed among nations of antiquity, hundreds, and, in some instances, thousands of years before Christ.

The doctrine of a miraculous CONCEPTION was common in ancient times. The story of Chrishna has already been given. Zoroaster also was believed to have been immaculately conceived by a ray from the Divine Reason. Mars was conceived by Juno touching a flower, and she conceived Vulcan by being overshadowed by the wind. An ancient work entitled Codex Vaticanus, gives an account of the immaculate conception of Quexalcote, the Mexican Savior. One of the sects in China worshiped a savior named Xaca, who was conceived by his mother, in her sleep, seeing a white elephant.[1]   Ya, the first Chinese monarch, was conceived by his mother being struck with a star while traveling.[2]   Another legend is that Yu, (probably the same as Ya), was conceived from a water-lily. Many cases might be mentioned of mortals who had an immaculate conception. Plato, Pythagoras, Tamerlane, Gengis Khan, Apollonius of Tyana and Augustus Cæsar, were all supposed to have been the product of immaculate conceptions.

Stars also presaged the birth of several of them.

At the birth of Confucius, five wise men from a distance came to the house, celestial music filled the air, and angels attended the scene.[3]

The title of SON OF GOD was very common among the ancients, and at the commencement of the Christian era. St. Basil says, "Every uncommonly good man was called the Son of God." When Apollonius, standing before Domitian, was asked, why men called him a god, his reply was, "Every good man is entitled to that appellation." An answer which Dr. Albert Réville, a theologian of Rotterdam, thought might throw a bright light upon the divinity of Christ.[4]

MIRACLES.—The belief in miracles has been common in all ages of the world. From the time of Uranus, father of the gods, down

(1.) History of China, by Alvarez Semedo, p. 89.
(2.) History of the Rajahs, by Col. Tod, p. 57.
(3.) See the Five Volumes.
(4.) See chapter of this work entitled "Apollonius."

through all the ages, the world has been filled with wonders. Esculapius raised Hippolytus from the dead—Hercules rescued Alcestis from the very hand of death—Actæon was changed to a stag—the walls of Thebes builded themselves to the music of the flute, while those of Jericho fell before the blasts of the priests of Israel. The daughters of Anius the high priest, changed everything they chose into corn, oil and wine, and the hair of Berenice was changed to a constellation of stars. Meanwhile, Prometheus lay bound on Mt. Caucasus, the vultures devouring his vitals, which grew as fast as eaten.

The heavens were full of gods, and earth, air and sea swarmed with myriads of angels, spirits and demons.

RESURRECTION.—Many cases of resurrection from the dead, are handed down in the ancient mythologies. Mithras, the "Mediator" of Persia, is said to have risen after three days. [1] So also, Quexalcote, of Mexico, Osiris of Egypt, and others.

Some of these, after their resurrection, ascended into heaven. Chrishna, after rising from the dead, and appearing to his disciples, ascended to Brahma, in heaven.

THE ATONEMENT.—This doctrine has in some form pervaded the religion of all countries. Offerings of propitiation, to appease the wrath of an offended God, or to satisfy the demands of justice, have been common in every period of the world. Sometimes they have consisted of fruits of the earth; at other times, of animals and men. As nations have advanced in civilization, the offerings have become less bloody in their character. In the Sandwich Islands, anciently, human beings were thrown as a sacrifice into the crater of Kileaua, the great volcano. Afterward animals were substituted, and finally products of the earth. The propitiary system of the Jews is well known. This is considered by Paul as a type of the higher Christian system.

THE TRINITY was an essential feature in the religion of many oriental nations. The Holy Ghost was the third member, under various appellations. In the Hindu trinity, it was Siva; the other members of the trinity being Brahma and Vishnu.

Mr. Maurice says, this notion of a third person in the deity, was diffused among all the nations of the earth. [2] Mr. Worsley considers the doctrine one "of very great antiquity, and generally received by

(1.) Pitrat, p. 105.

(2.) Ind. Antiq. vol. 4, p. 247.

the Gothic and Celtic Nations." [1]   In the Hindu   system, this third person was the Holy Breath, by which living creatures were made. [2] The Holy Ghost became visible in the form of a dove, a tongue of fire, etc.

The Holy Ghost was sometimes the agent in immaculate conceptions. In the Mexican trinity, Y Zona was the Father, Bascal the Word, and Echvah the Holy Ghost, by the last of whom Chimalman conceived and brought forth Quexalcote. [3] When Sesostris invoked the oracle, to know who, before him, could subjugate all things, the answer was, " First God, then the Word, and with them the Spirit." [4] Plutarch, in his 'Life of Numa', shows that the incarnation of the Holy Spirit was known to the ancient Egyptians.

The doctrine of the Word, as the creative power, is also very ancient. The Chinese Bible states that "God pronounced the primeval Word, and his own eternal and glorious abode sprang into existence." According to the Zend-Avesta, it was by the Word, more ancient than the world, that Ormuzd created the universe. The ancient Greek writer, Amelias, speaking of the god Mercury, says, "And this plainly was the Logos, by whom all things were made."

Plato taught a trinity of the soul, in which it is easy to see analogies, pointing to a higher form of the doctrine.

It is said there was an ancient Greek inscription on the great obelisk at Rome; thus: 1. The Mighty God; 2. The Begotten of God; and 3. Apollo the Spirit.

Confession and Remission of Sins.—These doctrines prevailed anciently in India; also among the ancient Persians, and Parsees. [5] In China, the invocation of Omito was held to remit the punishment of the greatest crimes. [6]

The doctrines of Original Sin, Fall of Man, and Endless Punishment, are all found in the religious systems of several ancient nations.

Sprinkling with water was a religious ceremony of much antiquity. [7] This may in some degree account for the change of the form

(1.) Enquiry, p. 42.
(2.) M. Dubois, p. 293.
(3.) Mexican Antiq. vol. 6, p. 1650.
(4.) Nimrod, vol. 1, p. 119.
(5.) Volney, p, 211.
(6.) Rev. Mr. Pitrat, p. 232.
(7.) See Potter's Antiquities, and Herbert's Travels.

of Christian baptism from immersion to sprinkling. The practice prevailed among the ancient Romans. 1

THE SACRAMENT OR EUCHARIST has also an ancient original. It was practiced by the Brahmins of India, and was introduced into the mysteries of Mithras. It prevailed, also, among the ancient Mexicans. 2

THE GOLDEN RULE was taught hundreds of years before Christ, by Confucius, Aristotle, and many others. 3

 (1.) Consult the writings of Virgil, Cicero and others.

 (2.) Travels of Father Acosta; Memoirs of Mr. Marolles, p. 215.

 (3.) Those who may wish to pursue this subject further, will find a mass of useful facts in the "Anacalypsis" of Godfrey Higgins; a rare work, in the preparation of which he was employed for twenty years; and from which some of the foregoing references, concerning the antiquity of prominent features of the Christian system, have been taken. Consult also, "The World's Sixteen Crucified Saviors, or Christianity before Christ;" by Kersey Graves, of Richmond, Indiana: an able and interesting work, containing a fund of very valuable information.

CHAPTER XXXIV.

Christian Writers of the Fifth Period.

Marcus—Aristo of Pella—Dionysius of Corinth—
Miltiades—Maximus — Pinytus — Modestas — Musanus—
Church of Vienne and Lyons—Florinus—Blastus—Mel-
ito of Sardis—Athenagoras—Claudius Apollinaris—
Theophilus of Antioch—Bardesanes—Hermogenes—Bac-
chylus of Corinth—Pantænus—Marcia—Hegesippus.

Marcus.—About A. D. 170.

Marcus was a native of Palestine, and a disciple of
Valentinus. "Valentinianism," says Baring-Gould,
"assumed two forms; broke into two sects; the
Marcosians and the Ophites."[1]

Marcus was considered a heretic. The most that
has been preserved concerning him, comes through
Irenæus, who treats of him and his followers, in
the work on Heresies, as follows :

"But there is another among these heretics, Marcus by name, who
boasts of himself as having improved upon his master. [Valentinus.]

(1.) Lost and Hostile Gospels, p. 287.

He is a perfect adept in magical impostures, and by this means drawing away a great number of men, and not a few women, he has induced them to join themselves to him, as to one who is possessed
of the greatest knowledge and perfection, and who has received the
highest power from the invisible and ineffable regions above. Thus
it appears as if he were really the precursor of Anti-Christ."

After describing some of the magical proceedings
of Marcus, he continues :

"Again, handing mixed cups to the women, he bids them consecrate
these in his presence."

Stating that, after the consecration of the cups,
Marcus would fill larger cups from the smaller ones,
Irenæus proceeds as follows :

"It appears probable enough, that this man possesses a demon as
his familiar spirit, by means of which he seems able to prophesy, and
also enables as many as he counts worthy to be partakers of his Charis,
themselves to prophesy.

"He devotes himself especially to women, and those such as are
well bred, and elegantly attired, and of great wealth; whom he frequently seeks to draw after him, by addressing them in such seductive
words as these:" [Here giving what purports to be an address of Marcus to the women, exhorting them to receive Charis, or the spirit of
prophecy.] The effect of this speech, he says, is, that the woman,
"vainly puffed up and elated by these words, and greatly excited in
soul by the expectation that it is herself who is to prophesy, her heart
beating violently, [from emotion], reaches the requisite pitch of
audacity, and idly as well as impudently utters some nonsense as it
happens to occur to her, such as might be expected from one heated
by an empty spirit."

Our author does not hesitate to add, that the woman, deeming herself a prophetess, out of gratitude
to Marcus, rewards him, not only by large possessions, but by yielding up to him her person.[1]

(1.) Irenæus, adv. Hær. bk. 1, 13.

ARISTO OF PELLA.—A. D. 175.

The Dialogue between Jason and Papiscus, has
been attributed to Aristo. Westcott thinks it uncertain whether he was the author. The same
writer adds that the words of the Dialogue do not
prove anything as to the existence of a New Testament canon.[1]

Of the Apology which Aristo is said to have delivered to Hadrian,[2] nothing is known.

In the 22d volume of the Ante-Nicene Collection,
are five small fragments attributed to Aristo. Four
of these are from the Dispute between Jason and
Papiscus, cited by Jerome and others. The other
is from Eusebius.

DIONYSIUS OF CORINTH.—A. D. 175.

Some fragments from this writer are supposed to
have been preserved by Eusebius, who, in his Ecclesiastical History, gives what purport to be extracts
from his writings.

There has been some controversy over certain
passages which Canon Westcott supposes to refer to
the New Testament; his conclusions being strongly
attacked by the author of Supernatural Religion.
It is not necessary to notice the discussion further;
since any fragments which appear only in Eusebius,
are absolutely unreliable.

This is the writer whom Eusebius cites in reference to the teaching and martyrdom of Paul and

---

(1.) Canon, pp. 84, 85.
(2.) Chron. Pasc. 477, of Routh, p. 104.

Peter. After giving an alleged quotation from Caius, a writer whose works are lost, Eusebius says he "superadds" the testimony of Dionysius, in order that the truth of his history may be still more confirmed.[1]

MILTIADES—MAXIMUS—PINYTUS.—About A. D. 175.

But little is known of these writers. Maximus was Bishop of Jerusalem. He is probably the one referred to by Eusebius,[2] who says he wrote on the origin of evil, and on the creation of matter.

The same writer refers thus to Pinytus:

Referring to the writings of Dionysius of Corinth, he speaks of an epistle to the Gnossians, in which Dionysius "admonishes Pinytus, not to impose upon the brethren without necessity, a burden in regard to purity, too great to be borne; 'but to pay regard to the infirmity of the great mass.' Pinytus, in reply, admires and applauds Dionysius, but exhorts him, at the same time, to impart, some time or other, stronger food, and to feed the people under him with writings abounding in more perfect doctrine, when he wrote again," etc.— [Ecclesiastical History, 4. 23.

MODESTAS—MUSANUS.—A. D. 176.

These writers are mentioned by Dr. Lardner,[3] as writers of the second century, whose works are lost.

CHURCHES OF VIENNE AND LYONS.—A. D. 177.

An epistle is said to have been written by these, to certain eastern churches, and the extracts from it occupy a prominent place in ecclesiastical history. The information comes through Eusebius. The

(1.) Ecclesiastical Hist. 2. 25.
(2.) Ibid. 5. 27.
(3.) Lard. Works, vol. 1, p. 436.

epistle is supposed to contain references to the Protevangelion Gospel.

FLORINUS—BLASTUS.—A. D. 177.

Florinus was a presbyter of the Roman Church. Was ejected for heresy. He maintained that God was the author of evil. Blastus was of the same school.

MELITO OF SARDIS.—A. D. 177.

It is supposed that some fragments of the lost writings of Melito, have been preserved in the Ecclesiastical History of Eusebius.[1] In these, some have found, as they have supposed, allusions to the New Testament writings. The inference is by others denied. Michaelis was inclined to the opinion, also, that Melito had testified to the existence of a Syriac version. But Bishop Marsh shows that the inference of Michaelis was illogical and unauthorized.[2] The fact is, we have not sufficient evidence as to what Melito wrote.

Some Syriac writings have appeared under the name of Melito, but they are not considered genuine. His Discourse, or Apology, and some other supposed fragments, are given in the 22d volume of Ante-Nicene.

ATHENAGORAS.—A. D. 177.

But little is known of Athenagoras, beyond the fact that he was an Athenian philosopher, became

(1.) Ecc. History, 4. 26.
(2.) Marsh's Michaelis, vol. 2, p. 552.

a Christian, and about the date above mentioned, is reputed to have presented to the Emperors Marcus Aurelius and Commodus an apology for Christians, which is still extant. A Treatise on the Resurrection is also attributed to him.

In his Apology, Athenagoras has been supposed to refer to some of the canonical gospels; but nothing definite can be determined in regard to it.

We may safely accept the conclusion of Dr. Donaldson, expressed as follows :

"Athenagoras makes no allusion to the inspiration of the New Testament writers. He does not mention one of them by name, and one cannot be sure that he quotes from any except Paul. All the passages taken from the gospels, are part of our Lord's discourses, and may have come down to Athenagoras by tradition."—[Hist. Ch. Lit. and Doct. 3. p. 172.

The passages referred to differ also from those in the canonical gospels, and may have exactly corresponded with older gospels then extant.

The fact that Athenagoras nowhere mentions either of the four gospels by name, becomes the more remarkable when it is considered that he cites by name, Moses, Jeremiah, Jonah, Thales, Plato, Homer, Hesiod, Orpheus, Herodotus, Pythagoras, Euripides, Aristotle, and others.

Though the Gospels of Luke and Mark, and possibly John, may then have been written, it is not probable that they were much known, or that any names of reputed authors were attached to them.

CLAUDIUS APOLLINARIS,—A. D. 178,

Was Bishop of Hierapolis. He is said to have

participated in the great paschal controversy. In
an extract purporting to be from a work written
by him on the passover, there is a reference to
what Matthew had said, and, by implication, to
the Gospel of Matthew. The extract is found in
the preface to the Paschal Chronicle, a work of the
seventh century. Its genuineness is, however,
generally discredited. [1] Three fragments are given
in Ante-Nicene, vol. 22.

THEOPHILUS OF ANTIOCH.—A. D. 180.

This writer occupies a prominent place in all the
works on the canon. He was Bishop of Antioch.
Of his writings three letters to Autolycus are preserved, in one of which the Gospel of John is expressly mentioned by name; [2] though it is not
stated it was written by an apostle.

Theophilus is reputed to have written a Commentary on the gospels, which is lost.

BARDESANES—HERMOGENES—BACCHYLUS OF CORINTH —PANTÆNUS.—A. D. 180.

The works of these writers are lost except a few
fragments. "The Discourse on Fate," of Bardesanes, is given in Ante-Nicene, vol. 22, pt. 2, p. 85.

Bardesanes was a native of Mesopotamia, and
lived at Edessa. He was a man of learning. [3]

Some have attributed to Bardesanes the author-

(1.) Donaldson, Hist. Ch. Lit. and Doct. 3. 247; Lardner, Credibility, etc., vol. 2,
p. 296.

(2.) Ad Autolycum, 2. 22.

(3.) Jerome, in Or. c. 10, p. 301; Augustine, de Civitate Dei, liber 22, c. 24.

ship of the Recognitions. Eusebius mentions him in his ecclesiastical History, 20. 30.

Hermogenes ascribed matter to an irregular motion. [1]

Bacchylus of Corinth was zealous in defending the faith against heretics. He was one of the bishops who convened local councils, at the request of Victor of Rome, to settle the paschal controversy.

Pantænus has been spoken of in connection with the Gospel of Matthew. [2]

Alexandria was the scene of his labors. He preceded Clement of Alexandria in the presidency of the catechetic school, or seminary, in that city. Soon after, he went as missionary to India. He is said to have been the author of commentaries on the scriptures.

MARCIA.—A. D. 183.

Marcia was a concubine of the Emperor Commodus. Dion Cassius says of her:

"She is related to have had a great affection for the Christians, and to have done them many good offices; she having a great ascendency over Commodus."—[Hist. 1. 72, p. 819.

HEGESIPPUS.—A. D. 185.

Hegesippus was a Jewish Christian of Jerusalem. He traveled extensively in order to become acquainted with the condition of the church, and

(1.) Lardner, vol. 4, p. 266.
(2.) See chapter XXXI.

came to Rome during the bishopric of Anicetus, sometime between the years 160 and 170.

Afterward, about 185, he wrote, it is stated, a historical work, called "Memoirs," in five books. It is said to have been a complete history of Christianity, down to his own time. It is now lost, except a few short fragments, most of them being only such as Eusebius has thought proper to preserve.

Hegesippus was an Ebionite, and, like the others of that sect, was violently opposed to Paul. The virulence of these Christians against the great apostle of the Gentiles, is well illustrated by a fragment of Hegesippus, preserved by Gobarus, of the sixth century. Referring to the words of Paul, in 1 Cor. 2. 9, "Eye hath not seen, nor ear heard, neither have entered into the heart of man, the things which God hath prepared for them that love him," Hegesippus says:

"These words are vainly spoken, and those who say these things give the lie to the divine writings, and to the Lord, saying, 'Blessed are your eyes that see, and your ears that hear.'"—[Photius, Bib. Cod. 232, col. 893.

This passage, cited by Hegesippus, is supposed to be taken from the Gospel of the Hebrews, which Eusebius says, Hegesippus used. [1] It will be noticed that the passage agrees in sense, while differing in phraseology, from Matthew.

Hegesippus, though he traveled extensively over the Christian world, makes no mention of the canonical gospels. Some supposed quotations from them have given rise to the usual discussion.

(1.) Ecc. Hist. 4. 22.

CHAPTER XXXV.

REVIEW OF THE FIFTH PERIOD.

INTRODUCTION OF THE FOUR GOSPELS AND ACTS OF THE APOSTLES, PREPARATORY TO THE ESTABLISHMENT OF THE PAPACY—THE SUBJECT INVOLVED IN MYSTERY—SOURCES OF INFORMATION GONE—SLAUGHTER OF THE INNOCENTS.

Though we find no mention of the four gospels during the fifth period, with the single exception of the Gospel of John, there is reason to believe they were all written during this time, as a part of the structure upon which Roman Catholic dominion was to rest. This relation to Roman Catholicism, is more particularly to be noticed in the Gospels of John and Matthew, and the Acts of the Apostles. The Gospels of Luke and Mark may have been composed without any special reference to the hierarchy; the one to counteract the influence of Marcion and his Gospel, and the other, to preserve, in a complete and comprehensive form, some of the older traditions of the church, which had been in circulation in various forms, particularly in the Gospel of Peter.

The Gospel of John was adopted, as settling in beautiful language, and in an acceptable form, the doctrine of the divinity of Jesus, and as indicating the unity of the church under Peter. The Gospel of Matthew, in still more explicit language, laid the foundations broad and deep, for the establishment of the supremacy of the papal power, on the authority of Christ as delegated to Peter; while the Acts of the Apostles bridged over the differences which had so long existed between the followers of Peter and Paul.

While thus much is apparent upon the surface, if we attempt to go deeper into the subject, we find everything involved in mystery.

All the most reliable sources of information are closed to the researches of the historian. Those writings of the second century to which he would naturally turn for information, commentaries and works written especially concerning the gospels then in circulation, are lost or destroyed, without a single exception.

Not one remains to give its testimony on one side or the other of any controverted question. Also many books written on the same subject, during the next two or three hundred years; while it is notorious that others, which have been preserved, have been tampered with and extensively interpolated.

Loss or Destruction of Evidence concerning the Four Gospels.

The following is some of the evidence of the

second century, which has disappeared.

1. THE COMMENTARIES OF BASILIDES.—A. D. 125.

Basilides is said to have written a Commentary on "the Gospel," in 24 books. A gospel is also attributed to him. But the better opinion appears to be that the Commentaries and the Gospel were one and the same.

These commentaries must have thrown a flood of light upon the history of the gospels then in existence. They would at least disclose the number and character of the principal ones then in circulation.

2. AGRIPPA CASTOR,—A. D. 130,

Wrote in refutation of the heresies of Basilides. This has perished with the commentaries of his adversary.

3. THE WORKS OF PRODICUS.—A. D. 120.

The followers of Prodicus boasted of having the secret books of Zoroaster. His writings would probably have disclosed the connection between Persian mythology and the Gospels of the Infancy.

4. APOLOGIES OF QUADRATUS AND ARISTIDES.
A. D. 126.

If these had been preserved, we could test the correctness of the assertion of Eusebius that the Apology of Quadratus referred to the miracles of Christ; which, in that case, would be, so far as known, the first reference to them in history. We

would know also what is meant by the statement
of the same historian, if there be any truth in it at
all, that Quadratus and others, at that time, delivered to those who had not heard the faith, the
books of the holy gospels. We would probably
learn from their writings what gospels were extant
in their day.

5. ARISTION,—A. D. 130,

According to Papias, as coming through Eusebius, preserved traditions concerning Christ. These
traditions would have thrown much light upon the
gospel history, and upon the earlier gospels.

6. JOHN THE PRESBYTER.—A. D. 130.

John, like Aristion, appears in Eusebius as one
of the informants of Papias, particularly concerning certain writings composed by Mark and Matthew; information which was long supposed to relate to the gospels bearing those names. It is now
thought they cannot be regarded as referring to any
of the canonical gospels. Had we the original traditions, or statements, in full, they would at once
settle the question.

7. CERINTHUS,—A. D. 145,

Was the reputed author of a gospel. His gospel
and writings are lost or destroyed.

8. VALENTINUS.—A. D. 150.

Valentinus had a gospel, called "The Gospel of
Truth." Irenæus places it sharply in antagonism

with the four gospels ; says they are false, if that
of Valentinus was the Gospel of Truth ; that if they
are true, Valentinus' was false. As the work of
Irenæus is preserved, and the four gospels, it is
much to be regretted, and must be considered
calamitous to the cause of impartial investigation,
that we have not the Gospel of Valentinus, and his
writings in support of it.

9.   PAPIAS,—A. D. 125,

Is said to have written five books, entitled "Exposition of the Oracles of the Lord." This must
have been a Commentary on the Oracles, or collections of the sayings of Christ; and would have
been invaluable ; giving those sayings, as they
stood early in the second century.

10.   THE WRITINGS OF MARCION.

Pure Christianity has suffered no greater loss
than that of the writings of Marcion, the great
theological thinker of the second century—the
compiler of the first complete gospel—the collector
of the epistles of Paul—the editor and publisher of
the first New Testament.

While the elaborate work against him, written
by Tertullian, who called him a "hound," has been
preserved, and the work of Epiphanius, who bestowed upon him the euphonious appellation of
"beast," the writings of Marcion have perished,
except such as are found in the references and citations of his adversaries. His works have shared
the common fate of the writings of the heretics of

the second century, none of which, in their original form, have been permitted to come down to us.

Marcion was an educated man, and a profound thinker, and no relic of Christian antiquity, next to the Epistles of Paul, would to-day be more valuable than his writings. Being himself a collector of gospel and New Testament manuscripts, his writings upon those subjects would forever set at rest the question as to what gospels were then in circulation.

11. THE WORK OF JUSTIN MARTYR AGAINST HERESIES.

As his Dialogue with Trypho contains an exposition of the Old Testament, his work against heresies would probably have thrown light upon the gospels in circulation in his day. It would at least have determined the much controverted question as to the gospels used by Justin himself.

12. THE WRITINGS OF APELLES.—A. D. 160.

Apelles was a Gnostic leader who had a gospel of his own, and whose writings must have referred to other gospels. His works are lost or destroyed.

13. PEREGRINUS,—A. D. about 160,

An erratic but talented Christian philosopher, held, for a time, a commanding position among the Christians of Palestine. "Some books" says Lucian, "he interpreted and explained, others he wrote." His writings would constitute an important chapter in the history of the times. We have sketches of the man from Lucian, Ammianus, Aulus Gellius and others, but his writings have all perished.

14. MARCELLINA.—A. D. 160.

It would scarcely be expected that the heretical writings of a woman would be preserved, amid such wholesale slaughter of the obnoxious works of the opposite sex. The writings of Marcellina have perished.

15. MONTANUS.—A. D. 170.

Much has been said about Montanism, but we have only such extracts from the works of its founder as his adversaries have chosen to preserve.

16. THE WRITINGS OF TATIAN.—A. D. 170.

Tatian wrote, it is said, a Harmony of the gospels. Though it is quite evident that he made use of the Gospel of the Hebrews, and his work was even known by some under that name, an attempt has been made to connect his Harmony with the four gospels, on the unsupported and suspicious testimony of Eusebius. He says it was called the Diatessaron, which he explains as meaning of or from the four. If we had the writings of Tatian himself or his Harmony, the question could speedily be determined.

17. MARCUS,—about A. D. 170,

Had, according to Irenæus, an innumerable multitude of apocryphal writings. He probably wrote in explanation of these books, and of their origin. Both the books themselves, with a few exceptions, and whatever he may have written concerning them, have perished.

18.   PANTÆNUS.—A. D. 180.

While it could not be expected that Pantænus, if he wrote the Gospel of Matthew, would admit the fact, yet if we had the account of his travels in India, and of his discovery there, as claimed, of an original Gospel of Matthew, we might have at least some light thrown upon the origin of that gospel.

19.   THE CHRONICLES OF HEGESIPPUS.—A. D. 185.

Hegesippus was the first church historian. He traveled over nearly all Christendom, for the express purpose of obtaining information, and then wrote the history of the church, from the beginning to his own time. This work is lost or destroyed. The extent of the loss cannot be over-estimated.

Eusebius was the next historian, writing 140 years afterward.

He had the history of Hegesippus before him.

After referring to the death of James, and the statement of Clement, that James was thrown from a wing of the temple, and beaten to death with a club, he says :

Hegesippus, also, who flourished nearest the days of the apostles, in the fifth book of his Commentaries gives the most accurate account of him, thus:

Here follows a lengthy account of the death of James. Eusebius then adds :

"Such is the more ample testimony of Hegesippus, in which he fully coincides with Clement."—[Ecc. Hist. bk. 2, 23.

Again, Eusebius gives an account of the grand-children of Judas, called the Lord's brother, who were examined before the Emperor Domitian. He concludes as follows: "Such is the statement of Hegesippus." [1]

Again, speaking of the martyrdom of Simeon, second Bishop of Jerusalem, he says :

"To this the same Hegesippus bears testimony, whose words we have already so often quoted."—[Ecc. H. 3. 32.

He then quotes several passages, further, from the same author. Subsequently, referring to ecclesiastical writers, he says :

"Among these Hegesippus holds a distinguished rank, many of whose writings we have already quoted, where we have given some things as he has delivered them from apostolic tradition. This author compiled, in five books, the plain tradition of the apostolic doctrine, in a most simple style of composition, and clearly shows the time in which he lived, where he writes respecting those who began to erect idols, etc." Here follows a quotation from Hegesippus, concerning the erection of cenotaphs, temples, etc.—[Ecc. Hist. 4. 8.

Again in the same book he says :

"Hegesippus, indeed, in the five books of Commentaries that have come down to us, has left a most complete record of his own views. In these he states that he conversed with most of the bishops, when he traveled to Rome, and that he received the same doctrine from all. We may also add what he says after some observations on the Epistle of Clement to the Corinthians."

(1.) Ecc. Hist. 3. 20.

He then quotes Hegesippus concerning the Church of Corinth. [1]

Continuing, Eusebius speaks of Hegesippus coming to Rome, and of the Roman Bishops, Anicetus, Soter and Eleutherus.

" 'In every succession, however,' says Hegesippus, 'and in every city, the doctrine prevails, according to what is declared by the law and the prophets, and the Lord.' "

He then quotes what Hegesippus says concerning the beginning of heresies, and the ancient heresies prevalent among the Jews. [2]

"He also speaks of many other matters," says Eusebius, "which we have in part already quoted, and introduced in their appropriate places. He also states some particulars from the Gospel of the Hebrews, and from the Syriac, and particularly from the Hebrew language, showing that he himself was a convert from the Hebrews. Other matters he also records, as taken from the unwritten tradition of the Jews. And not only he, but Irenæus also, and the whole body of the ancients called the Proverbs of Solomon, 'Wisdom,' comprehending every virtue. Also in discoursing on the books called apocryphal, he relates that some of them were forged in his day, by some of the heretics."—[Ecc. History, 4. 22.

From the foregoing it will be seen how much of the history of Hegesippus is incorporated into that of Eusebius. A few meager items, of comparatively no historical value ;—the manner of the death of James—an examination of a few individuals before Domitian—the martyrdom of Simeon —the worshiping of idols—the journey to Rome, and a few words concerning the commencement of heresies.

(1.) Ecc. Hist. 4. 22.
(2.) Ibid.

Not a word of what was important to be known ; —of the history of the progress of the church, and of the doctrines which had prevailed—of the controversies between the Jewish and Gentile Christians—of the history of Paul and Peter, and of the founding of the Church of Rome ; and above all, of the history of the gospels and New Testament books which Hegesippus found in circulation, showing by whom they were written, and how they had been preserved.

So far as can be learned, Hegesippus was profoundly silent concerning the four gospels, and spoke only of the Gospel of the Hebrews.

The History of Hegesippus must have been written after the accession of Eleutherus, Bishop of Rome ; and probably about A. D. 185. This was, if we have read history aright, in the infancy of the four gospels. Whether Hegesippus met with them, and if so, what estimate he formed of them, in comparison with the Gospel of the Hebrews, is a question of the utmost importance, but one upon which Eusebius is silent.

Since Eusebius had the history of Hegesippus in his possession, why did he not take measures to have it preserved, or else incorporate into his own history, the most important portions of it, and particularly the evidence, if any, in favor of the four gospels?

According to Eusebius, Hegesippus said, that in every city, the doctrine prevailed, according to the law and the prophets, and the Lord, and that he received the same doctrine from all. Eusebius would have his readers believe, that the doctrine of a Jewish Christian of the second century, was precisely the same as that which prevailed in every city. Again, Eusebius says that Hegesippus derived his information concerning apostolic doctrine from tradition. Is that consistent with the existence of gospels, which were everywhere received in the church as authoritative? Such gospels would have been superior to, and would have taken the place of all tradition concerning apostolic doctrine.

20. COMMENTARIES OF HERACLEON.—A. D. 190.

It is claimed that Heracleon wrote Commentaries on Luke and John. Clement of Alexandria quotes Heracleon in such a way as to indicate that he had commented on Luke or Marcion, or on some other gospel containing the sayings of Christ. The commentaries on John are inferred from some passages in Origen.

If these commentaries existed, their loss is irreparable.

21. THE WRITINGS OF SERAPION.—A. D. 190.

These, of which we have but a brief extract in Eusebius, would have enlightened us further in regard to the transaction at Rhossus. From Serapion, we could have learned something of the four gospels which he was substituting in place of the Gospel of Peter. He could inform us how long the four gospels had been in circulation—where he obtained them—what other gospels he had been obliged to suppress to make way for them, and whether he was acting under the direction of the Church of Rome. His writings have perished.

22. CLEMENT OF ALEXANDRIA,

Is said to have composed a work, specially upon the scriptures which were considered authoritative.

Eusebius says, that in the work called Hypotyposes, Clement gave abridged accounts of all the canonical scriptures. [1]

This work has perished, while most of the other more important writings of Clement have been preserved. [2]

This ends the list of works of the second century, either written expressly concerning the gospels and New Testament books in circulation at that time, or which would have thrown more or less light upon the subject;—more than fifty books, by more than twenty authors.

Nearly every thing written concerning the gospels to the year 325, and all the copies of the gospels themselves to the same period, are lost or destroyed.

(1.) Ecclesiastical Hist. 6. 14.

(2.) Besides the Hypotyposes, (Hupotuposeis), consisting of eight books of exposition of scripture, Clement wrote an Ecclesiastical Canon; (Kanon Ekkleesiastikos.) This also has perished.

CHAPTER XXXVI.

ASTERIUS URBANUS—CASSIANUS—HERACLEON—MURATOR-
IAN FRAGMENT—PTOLEMÆUS—MAXIMILLA—VICTOR—SERA-
PION, BISHOP OF ANTIOCH—THEODOTUS OF BYZANTIUM—
NARCISSUS, BISHOP OF JERUSALEM — RHODON — PALMAS—
POLYCRATES, BISHOP OF EPHESUS—MAXIMUS, BISHOP OF
JERUSALEM—NOETUS — PRAXEAS — SYMMACHUS — HERMAS—
SELEUCAS—PISTIS SOPHIÆ—ARTEMON—SECOND EPISTLE OF
CLEMENT—JULIUS AFRICANUS.

ASTERIUS URBANUS.—A. D. 188.

Of this writer, but little is known. According
to Cave, he flourished about the year 188.

CASSIANUS.—A. D. 190.

Julius Cassianus was a writer of the second century, who was quoted by Clemens Alexandrinus,
thus:

Wherefore Cassianus saith, that when Salome asked (Christ), when
the things should be known, concerning which she enquired, our
Lord answered, "When you shall despise," etc.

Which, Clement adds, was to be found in the Gospel according to the Egyptians. From which it is to be inferred that Cassianus made use of that gospel.

PTOLEMÆUS—HERACLEON.—A. D. 190.

These were prominent Gnostics.

Ptolemæus wrote a letter to Flora, which occupies a distinguished place in the literary history of the times. [1]

In this letter, Ptolemy, having commented upon the ceremonial and typical laws of the Pentateuch, as having been annulled by the appearing of the truth, adds :

"These things the other disciples of Christ taught, and also the apostle Paul." After which he tells Flora, that "he will explain to her the particulars of that doctrine he had just been mentioning, by the help of tradition received from the apostles, and handed down to them." But he adds, "All must be tried by, and made to square with, the doctrine of the Savior himself, which was to be the rule."—[Append. ad Iren. pp. 360, 361. Grabe, Spi. Pat. vol. 2, p. 77.

Heracleon is quoted by Clement and Origen, and is said to have written Commentaries on Luke and John. This, again, is denied by some critics. Origen shows that Heracleon made use of the Gospel of Peter.

THE MURATORIAN FRAGMENT.—About A. D. 190.

Nothing could better illustrate the paucity of materials from which to make up a correct judgment concerning the New Testament writings of the

(1.) See Epiphanius, Hær. 30. 3-7.

second century than the prominence which has been given to an anonymous manuscript, discovered in the last century, by the Italian scholar, Muratori.

This celebrated manuscript was found in the Ambrosian library at Milan, in a manuscript containing other writings of little importance.

It speaks of "the third book of the Gospel according to Luke," of "the fourth of the gospels of John, one of the disciples;"—of the Acts of the Apostles; 13 Epistles of Paul, an Epistle to the Laodiceans, and another to the Alexandrians, (supposed to be the Epistle to the Hebrews), "forged in the name of Paul, after the heresy of Marcion;" and "many others which cannot be received by the Catholic Church, as gall must not be mixed with vinegar."

The Epistle of Jude, and the 2d and 3d Epistles of John, are spoken of doubtfully, as among the received books. So also the Book of Wisdom. The Apocalypses of John and Peter were received, but some objected to reading in the church the Apocalypse of Peter. Special reference is made to the Pastor of Hermas, the writer thinking it should be read privately, but not publicly in the church.

It will be seen that the document exhibits a very confused condition of the canon.

The manuscript was estimated by Muratori himself, to be about a thousand years old. It bears internal evidence of being a transcript of an older document. How often it has been copied, cannot be known, nor even in what language it was originally written. It appears in Latin, and the text is very corrupt.

It is supposed by some to have been written in the latter part of the second century; the supposition being based, principally, upon the reference to the Pastor of Hermas. This, it states, "was composed very recently, in our own times, in the City of Rome, the Bishop Pius, his brother, sitting in the chair of the Church of the City of Rome." Pius was bishop about the middle of the second century.

There are eminent critics, however, who hold, that the original was not written earlier than the third century. [1] Their opinion is based upon internal evidence; particularly the expression, "sitting in the chair of the church." [2]

The document itself, a production of about the eighth century, cannot be looked upon as very satisfactory evidence of the condition of the canon in the second century.

VICTOR—SERAPION, BISHOP OF ANTIOCH—MAXIMILLA. A. D. 190.

We are not aware that any of the writings of these are extant, except a fragment or two of Serapion. They are given by Eusebius, and relate to the interdict of the Gospel of Peter, and the

(1.) Donaldson, Hug, Tayler, Eichhorn and others.
(2.) Donaldson, Ch. Lit. and Doct. 3. p. 212.

substitution of the canonical gospels, in its stead.

THEODOTUS OF BYZANTIUM.—A. D. 192.

A considerable fragment from this writer, is given by Clement of Alexandria. Theodotus taught that Christ was a man only. He used and cited the Preaching of Peter. He was excommunicated by Victor, Bishop of Rome. [1]

RHODON—NARCISSUS, BISHOP OF JERUSALEM.— A. D. 195.

There is a fragment in Eusebius, attributed to Rhodon, in which he vindicates the character of Apelles. [2]

The same historian relates of Narcissus, Bishop of Jerusalem, that when the oil failed, at the vigils of the great watch of Easter, Narcissus commanded that water from a neighboring well should be poured into the lamps. Whereupon, Narcissus having prayed over it, the water was changed into oil; of which, Eusebius says, a specimen had been preserved until that time. [3]

The same writer relates, that three men having slandered Narcissus, and sworn to their falsehoods, with imprecations of death upon themselves, by a miserable disease, by fire, and blindness, respectively, if their statements were not true, in each case the curse which had been invoked, was in-

(1.) Darras, Hist. Cath. Church, vol. 1, p. 163.
(2.) Euseb. Ecc. Hist. 5. 13.
(3.) Ecc. Hist. 6. 9.

flicted upon them by an omnipotent Providence. [1]

PALMAS—POLYCRATES, BISHOP OF EPHESUS.—A. D. 196.

These bishops were deputed by Victor, Bishop of Rome, to convene councils, to consider the question of the celebration of Easter.

Palmas convened the bishops of Pontus, and Polycrates those of pro-consular Asia. The latter refused to endorse the decree of the Italian Council, which provided that Easter should be celebrated on Sunday. Thereupon the Asiatic Churches were excommunicated. [2]

Eusebius says, Polycrates wrote a letter to Victor, and gives extracts from it. [3]

MAXIMUS, BISHOP OF JERUSALEM.—A. D. 200.

According to Eusebius, Maximus wrote on the origin of evil, and on the creation of matter. [4] A lengthy extract is given by Eusebius. [5]

NOETUS.—A. D. 200.

About this time, the controversy concerning the nature of Christ, was carried on with much spirit, by Theodotus, Hermogenes, Noetus, Vero, Beryllus, and Sabellius on the one side, and Artemon, and Paul of Samosata, on the other.

(1.) Ecc. Hist. 6. 9.
(2.) See next chapter.
(3.) Ecc. Hist. 3. 31, and 5. 24.
(4.) Ecc. Hist. 5. 27.
(5.) Evangelical Preparation, 7. 22.

Noetus was a native of Asia Minor. He maintained that Christ was the one God, both Father and Son. He was excommunicated.

The views of Noetus led to much discussion, which resulted in the Arian controversy, and the establishment of the doctrine of the Trinity.

Praxeas—Symmachus—Hermas—Seleucas.— A. D. 200.

These writers flourished near the close of the second century. But little is known concerning them. Seleucas is reputed to have written a number of the books in circulation in the second century, which were afterward pronounced apocryphal.

There is a strange confusion among the fathers in regard to his name. He is called Seleucas, Lucianus, Lucanus, Leucius, Lucian, Leuthon, Lentitius, and Leontius. Also Leucius Charinus. It was Seleucas who had published a version of the Gospel of the Infancy, which rendered it necessary for Jerome to give the bishops a better version.[1]

Pistis Sophiæ—A. D. 200.

This is a religious work, of the close of the second century, the author of which is unknown.

Second Epistle of Clement.—A. D. 200.

It is supposed to have been written about this time. The divinity of Jesus, which was not dis-

_____
(1.) See Supposed Gospel of the Birth of Mary.

tinctly taught in the earlier Clementines, (but rather the contrary doctrine), now more clearly
appears.

ARTEMON—JULIUS AFRICANUS.—A. D. 200.

But little is known of Artemon, beyond the fact
that he was prominent in the Noetian controversy.

Africanus was the writer cited by Eusebius, in
his forgery upon Thallus.

These names close the list of the more important
Christian writers of the first two centuries, except
the three great fathers, who will be briefly noticed
in the next chapter.

CHAPTER XXXVII.

IRENÆUS—CLEMENT OF ALEXANDRIA—TERTULLIAN.

Irenæus in Gaul, Clement in Egypt, and Tertullian in Northern Africa, were the three fathers, by whose influence the four gospels were introduced into general circulation, and who laid, broad and deep, the foundations of Roman Catholic supremacy.

It is not easy to form a just estimate of these men. That they were so far above the masses in general intelligence, as to give them an immense and controlling influence in the church, is certain; while, judged by the standard of more enlightened times, they themselves appear at a disadvantage.

The Rev. Dr. Davidson says of them :

"Irenæus was credulous and blundering; Tertullian, passionate and one-sided; and Clement of Alexandria, imbued with the treasures of Greek wisdom, was mainly occupied with ecclesiastical ethics."— [Davidson, Canon, p. 121.

Again, "Irenæus argues that the gospels should be four in number, neither more nor less, because there are four universal winds, and four quarters of the world.

"Matthew wrote his gospel while Peter and Paul were preaching in Rome, and founding the church. [Citing Iren. adv. Hær. 3. 1. 1.] Such assertions show both ignorance and exaggeration.

"Tertullian affirms, that the tradition of the apostolic churches, guarantees the four gospels, [citing adv. Marc. 4. 5.], and refers his readers to the churches of Corinth, Philippi, Ephesus, etc., for the authentic epistles of Paul. [Citing de Præs. Hær. 36.] What is this but the rhetoric of an enthusiast?

"Clement contradicts himself in making Peter authorize Mark's Gospel to be read in the churches; while in another place, he says the apostle 'neither forbade nor encouraged it.' [Citing Clement according to Eusebius, Ecc. Hist. 2. 15, and 6. 14.]"—Ibid.

The same writer continues thus:

"The three fathers of whom we are speaking had neither the ability nor the inclination to examine the genesis of documents surrounded with an apostolic halo. No analysis of their authenticity and genuineness was seriously attempted. In its absence, custom, accident, taste, practical needs directed the tendency of tradition. All the rhetoric employed to throw the value of their testimony as far back as possible, even up to or very near the apostle John, is of the vaguest sort. Appeals to the continuity of tradition and of church doctrine, to the exceptional veneration of these fathers for the gospels, to their opinions being formed earlier than the composition of the works in which they are expressed, possess no force.

"The ends which the fathers in question had in view, their polemic motives, their uncritical, inconsistent assertions, their want of sure data, detract from their testimony. Their decisions were much more the result of pious feeling, biased by the theological speculations of the times, than the conclusions of a sound judgment. The very arguments they use to establish certain conclusions, show weakness of perception. What are the manifestations of spiritual feeling, compared with the results of logical reasoning?"—[Davidson on the Canon, pp. 123, 124.

One great work of these fathers was the establishment of the four gospels, which had now appeared, and were being introduced into the churches.

Immediately connected with this was the establishment of the papal power on a definite basis.

Irenæus, in the third book against Heresies, written about A. D. 190, gave the opinion, that every church should agree with the Church of Rome on account of its pre-eminent authority. (See next chapter.) About five years afterward, he was called upon by the Roman Bishop, Victor, to assemble a council of the Bishops of Gaul, to consider the subject of the celebration of Easter; the question having already been passed upon by a council of Italian bishops. Irenæus presided in the council, and the result of its deliberations was, the approval of the decree of the Italian council. Other councils were in like manner held throughout the Christian world, and the result, with a single exception, was everywhere the same. The movement was to furnish a precedent for the jurisdiction of the Church of Rome over all questions of the kind.

It will be seen in the next chapter, that the views of Tertullian concerning the pre-eminence of the Roman Church, were, notwithstanding his difference with some of the Roman bishops, scarcely less decided than those of Irenæus.

As to Clement, he is less explicit in the assertion of any supremacy of the Roman Church; but there is little room to doubt that there existed an understanding among these fathers, and a concert of action, in upholding and establishing at the same time, the four gospels and the authority of the Roman Bishop.

IRENÆUS was Bishop of Lyons. He was born, according to Dodwell, in the year 97. According to Dr. Grabe, A. D. 108; Tillemont, about 120. Dupin, about 140. The last is probably the nearest correct.

About the year 178, he was sent by the Church of Lyons, to Eleutherus, Bishop of Rome, with an epistle, describing their sufferings during the persecution under Marcus Aurelius. On his return, he was elected Bishop of Lyons, in the year 180. He is supposed to have been martyred about A. D. 202. His martyrdom is denied by some critics.

CLEMENT OF ALEXANDRIA was born either at Athens or Alexandria, about the year 160. From 190 to 202, he presided over the catechetic school at Alexandria. In the latter year, he was compelled to leave that city, by the persecution under Severus. It is supposed by some, that he returned A. D. 211. His return is doubted by others. He died about the year 220.

TERTULLIAN was the first Latin father whose works have been preserved. He was born at Carthage, about the middle of the second century, and lived to a very advanced age.

He was converted about the year 185, and was married the year afterward. Was admitted to the priesthood in 192; became a Montanist in 199, and died about 220.

He was a vigorous, and, at times, powerful writer. But his works abound in looseness of argument, and in whimsical applications of scripture, such as were common in that day.

CHAPTER XXXVIII.

THE ROMAN CATHOLIC HIERARCHY.

It was during the sixth period, that the foundations were laid, of that great ecclesiastical power, which dominated the Christian world for thirteen hundred years, and whose supremacy is still acknowledged throughout a large part of Christendom.

For more than a hundred years after the foundation of the Church of Rome, there is no trace of its jurisdiction over other churches, outside of the Italian provinces.

In the latter part of the second century, a dispute existed concerning the celebration of Easter. The Latin churches claimed it should be on Sunday. The Eastern churches had been celebrating it on the 14th day of the month Nisan. The controversy had lasted nearly half a century. About A. D. 150, Polycarp, Bishop of Smyrna, visited Rome, and explained the views of the Eastern churches. He was treated by Anicetus, who was then bishop, as an equal; no attempt was then made to impose a different day upon the Asiatic churches. On the contrary, Polycarp and others celebrated Easter, according to their own views, in the City of Rome.

But in the time of Victor, the controversy becoming more heated, an attempt was made to settle it. A council was first called by Victor, of all the churches of Italy. At this council it was decreed that Easter should be celebrated on Sunday. Victor then issued a general letter, requesting local councils to be assembled by the following bishops: Theophilus of Cæsarea, Irenæus of Lyons, Bacchylus of Corinth, Demetrius of Alexandria, Palmas of Pontus, and Polycrates of Ephesus. [1]

The local councils were held. One consisted of the bishops in Gaul; another, of those in Palestine, another in Egypt, etc. All these approved the decree of the Italian Council, except the churches of pro-consular Asia, presided over by Polycrates. These refused to conform.

Thereupon Victor, encouraged and strengthened by all the other councils, proceeded to excommunicate the non-conforming Asiatic churches. (About A. D. 195.)

This appears to be the first assumption of su-

(1.) The Catholic Historian Darras, [Genl. History of the Catholic Church, vol. 1, p. 160], calls this letter an "order." According to Eusebius, it was a request. He quotes Polycrates, as writing to Victor, thus: "I could also mention the bishops that were present, whom you requested to be summoned by me, and whom I did call."—[Euseb. Ecc. Hist. 5.24.] It is more probable the letter was in the form of a request. The council called by Victor himself, consisted of all the bishops of Italy; which may be looked upon as indicating the extent of his jurisdiction at that time.

preme power by any Roman bishop. From this
time, the supremacy of the Church of Rome rapidly
culminated, both in theory and practice.   It is
true, that for a long time some churches remained
rebellious, but they were considered by the great
body of Christians as without the pale of the
church universal, as it had been established by
Christ, and had been represented by a regular succession of supreme pontiffs, commencing with
Peter.   For, as soon as the supremacy of the
Roman Church was once admitted, the Christians
of that day found no difficulty in believing that
such supremacy had continued from the times of
the apostles.   They were no more disposed to trace
back the title of a power which they found established, than they were to investigate the origin of
books which they found in circulation.

Protestant writers have claimed that the power
of the papacy was not established, nor its claims
admitted in the writings of the fathers, until several hundred years after Christ.   Even the fair-
minded Neander does not see in the writings of
Irenæus or Tertullian, any acknowledgment that
"the Roman Church held a prominence as the
Cathedra Petri, over all the other apostolic
churches." [1]   Whether as Cathedra Petri, or as the
Church of Peter and Paul, not only the prominence, but the supremacy of the Church of Rome,
would seem to be pretty clearly acknowledged, in
the following passage from Irenæus:

(1.) Church Hist. vol. 1, p. 290.

"Since, however, it would be very tedious, in such a volume as this, to reckon up the successions of all the churches, we do put to confusion all those who, in whatever manner, whether by an evil self-pleasing, by vain-glory, or by blindness and perverse opinion, assemble in unauthorized meetings; (we do this) by indicating that tradition derived from the apostles, of the very great, the very ancient, and universally known church, founded and organized at Rome, by the two most glorious apostles, Peter and Paul; as also (by pointing out) the faith preached to men, which comes down to our times by means of the successions of the bishops.

"For it is a matter of necessity that every church should agree with this church, on account of its pre-eminent authority; that is, the faithful everywhere, inasmuch as the apostolic tradition has been preserved continually by those who exist everywhere.

"The blessed apostles, then, having founded and built up the Church, committed into the hands of Linus, the office of the episcopate. Of this Linus, Paul makes mention in the Epistles to Timothy. To him succeeded Anacletus, and after him, in the third place, from the apostles, Clement was allotted the bishopric."

He then gives the names of nine bishops, following Clement, and proceeds as follows :

"In this order, and by this succession, the ecclesiastical tradition from the apostles, and the preaching of the truth, have come down to us. And this is most abundant proof, that there is one and the same vivifying faith, which has been preserved in the church, from the apostles until now, and handed down in truth."—[Irenæus adv. Hær. 3. 3.

In the time of Tertullian, some twenty years later, the Roman bishops issued peremptory edicts, and appealed to the authority of their predecessors. [1] They called themselves bishops of bishops ; episcopi episcoporum. [2]

Tertullian himself was scarcely less explicit than Irenæus :

"Since, moreover," he says, "you are close to Italy, you have Rome,

(1.) Tert. De Virg. Velandis.   (2.) Ibid. De Pudicitia, ch. 1.

from which there comes, even into our hands, the very authority. How happy is its church, in which apostles poured forth all their doctrine, along with their blood! Where Peter endures a passion like his Lord's! Where Paul wins his crown in a death like John's! Where the apostle John was first plunged, unhurt, into boiling oil, and thence remitted to his island-exile! See what she has learned, what she has taught, what fellowship she has had, even with churches in Africa! One Lord God does she acknowledge, the Creator of the Universe, and the Christ Jesus of the Virgin Mary, the Son of God, the Creator, and the resurrection of the flesh. The law and the prophets she unites in one volume, with the writings of the evangelists and apostles, from which she drinks her faith; this she seals with the water, arrays with the Holy Ghost, feeds with the eucharist, cheers with martyrdom; and against such a discipline thus she admits no gainsayer."—[Tertullian, Prescription against Heretics, ch. 36.

This passage is evidence, not only of the supremacy of the Roman Church, but that the New Testament then in circulation had been compiled under the same authority. The New Testament of Marcion, consisting of the Gospel and the Apostolicon, had been superseded by a larger collection containing the Acts of the Apostles, the Revelation of John, a larger number of Epistles of Paul, and in place of the one gospel of Marcion, four gospels, which were to stand as four pillars, to support the authority of the Church of Rome.

Irenæus, while he clearly concedes the supremacy of that church, at the same time shows the weakness of the foundation upon which the supremacy rested. He declares that the church had been founded by Peter and Paul, and that the episcopacy had been by them committed into the hands of Linus. From Linus it had gone to Anacletus, and "after him, in the third place from the apostles, Clement was allotted the bishopric." The tradi-

tion of the Catholic church has been, that Peter
was the first Bishop of Rome, and that the keys of
the kingdom, as well as the bishopric, were delivered immediately by Peter to Clement. This tradition is in accordance with the letter from Clement
to James, which was in circulation at an early day,
but it is not sustained by Irenæus.

This discrepancy has been the occasion of much
discussion. The most ingenious explanation is
given by Rufinus, the Latin translator of the Recognitions. He conjectures that Linus and Anacletus merely assisted Peter in the management of
the church, which was still, at the death of Peter,
delivered over to Clement. But then what becomes of the continuous "succession," dwelt upon
by Irenæus, in the chain of which two of the links
consisted of Linus and Anacletus?

The difficulty does not end here. According to
Irenæus, the next bishop to Clement was Evaristus. But this succession, though accepted by some
Catholic writers, is found by others not to accord
with the traditions of the church. Accordingly,
the Roman Almanac, entitled Gerarchia Cattolica, interposes Anacletus between Clement and
Evaristus. The third bishop, the second, exclusive
of Peter, according to this authority, was Cletus,
instead of Anacletus, while Anacletus came after
Clement, and ruled over the church twelve years;
from A. D. 100 to 112. Darras, the Catholic historian, whose work received the indorsement of
Pope Pius IX, has followed the succession as given

by Irenæus; stating that his chronology is that of the Chronologie de l'Histoire Ecclesiastique, on the model of the great work of President Henault, on the History of France.

But this author does not agree with other Catholic authorities. He has the bishopric of Peter commence in the year 33, fixing the very day; the 29th of June. This is nine years earlier than the time given in the Almanac, which on this point is supported by Alzog's Handbuch der Kirchengeschichte, a book very extensively used heretofore among Catholics, as a text book of church history.

Cletus, whose bishopric, according to the Roman Almanac, ends in 90, rules a year longer, according to Darras, his bishopric ending A. D. 91. Then comes Clement, his office terminating, according to both, in the year 100. After him, Evaristus, until 109, according to Darras, but according to the Almanac, until 121. Then Alexander, his bishopric, according to Alzog and Darras, ending in the year 119, but according to the Almanac, in the year 132.

After Alexander, the succession of the pontificates was as follows, according to these three authorities:

Sixtus,	according to the Almanac,	A. D. 132 to 142.
do.	do.	Alzog,	"	119 to 127.
"	"	Darras,	"	119 to 128.
Telesphorus,	"	Almanac,	"	142 to 154.
"	"	Alzog,	"	127 to 139.
"	"	Darras,	"	128 to 138.

Hyginus,	according to the Almanac,		A. D. 154 to 158.
"	"	Alzog,	" 139 to 142.
"	"	Darras,	" 138 to 142.
Pius I,	"	Almanac,	" 158 to 167.
"	"	Alzog,	" 142 to 157.
"	"	Darras,	" 142 to 150.
Anicetus,	"	Almanac,	" 167 to 175.
"	"	Alzog,	" 157 to 168.
"	"	Darras,	" 150 to 161.
Soter or Soterus,	"	Almanac,	" 175 to 182.
"	"	Alzog,	" 168 to 177.
"	"	Darras,	" 162 to 174.
Eleutherus,	"	Almanac,	" 182 to 193.
"	"	Alzog,	" 177 to 192.
"	"	Darras,	" 174 to 186.
Victor I,	"	Almanac,	" 193 to 203.
"	"	Alzog,	" 192 to 202.
"	"	Darras,	" 186 to 200.

Thus, in these eight pontificates, there are but two points in which any two of the three authors agree; the commencement of the bishoprics of Sixtus and Pius. In these particulars, Darras agrees with the Handbuch. But the Handbuch and Almanac do not agree in a single date; neither does Darras agree with the Almanac in a single date.

Darras and the Handbuch give the names of fourteen bishops previous to the year 200; the Almanac gives fifteen.

If Irenæus be brought into the comparison, while he does not give the dates of the pontificates he differs from all these authorities, in neglecting to say that Peter was bishop of Rome at all. On the contrary, he states that the church was founded by Peter and Paul, and by them handed over to Linus.

If, during all this time, the bishops of Rome had exercised supreme jurisdiction, can it be possible that nowhere throughout the Christian world there would have been kept a record of so much importance as the succession of the supreme bishops?   Would it not have been possible to arrive at a more harmonious result than this?

It will have been observed, that the Roman Catholic Church was established about the same time that the four gospels and the Acts of the Apostles were brought into general circulation. When Serapion, Bishop of Antioch, in the year 190, put aside the Gospel of Peter, and substituted in its stead the four gospels, he was engaged in the unification of the church.

And it is a significant fact, that Irenæus, the first writer who mentions the four gospels, was the first who acknowledged the supremacy of the Church of Rome.

CHAPTER XXXIX.

REVIEW OF THE SIXTH PERIOD—TESTIMONY OF HEATHEN
WRITERS—GENERAL REVIEW—CONCLUSION.

REVIEW OF SIXTH PERIOD.—1. The termination of the sixth period, which closes the century, finds the four gospels and the Acts of the Apostles coming into general circulation, with most of the other New Testament writings.

The condition of the church in reference to the New Testament books at the time, is well summed up by Rev. Dr. Davidson, in the closing paragraphs of his two volumes of Introduction to the New Testament :

"The following propositions," says he, "are deducible from an impartial survey of the history of the first two centuries:"

The propositions condensed are as follows:

1. Before A. D. 170, no book of the New Testament was termed "scripture."

2. No certain trace of the existence of the fourth gospel till after Justin Martyr. [This proposition might with equal truth be applied to the synoptic gospels, in their present form.]

3. The gospels of Matthew and Mark cannot be identified with the "logia" of Matthew, and the things "said and done" by Jesus, which Mark wrote, mentioned by Papias.

4. The writings of Paul were either not used, or little regarded, by the prominent ecclesiastical writers of the first half of the second century. After A. D. 150, they began to be valued.

5. The present gospels did not assume a canonical position till the latter half of the second century.

6. No canon of the New Testament, i. e., no collection of New Testament literature like the present one, supposed to possess divine authority, existed before A. D. 200.

[Davidson's Introduction to the New Testament, vol. 2, p. 520.   The last proposition cannot be accepted without some hesitation.   The reader will remember the words of Tertullian, written about the year 200:

"The law and the prophets she (the Church of Rome) unites in one volume, with the writings of evangelists and apostles," etc.

There is reason to believe, that very soon after the four gospels appeared, somewhere between the years 180 and 200, they were published under the authority and by the direction of the Church of Rome, in a volume with the Old Testament, and with the other New Testament books then in circulation.]

2. Closely following the introduction into general circulation of the books mentioned, was the establishment of the supremacy of the Bishop of Rome over the entire Catholic Church; the Gospels of John and Matthew being used as powerful agencies in the consummation of that object. Not that the gospels were considered of higher authority than the traditions of the church, but those traditions themselves were established upon the firmest foundation, by the sanction of gospels bearing the names of two of the apostles of Jesus.

And here it is worthy of remark, that while in the earlier gospels, attributed to Luke and Mark, neither of whom was an apostle, had been recorded the older legends and traditions of the churches, when, to aid the Bishop of Rome in assuming authority over the entire Christian world, it was thought necessary to have still other gospels, they were both attributed to apostles of Christ.

HEATHEN WRITERS.—Something is said in almost every complete work on the canon concerning the evidence of heathen writers. Such evidence is absolutely of no value in reference to the canon, because no mention is found in any heathen writer of any of the Christian writings before they are referred to by the Christians themselves.

Celsus, who, as quoted by Origen, is perhaps most relied upon as referring to the New Testament books, does not appear to have written the work cited by Origen, "The True Word," until early in the third century.

There is, however, important evidence concerning the life and death of Jesus at the time claimed by the Christians; facts which have been disputed by some learned writers. [1]

GENERAL REVIEW — CONCLUSION. — In taking a general review of the first hundred and seventy years of the Christian religion, the first thing that strikes the mind, is the dearth of material from which to construct a reliable history. It is seen at once, how much must rest upon probability in its different degrees—how much must be relegated to the province of speculation. The works of the

(1.) See Appendix, 1.

only church historian who wrote during that
period, lost or destroyed—the few fragments that
are left being of comparatively little value—the
writings of Porphyry and others who wrote against
Christianity, and those of the heretic Christians,
all destroyed—there remain only the works of some
of the orthodox fathers, and the text of those in a
mutilated and corrupted condition.

As from a few bones the scientist can reconstruct
the entire anatomy, so from these fragments can
the historian arrive at the frame-work of the orthodox religion of the second century. But the complete and living form of Christianity is wanting.

With the exception of the epistle of Clement of
Rome, written near the close of the first century,
and a few scattering writings afterward, there is
but little in the fathers of that day, to remind one
of the teachings of Jesus, or the fervid utterances
of the apostle to the Gentiles. The fathers of the
second century were, with united energies, engaged
in the work of suppressing heresy. Justin Martyr
was writing against the Jews, Tertullian against
Marcion, and Irenæus against all the heretics.
This raid against those who differed from the
established faith, left but little time to cultivate
the more kindly Christian graces, and finally culminated in the establishment of a power which
should be competent for the suppression of heresy
by force. The teachings of Paul concerning heresy
and his bitter denunciation of heretics, contributed
largely to this result.

Another thing that strikes the attention, in a comprehensive review of the period, is the ignorance and superstition, even of the most enlightened and best educated of the fathers. Their bigotry has been noticed—their ignorance and superstition were no less.

With rare exceptions, they were men who utterly despised that learning of the heathen which consisted in attempts to ascertain the laws of the material universe. Construing in the narrowest and strictest sense, the maxim, that the wisdom of this world is foolishness with God, they confined themselves, almost exclusively, to an exposition of the Jewish scriptures, and of the sayings of Christ, construed in the light of those scriptures; drawing oftentimes, in the application of the prophecies, the most fanciful and whimsical analogies.

Their credulity was unbounded. They had a sublime disregard for truth; not so much from perversity, as from carelessness, and indifference to its sacred character. Their unscrupulousness when seeking for arguments to enforce their positions, is notorious; as well as the prevalence among them of what are known as pious frauds. Jones, himself a zealous Christian writer, says that Justin Martyr, Clemens Alexandrinus and Lactantius made use of testimonies out of forgeries and spurious books, to prove the very foundation of the Christian Revelation; [1] and it is believed, on good grounds, that Irenæus was no better. This father,

(1.) Jones, vol. I, p. 364.

while engaged in the introduction of gospels which
show that the ministry of Christ lasted from one
to three years, not longer than three and a half,
himself declares that it lasted about twenty years,
and that he had the tradition from the elders of
Asia, who had obtained it from John and the other
apostles.

Such is the material at the hands of the historian. Of course he cannot rely implicitly upon
the unsupported assertion of any such writer, for
the truth of any historical fact whatever. In every
instance, he is obliged to scrutinize carefully, and
endeavor to ascertain whether any ulterior motives
may have prompted whatever statement may be
under consideration. If he can find none, and the
fact stands uncontradicted by other writers, it is
cautiously accepted. Under such circumstances,
progress is slow and uncertain. The most that any
writer can hope to accomplish, is to place in proper
shape what is already known, and to establish here
and there a landmark for the benefit of subsequent
historians.

In conclusion, as the result of this investigation,
it may be repeated, that no evidence is found of
the existence, in the first century, of either of the
following doctrines : the immaculate conception—
the miracles of Christ—his material resurrection.
No one of these doctrines is to be found in the
epistles of the New Testament, nor have we been
able to find them in any other writings of the first
century.

As to the four gospels, in coming to the conclusion that they were not written in the first century, we have but recorded the conviction of the more advanced scholars of the present day, irrespective of their religious views in other respects; with whom the question as now presented is, how early in the second century were they composed? [1]

Discarding, as inventions of the second century, having no historical foundation, the three doctrines above named, and much else which must necessarily stand or fall with them, what remains of the Christian religion?

All that is of any value—all that is in harmony with the immutable laws of the universe—all that is in accord with the eternal principles of right and justice, still remains. All else is fast passing away, and is destined to pass away forever.

(1.) Dr. Davidson does not think either of the four gospels, in its present form, written before the year 100. The Gospel of John not before 150. See his Introduction to the New Testament.

APPENDIX.

NOTES.

I.

Jesus Christ as a Historical Personage.

Some able writers, observing the confusion and uncertainty existing in the chronology of nearly all the events connected with the
early history of Christianity, have doubted whether such a person
as Jesus Christ lived at the time alleged. These doubts have, in some
instances, been expressed by writers of much learning, and cannot
well be disregarded.

There are three good and reliable witnesses of the first century;
one a Christian, one a Jew, and the other a heathen:

1. PAUL.—The Epistles of Paul stand out as a fact, utterly unex-
plainable, and incomprehensible, except upon the hypothesis of the
life and suffering of the central figure of them all.

That Paul wrote his Epistles in the first century, is attested by
Clement of Rome, A. D. 97, who refers to one of them expressly, and
by the fathers and writers of the first half of the second century, particularly Marcion, who, about 145, made a compilation of those then
in circulation, ten in number.

2. JOSEPHUS; who gives an account of the death of James, the
brother of Jesus, in the 9th chapter of the 20th book of the An-

APPENDIX.

tiquities. While narrating the particulars of the death of James, he speaks of him as "the brother of Jesus who was called Christ." We know of no good reason for doubting the authenticity of this passage.

3. TACITUS; who, in the 44th chapter of the 15th book of the Annals, speaks of Christus, "who, in the reign of Tiberius, was put to death as a criminal, by the procurator, Pontius Pilate."

II.

Zacharias.

There were four persons by that name, who have been referred to in the apocryphal and canonical gospels, and in the writings of the fathers, in such an indiscriminate manner as to create great confusion.

1. Zacharias, or Zechariah, the son of Jehoida. He was stoned to death in the court of the temple.—[2 Chron. 24. 20, 21.

2. Zacharias or Zechariah, the prophet, who was the son of Berechiah.—[Zech. 1. 1.] We have no account of his death.

3. Zacharias, father of John the Baptist.

In the Protevangelion, it is stated that because he would not disclose the hiding place of his son John, who had been concealed from Herod, he was murdered "in the entrance of the temple."

This account is referred to and accredited by the earlier fathers, including Tertullian and Origen. It does not appear who was the father of this Zacharias.

4. Zacharias, the son of Barouchos, who was murdered inside the temple, about A. D. 69.—[Josephus, Jewish War, bk. 4, ch. 5, 4.

Thus it will be seen, that three of the persons by that name were put to death in or near the temple. Of these, the first was the son of Jehoida; the father of the second not named; and the third was the son of Barouchos. This comes the nearest to the description of the Zacharias mentioned in Matt. 23. 35. We have therefore adopted the opinion of able writers, who consider the last the one referred to by the author of Matthew.

III.

Tatian and his Supposed Gospel.

It is claimed by Dr. George Moesinger, in a work published at Venice in 1876, that the Commentary of Ephraem the Syrian, of the fourth century, was based upon the Gospel of Tatian. We do not think such a theory can be sustained. On the contrary, since writing this History, and after reading the dissertation of Dr. Moesinger and his edition of Ephraem, and giving the subject a more thorough examination, we have come to the conclusion that it is extremely doubtful whether Tatian the Syrian ever wrote a gospel. It is not mentioned until Eusebius, who is entirely unreliable. Besides, it appears from some of the Syrian writers that Ammonius of Alexandria was also called Tatian; and it is more than probable that other writers have been misled by their references to the Gospel Harmony of Ammonius Tatianus, or, in the words of the Latin translator of one of the Syrian authors, "Ammonius, qui est Tatianus," supposing they referred to Tatian the Syrian.

IV.

The Philosophy of Oracles.

ATTRIBUTED TO PORPHYRY.

Gustavus Wolff, who has written two works upon Oracles, in the Latin tongue, published at Berlin, one in 1854, the other in 1856, treats the Philosophy of Oracles as the work of Porphyry. As Mr. Wolff gives all the references to it by ancient writers, scholars will here find the full strength of the case in favor of the genuineness of the work. But we do not think this author, with all his learning, has established its authenticity. The awkward fact still remains that all the references, with one exception, are to be traced directly or indirectly to Eusebius. What additional matter is furnished by Augustine, may fairly be looked upon as mere amplifications, such as were common among the early fathers of the Church. To the names of Fontenelle and Van Dale, given in the text, may be added that of the learned and celebrated Dr. Lardner against the authenticity.

V.

The Annals of Tacitus.

In a work put forth by Mr. Ross, in London, an elaborate attempt is made to prove that the Annals were forged in the 15th century by Bracciolini. The ingenious author comes as near to maintaining his position as can be expected, in face of the facts that the Annals were referred to by various writers, in the 3d, 4th, 5th, 6th, 9th and 12th centuries, and that several of the books were not discovered until after the death of Bracciolini.

VI.

Date of the Gospels.

THE ARGUMENT IN FAVOR OF AN EARLY DATE.

We say "The argument," because there is but one. There is no pretense that there is any direct evidence, carrying the gospels back to the first century, or even any definite tradition to that effect.

The argument, and it applies only to the synoptic gospels, is, that inasmuch as those gospels contain the prophecy of Jesus concerning the destruction of Jerusalem, if these books had been written after that event, they would certainly have referred to it. Since they do not do so, they must have been written before the destruction of Jerusalem; that is, before A. D. 70.

1. This argument, if it proves anything, proves too much, and is self-destructive. For, by the same process of reasoning, it could be proved that the Gospel of Marcion was written before A. D. 70; since that also contains the prophecy that not one stone of the temple should be left upon another, and contains no reference to the destruction of Jerusalem. But we know, with reasonable certainty, that this gospel was written about A. D. 145.

2. The Gospel of John is admitted by Canon Farrar himself, who lays great stress upon this argument, not to have been written until A. D. 90. Why does that gospel make no allusion to the destruction of Jerusalem?

If it be said that this gospel makes no mention of the prophecy of

Jesus concerning that event, then the question arises, why does it not, if it be true that such a prophecy was made? The author of that gospel had just as good an opportunity to emphasize the fact that the event had verified the prophecy as either of the synoptic gospel writers had, when writing after A. D. 70.

3. None of the apocrypal gospels make any mention of the destruction of Jerusalem. Yet it is not claimed that they were written before that event. Their silence concerning the prophecy is strong presumptive evidence that no such prophecy was made. On no other hypothesis can such silence be fully accounted for, whether they were written before or after A. D. 70.

Such is the argument in favor of dating the three gospels before A. D. 70; and when that conclusion is reached there is found but little difficulty in attributing them to Matthew, Mark and Luke.

But the objections to this authorship are such as make it simply absurd.

In the first place, neither of these men ever claimed or pretended to have written a gospel. Is it not wonderful, if such claim has any just foundation, that it was not made by them or by some one else for them in their life-time?

Again, why is the first person never used in these gospels? Why do not the writers say, "I," occasionally? Why does not Matthew say, "I was chosen?" On the contrary, the writer says:

"As Jesus passed forth from thence, he saw a man named Matthew sitting at the receipt of custom. And he saith unto him, Follow me. And he arose and followed him."

Is this the language a man would use, writing about himself?

The theory that these books were written by those men at that time or soon after, lays too heavy a tax upon the credulity of any thoughtful person.

It should be stated that even orthodox writers are not unanimous in dating all the synoptics before A. D. 70. Thus Reuss, speaking of the books of Luke and the Acts, says: "The date of the composition of this twofold historical work should not be put back too far. Even the first part of it, the Gospel, is later than the destruction of Jerusalem."—[Hist. of the N. T. by Eduard (W. E.) Reuss, Professor

in Emp. William's University in Strassburg: translated by Edw. L.
Houghton, from 5th German Ed., and published in Boston by
Houghton, Mifflin & Co., in 1884, p. 211.

YIELDING TO THE EVIDENCE.

The evidence of a late date for the four gospels, which has been
given to the public in this and other works during the last twenty
years, is having its effect in overthrowing the traditional theory that
those gospels were composed by Matthew, Mark, Luke and John, in
the first century. The more candid of religious writers are already
wavering, while some of them have actually abandoned the church
theory altogether.

A notable instance of this may be seen in the work entitled, "The
First Three Gospels;" written by J. Estlin Carpenter, M. A., Oxford,
and published in London in 1890, by the Sunday School Association.

This author, though careful and guarded in his language, concedes, with sufficient clearness, that the gospels had an uncertain
origin sometime in the second century.

Under the title of "THE FOUR SELECTED," he says:

"It is clear that in the last generation of the second century, the
four gospels, as we have them, were known and received from east to
west."—[The First Three Gospels, p. 4.

Again: "The four gospels, which come clearly into view in the
second half of the second century, had attained a unique position by
its close."—[Ibid. p. 26.

And speaking of the Gospel according to Matthew, he says:

"Certain it is that the work in its present form is not apostolic."—
[Ibid. p. 380.] He thinks the first decisive evidence of the existence
of this gospel was after A. D. 140.

This writer agrees also with the author of the History of the Christian Religion in the opinion that Matthew was the latest of the three
synoptic gospels.

Another instance, showing the tendency of modern thought on the
theological side, may be seen in a work entitled, "The Kingdom of
God; or Christ's Teaching According to the Synoptical Gospels;"
written by Alexander Balmain Bruce, D. D., Professor of N. T.

Exegesis at Glasgow, and published in New York by Scribner and Welford, in 1889.

This writer says:

"It would inspire great confidence in the synoptical records to be assured that they were compiled by certain of the men who 'had been with Jesus.' These men were eye and ear witnesses of Christ's ministry; they knew much, if not all, that He said and did, and they could be trusted to tell honestly and with substantial accuracy what they knew.

"But there is no sufficient evidence that any one of the first three gospels, in the form in which we have them, proceeded from the hand of an apostle. The most that can be said is, that their reports are based on apostolic traditions, preserved either orally or in written form."—[The Kingdom of God, etc., p. 2.

Again:

Washington Gladden, in his work entitled "Burning Questions, etc.," speaking of the objection that is made to the authenticity of the gospels, that they are mere compilations;—that the writers gathered and compiled oral tales and traditions about the Christ,— says:

"And there is, doubtless, some truth in this theory of the origin of the gospels. That is to say, the writers of the Gospel did compile narratives that were partly oral and partly written."—[Burning Questions, etc., by Washington Gladden, the Century Co., N. Y., 1890, p. 215.

This theory, which is now the prevailing one even among theologians themselves, that the gospels were composed partly from oral and partly from written tradition, is an entire abandonment of the other theory, so long and so tenaciously adhered to, that they were composed by eyewitnesses of the events related in them. The written statement of an eyewitness is neither oral nor written tradition. In fact, written tradition is nothing more nor less than oral tradition gathered up and committed to writing. To say, therefore, that the gospels were compiled partly from oral and partly from written tradition, is equivalent to saying that they were compiled, partly from oral traditions which had previously been committed to writing, and partly from oral traditions which were then, for the first time, reduced to writing. Thus, oral tradition constitutes the entire foundation.

VII.

Fulfillment of Prophecy.

CITATIONS FROM THE OLD TESTAMENT,
By the Author of the Gospel of Matthew.

In confirmation of the view taken by the author of this work, as to the inapplicability of the citations made from the Old Testament by the author of Matthew, the reader is referred to an able work by Professor Crawford Howell Toy, of Harvard University; published later than the earlier editions of the History of the Christian Religion.

In that work, which is entitled "Quotations in the New Testament," Professor Toy, writing with remarkable fairness, from a Christian standpoint, takes nearly the same view with the author of the History, though expressing himself in a somewhat more guarded manner.

Commenting on the passage in Isaiah, (vii. 14), cited by Matthew thus: "Behold a virgin shall be with child," etc. Professor Toy says:

"The rendering 'virgin' is inadmissible. The Hebrew has a separate word for 'virgin;' and the Greek versions, other than the Septuagint, here translate by 'young woman.'"

Again: "The article here shows that she was some well-known person, probably not the wife of the prophet (for she is elsewhere, Isa. viii. 3, called 'the prophetess'); possibly a wife of the King. But she is mentioned here only, and is of no importance in the prophecy for its prediction or its fulfillment. The child's birth is not represented as miraculous or in any way extraordinary, and there is nothing to prevent our supposing that the mother was a married woman."
—[Quotations in the New Testament by Crawford Howell Toy, N. Y., Chas. Scribner's Sons, p. 1 and note to p. 3.

Again: "The Jews seem never to have understood the passage Messianically. The name Immanuel occurs nowhere else in the New Testament (Luke has the birth from a virgin, but not this name), and was apparently never given to Jesus."—[Ibid. p. 3. and Note.

The Professor had previously explained that the name Immanuel given to the child, meaning "God with us," signified "that this same result (that is, that men should carry the riches of Damascus and the spoil of Samaria before the King of Assyria), should take place before the child in question had numbered more than a few years." "In this respect," the author continues, "Immanuel plays exactly the same part as Mahershalal-hash-baz and Shear-yashub, differing from them only in the fact that his mother's name is not given. He is merely the sign of a fact, not the instrument of its accomplishment. His person is to be the sign of the overthrow of Syria and Israel, and his name is to embody the great and consoling idea of God's presence with his people. He himself is passive, so far as the record goes; having fulfilled his function of acting as unconscious sign (for the fulfillment of the prediction is to take place while he is yet a child), he vanishes out of the history."—[Ibid. p. 3.

The Professor concludes by saying that the prophetic passage is understood by Matthew as a definite prediction of the historical fact of the birth of Jesus. To what extent the author thinks Matthew justified in thus understanding the prediction, may be gathered from the foregoing.

Again: In reference to the quotation from Jeremiah:

"In Rama was there a voice heard, lamentation and weeping, and great mourning, Rachel weeping for her children, and would not be comforted because they are not;" which the author of Matthew says was fulfilled when Herod slew the children of Bethlehem, Professor Toy says:

"The country had been overrun by the Chaldeans, and many of the people slain, and carried into captivity; and the prophet represents the nation, in the person of the ancestress Rachel (the best-beloved wife of Jacob), weeping over the loss of its sons. A repetition of this scene, and the fulfillment of a prediction, the evangelist sees in the mourning of the mothers of Bethlehem over their children, slain by order of Herod. The situations are in a measure alike, though the later is insignificant in extent in comparison with the earlier. Nebuchadnezzar inflicted a crushing blow on the nation; Herod may have slain ten or fifteen infants."—[Ibid. p. 11.

The author thinks the citation of a parallel event from Jeremiah natural and justifiable, but adds this significant statement:

"The prophet's words contain no prediction, Messianic or other; the context shows that he is thinking only of the present national calamity."—[Ibid.

Speaking, in his comments upon another passage, of the latitude allowed in those days, Professor Toy says:

"The principles of Scripture application of the day allowed the evangelist to take the words out of their connection, and use them as seemed to him best."—[Ibid. p. 9.

VIII.

Was Jesus an Essene?

By most writers the Essenes of Palestine and the Therapeutæ of Egypt have been confusedly treated as the same people; or if not the same, it has been supposed that one was a branch or colony of the other. Later scholarship has shown, however, that neither of these theories is correct.

THE THERAPEUTÆ.

All we know of these people can be traced back to a treatise entitled "Concerning a Contemplative Life;" attributed to Philo Judaeus, a Jewish writer of the first century. Attempts have been made by Professor Lucius, of Strassburg, and others, to prove that this was not a genuine work of Philo. But it cannot be said that these attempts have been successful.

Philo does not say that the Essenes and Therapeutæ were the same people. On the contrary it is manifest from the treatise itself that he did not consider them the same.

The Therapeutæ were a body of hermits living in Egypt. Philo's account of them is quite interesting, but as it is not of them we are now to speak, let us proceed to the consideration of

THE ESSENES.

What we know of the Essenes is derived from the writings of Pliny, of Philo Judæus, and of Josephus.

Philo was the earliest of the three. His writings must be placed in the first half of the first century.

Josephus is believed to have completed the Antiquities in the year 94, A. D. He had written The Jewish War some twenty years previous, about the time when Pliny was finishing his Natural History.

We will commence with Philo. His testimony is substantially as follows:

That there were living in Palestine and Syria, people called "Essenes;" that they numbered something more than 4,000; that they derived their name from their piety; that they did not sacrifice living animals. That they lived in villages, avoiding the cities.

"Among them," says Philo, "there are none attending to any employment whatever connected with war. * * They are utterly ignorant of all traffic, and of all commercial dealings, and of all navigation. * * There is not a single slave among them.

"Further, that the seventh day was accounted sacred; that in the synagogue one would take up the holy volume and read it while some man of the greatest experience would make explanations."

And still further, that "there is no one who has a house so absolutely his own private property, that it does not in some sense also belong to every one; for besides that they all dwell together in companies, the house is open to all of those of the same notions, who come to them from other quarters; then there is one magazine among them all; their expenses are all in common; their garments belong to them all in common; their food is common, since they all eat in messes."

That whatever they received for their wages was brought into a common stock; that they cherished respect for their elders, who were honored and cared for as parents by their children.

The next writer is Josephus. The most important account of the Essenes given by this writer is to be found in the 8th chapter of the 2d book of "The Jewish War," and is in substance as follows:

They were Jews by birth. They rejected pleasures as an evil, and esteemed continence and conquest over the passions to be virtuous. They neglected wedlock, and adopted children.

They were despisers of riches; had all things in common; were very communicative; thought oil a defilement; clothed themselves at stated times in white garments; had stewards appointed to take care of their common affairs. . . . .

"Whatsoever they say, also, is firmer than an oath. But swearing is avoided by them; and they esteem it worse than perjury. For they say, that he who cannot be believed without [swearing by] God, is already condemned. . . .

"They also take great pains in studying the writings of the ancients."

He who joins them must take an oath that "he will neither conceal anything from those of his own sect, nor discover any of their doctrines to others; no, not though anyone should compel him to do so at the hazard of his life."

Moreover, he must swear to abstain from robbery, "*and to preserve the books belonging to their sect,* and the names of the angels," [or messengers.]

Those caught in any heinous sin were cast out. The outcast, not being at liberty to partake of food elsewhere, often died in a miserable manner. Sometimes, when on the eve of starvation, he was taken back.

"They honor their legislator (Moses), and obey their elders and the majority. If any one blaspheme Moses, he is punished capitally. They are stricter than other Jews in the observance of the Sabbath."

"They are long lived also, insomuch that many of them live above a hundred years, by means of the simplicity of their diet; nay, as I think, by means of the regular course of life which they observe also. And as for death, if it will be for their glory, they esteem it better than living always." (Their fortitude in enduring sufferings in the Jewish war with the Romans, is here extolled and commented upon.)

"There are also those among them who undertake to foretell things to come by reading the holy books, and using several sorts of purifications, and being perpetually conversant in the discourses of the prophets; and it is but seldom that they miss in their predictions." —[Jewish War, B. II, ch. viii.

OTHER NOTICES BY JOSEPHUS.

Josephus has various other notices of the Essenes; some twenty altogether. The following are the most important:

FROM THE ANTIQUITIES OF THE JEWS.

1. "The sect of the Essenes affirm that fate governs all things, and

that nothing befalls men but what is according to its determination."—[A. J. Bk. XIII, ch. V, 9.

2. "But here one may take occasion to wonder at one Judas, who was of the sect of the Essenes, and who never missed the truth in his predictions. This man, when he saw Antigonus passing by the temple, cried out to his companions and friends, who abode with him as his scholars, in order to learn the art of foretelling things to come, 'That it was good of him to die now, since he had spoken falsely about Antigonus, who is still alive, and I see him passing by;' although he had foretold that he should die at the place called Strato's Tower, that very day, while yet the place is six hundred furlongs off, where he had foretold that he should be slain; and still this day is a great part of it already past, so that he was in danger of proving a false prophet.

"As he was saying this, and that in a melancholy mood, the news came that Antigonus was slain, in a place under ground, which itself was also called 'Strato's Tower.' "—[A. J. Bk. XIII, ch. XI, 2.

Substantially the same account is given in "The Jewish War," Bk. I, ch. III, 5.

3. "The Essenes, also, as we call a sect of ours, were excused by Herod from this imposition [taking the oath of fidelity.] These men live the same kind of life as do those whom the Greeks called Pythagoreans."

Josephus here relates how an Essene by the name of Manahem, once saw Herod, when he (Herod) was yet a child and going to school; and saluted him as King of the Jews. That he prophesied that he would excel all men in happiness, and would obtain an everlasting reputation, but would forget piety and righteousness.

That when Herod became king, he sent for Manahem, and asked him how long he should reign? Manahem was silent. Herod asked him whether he should reign ten years or not. "Yes, twenty, nay, thirty years;" but did not say how long.

"Many of the Essenes," adds Josephus, "have by their excellent virtue, been thought worthy of the knowledge of divine revelations." —[A. J. Bk. XV, ch. X, 4. 5.

4. "The doctrine of the Essenes is, that all things are best ascribed to God. They teach the immortality of souls, and esteem that the rewards of righteousness are to be earnestly striven for. When they send what they have dedicated to God, into the temple, they do not offer sacrifices, because they have more pure lustrations of their own; on which account, they are excluded from the common court of the

temple, and offer their sacrifices themselves; yet is their course of
life better than that of other men.

"This is demonstrated by that institution of theirs which will not
suffer anything to hinder them from having all things in common;
so that a rich man enjoys no more of his own wealth than he who
hath nothing at all.

"There are about four thousand men who live in this way. They
neither marry wives, nor are desirous to keep servants; as thinking
the latter tempts men to be unjust, and the former gives the handle
to domestic quarrels. But as they live by themselves, they minister
one to another. They also appoint certain stewards to receive the
income from their revenues, and of the fruits of the ground; such as
are good men and priests, who are to get their corn and their food
ready for them."—[Antiq. of the Jews, Bk. XVIII, ch. I, 5.

To which, in Whiston's Josephus, is the following note:

"It seems by what Josephus says here, and Philo himself elsewhere,
Op. p. 676, that these Essenes did not use to go up to the Jewish festivals at Jerusalem, or to offer sacrifices there, which may be one
great occasion why they are never mentioned in the ordinary books
of the New Testament."

But Josephus does not say that the Essenes "did not use to go up
to the Jewish festivals at Jerusalem." He says that they were "excluded from the common court of the temple;" that they sent into
the temple what they had dedicated to God, but did not offer sacrifices [with the other Jews], because they had purer lustrations of
their own. "They offer their sacrifices themselves."

When this is taken in connection with the fact that one gate of
the city was called the gate of the Essenes (B. J. V. 4, 2), the inference
is at least but a fair one, that either in another part of the temple or
in a part of the city outside the temple, they had their own peculiar
ceremonies, which, if not accompanied by actual sacrifices, were supposed to have a similar effect in the fulfillment of the law.

TESTIMONY OF PLINY (A. D. 77).

"Lying on the West of Asphaltites (the Lake of Sodom, or the
Dead Sea, called by Pliny Asphaltites, from the Greek *asphaltos*, on
account of the asphaltum floating on its surface), and sufficiently distant to escape its noxious exhalations, are the Esseni, a people who
live apart from the world, and marvelous beyond all others throughout the whole earth; for they have no women among them. To sex-
ual desire they are strangers; money they have none; the palm-trees
are their only companions.

"Day after day, however, their numbers are fully recruited by multitudes of strangers who resort to them, driven thither to adopt their usages by the tempests of fortune, and wearied with the miseries of life. Thus it is that through thousands of ages, incredible to relate, this people eternally prolongs its existence, without a single birth taking place there; so fruitful a source of population to it is that weariness of life which is felt by others."—[Nat. Hist. bk. v. ch, 17.

What have we now from Philo, from Josephus, and from Pliny?

1. There was in Palestine, in the first century, a Jewish sect of a peculiar character, of great antiquity. The date when they first appeared, by the name of Essenes, so far as can be gathered from Josephus, was about the middle of the second century before Christ. Pliny says that they had existed for thousands of ages.

He must have had other authority as to the antiquity of this sect than that of Philo or Josephus, since there is nothing in the works of either of those writers to justify the strong language used by Pliny.

2. The doctrines as well as the manners and customs of these people, bore a striking resemblance, in many respects, to those of the followers of Jesus the Galilean.

The resemblances may be epitomized as follows:

The Essenes were especially devoted to the service of God—lived principally in villages and in smaller settlements—were engaged in rural occupations—had scanty worldly possessions, which they threw into a common stock—were employed in daily labor, but had little, if any, commercial intercourse or business relations with those about them—lived on terms of social equality, aiding both each other and other like communities—inculcating obedience to law, and to the requirements of the lawful magistrate—observed the seventh day as the Sabbath—refused to sacrifice in accordance with the Mosaic law —had stated meetings for worship and for instruction— made use of ancient sacred scriptures—were abstemious in their habits—provided for the poor and the sick from a common stock—cherished respect for their elders—endured unflinchingly any hardship or cruelty rather than renounce their principles—had more love for one another than is customary among sects—looked upon pleasure as an evil, but thought continence and conquest of the passions a great virtue— neglected wedlock—guarded the virtue of women—clothed themselves at stated times in white garments—had stewards appointed to manage their common affairs—carried nothing with them when they traveled—had a person appointed to take care of strangers—said grace at their meals—abstained from oaths on ordinary occasions, but had their secret oaths of fidelity, etc.—were subject to trial and to expulsion for misconduct—were addicted to prophecy—believed in the immortality of the soul, and in the decrees of fate.

It has often been asked why neither Philo nor Josephus makes any mention of the Christians? There is no sufficient evidence that there were any people known by that name before the destruction of Jerusalem. According to the New Testament the disciples were first called Christians at Antioch, some thirty years before that event.— [Acts, 11.26.

It may be asked further, why, then, does not Josephus give an account of these people by some other name? Is it clear that he has not done so? What is lacking in his description of the Essenes, except the doctrine of the expected Messiah? His omission of that is no more wonderful of the Essenes, than of the other Jewish sects. Where has Josephus mentioned that doctrine at all?

Is it clear that the followers of Jesus were not alluded to in the following passage of Josephus?

"And now these imposters and deceivers persuaded the multitude to follow them into the wilderness, and pretended that they would exhibit manifest wonders and signs which should be performed by the Providence of God."—[Antiq. bk. xx, ch. 8, 6.

Again, Josephus says:

"These were such men as deceived and deluded the people under pretense of divine inspiration; but were for procuring innovations and changes of the government. These prevailed with the multitude to act like mad men; and went before them into the wilderness, as pretending that God would there show them the signal of liberty." [Jewish War, bk. ii, ch. 13, 4.

Again: Why has Josephus made no mention of Jesus, called Christ? Or, if he has mentioned him, why has he made no further mention? It is true that Josephus was not contemporary with Jesus if the latter was crucified at the time commonly supposed. But during the administration of Josephus in Galilee, the country must have been full of traditions of the crucified Galilean. But a single generation had passed, and the fame of Jesus being now spread abroad in other lands, could it have been any less in Galilee? Paul was contemporary with Josephus, and in his travels, if the accounts in the Acts of the Apostles can be at all relied upon, he must, more than once, have crossed the track of the Jewish priest and magistrate.

But is it clear that Josephus made no mention of Christ, or none other than those in the disputed passages?

Josephus knew of many persons in Galilee by the name of Jesus. Could any of these have been Jesus, called Christ?

Could he have been any one of the high priests by that name?

Could he have been Jesus, the son of Sapphias, "the leader of a seditious tumult of mariners and poor people?"—[Life of Josephus, sec. 12.

Was he Jesus, the brother-in-law of Justus, who [Jesus] had been "wisely put to death?"—[Ibid. sec. 35, 37.

Was he Jesus, the son of Ananus, "a plebeian and a husbandman," who came to the feast of the tabernacles, and began suddenly to cry aloud:

"A voice from the east and a voice from the west, a voice from the four winds, a voice against Jerusalem and the holy house, a voice against the bridegrooms and the brides, and a voice against the whole people;" and who, for seven years and five months, continued to cry, even though cruelly scourged, 'Woe, woe to Jerusalem!' "—[B. J. vi. 5, 3.

Or could he have been that unnamed person who "came out of Egypt;" who "said that he was a prophet, and advised the multitude of the common people to go along with him to the Mount of Olives;" and who "said further that he would show them from hence how, at his command, the walls of Jerusalem would fall down."—[A. J., bk. xx., ch. 8, 6.] The same Egyptian prophet led his followers into the wilderness.—[B. J., ii. 13. A. J., xx. 8. 6. See Acts, 21. 38.

Or, by a strange anachronism, could he have been connected with Judas of Galilee, who was "the author of the fourth sect of Jewish philosophy, who had inviolable attachment to liberty, and said that God was their only ruler and Lord; who did not value any kind of death, nor could any such fear make them call any man Lord;"—[A. J., xviii. 1, 6]; who "was a teacher of a peculiar sect of his own, and was not at all like the rest" of the leaders of the Jews?—[B. J., ii. 8. 1.

Again: Why is the New Testament silent concerning the Essenes? We have seen that the statement that they were not accustomed to go up to Jerusalem to sacrifice, is not a sufficient explanation, simply because it is untrue.

On the contrary, the fact that they did go up to Jerusalem and perform sacrifices or purifications of their own, would make them specially prominent. It was an important sect, and the oldest of any. Why is it not mentioned in the New Testament?

JESUS THE NAZARENE.

Fifteen times in the New Testament the Galilean is spoken of as "Jesous ho Nazoraios," in the original; which, in King James' translation, is, in every instance but two, translated "Jesus of Nazareth;" but which, in every instance, should have been rendered, "Jesus the Nazarite," or, which would also be unobjectionable, "Jesus the Nazarene." This (the latter rendering) is conceded in McClintock and Strong's Biblical Cyclopedia to be the better one. Under the title of "Jesus" it has the following:

"To distinguish our Lord from others bearing the name, he was termed Jesus of Nazareth (John 18. 7, etc.), strictly, Jesus the Nazarene, Jesous ho Nazoraios."

Now, why did King James' translators so pertinaciously insist upon a rendering which is admitted by the highest Biblical (orthodox) authority, not to be strictly correct?

That Jesus the Nazarene had lived in Galilee, is reasonably certain. And it is very possible that he lived in a place which was afterward named Nazareth. That the word Nazaret was derived from Nazoraios or Nazareenos is manifestly more probable than that these words were derived from Nazaret. The words Nazareenos and Nazoraios have a plain, etymological history; while taking Nazaret as an original word, commentators are all at sea as to its origin. Besides, we look in vain for any such place as Nazareth in the life-time of Jesus.

There is no sufficient evidence that there was any place known by the name of Nazareth before the destruction of Jerusalem. The word does not occur in the Old Testament, nor in Josephus. In the

New Testament it is to be found once in the Acts of the Apostles, a book written late in the second century. It occurs also several times in the Gospels, which were composed long after the destruction of Jerusalem.

It is said in Matthew that Joseph, the father of Jesus, dwelt in a city called Nazareth. But if there was any city by that name, it was near Tiberias; and how is it that no mention is made of it by Josephus? In his administration of the affairs of Galilee, he had his headquarters much of the time at or near Tiberias. He was perfectly familiar with all of that region, and made frequent mention of the principal places. Not only does he not speak of any such city, but he says expressly that there was no Jewish city near Tiberias.— [Life of Josephus, sec. 65; Whiston, vol. 2, p. 155.

It is certainly remarkable that while Paul, besides mentioning Christ by the name of Christ more than two hundred times, refers to him as Jesus, either alone or in connection with other names, more than two hundred times also, he does not once designate him as "Jesus of Nazareth." Had he known any such place, that he should have referred to Christ as "Jesus of Nazareth," would have been most natural.

We can now see why King James' translators insisted upon making, and why the translators of the revised version insist upon maintaining in most instances, the translation "Jesus of Nazareth."

It is because, for the purpose of giving credence to the legendary stories in Luke and in Matthew, concerning the birth and the childhood of Jesus, they wish it understood that the Bible is full of references to "Jesus of Nazareth;" whereas that phrase in the English version has its equivalent in Greek but three times in the entire New Testament; although Jesus is referred to by the name of Jesus only nearly six hundred times in the Gospels alone.

But while there is no sufficient evidence that there was any "Jesus of Nazareth" before the destruction of Jerusalem, and especially during the life-time of Christ, with "Jesus the Nazarene," the case is far different. The phrase occurs too many times not to believe that it was in the original manuscripts from which the New Testament Gospels were composed. It is more than probable that the place where Jesus had resided was afterward called Nazareth, from having been the residence of Jesus the Nazarene.

THE DISCIPLES OF JESUS WERE ESSENES— THE EVIDENCE.

It may be asked:

"What evidence have you that the followers of Jesus were Essenes?"

We reply, the testimony of Epiphanius:

"We should give the reason why those who gave to Christ his name were, before they took the name of Christians, called Jessenes; (Greek, *Iessaioi*.)

"I will remind you, it was because Jesse was the father of David, and they were therefore named from Jesse, or they obtained the name of Jessenes [*Iessaioi*] from Jesus Christ our Lord, being perfected in doctrine by Jesus, whose disciples they were; or else, finally, from the signification of the name by which our Lord was called.

"Jesus, in the Hebrew, signifies a healer, or physician. However that may be, this is the name by which they were known before they were called Christians."—[Epiph. Hæres. xxix. 4.

The word here used, Iessaios, is slightly different from that used by Philo, which is Essaios (Essene). Josephus, writing of the Essenes, has sometimes Essaios and sometimes Essenos.

Dr. Lightfoot says of this passage in Epiphanius, "From the connection the same sect seems to be meant." There is no doubt of it whatever; since in the same connection Epiphanius refers to what Philo had said about the same people.

THE NAZARITES.

As to what constituted a Nazarite, see the sixth chapter of Numbers.

To leave the locks unshorn while undertaking any difficult task in which divine aid was invoked, and to cut the hair and consecrate it after success, was practiced among various ancient nations.

Cyril of Alexandria considered that letting the hair grow "was taken from the Egyptians."

The Nazarite custom was continued down to the Christian era.

Josephus tells us of a vow of Bernice, the sister of Agrippa, who was staying at Jerusalem in order to perform her vow.—[B. J. ii. 15. 1.

In the fourth book of his Antiquities, Josephus alludes to the Nazarites in the following language.

"Moreover, those that have made a sacred vow, I mean those that are called Nazarites [Nazaraioi], that suffer their hair to grow long, and use no wine, when they consecrate their hair and offer it for a sacrifice, they are to allot what is shorn off to the priests."—[A. J., iv. 4. 4.

The ancient custom of the Nazarites prevailed among the Jewish disciples of Jesus, and Paul was required to conform to it in order to satisfy the Jews of his fidelity to their institutions. See Acts xxi. 23 to 26, where Paul was asked by Jewish believers to take four men who had a vow on them, and to purify himself with them, and be at charges with them, that they might shave their heads (cut their hair), thus satisfying the Jews that he did not look with contempt or indifference upon the ordinances of Moses. This Paul did accordingly. Some were Nazarites for life. Such were Samson and Samuel.

JOHN THE NAZARITE, CALLED JOHN THE BAPTIST.

Nazarite was *"Naziraios,"* or *"Nazaraios,"* which were equivalent. The Greek word applied to the followers of Jesus was *"Nazoraios,"* and this is a term by which they were known during the life-time of Jesus; since, even taking the statement in the Acts of the Apostles as it stands, it was not until after the death of the Galilean that his followers took the name of Christians. Before, it was Essenes and Nazarenes.

"Nazarene" is the English word which has been substituted for *"Nazoraios,"* and to carry the reader away from the true signification, "Nazarene" is rendered "of Nazareth." But *"Nazoraios"* was but another form for *"Nazaraios"* and *"Naziraios."* *"Naziraios"* and *"Nazaraios"* meant a Nazarite, one under a vow, and subjected to the ceremonial law prescribed in the sixth chapter of Numbers. Such was John the Baptist, who, like Samson and Samuel, was a Nazarite for life.

Appearing as such, and inviting Jesus to his baptism, he established a sect called "the Nazarites." Jesus attached himself to this sect, and, after the death of John, became its leader.

Jesus himself, although he fiercely denounced the Pharisees and the Sadducees, had nothing to say against the Essenes. Neither had John the Baptist. When he saw Pharisees and Sadducees coming to his baptism, he cried out: "O, generation of vipers, who hath warned you to flee from the wrath to come?"

If the Jews were divided into three sects, and John and Jesus were denouncing two of those sects, to which of them did John and Jesus themselves belong?

The brilliant De Quincey thought that Josephus, in describing the Essenes, was describing the disciples of Jesus and no other people whatever. But such a theory at once takes away all history of the Essenes as a previously existing sect.

JESUS THE NAZARITE.

That Jesus was a Nazarite, under the Mosaic law, is in the highest degree probable.

That he wore long hair is in accord with all the traditions in regard to his personal appearance. He was "separated" and devoted to the service of the Lord from his infancy. The author of the Epistle to the Hebrews speaks of Jesus as a high priest, "holy, harmless, undefiled, separate from sinners."—[Heb. 7. 26.

Jesus was a Jew, and observed the Jewish customs. He worshiped in the synagogues on the Sabbath—he participated in the national festivals—and there is no reason to doubt that he observed all the rites and ceremonies which were peculiarly incumbent upon those who, like himself, had been separated and consecrated to divine service, even from the mother's womb.

Again, the very name attached to Jesus, and by which he was distinguished from others of the name, indicates that he was a Nazarite. He was sometimes called the Galilean, and some thought him the Christ. But he was more usually called "Jesus the Nazarite" (*Iesous ho Nazoraios*); sometimes translated, properly enough, "Jesus the Nazarene." It is a fair inference that Jesus, as well as John, was a Nazarite from birth, and that his participation in John's baptism had much to do with the naming of the sect. Here was John the Nazarite baptizing, and Jesus the Nazarite coming to his baptism. What more natural than that the sect then formed should be called the Nazarites, or the Nazarenes?

There is every reason to believe that Luke, 7. 33. 34, is an interpolation. It is not in Marcion, the older Gospel, from which Luke was composed. The entire passage, from vv. 29 to 35 inclusive, is wanting in the Gospel of Marcion.

One historical book of the Hebrews, called "Juchasin," asserts that the Essenes were Nazarites. The author, who was Abraham Zachuth, calls the Essene, in Latin, translated from Hebrew, "Naziraeos" or "Nazaraeos," both forms meaning the same, Nazarite. The Hebrew word signifies "separated;" also "holy;" translated into the Greek (Septuagint) by the word "heegiasmenos." In the title of the work he writes:

"Nazarites, who are called Essenes."

Those who are curious to continue these investigations may consult the very learned work, edited by Ugolinus, entitled:

"Thesaurus Antiquitatum Sacrarum," etc., published at Venice in 1759. In the 22d volume of this work will be found much abstruse learning upon this interesting subject.

That Jesus was well known as "the Nazarite," is manifest from the Gospels, both the apocryphal and the canonical.

The exact relation subsisting between the Essenes and the Nazarenes, it is difficult to determine. For eighteen hundred years the efforts of those most interested have been directed to covering up and destroying what would have thrown light upon the subject.

How far these classes were involved in the war between the Jews and the Romans, is a question involved in mystery. We learn from Josephus that some of the Jewish leaders in the war were Essenes, and from the Gospels themselves that Jesus had armed followers. Beyond that, much is left to conjecture.

Scarcely any allusion is made in any of the New Testament writings to the insurrectionary war being carried on by the Jews against the Romans, though, according to Bible chronology, the history in the Acts of the Apostles is brought down to within a few years of the destruction of Jerusalem.

If the disciples and the followers of Jesus and the Jewish converts of Peter and Paul took no part in these transactions, why is there such a profound silence in regard to them in the New Testament writings?

The commencement of the Jewish war is generally dated at the time when Vespasian was sent into Judea with an army, A. D. 66. But if any reliance at all can be placed upon the accounts given by Josephus, Judea had been, for seventy years previous, the scene of constant tumults, revolts and insurrections against the Roman power. These resulted sometimes in the slaughter of thousands and even tens of thousands of people in Jerusalem, or in the immediate neighborhood. Yet of all this the New Testament authors are profoundly ignorant; and concerning such important and exciting events the books themselves are profoundly silent.

The Acts of the Apostles, which professes to give a history of the disciples for thirty years, A. D. 33 to A. D. 63, making Jerusalem and Judea the scene of much of the narrative, has not a word to say about the attempt made by Caius Caligula to set up his statue in Jerusalem, an attempt which created such a tumult that it came near ending in open war—[Jos. A. J. xviii. 8; B. J. ii. 10];—not a word about the difficulties under Cumanus, and the tumult in which ten thousand people were trampled to death—[B. J. ii. 12, 1];—no account of the insurrection of the Sicarii and of the magicians, and the attempt made by the Egyptian false prophet, who had a large force at his command which he led round about from the wilderness to the Mount of Olives and with whom Felix had a battle, though all these events took place within that thirty years. The curtain is raised sufficiently for Paul to be asked if he was not that Egyptian who, before those days, made an uproar, etc., when it suddenly falls again, as if it were an unintentional reference to scenes relegated to the darkness of oblivion.

Reference is made to one Theudas, Acts 5. 36, who had headed an insurrection about the time of the birth of Christ or soon after, but there is no reference to the Theudas who long afterward was at the head of a formidable insurrection [Josephus A. J. xx. 5, 1], although it occurred during the very time covered by the history of the Acts of the Apostles. Josephus knew nothing of the Theudas of the Acts, and the author of the Acts knew nothing or pretended to know nothing of the Theudas of Josephus.

When we consider this profound and mysterious silence of the New Testament books, we are prepared to accept the statement of

Epiphanius in regard to the connection of the followers of Jesus with the Essenes. Their participation in the Jewish war would naturally follow.

"The Essenes," says Thomas Goodwin in his Dissertation on the Theocracy of the Israelites, "adored Christ with unanimous consent."

IX.

The Zealots.

"In the progress of time," says Origen, "they (the Essenes) became separated; and not adhering to the same order of discipline, they were divided into four parties. Some of them are exceedingly religious." After giving illustrations of their religious zeal, which sometimes led to acts of violence, he adds:

"Wherefore, by chance they drew upon themselves the name Zealots. And by some they were called Sicarii."—[Origen against Heresies, ix. 26.

To the same effect is the testimony of Chrysostom, one of the earliest and most eminent of the Greek fathers. After saying that there were three sects among the Jews, viz: Pharisees, Sadducees and Essenes, speaking of the Essenes he says:

"The same are also Sicarii, because of their being Zealots." (*Hoi autoi de kai Sikarioi, dia to einai Zelotai.*)—[Homil. in Act. Apost. 46; on Acts 21. 18-38.

For a long time there had been a party among the Jews who had been called Zealots; but it was not until about the year 54 A. D., after the appointment of Felix as procurator, that they were called Sicarii. Afterward the words were used interchangeably.

Ugolinus speaks of these Jewish sects. After referring to the statement of Drusius, cap. xxi. in Scholia Graeca, in which he called the Essenes Sicarii, that is, Zealots, and after saying that Theophilactus writes the same, Ugolinus continues as follows:

"Not all of the Essenes were Sicarii; but those who transferred themselves to the sect of Judas, the Galilean. These, urged by a peculiar zeal for God, were called Zealots." (Latin, *Zelotes;* Greek,

Zelotai.)—[Ugolinus, Dissertation concerning the three sects of the Jews, cap. xiv., sec. 4; in his Thesau. Antiq., vol. 22, p. 162.

Concerning these people, sometimes called Sicarii and sometimes Zealots, Josephus gives us full information.—[Jewish War, bk. ii. 13, 3; ii. 17, 6; iv. 3, 9–14; ch. 4; ch. 5; ch. 6; ch. 7, 2; vii. 8–11.

The Sicarii, he says, derived their name from *sica*, the Latin word for dagger or dirk-knife. This weapon, called by Josephus in one place dagger, and in another place sword, was carried under the bosom [B. J., ii. 17. 6], and was suddenly thrust into the victim without the slightest warning.

From those of the Essenes who had joined the sect established by Judas the Galilean—"the fourth sect" spoken of by Josephus—came the disciples and followers of Jesus. They were "Zealots for the law." Though the Scribes and the Pharisees were constantly watching to entrap Jesus for non-observance of the law, they could never succeed; he was zealous for its observance as he construed it; and his disciples were more zealous for the law than were the Scribes and the Pharisees themselves.

In the first place, one of the Apostles was Simon Zelotes (Luke 6. 15: Acts 1. 13), or Simon the Zealot. In Matthew 10. 4, and Mark 3. 18, he is called Simon the Canaanite; but this is conceded to be a mistranslation. The word rendered "Canaanite" is the Syriac word *Kananites*, and means the same as the Greek word *Zelotes*, or the English word "Zealot."

The Douay version reads, "Simon the Cananean," both in Matthew and in Mark.

In the translation of the Diatessaron of Tatian, by Rev. J. Hamlin Hill, B. D., Edinburgh, 1894, the rendering of Luke 6. 15, is, instead of "Simon, called Zelotes," "Simon, which is called the Zealot."

In the translation by Agnes Smith Lewis, M. R. A. S., London and New York, 1894, of the ancient Syriac MS. discovered by Tischendorf, called the Sinaitic, and which is considered the oldest manuscript of the Gospels in existence, the reading is, both in Matt. 10. 4, and in Mark 3. 18, instead of "Simon the Canaanite," "Simon the Zealot."

McClintock and Strong, in their Biblical Cyclopedia, after giving the different names of this apostle, say: "Each of these equally points out Simon as belonging to the faction of the Zealots, who were conspicuous for their fierce advocacy of the Mosaic ritual."—[Art. "Simon."

Again: It appears from the Gospels themselves that Jesus was surrounded by armed Zealots as his followers when he was apprehended. He was told that there were two swords (*machairai*); and he said it was sufficient.—Luke 22. 38. The "*machaira*" was a dirk-knife; the same kind of a weapon as that which was called in Latin *sica*, and which gave their name to the Sicarii.

Afterward, one of those who were with Jesus drew his dirk-knife (*machairan*) and struck a servant of the high priest, cutting off his ear.—Matt. 26. 51; Mark 14. 47; Luke 22. 49, 50; John 18. 10. John gives the servant's name, and says that it was Simon Peter who struck the blow.

Again: The Gospels make frequent mention of the fact that those seeking to take Jesus feared the people.—Matt. 21. 46; Mark 11. 32; 12. 12; Luke 20. 19; 22. 2. Why should they stand so much in fear of an unorganized multitude, unless they knew that some of them, at least, were secretly armed?

Not only was Jesus surrounded by Zealots, but he was himself a Zealot. It was in execution of a Jewish law, called "the law of the Zealots," that, with a whip made of small cords, he scourged the money-changers and drove them from the temple.

Such is the opinion of Selden, than whom, perhaps, a man never lived more learned in the law. In his work, *De Jure Natur. et Gent.* bk. iv., c. iv., he goes into a thorough examination of the law of the Zealots. The chapter is entitled:

"Concerning the singular Law of the Zealots among the Hebrews; according to which those caught in various crimes were, by private persons, beaten with impunity, or put to death on the spot."

He gives, in this chapter, a full explication of the law, citing Sanhedrin, cap. 9, sec. ult.; Gemar Babylon, ib. fol. 81; b. & c. Hierosolymit. cod. tit. fol. 27, col. 2. These private avengers are denominated "pious men who are fired with zeal for God." "*Homines pii,*" says Selden, "*qui zelo Numenis accenderentur.*"

The next chapter he devotes to a consideration of the question, whether Christ was acting under this law in driving the money-changers out of the temple. After a very learned disquisition, in which he examines the various offenses which might be thus summarily punished, among which was desecrating the temple or the sacred utensils, he comes to the pious conclusion that Jesus, wishing to present himself as a perfect exemplar of absolute justice, was willing that all should see that what he was doing was according to law. Hence he scourged the money-changers in accordance with a law of the Hebrews, called "the Law of the Zealots;" a law authorizing private punishment for religious offenses.

This law is referred to by Philo, also, in one of his treatises. After speaking of the punishments of God, he says:

"But the punishments which are inflicted by men, are of various characters, being death or scourging, those men who are more excellent and more strict in their piety, inflicting death on such offenders, but those who are of milder dispositions, scourging them with rods publicly in the sight of all men."—[De. Spec. leg. 6. 7; Works. III, p. 261.

The influence of the Zealots, after the death of Jesus, is well illustrated by the following account from the Acts of the Apostles:

"And when we were come to Jerusalem, the brethren received us gladly.

"And the (day) following Paul went in with us unto James; and all the elders were present.

"And when he had saluted them, he declared particularly what things God had wrought among the Gentiles by his ministry.

"And when they heard (it), they glorified the Lord, and said unto him: Thou seest, brother, how many thousands of Jews there are who believe; and they are all zealous of the law [*zelotai tou nomou*, correctly translated in the Douay version, 'Zealots for the law;']

"And they are informed of thee that thou teachest all the Jews who are among the Gentiles to forsake Moses, saying that they ought not to circumcise (their) children, neither to walk after the customs.

"What is it, therefore? the multitude must needs come together; for they will hear that thou art come.

"Do, therefore, this that we say to thee: We have four men who have a vow on them;

"Them take and purify thyself with them, and be at charges with them, that they may shave (their) heads; and all may know that those things whereof they were informed concerning thee are nothing; but (that) thou thyself also walkest orderly, and keepest the law. * * *

"Then Paul took the men, and the next day purifying himself with them, entered into the temple, to signify the accomplishment of the days of purification, until that an offering should be offered for every one of them."—[Acts, ch. 21, vv. 17 to 26.

In order to understand fully this account, it is necessary to have recourse to a passage in the untranslated works of Origen.

Speaking of the Essenes, he says:

"Some there are who, when one of them hears some one discoursing concerning God and his laws, if he is not circumcised, when he catches such a man somewhere by himself, he threatens him with death, unless he becomes circumcised; and unless he is willing to comply, he does not spare him, but cuts him to pieces."—[Contra Hæreses, ix. 26. Series Græca, vol. 16, pt. 3, p. 3404.

From what Origen here says it is plain that Paul was in imminent danger of his life. No one knew this better than did Paul, who was himself a Zealot, and had been one of the fiercest Zealots for the law. He lost no time, therefore, in complying with the suggestion of his Jewish brethren. That he acted none too soon in this matter, is manifest from the statement in Acts, ch. 23, vv. 12 to 21, where it appears that more than forty of the Zealots had bound themselves by an oath, that they would neither eat nor drink till they had put Paul to death.

At a later day the spirit and zeal of the Jewish Zealots were transferred to the Christian converts. When these became consolidated into a compact ecclesiastical body, that spirit and zeal found a suitable field for activity.

X.

The Inquisition.

PETER AND PAUL.

Peter, according to the account in the Acts of the Apostles, struck dead Ananias and Sapphira because they had lied and kept back part of the price of land they had sold.

Dr. Doellinger, an eminent Catholic theologian, commenting on this transaction, says:

"When Ananias and Sapphira, through their hypocrisy and avaricious attempt at deception, had made the first assault on the authority of the apostles and the holy ghost ruling in the church, St. Peter inflicted a terrible punishment upon them."—[First Age of the Church, by John Ignatius Doellinger, D. D., 2d London Edition, 1867, p. 44.

Paul, before his conversion, persecuted the disciples, making havoc among them, entering into every house, haling men and women and committing them to prison. He continued to breathe out threatenings and slaughter against the disciples until his conversion, and after his conversion his persecution was transferred to the heretics within the church.

DOCTRINES OF PAUL.

BLOOD ATONEMENT.—It is difficult to understand how any one can deny that Paul taught the doctrine of the atonement. His views are set forth in language sufficiently explicit in the following passages, all taken from the epistles which are, by the German critics, admitted to be genuine:

"Whom God hath set forth to be a propitiation, through faith in his blood, to declare his righteousness for the remission of sins that are past, through the forbearance of God."—[Romans iii. 25.

"For when we were yet without strength, in due time Christ died for the ungodly.

"For scarcely for a righteous man will one die; yet peradventure for a good man some would even dare to die.

"But God commendeth his love toward us, in that while we were yet sinners, Christ died for us.

"Much more then, being now justified by his blood, we shall be saved from wrath through him.

"For if, when we were enemies, we were reconciled to God by the death of his Son, much more, being reconciled, we shall be saved by his life.

"And not only (so), but we also joy in God through our Lord Jesus Christ, by whom we have now received the atonement."—[Rom. v. 6–11.

"He that spared not his own son, but delivered him up for us all, how shall he not with him also freely give us all things?—[Rom. viii. 32.

"For I delivered unto you first of all, that which I also received, how that Christ died for our sins according to the Scriptures."—[1 Cor. xv. 3.

"Who gave himself for our sins, that he might deliver us from this present evil world."—[Galatians i. 4. See also Gal. iii. 13.

JUSTIFICATION BY FAITH.—Paul was equally plain in announcing this doctrine. See Romans i. 16; iii. 22-24; iii. 30; iv. 5; iv. 16; v. 1; Gal. ii. 16.

ELECTION AND PREDESTINATION.—These doctrines were promulgated by Paul in language, if possible still more explicit. See Rom. viii. 28, 30; ix. 11-24; xi. 5-7.

ORIGIN OF THESE DOCTRINES.

Sacrifice as an atonement for sin, was a doctrine with which the Jews were familiar. It had prevailed among all the nations of antiquity. The practice had its origin, as is well known, in the supposed necessity of placating an angry God. To appease the divine wrath offerings were made, at first of the fruits of the earth, then of animals. Among the Jews the prevailing doctrine is stated in the Epistle to the Hebrews: "Without shedding of blood is no remission."—[Heb. ix. 22.

If the blood of lambs and goats could so far appease the angry Deity as to induce him to remit the sins of a people, how natural the transition to the idea, that the death of a person of extraordinary merit, and especially one reputed to be the Son of God himself, should work the remission of the sins of the whole world. The greater the sacrifice, the more extensive the propitiation.

The ancients were familiar, also, with the idea of sacrifice in the form of crucifixion. Of these some of the more important were: Chrishna, of India, B. C. about 1200; the Hindu, Buddha Sakia, B. C. 600; Thulis, of Egypt, B. C. 1700; and Mithra, of Persia, B. C. 600.

Is it possible that Paul had heard nothing of these ancient saviors? And yet he was none the less sincere in believing that the true savior had now appeared. It is true that Jesus himself, at no time during his preliminary examination, either before the council or before Pilate, or on his way to execution, or at the crucifixion, gave any intimation that he was about to die for the sins of the world.

Nevertheless Paul, who had not participated in the Messianic dreams of the other apostles, and of Jesus himself, was logically impelled to look upon the suffering at the crucifixion as a sacrifice. If he was abandoning one religion of atonement, he must take hold of another, involving an atonement of a still higher character.

APPENDIX—THE INQUISITION.

This idea of a vicarious atonement, to which Paul was naturally and logically led, in his transition from the Jewish to the Christian faith, became with him the absorbing thought, the animating principle of his subsequent life. Henceforth he was to know only Jesus and him crucified for the sins of the world.

To the atonement, justification by faith was but a corollary. The sacrifice must be accepted by him for whom it was made. If his faith should be sufficient, he would be washed and purified by the blood of Jesus.

Predestination was but another form of the fatalistic doctrine of the Essenes. Though educated as a Pharisee, Paul had adopted many of the views of the Essenes, and was thoroughly imbued with the fatalism of that sect.

There are other doctrines of the Apostle which have hitherto been kept in the background, but which are of great importance in reference to the subsequent development of the Christian religion. These must now be considered.

INQUISITION DOCTRINES.

DESTRUCTION OF THE FLESH FOR THE SALVATION OF THE SPIRIT; OR, KILLING THE BODY TO SAVE THE SOUL.

"Ye are puffed up, and have not rather mourned, that he that hath done this deed might be taken away from among you.

"For I verily, as absent in body but present in spirit, have judged already, as though I were present, (concerning) him that hath so done this deed. . . . .

"To deliver such an one unto Satan for the destruction of the flesh, that the spirit may be saved in the day of the Lord Jesus. . . . .

"Therefore put away from among yourselves that wicked person." —[1 Cor. v. 2, 3, 5, 13.

What is Paul's meaning here? It is claimed that nothing more was meant than excommunication from the church.

Such, however, was not the language used by the apostle, to direct exclusion from the church. The brethren were to "withdraw" themselves from such (1 Tim. vi. 5; 2 Thess. iii. 6); or "from such" they were to "turn away" (2 Tim. iii. 5); or they were to "avoid them" (Rom. xvi. 17); or to "note" or notify them, and to "have no company" with them (2 Thess. iii. 14).

Paul commanded the church at Corinth to "put away" from among themselves that wicked person. The word here used is *exareite* from *exairo;* or, according to the better reading, *areite*, from *airo*.

Now, what is the meaning of *airo* and *exairo?*

The following is one of the definitions given by Liddell and Scott: "To lift and take away, to take away, put an end to: later, to kill."

So, one of the definitions of *exaireo*, of which *exairo* is a contracted form, is, "to make away with."

This use of the phrase "take away," is recognized by us; as when we say of a friend, "He has been taken away." In fact, this has been a common use of the phrase and of its equivalents in other languages for more than two thousand years.

In the New Testament there are frequent examples of the use of the verb *airo* in this sense.

For instance:

Matt. xxiv. 39: "And knew not until the flood came, and took them all away;"—*kai eeren* (from *airo*) *hapantas*.

Luke xxiii. 18: " And they cried out all at once, saying, Away with this man (*aire touton*, take away this man), and release unto us Barabbas." See also John xix. 15, and Acts xxi. 36.

John xvii. 15: "I pray not that thou shouldest take them (*arees*, from *airo*) out of the world."

John xv. 2: "Every branch in me that beareth not fruit he taketh away;" (*airei* from *airo*).

John xi. 48–50: "If we let him thus alone, all will believe on him; and the Romans will come and take away (*arousin* from *airo*) both our place and nation."

Acts viii. 33: "In his humiliation his judgment was taken away (*eerthee*, from *airo*); and who shall declare his generation? For his life is taken (*airetai*) from the earth.

Acts xxii. 22: "And they gave him audience unto this word, and (then) lifted up their voices, and said: Away with such a (fellow) (*aire ton toiouton*, take away such a one) from the earth; for it is not fit that he should live."

Thus the philological evidence is overwhelming.

But if there were any doubt remaining as to the meaning of this chapter, and the intent of the apostle, it should be removed by a perusal of his subsequent letter to the same church, in which he alludes to the same transaction. In that subsequent letter he says:

"Though I made you sorry with a letter, I do not repent, though I did repent; for I perceive that the same epistle hath made you sorry, though (it were) but for a season.

"Now I rejoice, not that ye were made sorry, but that ye sorrowed to repentance; for ye were made sorry after a godly manner, that ye might receive damage by us in nothing.

"For godly sorrow worketh repentance to salvation not to be repented of; but the sorrow of the world worketh death.

"For behold this self-same thing, that ye sorrowed after a godly sort, what carefulness it wrought in you, yea, (what) clearing of yourselves, yea, (what) indignation, yea, (what) fear, yea, (what) vehement desire, yea, what zeal, yea, (what) revenge! In all things ye have approved yourselves to be clear in this matter.

"Wherefore, though I wrote unto you (I did it) not for his cause that had done the wrong, nor for his cause that suffered wrong, but that our care for you in the sight of God might appear unto you."—[2 Cor. vii. 8–12.

The apostle cared nothing for the accused party. Neither did he care anything for him who had been wronged. His only care was for the church. And now that the church had aroused itself, and in its indignation and zeal had taken vengeance on the offender, he, Paul, was satisfied.

He had already condemned the offender, and had pronounced sentence, and he made it sufficiently clear that he desired the sentence to be executed. That this had been done, clearly appears also from the language of the second epistle.

The conclusion drawn from this chapter by Tertullian, Ambrose, and other fathers of the church, was, "that the individual may be destroyed in order that the church may be saved."

Nor do modern commentators find it easy to come to any other conclusion.

In Scott's Henry's Comm., Phil., 1855, it is suggested that Paul was to strike the offender with a dreadful disease in the midst of them, while assembled together, so that they would be obliged on account of this disease to carry him forth from their assembly.—[Page 272, citing Bloomfield and Rosenmueller.

Olshausen admits that the phrase *airein ek meso*, "to put away from the midst," really means "to remove, i. e., to kill;" but he thinks the exclusion from the church is to be understood as a spiritual death.—[Comm. on 1 and 2 Cor. in 20th vol. Clarke's Theo. Lib. Ed. 1855, p. 88.

Dean Stanley frankly admits that Paul probably intended the death of the offender.—[On the Epistles to the Corinthians, 5th edition, London, 1882, pp. 77, 78.

FURTHER FOUNDATIONS OF THE INQUISITION.

"I would they were even cut off who trouble you."—[Galatians v. 12.

This also we are kindly asked to understand as merely an expression of the apostle's wish that certain persons might be excluded from the church. But he claimed and exercised the right to direct the exclusion of members from the church. Such directions had repeatedly been given.—[1 Tim. vi. 5; 2 Tim. iii. 5; 2 Thess. iii. 6, 14.

In this case he "would" that something might be done which he had not the power absolutely to order.

Again: "I would they were *even* cut off." Is exclusion from the church such an extreme punishment as to justify the use of the word "even"?

"I would they were even cut off (*apokopsontai*) who trouble you." *Apokopsontai* from *apokopto*. What is the meaning of this verb?

The first definitions of the verb *kopto*, given by Liddell and Scott, are as follows:

1. To strike, smite, cut.
2. To knock down, fell, slay.
3. To cut off, chop off.

The Greek preposition *apo* meaning *from*, the verb *apokopto* is defined by the same authority, "*to cut off, hew off, knock off.*"

Let us look at the other places in the New Testament where it is used:

1. Mark ix. 43: "And if thy hand offend thee, cut it off; (*apokopson auteen*.)"

2. Mark ix. 45: "And if thy foot offend thee, cut it off; (*apokopson auton*.)"

3. John xviii. 10: "Then Simon Peter having a sword drew it, and smote the high priest's servant, and cut off (*apekopsen*) his right ear."

4. John xviii. 26: "One of the servants of the high priest (being his kinsman whose ear Peter cut off)" (*apekopse*) etc.

5. Acts xxvii. 32: "Then the soldiers cut off (*apekopsan*) the ropes of the boat, and let her fall off."

Can there be any doubt about the meaning of this word? Paul wished these churches to do what he desired the Church at Corinth to do. He wished the offenders cut off from the face of the earth.

In Adam Clarke's Commentaries we find the following comment on this passage:

"At first sight it seems as if the apostles were praying for the destruction of the false teachers who had perverted the churches of Galatia."

The learned commentator does not inform us how the first impression made by reading the passage is to be removed.

Olshausen says: " An imprecation of punishment against his opponents."

The Pulpit Commentary of Spence and Extell favors the theory of self-mutilation—a wish that they would mutilate themselves; and it expressly disavows the construction which makes the apostle refer merely to excommunication.—[Commentary on Galatians, p. 248.

The self-mutilation theory is simply absurd. According to that view, Paul says: "I would they who trouble you would even mutilate themselves." How would that relieve the church?

No; Paul wanted these heretics to be put to death.

He had already pronounced them accursed:

"There be some that trouble you (the same expression), and would pervert the Gospel of Christ.

"But though we, or an angel from heaven, preach any other gospel unto you than that which we have preached unto you, let him be accursed."—[Gal. i. 7, 8.

And again:

"As we said before, so say I now again, if any (man) preach any other gospel unto you than that ye have received, let him be accursed."—[Verse 9.

Now, what is the significance of being accursed?

In Joshua vi. 17, we read as follows:

"And the city shall be accursed, (even) it and all that (are) therein, to the Lord: only Rahab the harlot shall live," etc.

Again, in chapter vii. verse 12:

"Therefore the children of Israel could not stand before their enemies, (but) turned (their) backs before their enemies, because they were accursed: neither will I be with you any more, except ye destroy the accursed from among you."

Among the Jews, to be accursed was to be subject to condign punishment. "He that is hanged (is) accursed of God."—[Deut. xxi. 23.] Any one who stood accursed might be lawfully put to death.

Paul had been a persecutor before his conversion—he was a persecutor still. The spirit of persecution pervades his writings.

"If any man love not the Lord Jesus Christ, let him be anathema maran-atha."—[1 Cor. xvi. 22.

In 2 Thess. i. 8, the Lord Jesus is spoken of as "taking vengeance" on those who obey not his Gospel.

In 1. Tim. i. 20, Hymeneus and Alexander, who had departed from the faith, he had "delivered unto Satan."

In 2 Tim. iv. 14, "Alexander the coppersmith did me much evil; the Lord reward him according to his works."

In Titus i. 11, referring to those in the church who were unruly, and vain talkers and deceivers, it is said:

"Whose mouths must be stopped."

In Acts xiii. 8-11, he is represented as punishing with blindness Elymas, that "child of the devil," who had withstood Barnabas and Paul, seeking to turn away the deputy from the faith.

Thus was Paul strengthening the foundations of the Inquisition. Those foundations had already been laid by his own doctrines and by the teachings and example of Peter; and these apostles found encouragement in the denunciations of Jesus himself against unbelievers. Those who founded the Inquisition also found encouragement in his sanction of punishment by torture. (According to Matt. xviii. 34, 35.)

We shall have occasion, as we proceed, to notice how these foundations were gradually strengthened as time progressed. But one additional circumstance need here be mentioned. There was a document in general circulation in the early ages of the church, and at that time considered of high authority. It was entitled, "The Epistle of Clement to James." It is translated in the 17th volume of the Ante-Nicene Christian Library.

In this epistle, Clement describes his ordination. He says that when Peter was about to die, the brethren being assembled (at Rome), he laid his hands on Clement, as the Bishop, and communicated to him the power of binding and loosing, etc., and as to him who should grieve the President of the Truth, after declaring that such a one sins against Christ and offends the Father of all, Peter proceeded as follows:

"Wherefore, *he shall not live;* and therefore it becomes him who presides to hold the place of a physician; and not to cherish the rage of an irrational beast."

JEROME AND AUGUSTINE.

These are the most eminent of the Church Fathers. They were the expounders of the Nicene Creed, and the highest authorities on faith and doctrine.

Since these fathers stand as the great landmarks of Christian piety and learning, and the great exponents of Christian doctrine, their views on the subject of persecution, and especially concerning the persecution of heretics, become of the highest importance.

JEROME.

Under Constantine and his sons, commissions had been issued against heretics, especially against the Donatists, who were visited with the most rigorous punishment. In 382, under Theodosius I., an edict was published against the Manichæans and other sects. A law of Honorius, in 398, threatened the professors of certain heresies, in particular the priests of the Montanists and the Eunomians, with banishment and death if they persisted in bringing people together. The decrees for the extirpation of heathenism were even more severe. Jerome and Leo the Great were in favor of the death penalty.

Let us look at the teachings of Jerome:

"We may ask," says he, "whether God is good, who has given the law and the prophets, seeing the life of the wicked is prospered, and they do not suffer anything from him, according to their deserts. They have abounded indeed, all those who have separated themselves in contumely—those who with rabid jaws bark against their maker— who reproach him with blasphemous speeches.

"These have abounded—they have been planted, and have sent forth roots. They have begotten sons, and have brought forth fruits. What fruits has Marcion brought forth, begetting sons of Infidelity? What Basilides? What Valentinus? Concerning whom, indeed, it is prophesied, saying: 'They have begotten sons, and have brought forth fruit. Near art thou to their mouth, but far from their heart.' 'They call upon Jesus; but they have him not, neither do they confess him as Christ. And thou, Lord, hast known me, and hast tried me in thy sight. *Sanctify them in the day of their killing.*' (Jer. xii. 3.) In what way would I expound this? *He calls the torments of those who are tortured, sanctification.* (Tormenta sanctificationem vocat eorum qui torquentur.) 'Sanctify them,' he says, 'in the day of their killing.' That is, 'by that thou killest them, sanctify them.'" (Id est, per hoc quod interficis eos, sanctifica eos.)—[Works of Jerome, Vol. v, 818.

Here is the doctrine of Paul—the destruction of the flesh that the spirit may be saved in the day of the Lord Jesus. But Jerome has improved upon the Apostle, and has explained that the flesh may be destroyed by torture, and that the torments will result in sanctification.

AUGUSTINE.

In his earlier days, Augustine taught religious liberty. But these were the generous impulses of youth. As he advanced in years, he saw his error. In his "Retractations," he retracted his previous teaching on this subject:

"There are two books of mine," he says, "the title of which is, 'Against the Party of Donatus.' In the first of these books I said that I did not favor violently bringing into the communion schismatics by the force of any secular power. Indeed, I did not then favor it, because I had not yet found out by experience, either to how much evil impunity would embolden them, or to how much better conditions the diligence of discipline might bring them."—[Retractationes, Liber II, Caput V.

Having learned by experience the good results of "the diligence of discipline," he was, from this on, outspoken in his advocacy of persecution.

In his letter to Vincentius, A. D. 408, he says:

"We are precluded from rest by the Donatists; the repression and correction of whom, by the powers which are ordained of God, appears to me to be labor not in vain. . . .

"You are of opinion that no one should be compelled to follow righteousness; and yet you read that the householder said to his servants, 'Whomsoever ye shall find, compel them to come in.' . .

"Paul was given up to be imprisoned and bound; but Satan is unquestionably worse than any jailor; yet to him Paul himself gave up one man for the destruction of the flesh that the spirit might be saved in the day of the Lord Jesus. . . .

"Whatever, therefore, the true and rightful mother does, even where something severe and bitter is felt by her children at her hands, she is not rendering evil for evil, but is applying discipline to counteract the evil of sin, not with the hatred which seeks to harm, but with the love which seeks to heal. If to inflict persecution were in all cases blameworthy, it would not have been written in the sacred books: 'Whoso privily slandereth his neighbor, him will I persecute' (cut off). In some cases, therefore, he who suffers persecution, is in the wrong; and he who inflicts it, is in the right. . . .

"Truly, if past events recorded in the prophetic books were figures of the future, there was given, under King Nebuchadnezzar, a figure both of the time which the Church had under the apostles, and of that which she now has. In the age of the apostles and the martyrs, that was fulfilled which was prefigured when the aforesaid king compelled pious and just men to bow down to his image, and cast into the flames all who refused. Now, however, is fulfilled that which was prefigured soon after in the same king, when, being converted to the worship of the true God, he made a decree throughout his empire, that whosoever should speak against the God of Shadrach, Meshach and Abednego, should suffer the penalty which their crime deserved. The earlier time of that king represented the former age of emperors who did not believe in Christ, at whose hands the Christians suffered because of the wicked. But the later time of that king represented the age of the successors to the imperial throne, now believing in Christ, at whose hands the wicked suffer because of the Christians."—[Letters of Augustine, p. 395, et seq.

Again, speaking of heretics, he says:

"Let death seize upon them, and let them go down quick into hell; like Dathan and Abiram, the authors of an impious schism."—[Letters of Augustine, pp. 395–420.

These were the teachings in accordance with which the burning of heretics was soon after commenced, and was continued at intervals until the twelfth century, when it was reduced to a system, and carried on extensively over the Christian world for nearly five hundred years.

JESUS AND PAUL.

Jesus, according to the Gospel, taught the doctrine of punishment in hell-fire; using Gehenna, or the valley of Hinnom, where the corpses of the worst malefactors were burnt, as a symbol of the place where evil doers would be punished in the future. And according to the author of the Gospel of Matthew, he expressly sanctioned punishment by torture.

"And his lord was wroth, and delivered him to the tormentors, till he should pay all that was due unto him.

"So likewise shall my heavenly Father do also unto you, if ye from your hearts forgive not every one his brother their trespasses."—[Matt. xviii. 34, 35.

The punishment in hell-fire was to be everlasting.—[Matt. xviii. 8; xxv. 41, 46.

Paul, with the view of relieving the offender from this terrible doom, and at the same time meting out to him punishment in this life, taught that the body may be destroyed, in order that the spirit may be saved in the day of the Lord Jesus.

If Jesus said what he is reported to have said in the Gospel according to Matthew, there must have been traditions of those sayings in circulation in the time of Paul, and known to him; in which case it is possible that Paul took this idea from the sayings of Jesus, as reported in the fifth chapter of Matthew:

"And if thy right eye offend thee, pluck it out, and cast (it) from thee; for it is profitable for thee that one of thy members should perish, and not (that) thy whole body should be cast into hell.

"And if thy right hand offend thee, cut it off, and cast (it) from thee; for it is profitable for thee that one of thy members should perish, and not (that) thy whole body should be cast into hell."—[Matt. v. 29, 30.

A logical extension of the doctrine would require that if the offense extend to the whole body, the whole body should perish rather than be cast into hell.

The doctrine of substitution, and of expiatory suffering with which Paul, with whom the atonement was a favorite doctrine, was so familiar, naturally favored also his idea of the destruction of the body for the salvation of the soul. It was but another form of expiatory suffering. Instead of one person suffering in place of another, it was the same person suffering in this life, in place of suffering in the life to come. It was suffering for a short time here instead of suffering throughout endless ages hereafter.

In that view, the infliction of the necessary pain here was an act of mercy.

The merciful and compassionate character of the proceedings, as seen from an orthodox Christian standpoint, will account for some of the phrases in use by inquisitors—phrases which, it has been supposed by some, were used in derision.

The heretic was admitted to an "audience"; he was "put to the question" (by torture); he had preparatory "instruction" and "monition"—if he was to suffer everything but death, he was "reconciled"; if he was to be burnt alive, he was to be "relaxed." The motto of the Inquisition was, "mercy and justice."

UNDER CONSTANTINE.

"Not a moment was lost," says Gibbon, "in excluding the ministers and the teachers of the separated congregations from any share of the rewards and the immunities which the emperor had so liberally bestowed on the orthodox clergy. But as the sectaries might still exist, under the cloud of royal disgrace, the conquest of the East was immediately followed by an edict which announced their total destruction."—[Citing the Life of Constantine by Eusebius, vol. iii, ch. 63–66.

Under Constantine and his sons commissions were issued against the Donatists, who were visited with the most rigorous punishment. Under Theodosius I, in 382, heretics were searched out and punished; and from this time the terms "inquisition" and "inquisitors" came into general use. In 385, Priscillian, the Gnostic and Manichæan, was tried by Maximus, at Treves, by the use of torture, and was put to death, with six of his disciples.

FIFTH CENTURY.

Having thus been brought into existence in the fourth century, the Inquisition was in full blast early in the fifth century, during the time of Jerome and of Augustine, who were well acquainted with the workings of the same. This is sufficiently manifest from the Letters of Augustine himself.

In Letter civ, directed to Nestorius, he says:

"Have you perchance heard some report, which is as yet unknown to us, that my brother Passidius had obtained authority for proceedings of greater severity against your citizens, whom—you must excuse me for saying this—he loves in a way more likely to promote their welfare than you do yourself? For your letter shows that you apprehend something of this kind, when you charge me to set before my eyes 'the appearance presented by a town from which men doomed to torture are dragged forth,' and to 'think of the lamentations of mothers and of wives, of sons and of fathers, of the shame felt by those who may return, set at liberty, indeed, *but having undergone the torture*, and of the sorrow and groaning *which the sight of their wounds and scars* must renew.' "—[Letters of Augustine, vol. 2, p. 64.

Again: In Letter cxxxiii, (A. D. 412,) to Marcellinus, he says:

"Fulfill, Christian judge, the duty of an affectionate father. Let your indignation against their crimes be tempered by considerations of humanity. Be not provoked by the atrocity of their sinful deeds, to gratify the passion of revenge, but rather be moved by the wounds which those deeds have inflicted on their own souls, to exercise a desire to heal them. Do not lose now that fatherly care which you maintained when prosecuting the examination, in doing which you *extracted the confession* of such horrid crimes, not by stretching them on the rack, not by furrowing their flesh with iron claws, not by scorching them with flames, *but by beating them with rods*—a mode of correction used by schoolmasters, and by parents themselves in chastising children, and often also by bishops, in the sentences awarded by them.

"*It is generally necessary to use more vigor in making inquisition*, so that when the crime has been brought to light, there may be scope for displaying clemency."—[Ib. p. 170. . . .

"Do not call for the executioner now, when the crime has been found out, after having forborne from calling in the *tormentor* when you were finding it out."—[Ibid.

Augustine was here urging clemency in a particular case. If in this case the party addressed had refrained from "calling in the tormentor," was there not a tormentor at hand ready to be called in when it should be thought the exigencies of the case required it?

When the wrath of Jerome was excited by Vigilantius forbidding the adoration of relics, he expressed his wonder that the bishop of the hardy heretic had not destroyed him in the flesh for the benefit of his soul; and argued that piety and zeal for God could not be cruelty.

Rigor, in fact, he argues, in another place, is the most genuine mercy, since temporal punishment may avert eternal perdition.— [Epist. 109, *ad Rip.* Comment. in Naum, 1, 9.

SIXTH CENTURY.

Not only was the Inquisition flourishing in the days of Jerome and of Augustine, but it was expressly provided for in the Code of Jus· tinian.

"The inquisition may be extended, also, to death." (*In mortem quoque inquisitio tendatur.*)

The Eleventh Section is entitled, "Manichæans, wherever found, are to be visited with capital punishment." (*Manichaei ubicunque reperti capitali poena plectuntur.*)

FROM THE SIXTH TO THE TWELFTH CENTURIES.

After the time of Jerome and Augustine, it soon became the general doctrine of the church, as expressed by St. Isidor of Seville (A. D. 620), that princes are bound, not only to be orthodox themselves, but to preserve the purity of the faith, by the fullest exercise of their power against heretics.

Under the Patriarch, Michael Oxista, the penalty of burning alive was introduced as the punishment of the Bogomili. This was in 1119.

If the fires of the Inquisition were slumbering from the sixth to the twelfth century, it was because heretics, during that time, were neither so numerous nor so aggressive as to cause much trouble to the church.

But it is a great mistake to suppose that the institution was first established in the twelfth century in any other sense than that it was then more completely organized, and made more effective than ever before.

In 1163, the Cathari, detected in Cologne, were sentenced to be burned by judges appointed for that purpose.

In 1212 eighty heretics were burned in Strassburg.

In England, the writ of *de heretico comburendo,* "concerning the burning of heretics," was created by statute in 1401.—[Lea's Hist. Inq., vol. 1, p. 221.

In FRANCE, something was done, in the latter part of the twelfth century. But early in the thirteenth century, Pope Innocent III determined, in order to efface forever the last vestige of heresy, to make the Inquisition a permanent institution. In accordance with the decisions and the directions of the Lateran Council of 1215, heretics were hunted out and punished.

In 1232, it was placed under control of the Dominicans.

The institution prevailed in France until about the middle of the sixteenth century.

In GERMANY, the first inquisitor was Conrad of Marburg, who organized the "holy office," and exercised its functions with terrible severity in 1231-33. The institution lasted in Germany in a modified form until the Reformation.

In ITALY the Inquisition had a chequered history for nearly six hundred years, until Napoleon, as King of Italy, put an end to it in 1808. It was re-established afterward, and continued in Sardinia until 1848, and in Tuscany until 1859.

In ENGLAND all attempts of Rome to introduce its Inquisition failed; but the Protestant Inquisition took its place, and proved to be no mean rival, whether we consider the extent of its operations or the ferocity with which they were carried on.

THE NETHERLANDS.—For more than three hundred years the horrors of the Inquisition were practiced in the Netherlands. Particularly was this the case under the bloody Duke of Alva, during the reign and by the command of Philip II, of Spain.

On the 16th of February, 1568, by a sentence of the Holy Office, all the inhabitants of the Netherlands were condemned to death as heretics. From this universal doom only a few persons, specially named, were excepted. "Three millions of people," says Motley, "men, women and children, were sentenced to the scaffold in three lines."—(Rise of the Dutch Republic, ii, 155.) Nothing but the want of the requisite power prevented this bloody sentence from being carried into execution.

The Holy Office was established in Aragon, by the Dominicans, in 1242.

Toward the close of the fifteenth century the Inquisition was re-organized in Spain and carried on its work with thoroughness and completeness.

Much has been said concerning the position occupied by Isabella of Castile, in reference to the Inquisition, and much abuse and denun-ciation of that great queen has been indulged in on account of her connection with it. But the Inquisition had been a cherished insti-tution there for two hundred and fifty years. Isabella was not re-sponsible for it. She was in the hands of the priests; and to their bloody projects she was obliged to yield, though she did so not with-out a struggle.

Even McClintock and Strong exonerate Isabella.—[Article, "In-quisition."

The power of Isabella was limited by the Cortes. Had she failed to sanction the Inquisition, her reign would have been of very brief duration.

Torquemada and his successors organized the work and carried it on with great success for more than three hundred years. In 1808, the Inquisition was abolished in Madrid by an edict of Joseph Bona-parte. In 1814, it was re-established by Ferdinand VII. In 1820, the palace of the Inquisition was destroyed by the people. In 1826, the old tribunal was restored. It was suspended in 1834, and made nuga-tory by the Constitution of 1855. Notwithstanding which, we find it in force as late as 1857. Such has been the difficulty in putting an end to this institution, which has hung on to life with desperate ten-acity, claiming for its existence the same sanction which perpetuates the most sacred and the most ancient ordinances and institutions of the church.

No *Auto da Fe*, or public burning of heretics, has taken place in Spain for nearly a hundred and fifty years. But for a long time after these spectacles ceased, the sentences were carried into execution privately in the buildings of the Inquisition. Executions were con-tinued for another hundred years.

Thus did the Inquisition do its bloody work for ages.

All the inquisitors in all these countries, and during all these centuries, were engaged in the same great work. They were giving their victims an opportunity to expiate endless ages of torture and of burnings in the life to come, by a brief season of torture or burning in this present life.

They were all following the teachings of Paul, of Jerome and of Augustine.

They were engaged in the destruction of an immense number of bodies, in order that a great multitude of souls might be saved in the day of the Lord Jesus.

XI.

When Was the Bible Completed ?

"Each individual book of Scripture is an integral part of the organic whole of Scripture. . . .

"The vision is shut up and the book is sealed. No hope has been given us that the seals will be broken, or a new page added."—[The New Testament Scriptures, by A. H. Charteris, D. D., Professor of Biblical Criticism, etc., in the University of Edinburgh; N. Y., Robt. Carter & Bro.; 1882, pp. 218, 222.

Such being the nature and condition of the Bible, it becomes important to know when it was completed; when the vision was shut up, and the book sealed.

We will let Professor Charteris himself answer this question:

"There is not in the whole history of the Church of Christ down to the Council of Trent in 1546, any decree or formal utterance of the Church fixing the Canon."—[The New Testament Scriptures, p. 188.

Again:

"The Eastern Church was as completely without a fixed Canon as the Western at the Reformation."—[Ibid. p. 199.

Now, since all the books composing the New Testament were written, as is claimed, either in the first or second century, how is it that for fourteen hundred years it could not be determined which of those books were entitled to a place and had a right to be considered Scripture, to the exclusion of others for which the same claim was made?

Is it not plain that there was not sufficient evidence to determine which were genuine and which were not, and that there was no satisfactory rule by which to settle the question? And if the relative validity and merit of the books as between each other could not be determined during all that time, how can we know whether the bishops of the second century decided correctly, when they selected the four gospels now in the New Testament to the exclusion of others which were afterward called apocryphal?

GENERAL INDEX.

———

(The figures in parenthesis indicate the year when the person lived or flourished.)

Alford, Greek Testament, 38.
Alvarez, Semedo, 436.
Alzog, 479-481.
Amasis, king of Egypt, 107.
Ambrose, Latin father of 4th century, 11, 92, 148, 385.
Amelias, an ancient Greek writer, 438.
Ammianus Marcellinus, a writer, 3d century, 322, 454.
Amuphis, an Egyptian magician, 138.
Anacletus, bishop of Rome, 477-499.
Ananias and Sapphira, 30.
Ananus, high priest, 38.
Andrew, the Apostle, 66, 140, 399.
Angels in the Jewish system, 131, 132.
Anicetus, bishop of Rome, 448, 458, 474, 481.
Anius, the high priest, 437.
Anna, grandmother of Jesus, 144, 145.
Anna, the prophetess, see Hannah.
Annas and Caiaphas, high priests, 16, 17, 204, 208, 210, 237.
Announcement to Mary, 145, 152, 153, 184, 309, 363.
Anonymous writings, 259, 260.
Ante-Hieronymian versions, 347.
Antinous, the favorite of Hadrian, worshiped as a god, 131.
Antiquity of Christian doctrines, 436-439.
Antonine column, sculpture on, 138.
Antonius, an ascetic [3d century], 84.
Antonius, father of Simon Magus, 119.
Antoninus Pius, emp. (138-161), 138, 305, 336.
Apelles (160), a Gnostic leader, sketch of, 91, 319, 320, 385, 386, 466; his writings lost, 454.
Apocalypse of Bartholomew, 100.
" of Cerinthus, 36.
" of Esdras, 140.
Apocalypse of John, in N. T., 36, 100, 140, 307, 464, 478; not generally received by the ancients, 36; omitted from the canon by the Asiatic churches, 36, 39; references to passages in, 97; supposed to have been written by John the Presbyter, 258; not in Marcion's N. T., 274.
Apocalypse of John (another), 100, 140.
" of Moses, 140.
" of Paul, 100, 140.
" of Peter, 100, 464.
Apocryphal acts, epistles, revelations, etc., 100, 140.
Apocryphal gospels and writings, 88-100, 139, 169, 257, 352, 455.
Apollo, 129, 438.
Apollonius, Christian writer [3d century], 323.

Apollonius of Tyana [1st century], 101-116, 128, 130, 321, 322, 421, 436: biography of, by Philostratus, 101-111; estimate of his character by different writers, 112-116; extracts from his epistles, 114-116.
Apostles of Christ, 21-39, 470, 487.
Apostolic fathers, 40-61, 263.
Apuleius, Pagan philosopher of the 2d century, 130.
Aquila, brother of Clement of Rome, 44, 119-121.
Archelaus, king of Judea, 169, 184, 331, 332, 364.
Aretas, king of Petræa, 19.
Arian controversy, 427, 468.
Aristeas of Proconnesus, 131.
Aristides (126), author of an Apology, 451; sketch of, 255; epistle to Diognetus attributed to, 270.
Aristides the sophist (176), 416, 417.
Aristion (130), 257, 258, 269, 452.
Aristo of Pella (175), 442.
Aristotle, 103, 189, 343, 439, 445.
Arnobius, Christian writer early in the 4th century, 136.
Artemon (200), 467, 469.
Ascension of Jesus, 236, 238, 376.
Asceticism, 81-84.
Astarte, 189.
Asterius Urbanus (188), 462.
Asterius, writer [4th century], 222.
Athanasius (373), 173.
Athenagoras (177), Athenian philosopher and Christian writer, 305, 321; sketch of, 444, 445; held to a material resurrection, 423.
Atonement, the, 429, 430, 437.
Augustine (420), 89, 136, 272, 385, 399, 446; relates astonishing miracles, 137; discussion with Faustus the Manichæan, 340-345; his explanation of the genealogy of Christ, 362; developed the doctrine of original sin and inherited guilt, 430.
Augustus Cæsar, 139, 157, 175, 203, 436.
Aulus Gellius, early in 2d century, 322, 455.
Aurelian (emp. 270-275), 112.
Aurelius, Lucius Commodus, 305.
Aurelius, Marcus (emp. 161-180), 50, 137, 305, 445, 473.
Austin (600), Christian writer, 149, 320.
Avenging of the Savior, 248.

Bacchylus of Corinth (180), sketch of, 447, 475.
Baldæus, 194-196.
Baptism, 433-435; form of was immersion, 433; change from immersion to sprinkling, 439.
Baptism of Jesus, 16, 66, 68, 172, 173, 181, 312, 319, 357.

548

GENERAL INDEX.

Final restoration, believed in by Origen, 431.
Fire in the Jordan, 260, 312.
Fire worshipers, 168, 182.
Fleury, 306.
Flora (190), 352, 463.
Florinus (177), 444.
Fontenelle (1700), 336.
Forbes' Oriental Memoirs (1800), 199.
Freedom of the will, 428.
Froude, the historian, 113, 128.

Galba, emp. (68-69), 107.
Gamaliel, 415, 416.
Gelasius, decree of (494), 12, 71, 85, 87, 89, 97-100, 149, 264.
Gelasius, Pope (494), 71, 90, 92, 99, 100.
Genealogies of the Desposyni, 96.
Genealogy of Jesus, see Jesus Christ.
Genesis, 121.
Gengis Khan (1220) 436.
George, Bishop of Nicomedia, 149.
Gerarchia Cattolica, the Roman Almanac, 479.
Germanus, Bishop of Constantinople (715), 148.
Gestas, 228, 230, 231.
Gfroerer (1850), 131.
Gibbon (1780), 112.
Gnostics and Gnosticism, 54, 88, 89, 90, 92, 118, 252, 262, 263, 267, 319, 322, 324, 424, 432, 463.
Gobarus [6th century], 448.
Golden Rule before Christ, 439.
Gospel of Andrew, 89; written before Luke, ib.
Gospel of Apelles, 80, 94, 320, 385, 386; written before Luke, 80, 320.
Gospel of Barnabas, 94-96.
Gospel of Bartholomew, 80, 89, 90, 385, 413; written before Luke, 80, 385.
Gospel of Basilides, 80, 96, 253, 385, 386; written before Luke, 80, 386.
Gospel of the Birth of Mary (a supposed gospel), nothing but a translation by Jerome of a portion of the Gospel of the Infancy, 244-246, 365, 468; this gospel was asserted by Jerome to be in the handwriting of Matthew, 72, 244, 351.
Gospels, Canonical, the four, vii, viii, 6, 10, 29, 40-42, 54, 57-61, 72, 80, 81, 87, 142, 169, 174, 196, 210-241, 253, 256, 264, 267, 273, 307-309, 314, 315, 324, 326, 337-340, 344, 373, 377, 379, 385, 423, 445, 448, 449, 452, 453, 459, 460, 470, 471, 478, 82, 489; when written, 359; selected for the use of the churches from a large number of gospels, 10. 352; a support to Roman Catholic supremacy, 478, 482.

Gospel of Cerinthus, 96, 99, 265, 266, 386, 452; written before the Gospel of John, 266; before Luke, 386.
Gospel of the Ebionites, a version of the Gospel of the Nazarenes, 72.
Gospel of the Egyptians, 78-88, 463; frequently cited by Clement of Alexandria, 81; written before Luke, 80, 81, 385.
Gospel of the Encratites, referred to by Epiphanius, 96.
Gospel of Eve, a doubtful gospel, referred to by Epiphanius, 88, 91, 92.
Gospels, the four Canonical, see Gospels, Canonical.
Gospel of the Gnostics, properly no such gospel, though the term sometimes used; 97.
Gospel or Harmony of Tatian, 12, 96, 100, 339, 405; history of, 324, 326; not a harmony of the four Gospels, 339; based on the Gospel of the Hebrews, 325, 455.
Gospel of the Hebrews, 12, 15, 62-77, 81, 84, 85, 90, 91, 96, 98, 118, 185, 259, 269, 303, 312, 313, 317, 422; claimed by Jerome and Epiphanius to be the Hebrew Gospel of Matthew, 62-69, 402, 403; written before the Canonical Gospels, 80, 81, 385; used by Justin Martyr, 271; supposed to have been used by Tatian, 324, 325, 455; used by Hegesippus according to Eusebius, 448, 458, 459.
Gospel of the Infancy, attributed to Thomas, 54, 72, 88, 89, 144, 158, 163, 165, 167, 169, 172, 174, 176, 178-188, 196, 197, 213, 244-246, 311, 312, 339, 351, 363, 365, 406, 414, 451; written before Luke and Matthew, 80, 338; synopsis of its contents, 167-172; testimony of the fathers, 172-174; compared with the first two chapters of Luke and Matthew, 175-187; origin and history of, 188-201.
Gospel of James, same as the Protevangelion, 98, which see.
Gospel according to John, 37, 39, 57, 142, 193, 213, 214, 229, 240, 258, 271, 307, 315, 318, 324, 338, 351, 353, 358, 359, 367, 368, 370, 371, 373-375, 377, 378, 416, 445, 446, 449, 450, 460, 463, 484, 489; references to and specific passages in, 213-219; 230, 233, 302; written subsequent to Cerinthus, 266; not known to Justin Martyr, 307, 315; when written, 359; the first Canonical Gospel mentioned in Christian history, 344, 489; radically different from the synoptics, 353, 354; critically examined, 394-401.
Gospel of Judas Iscariot, 93, 98; mentioned by Irenæus, 93.
Gospel of Jude; same as Gospel of Judas Iscariot.
Gospel of Justin, sometimes employed to designate the gospel principally used by Justin Martyr, 98; this supposed to have been the Gospel of the Hebrews, ib.

Miraculous or immaculate conception, x, 21, 195.
Mithras, a god of Persia, 437.
Modestas (176), 443.
Mohammed (620), 95.
Montanists and Montanism, 323, 455, 473; Tertullian a Montanist, 473.
Montanus (170), 323, 455.
Moor, Major, ix.
Moses [B. C. 1500], 122, 178, 189, 206, 278, 279, 283, 294, 297, 310, 396, 397, 407, 425, 445.
Mosheim (1726), 42, 117, 118, 266.
Moyle (1720), 138, 321.
Mozley, 143.
Muratori (1672), 464, 465.
Muratorian Fragment, 34, 263, 463-465.
Musanus (176), 443.

Narcissus, Bishop of Jerusalem (195), 139, 466.
Narrative of Joseph of Arimathea, 243.
Nathan's embassy, 248.
Nathaniel, apostle, 39.
Nazarenes, 7, 11, 14, 63, 65, 67-70, 72-74, 76.
Neander (1840), 37, 270, 304, 320, 422, 431, 432, 476.
Nero, emp. (54-68), 106, 125-127, 247.
Nerva, emp. (96-98), 108, 111.
Newman, Cardinal (1840), 138, 139.
New Testament, 36, 39, 58, 80, 85, 102, 265, 267-269, 316, 341, 343, 346, 349, 350, 352, 417, 429, 442-445, 459, 463, 483, 488, published by the Roman Catholic church; 478, 484.
New Testament of Eusebius, 36.
New Testament of Marcion (145), 28, 478; the first ever published, 274, 453; what it contained, 274.
Nicephorus, the historian (800), 90, 95, 222.
Niceta, a brother of Clement of Rome, 44, 119, 124.
Nicodemus, 119, 206-210, 225, 226, 234.
Niemeyer, Dr. (1790), 72.
Nimrod, 438.
Noetian Controversy, 469.
Noetus (200), notice of, 467, 468.
Norton (1846), 12, 34, 39, 74, 84, 88, 91, 306.

Œcumenius (950), 11, 268.

Old Testament, citations from: Genesis, 121; Exodus, 121; Deuteronomy, 341; Psalms, 28, 94, 399; Proverbs, 458; Isaiah, 141, 174, 311, 367; Jeremiah, 163, 164, 383; Hosea, 183; Micah, 165, 177, 183; Zechariah, 383.
Olshausen (1830), 383.
Omito, a Chinese god, 438.

Onisephorus, 33.
Ophites, 88, 91, 440.
Oracles of Christ, by Matthew, 3, 13-15, 41, 75, 76, 85, 253, 269, 270, 357, 393, 414.
Ordination of Clement of Rome, 31, 42.
Origen (230), 10, 11, 14, 43, 51, 63, 64, 68, 79, 80, 84, 87, 92, 93, 135, 140, 144, 146, 147, 149, 259, 301, 385, 422, 423, 430, 431, 460, 463, 485; references to and quotations from his writings, 10, 79, 92, 131, 135, 147, 172, 173, 256, 259, 264, 311, 312, 332, 333, 352, 385, 428, 435.
Original Acts of Pilate, 250.
Original sin, 430, 438.
Ormuzd, a Persian god, 438.
Orpheus [B. C. 1200], 112, 445.
Oschedermah and Oschederbami, 191, 192.
Osiris, of Egypt [B. C. 2000], 437.
Otho, emp. (69), 107.
Otto (1150), 304.

Page (1650), 304.
Palmas (196), 467, 475.
Pamphilius (300), 67.
Pandava, ix.
Pantænus (180), 90, 413, 414, 447, 456.
Papias, Bishop of Hierapolis (125), 13, 14, 65, 74, 258, 267-270, 351, 432, 452, 453, 484; sketch of, 268-270.
Paschal Chronicle [7th century], 446.
Paschal Controversy, 384, 446, 447.
Paschal Supper, 384.
Paul the Apostle, 3-6, 13, 14, 21-30, 32, 33, 45, 59, 91, 95, 127, 256, 260, 262, 264, 273-275, 287, 316-318, 357, 376, 413, 417-419, 424, 433, 437, 445, 448, 450, 453, 454, 459, 464, 471, 476-478, 482, 484, 486; Paul a spiritualist, 29, 45, 140, 376, 422, 423, 429, 442.
Epistles of Paul:
  Epistle to the Colossians, 274, 433.
  1st Epistle to the Corinthians; 4, 27, 44, 59, 68, 274, 448.
  2d Epistle to the Corinthians, 27, 30, 274, 424, 448.
  Epistle to the Ephesians, 28, 59, 274.
  Epistle to the Galatians, 5, 23, 27, 418, 419.
  Epistle to the Hebrews, 28, 39, 464.
  Epistle to Philemon, 274.
  Epistle to the Philippians, 59, 274, 424.
  Epistle to the Romans, 4, 27, 30, 264, 274, 422.
  1st Epistle to the Thessalonians, 274.
  2d Epistle to the Thessalonians, 4, 241, 274.
  Epistle to Timothy I, 28, 477.
  Epistle to Timothy II, 28, 477.
  Epistle to Titus, 28.
Paul of Samosata (200-260), 467.

Paul of Thebais, an Egyptian, the first Christian monk, 84.

Paulina, sister of Hadrian, 83.

Pauline Gospels, 88, 91, 92, 94.

Paulus and Papinian (210), 101.

Pearson, Bishop (1672), 148, 204.

Pehlvian and Parsian Books of the Persians, 191.

Pepuzians, a sect who permitted women to baptize, 324.

Peregrinus (150-169), sketch of 320-322; his writings have perished, 454.

Perpetua, story of, 26, 140.

Persian history of Christ, 100.

Persians, and Persian religion and mythology, 188-194, 199, 451.

Peshito version, 34-36, 39, 346, 349, 350.

Peter, 7-15, 23, 27, 30-34, 42, 43, 44, 66, 71, 83, 119-127, 191, 238, 247, 259, 262, 269, 274, 277, 279, 284, 293, 294, 317, 354, 378, 393, 399, 400, 403, 407, 410-413, 417-419, 443, 450, 459, 471, 476-482; the first bishop of Rome, according to Catholic authorities, 479-481; but not so stated by Irenæus, 481; his discussion with Simon Magus, 121-124; dispute with Simon before Nero, 125-127; did Peter go to Rome? 32, 33; Epistles of Peter, 34.

1st Epistle of Peter, 34.

2d Epistle of Peter, 34, 36, 39.

Epistle of Peter to James, 259.

Peter, book of the doctrine of, 76, 259, 260.

Peter, book of the preaching of, 11, 76, 83, 259, 260, 270, 466; written by Mark, 83.

Petrine Gospels, 84.

Philip, apostle and evangelist, 3, 90, 91, 140, 269, 357.

Philip, Tetrarch of Trachonitis, xiii, 16, 18.

Philip, a writer (170), 323.

Philo Judæus [1st century], 81-83, 318, 426.

Philostratus (210), 101-111, 322.

Philumene [2d century], 320.

Phlegon (150), 83, 332-335.

Photius (877), 99, 222, 448.

Pilate, death of, 248.

Pilate, Pontius, 16, 20, 33, 202-210, 214, 224, 226-228, 230, 233, 234, 247, 248, 299, 305, 313, 314, 354, 372-374; 383; Letter of, 247; giving up of, 248; newly discovered Acts of 249, 250.

Pinytus (175), 443.

Pious frauds, prevalent among the fathers, 487.

Pistis Sophiæ (200), 468.

Pitrat, 437, 438.

Pius I, Bishop of Rome, 263, 465, 481.

Pius IX, Pope (1846), 479.

Plato [B. C. 375], 103, 343, 436, 438, 445.

Pliny the Elder (75), 189.

Pliny the Younger (105), 424.

Plutarch (100), 189, 438.

Polycarp (116), 48, 52, 55, 57, 61, 268, 371, 474; Epistle to the Philippians, 51, 55, 56, 59, 429, 474; 475.

Polycrates, Bishop of Ephesus (196), 467, 475.

Polytheism, 121, 425.

Pontius Pilate, see Pilate, Pontius.

Popes, or Bishops of Rome, to A. D. 200, 477-482.

Porphyry (300), 335, 336, 486; wrote against the Christian religion, 335; his works, destroyed by order of the Emperor Constantine, 335, 336.

Potter's Antiquities (1700), 438.

Praxeas (200), 468.

Preaching of Paul, 11, 259, 312, 466.

Predestination, doctrine of, 429.

Prideaux, Dr. (1700), 190.

Priestley, Dr. (1793), 317, 323.

Procla, wife of Pilate, 247.

Proclus, 32.

Prodicians, followers of Prodicus, 91; a Christian sect who had the secret books of Zoroaster, 193, 254.

Prodicus (120), 193, 254, 451.

Prometheus, 104, 437.

Protevangelion, or Book of James, 10, 11, 98, 144-166, 168, 175, 176, 181-188, 303, 331, 361, 444; Justin Martyr acquainted with it, 309-311; written before Luke and Matthew, 150-166, 339.

Proverbs of Xystus, 258.

Providence, doctrine of, 431.

Pseudo-Matthew, 243.

Ptolemæus (190), 369; letter to Flora, 352, 463.

Punishment, endless, see Eternal.

Punishment, nature and object of, 431.

Puranas, sacred books of the Hindus, 199-201.

Pythagoras [B. C. 530], 103, 104, 254, 436, 445.

Quadratus (126), Apology of, 255, 451, 452; Epistle of Diognetus attributed to, 270.

Quexalcote, 436, 437, 438.

Rachel, mother of Simon Magus, 119, 123.

Recognitions, 27, 42, 43, 44, 119-127, 190, 271, 272, 433, 434, 479; attributed to Bardesanes, 447.

Regenerating grace, 430.

Renan, 98.

Report of Pilate, 204, 247.

Resurrection of Christ, see Jesus Christ.

Resurrection of Saviors, 437.

Revelation, 97, 274, 478.

Revelations of Adam, 97.

Revelations of Antichrist, 260. For other
Revelations, see Apocalypse.
Reville, Albert, 112, 116, 436.
Rhodon (195), 466.
Ritschl (1850), 277.
Roman Catholic Hierarchy, 400, 410, 412,
417-419, 449, 450, 474-482.
Rosenmueller (1800), 74.
Routh (1814), 441.
Rufinus (410), 43, 427, 479.

Sabbath, the, 432, 433.
Sabellians and Sabellianism, 80, 86, 427.
Sabellius (200-250), 467.
Salome, 78, 79, 85, 87, 146, 462; a daughter of
Joseph, 148.
Sanday, Rev. Mr. (1876), 49, 54, 57, 359, 389,
393.
Sapphira, 30.
Saturninus (125), 251, 252.
Sayings of Christ, 54-57, 121, 253, 258, 308,
315, 316, 402, 445, 453, 460.
Scaliger (1600), 138, 328, 335.
Schleiermacher (1820), 150-152, 154, 156-159,
177, 187, 224, 288, 303, 356, 360, 364, 366,
379, 381, 389, 390, 392, 406-408.
Schmidt, J. Alexander, 288.
Scholten, 50.
Scripture, when the term applied to New
Testament books, 488.
Secrecy of the Christians, 434, 435.
Secret books of Zoroaster, 193, 254.
Seleucas, otherwise Leucius, etc. (200),
244-246, 415, 468.
Semedo, Alvarez, 436.
Semisch, 304.
Semler (1783), 288, 346.
Serapion, Bishop of Antioch (190), sup-
pressed the Gospel of Peter, 7, 460, 465,
482.
Serapis, 83, 136, 173.
Serarius (1600), 84.
Servianus, 83.
Sesostris [B. C. 1400], 438.
Severus, Alexander, emp. (222-235), 112,
222.
Severus, Septimius, emp. (193-211), 100, 473.
Shedd, Dr. (1871), 427, 429, 430.
Shepherd of Hermas, see Hermas.
Shepherds, the, 176, 177, 185, 363.
Sibylline Oracles, 259, 260.
Sidonius Apollinaris (475), 113.
Sike (1700), 167.
Simeon, 168, 178, 179, 208, 209.
Simeon, second Bishop of Jerusalem, 457,
458.
Simeon, brother of Jesus, 148; 157.

Simon the Cyrenian, 254, 373.
Simon, Father (1689), 72, 385.
Simon, the high priest, 18.
Simon Magus, 43, 117-127, 247, 251, 252, 421;
discussion with Peter, 121-124; before
Nero, 125-127; his death, 127.
Simon Peter, see Peter.
Simon Zelotes, 31, 66.
Siva, third member of the Hindu trinity,
437.
Sixtus I, Bishop of Rome, 480, 481.
Sixtus Senensis (1560), 260.
Slaughter of the children, 146, 163, 183, 185,
198, 205, 363.
Socrates, historian (440), 312.
Son of God, common among the ancients,
436.
Sosiosh, a prophetic son of Zoroaster,
192.
Soter, Bishop of Rome, 323, 458, 481.
Soterichus Oasites, 112.
Soul, nature of the, views of Tertullian
and Origen, 428.
Sousa, Alfonso, 199.
Sozomen, historian (439), 84, 174, 222, 312.
Spanheim (1680), 84, 204.
Spiritualism, 45, 135, 376.
Sprinkling, 438.
Stars, 54, 188-193, 436; the Jews believe
them to be animated beings, 131; so
also Origen, 136; the star in the east,
162, 163, 168, 182, 188.
Statue of Christ, 222.
Stephanus, who assassinated Domitian
110.
Stowe, Prof. (1867), 337, 385.
Strauss, (1865), 89;
Stroth (1780), 73, 74.
Suetonius (125), 125, 127.
Suidas [10th century], 95, 111.
Sunderland, Rev. Dr., 32.
Sunderland, J. T. (1878), 27, 357.
Supernatural Religion, 30, 49, 131, 277, 308,
442.
Symmachus (200), 468.
Syriac documents, 260, 444.
Syriac epistles, see Ignatius.
Syriac New Testament in 1562, 35, 36.
Syriac Version, 36, 38, 39, 51, 62, 444.

Tacitus [Annals, 117], 372.
Tamerlane (1400), 436.
Tanaquil Faber (1665), 330.
Tatian (170), vii, 7, 12, 324; sketch of, 324-
326; used the Gospel of the Hebrews,
74, 271, 324; his writings lost, 455; did
not believe in the immortality of the
soul, 428.

Printed in March 2024
by Rotomail Italia S.p.A., Vignate (MI) - Italy